BEGINNER'S ASSYRIAN

D.G. Lyon

HIPPOCRENE BOOKS, INC.
New York

For information, address:
HIPPOCRENE BOOKS, INC.
171 Madison Avenue
New York, NY 10016

ISBN 0-7818-0677-1

Printed in the United States of America.

PREFACE.

THIS book is designed to meet the needs of those who desire to become acquainted with the Assyrian language but who cannot easily have access to oral instruction. It is believed that this class is not a small one and that it will rapidly grow. The Assyrian remains are so rich in the most valuable materials that the language is no longer a luxury to be enjoyed by the few, but has become a necessity to the specialist in Semitic history, religion and linguistics. The points of contact with the Hebrew language and literature in particular are so numerous and of such interesting character that no Old Testament exegete can ignore the results of Assyrian study. Two great obstacles have stood in the way of those who desire to become acquainted with the language, the lack of suitable books for beginners and the large demand made on the memory for the acquisition of the cuneiform signs. It is the task of learning the signs which constitutes the chief difficulty. Indeed, apart from this, the language is not very difficult. But for this, one who is fairly well acquainted with Hebrew, might read ordinary prose Assyrian with much less labor than it costs to learn Hebrew. That is, Assyrian written in Hebrew or in Latin letters, is one of the easiest of the Semitic languages. No student, of course, can ever be an independent worker unless he also acquires the cuneiform signs, and that for the reason that the values of many of the signs are variable. But supposing the signs to be correctly transliterated, it is possible to have a good acquaintance with the language without learning any of the signs. It is true of the Assyrian as of all languages, that it lies not in the characters which represent the sounds, but in the sounds themselves. The recognition of this fact constitutes the chief peculiarity of the *Assyrian Manual.* The author has learned by several years' experience in teaching, that the best beginning is made by the use of transliterated texts. Thus by the time the student has learned the most necessary cuneiform signs, he has already gathered a small vocabulary and begins to appreciate the grammatical structure of the language. Each step in this direction increases his interest in the study and lightens the task of committing the signs to memory. Some persons will content themselves without the signs. Those who have more time, or who wish to be independent of transliterations made by others, will not fail to acquire the signs, however irksome the task may be.

The central feature of the *Assyrian Manual* is the collection of transliterated texts, pages 1–52. The originals to these texts are nearly all found in volumes I and V of "The Cuneiform Inscriptions of Western Asia," and the suspended figures represent in each case the line, so that the original can be readily consulted. There is perhaps no more satisfactory method of learning the cuneiform signs than by reading inscriptions with the aid of transliterations. It is to be observed that in the transliterated texts in this book words in smaller type represent determinatives, words divided into syllables represent such as are written syllabically, and those not so divided represent such as are written by an ideogram; cf. pp. xxv–xxvi. Ideograms about whose reading I am in doubt have been indicated by **bold-face** type. Groups of signs have also been sometimes thus indicated, some of which may turn out to be ideograms and others syllables. In the case of words ideographically written and also in the glossary, I have undertaken to indicate the length of the vowels, though I have not in all cases done so. This task is a difficult one, and the decision must in many cases be based upon analogy. The texts selected, excepting those of Nabonidus and Cyrus, all fall within what might be called the classic Assyrian period.

For the transliterated texts the chronological order has been followed, except that it seemed desirable to place the translated passage, with which the student should first begin (pp. 42–49), near the cuneiform original (pp. 53–57). Pages 50 and 51 are intended for study immediately after the foregoing section, while page 52, which is not in chronological order, is placed where it is because its contents are essentially unlike those of the other transliterated texts. The system of transliteration adopted here is essentially that in use among German students of Assyrian. In the case of words containing the signs *ki* (*ḳi*) or *ka* (*ḳa*), I have generally written *ki*, *ka*, these being the most frequent values of the signs. The student must therefore bear in mind that *k* sometimes corresponds to a ק.

The texts have not been divided into sentences and paragraphs as fully as might have been done. The Assyrian, it must be remembered, indicates but rarely such divisions.

The selection of *cuneiform* texts, besides the original of the Egyptian Campaign, had special reference to the intrinsic interest of the passages chosen. It is believed that these passages, excepting a few difficult words, will be within the reach of those who have mastered the syllabic signs (pp. xiii–xvi) and some pages of the transliterated texts.

The *notes* (pp. 65–94) are not intended as a commentary, but only as brief suggestions to aid the student's progress. They are fullest on the passage for beginners (pp. 42–49). It has not seemed necessary to comment in each case on words of whose meaning I am in doubt, that doubt having already been sufficiently expressed in the transliteration or in the glossary. Notes on pp. 53–57^{15} have not been given, because those on pp. 42–49 cover this passage. The references with § before them are to the outline of grammar (pp. xxv–xlv). I have in the notes rarely divided into syllables the words commented on, because the student knows from the transliteration in each case whether a word is an ideogram or is written syllabically. Nor have I ordinarily divided into syllables Assyrian words quoted in the comments.

In the *glossary* the etymological arrangement has been followed, but for ease of reference most words with formative prefixes have been twice entered. In the case of weak stems, there are, of course, many instances in which a doubt exists about one or more letters. In such cases the provisional stem indicated by Hebrew letters is only intended to aid in using the glossary. Progress in the study will undoubtedly make many corrections in any attempt to assign to each word its tri-literal stem. The first word in **bold-face** type after the Hebrew letters is in the case of verbs the infinitive of the form I 1 (Qal), the Hebrew letters, however, being regarded as sufficient in cases where I was in doubt as to the Assyrian form of the infinitive. In the case of other words than verbs the word in **bold-face** type represents the absolute form of the noun, etc. Only those forms which are followed by a reference to page and line actually occur in this collection of texts. The division of the word into syllables is the same as explained above. Words for which I have no definition are followed by five dots (. . . . .). I have tried to make the references complete in the case of words occurring but few times, but this course did not seem necessary in the case of those which occur with great frequency.

A list of the proper names which occur in the texts has not been added, because in a book for beginners such a list does not seem to me necessary.

The *list of signs* includes an almost complete list of the phonograms (pp. xiii–xvi), together with a full list of the ideograms (pp. xviii–xxiv) occurring in the cuneiform texts (pp. 53–64) and in the originals on which the transliterated texts (pp. 1–52) are based. In case of the texts written in Babylonian characters (pp. 23, 24, 35–41), the Assyrian form of the sign is given. A complete list of phonetic values is not yet possible, but the one here given is sufficiently full for all practical purposes. A complete set of ideograms and ideographic values is also impossible and lies outside of the scope of this book. The signs are arranged in the order of complexity, reference being had in each case to the first wedge or wedges on the left of the sign. Thus *zu*, No. 5, though composed of more wedges than *is*, No. 135, comes before it, because *zu* begins with only one horizontal wedge, while *is* begins with two. The order is first those signs beginning with horizontal wedges, then those with oblique wedges, afterwards those with the double wedge and lastly those with perpendicular wedges. These groups are further subdivided on the basis of the number of wedges with which each sign begins.

The *outline of grammar* (pp. xxv–xlv) is intended as a bare sketch, yet it is believed that the important facts of the grammar are here presented. A reference has been given for nearly every word quoted as an illustration, and so far as possible the reference is to texts in this book. The student can thus easily turn to the passage and see the word in its connections. In the treatment of the weak verb, §§ 25–32, an attempt has been made to refer existing forms to the original forms from which they come, though it must be admitted that in most cases such original forms were no longer in use when the language entered on its literary stage.

The plan to be pursued in the use of this book will depend on one's methods of study. For those who have no teacher I would recommend the following plan: Read the outline of grammar two or three times. Then read several times the Egyptian Campaigns with the translation (pp. 42–51). Much of the grammar will at once be clear and many Hebrew equivalents will present themselves. Then go over the same passages in connection with the notes and glossary, looking up all the grammatical references. At the same time commit to memory each day a few of the most common phonograms (pp. xvi–xvii), and practise those learned, by writing them and by pointing them out in the cuneiform texts. After the Egyptian Campaigns the selection beginning on page 21 may be studied, then the one on page 27, after this the Syrian Campaign of Sennacherib, pp. 10–12. The student may then read the remaining selections in order, the most difficult being those of Nabonidus and Cyrus (pp. 35–41), the difficulty in the latter case being largely due to the fragmentary condition of the original. So soon as the Egyptian Campaign has been mastered in transliteration, or even before, the student may turn his attention to the original, pp. 53–57. He should make himself so familiar with this that he could write out a transliteration, or could reproduce the original from the transliteration. When he has done this, it is probable that he could make very good headway with the remaining cuneiform selections, pp. 57–64. In reading these he will turn to the list of signs for any syllable or ideogram which may be unknown. But his acquaintance with the structure of the language, gained from reading transliterated texts, will generally enable him to decide whether a sign is syllable or ideogram. It is desirable to make constant reference to the original in reading the other selections also, and thus to gain familiarity with the signs. Long before the student has accomplished all that is here marked out, he will be delighted to find that, if he is tolerably familiar with the list of signs, he will be in position to translate with a good deal of confidence untransliterated historical texts. For practice it is particularly desirable to have volume V of "The Cuneiform Inscriptions of Western Asia."

To the published works of my co-laborers in Assyrian I am under obligations for many suggestions as to reading and meaning of words. I have not thought it necessary in each case to cumber the notes by an acknowledgment. The cases may be few where I have assigned to words meanings which have not been assigned by some predecessor. But besides the acknowledgments made in the notes I desire here to express in particular my obligations to the works of Prof. Friedrich Delitzsch. The *Schrifttafel* in Prof. Delitzsch's *Assyrische Lesestücke*, ed. 3, is the most valuable collection of cuneiform signs which has yet appeared.

The printers, Messrs. J. S. Cushing & Co., have brought to the mechanical execution of the book that good taste and faithfulness which characterize all their work. If the book shall supply the need which seems to me to exist, and shall make it possible more easily than heretofore to possess oneself of the rich treasures of the Assyrian language, I shall be amply rewarded for all the time and labor which its preparation has cost.

D. G. LYON.

CONTENTS.

ABBREVIATIONS.

Asb., Asb. Sm., Assurb. Sm.: History of Assurbanipal, by George Smith. London, 1871.

Beh.: Behistun-Inscription of Darius, III R 39–40.

Busspsalmen: Babylonische Busspsalmen, by Heinrich Zimmern. Leipzig, 1885.

D., NR., S.: short Achaemenian inscriptions, published by Paul Haupt in Bezold's Die Achämenideninschriften. Leipzig, 1882.

Lay., Layard: Inscriptions in the Cuneiform Character, by A. H. Layard. London, 1851.

Lesest.[3]: Assyrische Lesestücke, ed. 3, by Friedrich Delitzsch. Leipzig, 1885.

Paradies: Wo lag das Paradies?, by Friedrich Delitzsch. Leipzig, 1881.

KAT[2]: Die Keilinschriften und das Alte Testament, ed. 2, by Eberhard Schrader. Giessen, 1883.

Khors: Grande Inscription du Palais de Khorsabad, by J. Oppert and J. Menant. Paris, 1863.

Nimrodepos: Das Babylonische Nimrodepos, by Paul Haupt. Leipzig, 1884.

Pinches Texts: Texts in the Babylonian Wedge-Writing, by T. G. Pinches. London, 1882.

R: The Cuneiform Inscriptions of Western Asia, by Sir Henry Rawlinson and others. 5 vols. London, 1861–1884. The number before R indicates the vol., the numbers after R indicate page and line. Thus IV R 9, 6 a means vol. IV, p. 9, l. 6, col. 1.

S^a, S^b, S^c: The Syllabaries in Delitzsch's Assyr. Lesest.[3]

Sargontexte: Keilschrifttexte Sargon's, by D. G. Lyon. Leipzig, 1883.

Sargon Cyl., Sargon St.: The Cylinder-Inscription and Bull-Inscription in Lyon's Sargontexte.

Strassm.: Alphabetisches Verzeichniss der Assyrischen und Akkadischen Wörter, etc., by J. N. Strassmaier. Leipzig, 1882–1886.

Tiglathpileser: Die Inschriften Tiglathpileser's I, by Wilhelm Lotz. Leipzig, 1880.

ZKF.: Zeitschrift für Keilschriftforschung, by Carl Bezold and others. Leipzig, 1884–1886.

---

det., determ.: determinative. — **id.** (pl. **ids.**): ideogram. — **perm.**: permansive. — **st.**: stem. — **var.**: variant. The other abbreviations will be familiar.

Phonograms.

1. áš, rum, dil.
2. ḫal.
3. mug (k, ḳ).
4. ba.
5. zu, ṣu.
6. su, rúg (k, ḳ), kús (š).
7. rug (k, ḳ), šun, šin.
8. , tar, ṭar, kud (ṭ, t), ḳud (ṭ, t), šil, ḫaz (ṣ), dím, tím.
9. , bal, pal, bùl, pùl.
10. = na.
11. ád (ṭ, t), gír.
12. bul, pul.
13. , = ti.
14. an.
15. ka.
16. nag (k, ḳ).
17. ír, ál, ŭr.
18. kál.
19. šaḫ, sáḫ.
20. la.
21. pin.
22. maḫ.
23. tu.
24. , , li.
25. bab, pap, kúr, ḳúr.
26. gul, kul, ḳul, zir.
27. mu.
28. ḳa.
29. kad (ṭ, t).
30. gil, kil.
31. kad (ṭ, t).
32. ru, šub (p).
33. bí, bad (ṭ, t), mid (ṭ, t), til, ziz.
34. na.
35. = , No. 32.
36. šir.
37. = , No. 26.
38. ti.
39. = .
40. = , No. 32.
41. = ba.
42. = , No. 5.
43. = , No. 6.
44. bar, bìr, pár, mas (š).
45. nu.
46. gun, kun, ḳun.
47. , ḫu, bag (k, ḳ), pag (k, ḳ).
48. , , nam.
49. , ig (k, ḳ).
50. mud (ṭ, t).
51. kad (ṭ, t), gad (ṭ, t), gum, kum, ḳum.
52. dim, tim.
53. mun.
54. = .
55. , ag (k, ḳ).
56. rad (ṭ, t).
57. zi.
58. gi.
59. = .
60. , ri, dal, ṭal, tal.
61. ín.
62. , nun, zil, ṣil.
63. , kab (p), ḫúb (p).
64. ḫub (p).
65. sur, šur.
66. suḫ.
67. sa.
68. gán, kán, ḳár.
69. tig (k, ḳ).
70. dúr, ṭur, tùr.
71. gur, kùr, ḳur.
72. si.
73. dar, ṭar.
74. šag (k, ḳ), riš.
75. , dir, ṭir.
76. dab (p), ṭab (p), tab (p).
77. ták (ḳ), šum.
78. ab (p).
79. nab (p).
80. mul.

81. ug (k, ḳ).
82. az (s, ṣ).
83. um, muš.
84. dub (p).
85. ta.
86. i.
87. gan, kan.
88. dùr, ṭúr, tur.
89. ad (ṭ, t).
90. ṣi.
91. ya.
92. in.
93. rab (p).
94. sar, šar, sìr, šír, ḫir.
95. sí, šúm.
96. kaz (s, ṣ), ras (š).
97. = ta.
98. =
99. =
100. gab (p), káb (p), ḳab (p), daḫ, ṭaḫ, taḫ, duḫ.
101. ṭáḫ, dáḫ.
102. =
103. =
104. am.
105. šìr.
106. ní, ṭì, bì, bíl, kúm, ḳúm.
107. bil, pil.
108. zig (k, ḳ), ṣig (k, ḳ).
109. ḳu, ḳùm.
110. gaz (s, ṣ), káz (s, ṣ).
111. šám.
112. ram.
113. = ta.
114. ìr.
115. il.
116. du, gub (p), kub (p), ḳub (p), kìn.
117. =
118. dum, tum, ib.
119. = ta.
120. uš, nit.
121. iš, mil.
122. bi, kàs, kaš, gás, gaš.
123. šim, rig (k, ḳ).
124. kib (p), ḳib (p).
125. tag (k, ḳ).
126. kak, ḳak, dá.
127. ni, zal, ṣal.
128. = No. 125.
129. ir.
130. mal.
131. dag (k, ḳ), pàr.
132. pa, ḫad (ṭ, t).
133. sab (p), šab (p).
134. sib (p).
135. iz (s, ṣ), giš.
136. al.
137. ub (p), ár.
138. mar.
139. í.
140. dug (k, ḳ), lúd (ṭ, t).
141. gíd (ṭ, t), kid (ṭ, t), ḳid (ṭ, t), siḫ, saḫ, lil.
142. rid (ṭ, t), šid (ṭ, t), lag (k, ḳ), mis (s, š), kil.
143. ú, šam, sam, guš.
144. ga.
145. laḫ, liḫ, luḫ, riḫ.
146. kal, kàl, rib (p), lab (p), lib (p), dan, ṭan, tan.
147. = No. 96.
148. un.
149. bit (t), pit, ì.
150. nir.
151. ra.
152. sis, šiš.
153. zag (k, ḳ), sag (k, ḳ).
154. = in.
155. = No. 94.
156. = No. 95.
157. gar, ḫàr, ḳar.
158. id (ṭ, t).
159. da, ṭa.
160. lil.
161. aš.
162. ma.
163. gal, ḳal.
164. bàr.
165. biš, piš, gir, kir.
166. mir.

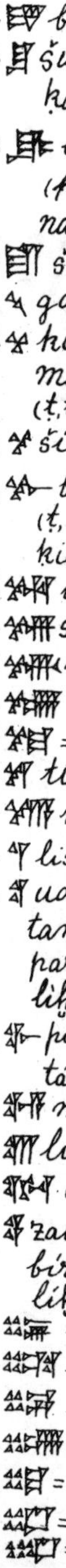

167. bur, pur.
168. šú, kàd(ṭ, t), kad(ṭ, t).
169. lib(p), lub(p), lul, nar, paḫ.
170. šá.
171. gam, gúr.
172. kur, lad(ṭ, t), mad(ṭ, t), nad(ṭ, t), šad(ṭ, t).
173. ší.
174. bu, pu, gid(ṭ, t), kíd(ṭ, t), ḳid(ṭ, t), sir.
175. uṛ(s, ṣ).
176. sír, šud(ṭ, t).
177. muš, ṣir.
178. tir.
179. =  tu.
180. tí.
181. kar.
182. lis(š).
183. ud(ṭ, t), tú, tam, bár, par, pìr, láḫ, liḫ, ḫis(š).
184. pi, mì, tù, tál.
185. má.
186. líb(p), šà.
187. úḫ.
188. ẓab(p), ṣab(p), bír, pir, làḫ, liḫ.
189. =  in.
190. =  li.
191. = 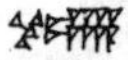 tir.
192. =  tir.
193. = 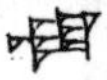 tu.
194. = 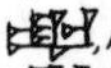, No. 94.
195. = 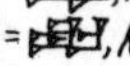, No. 94.

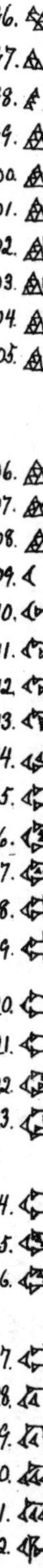

196. = 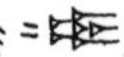, No. 87.
197. = , No. 241.
198. ẓib(p), ṣib(p).
199. ḫi, ṭí, šár.
200. 'a, 'i, 'u, a', i', u'.
201. aḫ, iḫ, uḫ.
202. kam, ḫam.
203. im.
204. bir, pír.
205. ḫar, ḫír, ḫur, ḫám, ḳin, mur, ùr.
206. ruš.
207. súḫ.
208. ṣun.
209. u.
210. muḫ.
211. =  ba.
212. = , No. 5.
213. = , No. 6.
214. = .
215. lid(ṭ, t), rím.
216. kir.
217. kis(š), ḳis(š).
218. mi.
219. gúl, kúl, ḳúl, sun.
220. nim, num.
221. lam.
222. túm.
223. , , 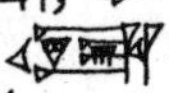 kir.
224. ṣur.
225. ban, pan.
226. ,  gim, kim.
227. ul.
228. =  ba.
229. = 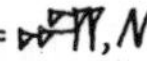, No. 5.
230. = , No. 6.
231. = 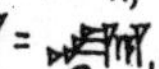, No. 7.
232. ši, lim, ini.

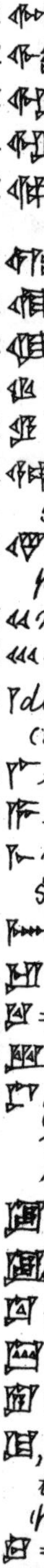

233. ar.
234. pá.
235. ,  ù.
236. ḫul.
237. di, ṭi, šál, šúl.
238. = 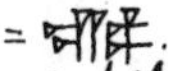.
239. tul, ṭíl.
240. ,  ki, ḳí.
241. din, tin.
242. = , No. 32.
243. dun, sul, šul.
244. bád(ṭ, t), pad(ṭ, t), šuk.
245. man, niš.
246. íš, ẓin, sin.
247. diš, ṭiš, tiẓ(s, š), ana.
248. lá, lal.
249. lál.
250. mí, sib(p), šib(p).
251.  míš.
252. ib(p).
253. = , No. 276.
254. = , No. 63.
255. gil, kil, ḳil, ḫab(p), kír, rim, rin.
256. ẓar, ṣar.
257. 'ú.
258. pú.
259. búl, púl.
260. ẓug(k, ḳ), suk.
261. ,  ku, dur, túr, tuš, úb(p).
262. = , No. 261.

Phonograms.

263. lu, dib(p), tib(p), tib(p).
264. ki, kin, kin.
265. šik.
266. šu.
267. sal, šal, rag(k, k).
268. ṣu, zum.
269. nin.
270. dam, tam.
271. gu.
272. amat.
273. nik(ḳ).
274. il.
275. lum, ḫum, kuz(s, ṣ).
276. tuk(ḳ), dúg(k, ḳ).
277. ur, lig(k, ḳ), das, tas(š), tan, tíz, tíš.
278. a.
279. a-a, â, ai.
280. za, ṣa.
281. ḫa.
282. gug.
283. sig(k, ḳ), šig(k, ḳ), zik, pik.
284. ṭu.
285. ša, gar.
286. yá, à.
287. àš.

Selected Phonograms.

(Those most used)

áš.
ba.
zu.
su.
an.
ka.
la.
tu.
li.
mu.
ḳa.
ru.
na.
ti.
nu.
ḫu.
ig, ik, iḳ.
ag, ak, aḳ.
zi.
gi.
ri.
in.
sa.
si.
ab, ap.
ug, uk, uḳ.
az, as, aṣ.
um.
ta.
i.
ad, at, aṭ.
ṣi.
ya.
in.
am.
ḳu.
úr.
il.
du.
uš.
iš.
bi.
ni.
ir.
pa.
iz, is, iṣ.
al.
ub, up.
í.
ú.
ga.
un.
ra.
id, it, iṭ.
da, ṭa.
aš.
ma.
šú.
ša.
ší.
bu, pu.
uz, us, uṣ.
ti.
ud, ut, uṭ.
pi.
ḫi.
'a, 'i, 'u, a', i', u'.
aḫ, iḫ, uḫ.
im.
u.
mi.
ul.
ši.
ar.
di, ṭi.
ki.
iš.
mí.
ib, ip.
ku.
lu.
ki.
šu.

ṣu.	il.	a.	tu.
gu.	ur.	za, ṣa.	ša.
		ḫa.	

Determinatives.

(Those marked × are placed after their words.)

ilu: god.	× kam: number.
alu: city.	× pl.
arḫu: month.	× ki: place, country, city.
× iṣṣuru: bird.	m.: masculine proper nouns.
kakkabu: star.	× pl.
× ta-a-an: number.	f.: fem. proper nouns, female animals, fem. adjectives used as nouns.
× kan: number.	ku: clothing.
imiru: animal.	kirru: lamb.
abnu: stone.	× a-an: number.
iṣu: tree, wood.	nâru: stream, body of water.
karpatu: vessel, pot.	× nûnu: fish.
amilu: official, tribe, people.	
mâtu: land, country. šadû: mountain.	

Ideograms.

1. ina: in, with, by; nadânu: to give.
2. Diklat: Tigris.
3. apsû: ocean, abyss.
4. mašku: skin; rabû: to increase.
5. sûḳu: road, street.
6. , naḳû: to sacrifice; palu: reign, year of reign; šupiltu: pudenda.
7. patru: dagger.
8. ilu: god; šamû: heaven.
9. anaku: lead.
10. išâtu: fire.
11. ṣalu(?)-lum: shadow(?).
12. parzillu: iron.
13. = Bil: god Bil.
14. Aššur: god Aššur.
    Aššur: city Aššur.
    Aššur: Assyria.
15. pû: mouth, exit (of a stream); ḳibû: to speak, command; šinnu: tooth, tusk.
16. šaptu: lip.
17. taḫazu: battle.
18. Šumiru: land Šumir.
19. alu: city.
20. puḫru: totality, assembly.
21. Marduk: god Marduk.
22. = Ištar: goddess Ištar.
23. = Nabû: god Nebo.
24. = Bil: god Bil.
25. ardu: servant; zikaru: male, manly.
    Dibbara: god of pestilence.
    , šu(?): tame sheep.
26. , arḫu: month.
27. šaḫu: a kind of wild beast.
28. dišu(?): grass(?).
29. uššu: foundation.
30. ṣiru, f. ṣirtu: exalted.
31. iribu: to enter.
    summatu: dove.
    a precious stone of some kind.
32. aḫu: brother; nakru: hostile; napḫaru: sum total, all; naṣâru: to protect.
    ( ) nakru: enemy.

33. 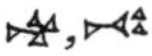 ziru: seed.
34.  zakâru: to speak, mention; nadânu: to give; šumu: name.
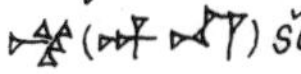 šattu: year.
35.  innu: lord; dâmu: blood; naḳbu: canal, stream.
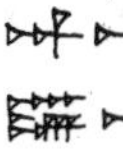 Bíl: god Bíl.
pagru: corpse.
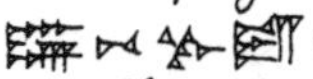 some high official.
36.  balâṭu: life.
ti-amat: the sea, also the sea personified.
37. 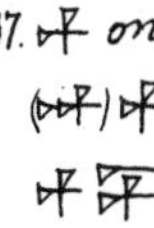 one half.
Adar: god Adar.
ṣabitu: gazelle.
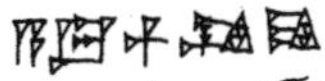 Diklat: river Tigris.
38.  lâ: not, without.
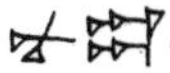 nisakku: prince.
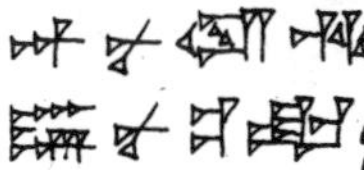 god Ìa.
gardener.
39.  iṣṣuru: bird.
40. 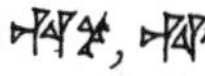 šîmtu: fate, destiny.
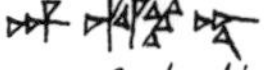 Nam-tar: god of destiny.
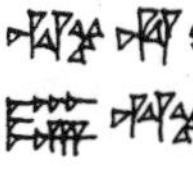 sinuntu: swallow.
piḫâtu: satrap.
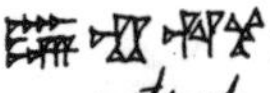 bíl piḫâti: satrap, governor.
41.  daltu: door.
42. kitu: a kind of clothing.

43.  ṭâbtu: goodness.
44. 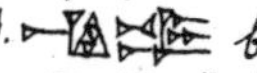 bûlu: cattle.
 šuttu: dream, vision.
45. 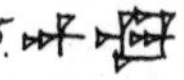 Nabû: god Nebo.
46. 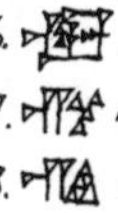 taḫazu: battle.
47. napištu: life.
48. ḳanû: reed.
 kânu: to be established; kînu: firm, lasting; kittu = kintu: right, justice.
49. 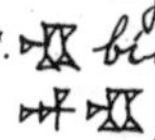 bílu: lord, possessor.
god Bíl; also bílu: lord.
 ḳipu: chief, governor.
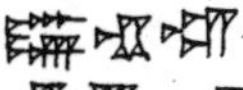 ḳipu: chief.
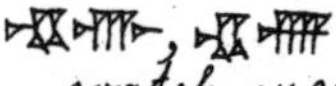 maṣartu: watch, guard.
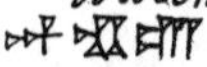 Bíl: god Bíl.
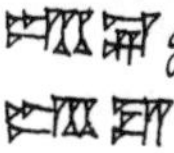 god Bíl & bílu: lord.
Sin: god Sin.
[illegible] kuṣṣu: hurricane.
50. 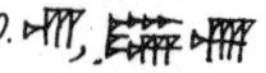 rubû: prince.
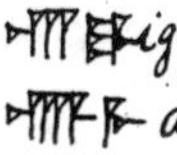 igigi: spirits of heaven.
abkallu: leader.
51.  šumílu: left hand.
52. 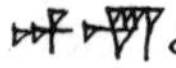 Ištar: goddess Ištar.
53.  dišpu: honey.
54. kišadu: neck, bank of a river.
55.  talent; biltu: tribute.
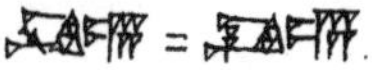
56. 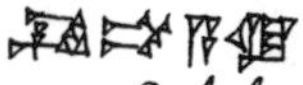 Kûtu: name of a Babylonian city.
57. 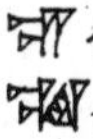 ḳarnu: horn.
58. birmi: variegated clothing.
59. 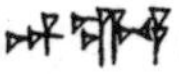 šídu: bull colossus.

60. rîšu: head; ašâridu: chief, leader.
kakkadu: head.
ašâridu: leader.
išâru: to prosper.
61. ilippu: ship.
malahu: seaman, pilot.
Mâ-kan: land M.
62. arba': four.
Arba'-ilu: Arbela
63. lapâtu: to fall.
64. stalk (?).
65. kakkabu: star.
66. iru: bronze.
67. Ninâ: Nineveh.
68. bâbu: gate.
abullu: city-gate.
Bâbilu: Babylon.
69. duppu: tablet.
70. ištu, ultu: from.
det. after numbers.
71. nâ'du: exalted.
i-gi-gi; cf. No. 50.
askuppu: threshold.
= i-na: in.
72. higallu: abundance.
šûku (?): abundance.
72a. ṣihru, ṣahru: small; mâru, aplu: child, son, inhabitant.
bin-bini: grandson.
aplu: son.
bintu: daughter.
apal-šarrûtu: prince regent, regency.
73. abu: father.
74. šarru: king.
Šarru. god Šarru.
75. kiru: park.
76. dûru: wall, castle.
Dûr-ilu: city D.
bît-dûru: stronghold.
77. nadânu: to give.
a festival (?).
78. harranu: road, campaign.
kasbu: double hour, journey of two hours.
79. irtu: breast, front.
80. ṣîru: top; ṣîr: above, upon, against; ṣîru: a plain.
kultaru: tent.
81. pîru: elephant.
82. šîru: flesh, members of the body.
83. išâtu: fire.
abu: month Ab.
84. dâku: to kill.
85. alâku: to go.
86. amilu, det. =
87. šarru: king.
88. imiru: ass; as det., animal.
purimu: wild ass.
gammalu: camel.
sisû: horse.
paru: mule.
gammalu: camel.
Dimašku: Damascus.
89. arkû: the rear; arka: after (adv.); arki: behind, after; arkânu: afterwards.
90. karanu: wine.
vine (?).
91. zikaru: male, manly; ridûtu: coition.
92. zikaru: man, servant.
93. ipru: dust.
94. kurunnu: wine.
95. rikku: aromatic plant.

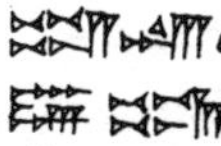

a kind of plant.

96. some official name(?).

97. 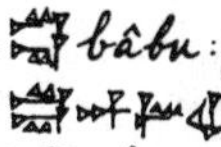 bâbu: gate = No 68.

Bâbilu Babylon

98.  abnu: stone

99. ipišu: to do, make; banû: to build, create, beget; kâlu: all.

100. 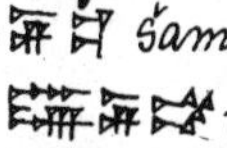 šamnu: oil.

kipu: guard.

101. 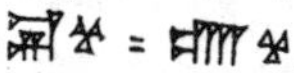 = , No. 122.

102. 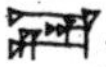 ummu: mother; rapšu: broad, numerous.

103. šamnu: oil; kisallu: floor, platform, altar(?).

104. 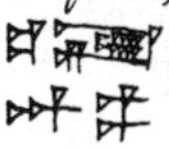 gušuru: beam.

105. Nabû: god Nebo.

ḫattu: scepter.

a kind of stone.

106. 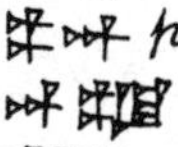 parṣu: command.

107. Nusku: god N.

108. 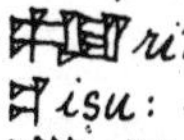 ri'u: shepherd, king.

109. iṣu: tree, wood.

110.  worshiper(?).

111. Šamaš: god Š.

112. 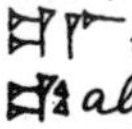 tukuntu: battle.

113. alpu: ox.

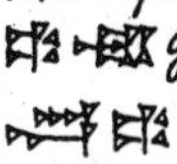

gû-maḫḫu: ox.

âru: name of a month.

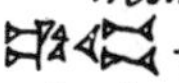

buffalo(?).

114. 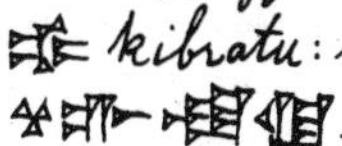 kibratu: region.

115. Aḫarrû: the West-land, Syria.

116.  karpatu: pot, vessel.

117. šangu: priest.

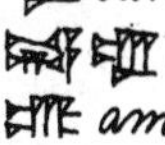

a kind of stone.

118. ammatu: cubit.

119. sukkallu: servant, messenger.

120. 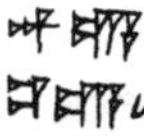 lamassu: bull colossus.

usû: a kind of wood.

121. nišu: people, inhabitants.

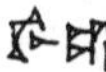

zikartu: female, woman.

122.  bîtu: house.

iširtu: shrine.

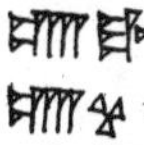

ikallu: palace.

ikur: temple.

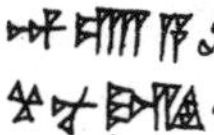

Ia: god I-a.

123. mâtu lâ târat: the underworld.

124. 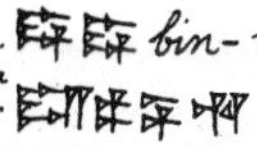 bin-bini, cf. No. 72.

124a. surdû: owl.

125.  amilu: man, officer, tribe.

126. aḫu: brother; naṣâru: to protect.

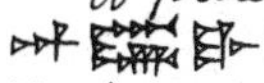

Nirgal: god N.

127. imnu, imittu: right hand.

128. 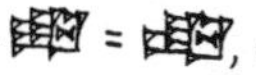 = , No. 76.

129. idu: hand, side; imuku: power, troops.

našru: eagle.

130. dârû: lasting.

131.  ḳablu: midst; ḳabaltu: waist.

132. 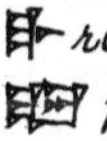 rabû: large.

133. parakku: sanctuary.

134.  agû: crown.

135. biltu: queen.

Šarrat: goddess Š.

136. ḳâtu: hand.

ubanu: finger, peak.

137.  male musicians.

female musicians.

138. 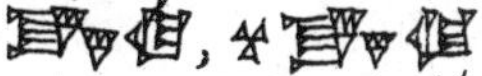 , Akkadu: land Akkad.

139. kašâdu: to reach, capture; kišittu: capture,

booty; mâtu: land, country; šadû: mountain.

a kind of bird.

140. magiru: gracious, favorable.

nirba: a species of grain.

141. a kind of bird.

142. rûḳu: distant.

143. kištu: forest.

144. gallu: demon.

145. mark of separation.

146. = , No. 76.

147. ûmu: day; šamšu (babbar): sun; piṣû: white; piru: scion, sprout.

šamšu: sun; Šamaš: Sun-god.

sît šamši: sunrise.

siparru: copper.

aṣû: to go out.

Sippar: city S.

Sippar: city S.

Purattu: Euphrates.

urru: light.

Larak: city L.

148. , uznu: ear.

149. libbu: heart.

150. ( ) ṣâbu: soldier.

( ) ummânu, ummânâti: army.

nirarû: help.

some precious stone.

151. kiššatu: totality, power.

Aššur: god Aššur; 62'' god Šár.

Aššur: Assyria.

ṭâbu: good.

152. det. after numbers.

153. šâru: wind.

Ramân: god R.; Addu: god A.

imbaru: storm.

nâ'du: exalted.

154. šimiru: ring.

155. pl. sign.

156. Ramân: god Ramân.

157. íli: at, upon, about, against.

158. = , No. 4.

159. Nirgal: god N.

160. iršu: bed.

161. kiššatu: totality, power.

162. ṣillu: shadow.

163. ḳaštu?: bow?.

Ílamtu: Elam.

birku: lightning.

kirru: lamb.

164. Marduk: god M.

165. niḳu: sacrifice.

niḳu: sacrificial lamb.

bíl niḳâni: priest.

166. ( ) ḳaštu: bow.

167. , kîma: like, as.

168. padanu: road, region; šípu: foot.

, šípu: foot.

šakkanakku: governor.

skeleton, bones.

169. , kabtu: heavy.

170. 1000.

abiktu: defeat.

171. ínu: eye.

172. concubine.
173. damku: gracious, favorable; damiktu: grace.
174. bilu: lord.
175. limuttu: evil (noun).
176. šulmu: peace, sunset.
dânu: judge.
sacrifice (?).
177. šarâpu: to burn.
178. tilu: hill, mound.
179. irṣitu: earth, land, site; ašru: place.
karašu: camp.
šupalû: lower; šaplitu: lower part.
kaspu (?): silver (?).
180. sign of repetition.
181. balâṭu: life.
182. illu: brilliant.
ḫurasu: gold.
kaspu: silver.
183. Ištar: goddess I.
184. šarru: king.
185. Sin: god Sin.
purussu: decree, decision.
186. = , No. 76.
187. det. for a man; ana: to, unto, for, against.
ištin: one.
188. našû: to bear.
189. one hundred.
190. plural sign.
191. seventy.
192. ṣinu: small domestic animals, sheep & goats.
193. narkabtu: chariot.
194. tukultu: confidence, aid.
urkarina: a kind of wood; kakku: weapon, battle; tukultu: confidence, aid.
tišrîtu: month Tishri.
195. irinu: cedar.
196. kiššatu: totality, power; šanîtu: time, repetition.
irib šamši: sunset.
197. = , No. 177.
198. nîru: yoke.
199. ḫidûtu: joy.
200. det. for females; aššatu: woman; zinnišu: female (adj.).
201. aḫâtu: sister; biltu: queen; mimma: whatever.
Bilit: goddess B.
Nin-ki-gal: goddess N.
Adar: god Adar.
202. aššatu: woman, wife.
203. kussu: throne.
guzalalu: throne-bearer.
204. libittu: brick.
god of bricks.
simânu: month Simân.
igaru: wall.
205. dual sign.
206. šumilu: left hand.
207. išû: to be, have.
208. nišu: lion.

209. barbaru: jackal.
kalbu: dog.

210. aplu: son; mû: water.
det. after numbers; zunnu: rain.
tâmtu: sea.
mîlu: overflow, flood.
nâru: stream, body of water.
Nâru: god Nâru.
Purattu: Euphrates.
A-šur: god Aššur.
anunnaki: spirits of the deep.
iklu: field, territory.
šigû: prayer or hymn.
Anum: god Anu.
god Malik(?).
allaku: messenger, courier.

211. uknu: crystal.

212. nûnu: fish.

213. inšu: weak.

214. šiklu: shekel.

215. šakânu: to establish; šaknu: governor, prefect.
a kind of chariot.
kudurru: crown, boundary stone.
makkuru: treasure.
ḫaṭṭu: scepter.
bušû: possession.
šaknu: governor.
bušû: possession.
a kind of chariot.
parab: five sixths.
igigi, cf. No. 50.

Numbers.

When not written syllabically, numbers are thus expressed:

= 1	= 12	= 200
= 2	= 20	= 1000
= 3	= 30	= 2000
= 4	= 70	= 20000
= 10	= 80	= 1886.
= 11	= 100	

OUTLINE OF GRAMMAR.

§ 1. **The language.** Assyrian is the language of that great Semitic empire of the Mesopotamian valley, which came to an end with the capture of Babylon by Cyrus in 538 B.C. This language has been preserved in inscriptions carved on stone and metals and stamped on clay. The oldest known specimens are from the time of Sargon I, whose date is given as about 3800 B.C. (cf. 37[38]). The written language continued in use through the Persian and Greek periods till after the beginning of our era, particularly for recording commercial transactions. The most flourishing literary period was the time of the last Assyrian dynasty, 722–606 B.C. The language, with very slight dialectical differences, was the same in Babylonia as in Assyria. Such a difference is the Babylonian preference for a softer pronunciation, as *íbíšu* 38[21] for *ípíšu* to make, *gâtu* 36[31] for *ḳâtu* hand, *irzitu* for *irṣitu* earth. The Assyrian belongs to what is known as the northern group of Semitic languages, including Hebrew, Aramaic, etc.

§ 2. **The written character.** The Assyrian language, which is read from left to right, is written in wedges, whence the name cuneiform (Lat. *cuneus*, a wedge, and *forma*), the common designation of this kind of writing. This character, which was employed by various other peoples besides the Babylonians and Assyrians, is believed to have been of non-Semitic invention. The Persians used a simplified form, which they reduced to an alphabet.

§ 3. **Ideograms.** Cuneiform writing was originally picture writing, each sign representing an object or idea. Thus a circle was the sun, four lines crossing at a point, a star, and five horizontal lines, a hand. It was perhaps owing to the difficulty of tracing on soft clay that the curves and straight lines developed into wedges. In the cuneiform signs as we now have them the original picture is in most cases no longer discernible. Signs representing objects and ideas are called *ideograms*. Some ideograms have several significations, but in many cases a relation between the several meanings is evident. Thus the sign for mouth represents the verb to speak, and the sign for booty represents also the verb to capture.

§ **4. Phonograms.** A second stage in the development was the use of some of the cuneiform signs to represent syllables. Such signs may be called *phonograms.* The syllabic or phonographic value comes directly from the name of the object represented by the ideogram. Thus the same sign stands for *rîšu* head as an id., and for *riš* as a phonogram; the id. *ḳâtu* hand gives the phon. *ḳat.* Some signs have several syllabic values, but in such cases there is generally one most frequently used, and practice will soon teach which of several values the reader should select. In transliterating it is customary to divide into syllables words written by phonograms, as *ak-šu-ud* I captured and to write without division words written ideographically, as *akšud.* Of the several hundred phonograms there are many of rare occurrence, while there are about a hundred which are used perhaps more than all the others combined. Most Assyrian writing is a union of ideograms and phonograms in proportions which vary greatly. Ordinarily the fewer the ideograms, the easier the reading.

§ **5. Determinatives, Phonetic complements.** The reading of Assyrian is greatly helped by the fact that certain of the ideograms are generally used to show to what class of objects the words they accompany belong. Such signs are called *determinatives,* and are used with names of gods, men, women, animals, countries, rivers, etc. The name itself may be written syllabically or ideographically. Most of the determinatives precede the words which they define. In transliterating, determinatives are usually indicated by difference of type. A *phonetic complement* is a syllable used after an id., to show how the word represented by the id. terminated. Thus if the id. for to capture be followed by the phonogram *ud,* we should have to read some form of the verb terminating in ud, as *ikšud, takšud, akšud.*

§ **6. On reading cuneiform inscriptions.** In reading a text in the original the first task is to group the signs into words and the words into clauses. Besides the aid given by determinatives and phon. complements, the student finds great help in a knowledge of the grammatical forms. The connectives and pronominal suffixes show the terminations of words. It is extremely rare that the Assyrians divided a word at the end of a line. Rather than do this they sometimes overcrowded the end of a line. In choosing between several syllabic values of a sign, that one is generally preferable which will give a tri-literal stem to the word under examination.

PHONOLOGY.

§ **7. Phonic material.** 1. Vowels. The language contains the vowels *a, i, u, â, î, û*. We may suppose that the vowels *e* and *o* also existed, but the Assyrians seem not to have employed special signs for these sounds. Some students believe that they did have separate signs for *e*-syllables[a], but it is clear from an examination of the cuneiform texts that the signs for *i* and those supposed to represent *e* are used interchangeably. The marks over the vowels, as *ú, ù, í, ì*, etc., in the transliterated texts (p. 1–52), represent neither accent nor difference of sound, but simply a difference of sign. In order to mark a vowel as long the Assyrians repeated the vowel sign, as *la-a* = *lâ*, *pu-u* = *pû*, but ordinarily the length of a vowel is not indicated at all. Such a repetition as *lu-ul* does not mark a vowel as long.

2. Consonants. The consonants are ב, ג, ד, ז, ח, ט, כ, ל, מ, נ, ס, פ, צ, ק, ר, שׁ, ת, or as transliterated *b, g, d, z, ḫ, ṭ, k, l, m, n, s, p, ṣ, ḳ, r, š, t*. The ח corresponds to the Arabic strong ח, the weak ח being lost in Assyrian. All the other gutturals (א, ה, ע) and also ו and י have been lost. In characterizing word stems the symbol א is however used to represent the lost gutturals, $א_1$ = א, $א_2$ = ה, $א_3$ = weak ח, $א_4$ = weak ע, $א_5$ = strong ע. These lost gutturals are frequently indicated by ' in transliteration. The Assyrian has a sign which stands for any one of the lost gutturals in connection with a vowel. The original presence of a guttural, especially of $א_{3\ 5}$, is seen in many words in the change of an original *a* to *i*, these gutturals preferring the *i* vowel (§ 8. 1), as *niribu* entrance for *na'ribu*, st. ערב. The presence of an original ו or י may also be seen by the influence of the consonants on the vowels, as *ušib* I sat = *a*ו*šib*, *idi* I knew = *a*י*da*ע. The Assyrians do not seem to have had the fricated forms of the letters ב, ג, ד, כ, פ, ת, nor to have distinguished between שׂ and שׁ.

§ **8. Phonic changes.** 1. Vowels. The change of *a* to *i* under the influence of a guttural is very frequent, as *ílî* I ascended for *a'lî*

---

a. I shared this view when I published *Keilschrifttexte Sargons*, J. C. Hinrichs, Leipzig, 1883, but renewed investigation has led to a change of opinion. I have collected considerable material on the subject which I hope some day to publish.

st. עלי, *rímu* grace Heb. רַחַם.—We have also in stems without a guttural *i* instead of the normal *a*, as *mu-šim-ḳít* 9[24] for *mu-šam-ḳít* one who casts down, *u-šik-ni-ša* 5[25] for *u-šak-ni-ša* he subdued.—The loss of a short *a* or *i* is common, as *bíltu* queen = *bílatu*, *ubla* he brought = *ubila*.—The diphthongs *a*ו and *a*י have become *u* and *i* respectively, as *ušib* 7[21] I sat = *a*ו*šib*, *iši* 58[6] I had = *a*י*ši*.—Vowel contraction is frequent, as *ukîn* 10[28] I placed = *uka*וו*in*.

2. Consonants. *a. Sibilants.* A sibilant (*z*, *s*, *ṣ*, *š*) if vowelless (i.e. not followed by a vowel) before a dental (*d*, *ṭ*, *t*) often becomes *l*, as *manzaltu* 50[15] position = *manzaztu*, *riḫiltu* 3[19] overflow = *riḫiṣtu*, *lubultu* 48[10] clothing = *lubuštu*. Here belongs perhaps *Kal-da-a-a* the Chaldean, cf. Heb. כַּשְׂדִּים. The same change often takes place when *š* precedes another sibilant, as *ulziz* 22[8] I stationed = *ušziz* = *ušaziz* = *ušazziz* = *ušanziz*, *alsâ* 15[27] I cried out = *aššâ*. *Š* after a vowelless dental and often after another sibilant becomes *s*, as *libnât-su* 36[18] its bricks = *libnât-šu*, *ulabbi-su* 48[11] I clothed him = *ulabbiš-šu*. After change of *š* to *s* the preceding letter may be assimilated and may then fall away, as in *ulabbi-su* (cf. *b.*).

b. Dentals. Vowelless dentals (*d*, *ṭ*, *t*) are often assimilated to a following sibilant or dental, sometimes falling away after assimilation, as *ḳaḳḳa-su* 18[22] his head = *ḳaḳḳad-su* (cf. *a*) = *ḳaḳḳad-šu*, *baltûs-su* 28[31] his life (i.e. him alive) = *balṭût-su* = *balṭût-šu*, *kišitu* 4[26] booty = *kišit-tu* = *kišid-tu*, *nubattu* 31[8] celebration (?) = *nubaṭ-tu*.

After a vowelless sibilant (*z*, *s*, *ṣ*, *š*) *t* in reflexive verb stems is sometimes assimilated to the sibilant, as *iṣṣabat* 13[27] he took = *iṣtabat*, *izzakkar* 52[13] she speaks = *iztakkar*.

T often becomes *d* after vowelless *m*, and *ṭ* after vowelless *ḳ*, as *tâmdu* 7[24] sea = *tâmtu*, *amdaḫiṣ* 4[9] I contended = *amtaḫiṣ*, *aḳṭírib* 8[2] I approached = *aḳtarib* (cf. § **8.** 1).

c. M. Vowelless *m* before dentals (*d*, *ṭ*, *t*), *ḳ* or *š* frequently becomes *n*, as *ṣindu* 14[29] span = *ṣimdu*, *lišanṭil* 37[13] may he prolong = *li* + *ušamṭil*, *mundaḫṣu* 24[25] soldier = *mumtaḫiṣu* (cf. § **8.** 1, and *b* above), *dunḳu* 46[28] favor = *dumḳu*, *ṭínšu* 28[19] his design = *ṭímšu* st. טעם, *ḫanšâ* II R 62, 45 fifty = *ḫamšâ*. In rare cases after change of *m* to *n* assimilation to a following letter takes place, as *attaḫar* I R 22, 88 I received = *antaḫar* = *amtaḫar*.

By a process of dissimilation vowelless *m* sometimes occurs instead of a doubled letter in order to mark an accented syllable, as *inambû* 39[15] they will name = *inabbû* = *inábû*, *inamdinû* 33[28] they were giving = *inádinû*.

In *irum-ma* 23[25] he entered and = *irub-ma* a vowelless *b* has been assimilated to *m*.

d. *N*. Vowelless *n* is usually assimilated to a following letter, as *akkis* 8[22] I cut down = *ankis*, *aššî* 42[14] I lifted = *anšî*, *limuttu* 39[25] evil = *limun-tu*. Occasional exceptions occur, as *ušanṣir* 31[25] I caused to keep, *mandattu* 10[27] gift. After assimilation the *n* often falls away, as *mâdâtu* 8[3] gift = *mandantu*, *akis* 7[27] I cut down = *ankis*. Sometimes only a partial assimilation takes place, the *n* becoming *m*, as *ambi* Sargon Cyl. 68 I named = *anbi*, *namba'u* 31[24] spring = *nanba'u*. In *ušamkir* 27[30] he made hostile = *ušankir* (?) there seems to be a case of dissimilation.

An initial *n* is lost in imperatives I I (cf. § 21), as *izizi* 52[23] stay = *nizizi*, *uṣur* protect = *nuṣur* (e.g. in the proper name *Nabium-kudurri-uṣur* I R 65, 1), *išî* lift up = *nišî* cf. *i-ša-an-ni* V R 21, 24 lift me up.

e. *Gutturals* and ו. A guttural instead of being lost is sometimes assimilated to a following or preceding letter, as *allik* 1[22] I went = *a*ח*lik*, *innabit* 10[20] he vanished = *in*א*abit*. Similarly in the reflexive stems of verbs initial ו the ו is assimilated to the following *t*, as *attašab* 59[23] I sit down = *a*ו*tašab*.

MORPHOLOGY.

PRONOUNS.

§ **9. Personal pronouns.** 1. SEPARABLE PRONOUNS.

a. *As subject*.

		SING.	PL.
1.	c.	*anâku*	*(a)nîni*
2.	m.	*atta*	*attunu*
2.	f.	*attî*	*attina* (?)
3.	m.	*šû*	*šûnu*
3.	f.	*šî*	*šina*

Illustrations: *a-na-ku* 19[17] (sometimes written *ana-ku*, as I R 17, 34 var.); *atta* 14[24]; *at-ti* V R 25, 30; *šû* 12[23]; *šî* V R 6, 110: *anîni* Strassm. No. 492 *a-ni-ni ni-il-la-ka* we will go; *attunu* Strassm. No. 923; *šûnu* V R 4, 121; *šina* III R 40, 100.

b. *As object* (with force of Acc., Dat., etc., me, to me, as for me, etc.).

		SING.	PL.
1.	c.	*yâtu*, *yâti*, *yâši*, *a-a-ši*	——
2.	m.	*kâtu*, *kâti*, *kâša*	*kâšunu*
2.	f.	*kâti*, *kâši*	——
3.	m.	*šâšu*	*šâšunu*
3.	f.	*šâši*	——

Illustrations: *yâtu* Strassm. No. 3557, *yâti* 22^{17}, *yâši* 24^{8}, *a-a-ši* V R 6, 4 var.; *kâtu* IV R 9, 60 a, *kâša* IV R 50 col. I 10; *šâšu* 11^{10}.

2. PRONOMINAL SUFFIXES.

			NOMINAL.	VERBAL.
SING.	1.	c.	*-î, -ya, -a*	*-ni*
	2.	m.	*-ka*	*-ka*
	2.	f.	*-ki*	*-ki*
	3.	m.	*-šu, -š*	*-šu, -š*
	3.	f.	*-ša, -š*	*-ši, -š*
PL.	1.	c.	*-ni*	*-nâši*
	2.	m.	*-kun(u)*	*-kunûši*
	2.	f.	*-kina* (?)	——
	3.	m.	*-šun(u), -šunûti*	*-šunu, -šunûti, -šunûtu, -šunûši*
	3.	f.	*-šin(a)*	*-šina, -šinâni, -šinâti, -šinîti.*

The nominal suffixes *î* and *ya* are appended to forms ending in *i*, while *a* is appended to forms ending in *a* or *u*, rarely to forms ending in *i*, as *bílû-ti-a* 5^{17}. The first consonant of the suffixes is frequently doubled when appended to forms ending in a vowel, thus giving *-anni*, *-akka*, etc. — The suffixes, nominal and verbal, of the 1st and 2nd persons pl. are comparatively rare. — For the 3rd m. pl. *-šun*, *-šunu* are the prevailing forms with nouns and *šunûti* with verbs. — The verbal suffixes generally express the direct object, but often also the indirect object.

Illustrations. 1) Nominal: *libbî* 42^{13} my heart, *ḳâtî-ya* 42^{14} my hands, *abû-a* 23^{10} my father; *ummân-ka* 14^{22} thy army; *šum-ki* 52^{24} thy name; *kakku-šu* 9^{6} his weapon, *napšatuš* 14^{13} his life; *siḫírti-ša* 1^{22} its extent; *put-ni* 61^{24} our side, *biri-inni* 61^{24} our midst; *libbi-kun* I R 9, 19 of your heart, *libbi-kunu* IV R 52 No. 1, 2; *maḫar-šun* 10^{11} before them, *šarrâni-šunu* 1^{2} their kings, *libba-šunûti* 46^{11} their heart; *bâbî-šin* Sargon St. 74 their gates, *kâli-šina* 5^{14} all of them.

2) Verbal: *uma'ira-ni* I R 12, 52 he sent me, *umašširanni* 27^{27} he forsook me, *ušíšibu-inni* 20^{23} they seated me; *išannan-ka* IV R 26, 57 he rivals thee, *tušannakka* Assurb. Sm. 125, 63 she addresses thee; *išassu-ki* IV R 29, 58 b he calls to thee; *isḫup-šu* 48^{22} it cast him down, *ušatlimu-š* 50^{22} he granted to him, *ura-aššu* 11^{11} I carried him; *ušarriḫ-ši* 6^{25} I made it powerful; *ikarrabannâši* 61^{24} he blesses us, *itbuḫu-kunûši* IV R 52 No. 1, 4; *alḳa-šunûti* 1^{18} I took them, *dûku-šunûtu* III R 39, 48 kill them, *inadin-šunûši* II R 11, 27 b he gives them; *ištín'í-šinâtim* 40^{11} he provided for them.

§ **10. Demonstrative pronouns.** There are four demonstrative stems, the *n*, the *l*, the *š* and the *g* stems.

1. *annû*, this, this one (gen. *annî*, acc. *annâ*, pl. *annûti*, *annûtu*; fem. *annîtu*, gen. *annîti*, acc. *annîta*, pl. *annâti*, *annâtu*, *annîti*, *annîtu*).

Illustrations: *an-nu-u šar-a-ni* III R 15 col. I 25 this one is our king, *û-mí an-ni-i* V R 6, 2 of this day; *šarrâni an-nu-ti* 46[1] these kings, *an-nu-tu* Strassm. No. 549: *šutta an-ni-tu* 22[14] this vision, *í-li šutti an-ni-ti* V R 5, 102 upon this vision; *ip-ší-í-ti an-na-a-ti* 26[27] these deeds, *an-na-a-tu matâti* III R 39, 40 these are the countries, *an-ni-ti matâti* NR. 8 these countries, *matâti an-ni-tu* NR. 25 these countries.

2. *ullû* that, that one, the former (gen. *ullî*, acc. *ullâ*, pl. *ullûti*, *ullûtu*).

Illustrations: *ina ṭur-ri ul-lu-u* S. 9 on that hill (?), *ul-tu ul-la* 34[9] from that (time) = from of old; *û-mí ul-lu-u-ti* 27[4] former days, *tab-ba-nu-u ul-lu-u-tu* D. 15 those buildings.

3. *šû'atu*, *šû'ati*, *šâtu*, *šâti* (= 3 pers. stem *šû* + *tu* etc.) that one, the same one (pl. *šû'atunu*, *šâtunu;* fem. *šî'ati*, pl. *šû'atina*, *šatina*).

Illustrations: *ala šu-a-ta ak-šud* 4[21] that city I captured, *ši-pir šu-a-ti* 24[14] that building, *ala ša-a-tu* . . . *aš-ru-up* I R 10, 34 that city I burned; *na-gi-i šu-a-tu-nu* Khors. 71 those provinces, *šarrâ-ni ša-tu-nu* I R 13, 10 those kings: *ina šatti-ma ši-a-ti* Lay. 89, 50 in that same year; *matâti šu-a-ti-na* II R 67, 23 the same countries, *si-gur-ra-a-tu ša-ti-na* I R 16, 53 the same towers (?).

So, also, the simpler forms (given above as 3 pers. pronouns), as *alu šû* 6[18] that city, sometimes strengthened by the pronominal elements *ti*, *tina*, as *abullî šinâti* I R 56 col. VI 19 these gates, *matâti šinâtina* I R 12, 32 these countries.

4. *agâ* this, this one, belongs chiefly to the Persian period. *agâ* Beh. 4, pl. *aganûtu* Beh. 106, *aganûti* IV R 52, 37; fem. *agâta* Beh. 10, pl. *aganîtu* Beh. 8. The adverb *agannu*, *aganna* here, is composed of *agâ* and *annu*. For *aganna* cf. Pinches Texts 7, 7 (in a report sent by an officer to Sargon) and Assurb. Sm. 125, 63 *a-gan-na lu aš-ba-ta* here shalt thou remain.

§ **11. Relative pronoun.** The relative pronoun is the indeclinable *ša*, used for all persons, genders and numbers, as 1[2,21]. The relative is frequently used for the one who, whoever, as Sargon Cyl. 76 *ša ipšit ḳâti-ya unakkaru* whoever shall change the work of my hand. As a weakened relative *ša* is much used to express the genitive relation, as *bamâti ša šadî* 1[18] heights of the mountains. As anticipative of a pronominal suffix *ša* often occurs, as *ša . . . kakku-šu* 9[6] whose weapon, *ša . . . abikta-šu* 42[3,4] whose defeat. The relative is frequently omitted, as *ṭâbtu ipussunûti* 46[10] the good which I had done to them, *ašar ikaššadu* 17[2] wherever they catch them. Those forms of the verb regularly terminating in a consonant take in relative sentences the vowel termination *u* or *a*, as *akšudu* 4[27] I captured, *azkura* 20[16] I mentioned. This usage holds in cases where the relative is omitted, as *ultu . . . ímídu* 21[25] after I had subdued (= *ultu ûmi ša . . . ímídu*, from the day when . . . I subdued), *ultu ipšîti annâti ítíppušu* 26[27] after I had done these things.

§ **12. Interrogative pronouns**: *mannu* who?, *minû* what? (gen. *minî*, acc. *minâ*). Illustrations: *ina šamî man-nu ṣîru* IV R 9, 54 in heaven who is exalted?, *minâ íkul ínnî* II R 56, 16 what has my lord eaten?, *ina íli minî* 32[22] wherefore? *amminî* 63[7] wherefore? (= *ana minî*).

§ **13. Indirect interrogative and indefinite pronouns**: *mannu* whoever, *manman*, *mamman*, *mamma*, *manma*, *manama*, *manamma*, *maman* any one, any one at all; *manma*, *mimma* anything at all, whatever, whatsoever.

Illustrations: *mannu atta* 39[14] whoever thou be, *ana maḫar mamman lâ illikamma* II R 67, 26 into the presence of no one did he come, *ša . . . mamma lâ iškupu* I R 15, 20 which no one had planted, *manama šarru* 37[33] any king, *apal lâ maman* I R 18, 76 son of a nobody; *manma ša ina matâti ítípuša* Layard 90, 72 whatever I had done in the countries, *mimma šumšu* 12[29] whatever its name, cf. *mi-im-ma šu-um-šu* I R 53 col. II 32.

§ **14. Reflexive pronoun.** To express the reflexive idea the pronominal suffixes are attached to the word *ramânu* self, as *í-muḳ ra-man-i-šu* 22[27] the power of himself, *ra-man-šu im-nu* 25[23] he reckoned himself, *ša ra-man-šu iš-ku-nu* 28[18] who had appointed himself (as king).

NOUNS.

§ **15. Noun formation.** 1. Simple stem. Many nouns present, of course, only the simple stem consonants, with large variety in the sequence of vowels, as *danânu* 34[30] might, *gašîšu* 33[32] stake, *šaruru* 37[3] brilliance, *šâninu* 2[19] rival, *kišadu* 19[15] neck, *ḳurâdu* 2[16] warrior; and the segholates, as *malku* 9[7] prince, *šiknu* 24[30] appointee, *dunḳu* 46[28] favor. The segholate formation is a favorite one from stems initial ו, as *biltu* 10[27] tribute Aram. בְּלוֹ st. ובל, *šubtu* 6[22] abode Heb. שֶׁבֶת st. ישב, *šuttu*

35[14] dream Heb. שֵׁנָה st. ושן, *riḳḳu* 36[15] plant Heb. יֶרֶק st. ורק, *ṣîtu* 6[10] exit Heb. צֵאת st. וצא.

2. Reduplicated stem. The reduplication may affect the second letter, or the third letter, or the whole stem: as *ḫabbilu* 14[11] bad, *ḳullultu* 12[3] shame; *agammu* 14[12] marsh, *ḫušaḫḫu* 61[17] famine; *dandannu* 7[8] all-powerful, *ḳalḳaltu* 30[10] hunger. (It must be borne in mind that the doubling of a letter is also often purely orthographic.)

3. Formative elements. Many other nouns are made by formative elements, prefixed, inserted or appended. *a. Prefixes:* א, *m*, *n*, *š*, *t*, the most frequent being *m*, *n*, and *t*. Illustrations: א, *iḳribu* 24[17] prayer; *m*, *manzazu* 32[29] position, *maṣartu* 31[24] guard = *manṣartu*, *mûšabu* 28[13] abode st. ושב, *mušpalu* 6[20] depth, *mîšaru* 40[11] righteousness st. ישר; *n*, *namkuru* 1[15] possession, *nabnîtu* 7[17] offspring, *narâmu* 20[19] favorite st. ר$_3$אם, *nimíḳu* 36[12] wisdom st. $_4$אמק, *nišbû* 30[31] sufficiency; *š*, *šupšuḳu* I R 12, 54 steep, *šûturu* 7[5] powerful st. ותר; *t*, *tamḫaru* 1[4] battle, *tamirtu* 11[26] vicinity st. $_1$אמר, *taḫlubu* 36[22] roof, *tínišítu* 19[25] mankind st. $_1$אנש, *talittu* 20[28] birth = *ta*ו*lid-tu*, *tidûku* 8[18] slaughter st. דוך.

b. Infix: *t* after the first radical, as *bitḫallu* 8[19] riding-horse, *gitmalu* 7[8] mature, *mitḫuṣu* 12[10] battle, *ḳitrubu* 12[10] attack, *itpíšu* Sargon Cyl. 34 wise st. אפש.

c. Affixes: *â* (written *a-a*) making gentilic nouns, *ût* (the fem. *t* appended to the stem in *û*) making abstract nouns, and *ân*. Illustrations: *â*, *As-du-da-a-a* 11[8] the Ashdodite; *ût*, *nirarûtu* 2[12] help, *šarrûtu* 20[4] royalty, *bílûtu* 12[5] dominion; *ân*, *ḳurbânu* II R 38 11 offering, *bârânu* Sargon Cyl. 32 robber st. באר, *ušmânu* 8[20] camp st. $_3$אשם.

§ **16. Inflection.** 1. Gender. Masculine nouns have no distinctive ending. Feminines are made by the termination *t*, as *šarratu* 52[24] queen from *šarru* king, *šalimtu* 41[13] peace. Some feminines are without the distinguishing *t*, as *ummu* 7[10] mother, *ínu* 37[11] eye, *girru* 10[18] way, campaign, *ímuḳu* 50[22] power st. $_4$אמק.

2. Number. The dual, terminating in *â*, is little used, except in the names of objects occurring in pairs, and even here not always, as *i-na* IV R 48, 6 eyes, but also *i-ni* 37[11] eyes.

Plurals masc. are made in *û*, *î*, *âni* (*ânu*), *ûti* (*ûtu*), the most frequent being *î* and *âni;* as *mušarbû* 7[12] those who enlarge, *šadî* 6[8] mountains, *ḳípâni* 42[7] governors, *amílûti* 32[8] men. Occasionally plurals are found, both masc. and fem., which have lost the vowel terminations, as *malik* 23[16] kings, *kibrât* 5[6] regions (fem.).

Plurals fem. are made in *âti*, *îti*, some feminines, however, not differing in form from masculines; as *napšâti* 17^{1} from *napištu* life, *girrîti* 21^{4} from *girru* road, *ímuḳî* 50^{22} powers, *idân* Sargon Cyl. 24 forces.

In adjectives and participles plurals masc. are made in *ûti* (*ûtu*), plurals fem. in *âti* (*âtu*), as *kašidûti* 29^{28} victorious, *ṣîrûtu* 36^{23} lofty, *ṣîrâti* 38^{9} lofty.

3. Case. The terminations *u*, *i*, *a* correspond to the nom., gen. (dat., loc., etc.) and acc., as in classic Arabic, as nom. *šarru*, gen. *šarri*, acc. *šarra;* but the distinction is not always consistently observed, as *ḫarranu* 13^{27} way (acc.), *dannu* 23^{17} mighty (gen.), *libba* 11^{23} heart (nom.). After prepositions the form in *i* is generally used, unless the noun be also in the construct state, in which case the final vowel would be regularly omitted, as *ina niš ḳâti-ya* 23^{7} at the lifting up of my hands. In the plural there is no distinction of case by the form, *šarrâni*, for instance, representing all the cases.

To noun forms terminating in a vowel one sometimes finds an *m* appended, which is generally known as the *mimmation*, as *ḫattum* 13^{25} fear, *karanam* I R 65 col. I 22 wine, *tâmtim* 10^{20} sea.[a]

4. Construct state. In the construct state the first of the two nouns loses its final vowel and the second is used in the genitive, as *nâš bilti* 1^{3} bearer of tribute, *mítíḳ narkabâti* 2^{7} passage of the chariots, *šalmât ḳurâdî* 1^{11} corpses of the warriors. Sometimes the form in *i* instead of the form without a final vowel is used in the construct state, as *tukulti* 1^{6} aid, *puluḫti* 29^{27} fear. In segholates the noun becomes dissyllabic, as *arad* 25^{8} from *ardu* servant, *uzun* 52^{2} from *uznu* ear, *gimir* 2^{19} from *gimru* totality. In feminine segholates the original *a* vowel of the feminine returns, as *napšat* 26^{7} from *napištu* life, *gimrat* 7^{1} from *gimirtu* totality, *irat* 9^{16} from *irtu* breast. The construct of nouns from stems ע״ע generally loses the final consonant, as *šar* 3^{6} from *šarru* king. The construct form of the noun is very common before suffixes, as *mât-su* 42^{4} for *mâta-šu* his land, *ḳât-su* 5^{13} his hand, *ummân-ka* 14^{22} thy army, *šubat-su* 18^{18} its dwelling; *libnât-su* 36^{18} its bricks (§ **8**. 2 *a*).

§ **17. Numerals.** Some of the numerals occur very rarely written syllabically. Of the cardinals whose pronunciation is known to me $1 =$ *ištín* 6^{11} (cf. Heb. עַשְׁתֵּי־עָשָׂר $= 1 + 10 = 11$); $2 =$ *šinâ* IV R 7 col. I 21; $3 =$ *šalašti* V R 12, 34, *šalalti* S^{c} 124, *šílalti* IV R 5 64 a; $4 =$ *arba'i* 2^{22}

---

a. This *m* seems to be identical with the pronominal enclitic *ma* (§ 18), and also to exist in Hebrew and Sabean, but, whatever its origin and original function, the *mimmation* has become in Assyrian a petrifaction, without perceptible influence on the meaning of the word with which it occurs.

fem. *irbittu* 35[2]; 5 = *ḫamilti* II R 62[51] (§ **8.** 2 *a;* the masc. form *ḫamiš* is seen in the word for fifteen); 7 = *siba* II R 19, 14 fem. *sibitti* IV R 2 col. V 31; 8 = *samnu* (so one may conclude from the name of the 8th month *Araḫ-samnu* Delitzsch Lesest.[3] p. 92); 10 = *išírit* II R 62, 50; 15 = *ḫamíššírit* ib. 49; 20 = *íšrâ* ib. 48; 30 = *šílašâ* ib. 47; 40 = *irba'a* ib. 46; 50 = *hanšâ* ib. 45 (§ **8.** 2 *c*); 60 = *šušu* ib. 44; 600 = *nír* V R 18, 23; 3600 = *šar* S[c] 79, the last three names being derived from the sexagesimal system which existed beside the decimal system of counting.

The ordinals known to me are 1st *maḫrû* 42[1]; 2nd *šanû* IV R 5, 15; 3rd *šalšu* 10[18] fem. *šalultu* 35[25]; 4th *ribû* 60[6]; 5th *ḫaššu* IV R 5, 22 (§ **8.** 2 *c*); 6th *šiššu* IV R 5, 24; 7th *sibû* 59[16].

PARTICLES.

§ **18. Conjunctions.** The connectives are *û*, joining single words, as 1[3], or introducing paragraphs, as 11[8], and *ma*, joining sentences, as 1[18]. *Ma* is always attached to the end of the first sentence. Frequently *ma* is attached to a word not as a connective, but as an emphatic demonstrative, as *ušabrišuma* 22[11] he caused him to see; in other cases it makes its word more indefinite, as *ya-um-ma* 1[4] any one at all.

Other frequent conjunctions are *adi* 37[29] while, during, *aššu* 22[26] (= *ana* + *šu*) because, in order to, *ištu* and *ultu* 21[25] after, from the time when, *kî* 14[14] as, when, surely.

Lû or *lî* is a particle of wishing or of asseveration prefixed to verbs. Its vowel frequently unites with the initial vowel of the verb, as *lu-šar-di* 1[18] I caused to flow = *lû* + *ušardî*.

§ **19. Adverbs.** Any noun or adjective, sing. or pl., may form an adv. terminating in *iš*, as *damḳíš*, 41[13] graciously, from *damḳu* grace. One sometimes meets the form in *iš* preceded by a preposition as *ana ma'diš* 8[15] very much. Such usage seems to show that the adverb in *iš* was originally only a shortened form of the demonstrative *šu* or *ša* appended to the noun form in *i*.

1. Adverbs of manner. Nearly all the adverbs in *iš* denote manner, as *míšíriš* 2[22] righteously, *abubâniš* 7[19] like deluges. Other adverbs expressing manner are *kîam* 63[8] thus, *mâ* I R 21, 50, and *umma* 22[12] thus (introducing oratio recta). Adverbs of affirmation and negation are *lû* 1[9] verily, *lâ* 8[23], *ul* 1[8] and *â* 46[18] (written *a-a*) not.

2. Adverbs of time: *ullâ* of old, *ininna* 26[23] now, *itimali*, *timali* yesterday (אֶתְמוֹל), *arka* 14[6] and *arkânu* 20[4] after, afterwards, *matî*

when?, *adi matî* IV R 29, 54a how long? (עַד־מָתַי), *matîma* ever, at any time, *lâ matîma* 21[8] never, *pana*, *panama* before.

3. Adverbs of place: *agannu* Beh. 12 *aganna* Assurb. Sm. 125, 63 here, *kilallan* 35[16] around, about, *íliš* 62[4] above, *šapliš* 62[5] below.

§ **20. Prepositions**: *adi* 3[24] 11[30] as far as, together with, *ana* 32[5] to, unto, against, etc., *arki* 25[2] 50[7] after, behind, *íli* 6[19] over, above, upon, more than, to, against, *íllamu* 11[26] before, in front of, *ina* 21[4] in, with, by, at the time of, *ištu* 5[22] out of, from, *itti* 1[9] with, against, *ultu* 9[8] 21[29] out of, from, *balu* I R 35 No. 2, 6 without, *birit* 30[8] between, *gadu* 17[29] together with, *kî* Sargon Cyl. 51 and *kîma* 5[21] like, according to, *kum* 29[13] instead of, *lapan* 14[13] before, in front of, *maḫar* 39[9] before, in front of, *ṣîr* 15[26] upon, against.

In such expressions as *ina íli* above, *ultu kirib* out of, *ina maḫar* in front of, the words *íli*, *kirib*, *maḫar* preserve their original nominal force. On the form of the noun after prepositions cf. § **16**. 3.

Instead of a preposition and noun one often meets a form of the noun in *u* without a preposition, as *mâtuššun* 17[15] to their country = *ana mâti-šun*, *šípû-a* 10[26] to my foot = *ana šípi-ya*, *aluššu* Sargon Cyl. 32 out of his city = *ištu ali-šu*.

VERBS.

§ **21. Verb stems.** The Assyrian verb has four primary, four secondary and two tertiary stems, the secondary and tertiary being formed from the primary by the aid of the syllables *ta* and *tan*, according to the following scheme:

PRIMARY.	SECONDARY.	TERTIARY.
I 1 *Pe'al*	I 2 *Ifte'al*	I 3 *Iftane'al*
II 1 *Pa'el*	II 2 *Ifta'al*	——[a]
III 1 *Shafel*	III 2 *Ishtafal*	——[a]
IV 1 *Nifal*	IV 2 *Ittafal* (= *Intafal*)	IV 3 *Ittanafal* (= *Intanafal*)

With the verb *šakânu* to set, place, establish, this scheme would give in the 3rd sing. of the second impf. (§ **22**):

I 1 *iškun*	I 2 *ištakin*	I 3 *ištanakin*
II 1 *ušakkin*	II 2 *uštakkin*	——
III 1 *ušaškin*	III 2 *uštaškin*	——
IV 1 *iššakin* (= *inšakin*)	IV 2 *ittaškin*	IV 3 *ittanaškin*

a. I should suppose that the language had also the stems II 3 and III 3, but I have met no examples of them. The stems IV 2–3 are rare.

1. The use of the numerals to represent the various stems has been found to be very convenient. Observe that the formative syllables *ta*, *tan* come immediately after the first consonant of the various stems, and therefore before the first radical in the stems III and IV, i.e. in stems with formative prefixes.

2. Besides these ten stems, one occasionally meets a stem III–II, a Shafel of a Pa'el, as *ušḫammiṭ* 18[16] I caused to hasten, *ušrappiš* I R 7 No. F. 18 I made broad. The stem III–II is particularly frequent with the verbs *malû* to be full and *rabû* to be large.

3. Such forms as *upaḫir* 20[2], variant for *upaḫḫir* he collected, are only orthographically different from regular Pa'el forms. On the other hand, the doubling of a consonant seems in many cases to be intended to mark an accented syllable, as *išaṭṭaru* 24[20] for *išáṭaru* I 1 he shall write.

4. In *meaning* I 1 is the simple stem (Heb. Qal), II 1 intensive, causative or (when I 1 is intransitive) transitive (Heb. Piel), III 1 causative (Heb. Hifil), IV 1 passive, rarely reflexive (Heb. Nifal). The stems with *ta*, *tan* have reflexive force, being sometimes equivalent to a Greek middle voice, but are often used interchangeably with the primary stems.

Illustrations: I 1 *ikšud* 3[31] he captured, I 2 *iṣṣabat* 13[27] (= *iṣtabat* § **8.** 2 *b*) he took, I 3 *ištanapara* 22[26] he was sending, II 1 *urakkis* 21[4] I erected, II 2 *uktîn* 60[17] (= *uktawwin* §§ **7.** 2; **8.** 1 st. כון) I arranged, III 1 *ušaṣbit* 6[18] I caused to work, III 2 *ultašpiru* 9[9] (= *uštašpiru* § **8.** 2 *a*) he ruled, IV 1 *iššakin* 23[10] it was established, IV 2 *littapraš* IV R 4, 2 b (= *li* + *intapraš*) may he fly, IV 3 *ittanabriḳ* IV R 3, 4 *a* it lightens.

§ **22. Tense and mood.**[a] Each stem has two forms of the Imperfect, a Permansive, an Imperative, an Infinitive, and a Participle.

1. The mark of the first impf. I 1 is the vowel *a* after the first radical and *a* (rarely *u* or *i*) after the second radical, as *ikaššadu* 17[2] (= *ikašadu* § **21.** 3) they were catching, *adabuba* 20[16] I was planning, *inakimu* I R 16, 68 he will heap up. The second impf. I 1 has no vowel after first radical, while the second radical has *u*, *a*, or *i*, as *ikšud* 3[31] he captured, *iṣbat* 25[22] he took, *iddin* 60[3] (= *indin*) it gave. In the other stems the two imperfects are distinguished by the vowel after the second radical, this vowel being generally *a* in the first and *i* in the second

---

a. Although these terms are objectionable in speaking of the verb in Semitic languages, they are here retained because we have no convenient substitutes for them.

impf.; as II 1 *urasapu* 17² (= *urassapu* § **21**. 3) they were piercing (first impf.), *urassip* 25¹ he pierced (second impf.).[a]

2. The office of the impf., in general, is to mark an action as inchoative, continuing, repeated.

The first impf. expresses continuous action whether in past, present or future time, as *irtammam* 58¹² he was thundering, *ibanna-ši* 61⁸ he does it, *izannanû* Delitzsch Lesest.³ 103, 86 var. they will rain st. *zanânu.*

The second impf., which is the ordinary narrative tense, is chiefly used to mark an action as occurring at a point of time, as *aškun* 1¹¹ I accomplished, *iṣbatû* 1⁶ they took, *allik* 1²² I went.

Both forms of the impf. are employed in expressing wish, but the second impf is most used, as *lisaḫrûni* I R 16, 24 may they turn (= *li* + *isaḫarûni*, § **8**. 1), *lišṭur* 24¹⁶ may he write (= *li* + *ištur*). In prohibition the first impf. is used, as *lâ tanaša* 52²³ do not lift up, *lâ tapalaḫ* IV R 68, 16 b do not fear, *ana ili šanima lâ tatakkil* I R 35 No. 2, 12 do not trust in any other god (but Nabu).

3. The permansive differs in form from the impf. in that it has no preformatives, the pronominal elements (shortened forms of the personal pronouns) being placed after the verb stem. The 3rd pers. sing. and pl. of the permansive is without such pronominal addition, the *t* in 3rd fem. sing. being the same as in nouns.

The permansive has generally intransitive meaning, and denotes continuance of a state or quality. It may have other vowels in the stem I 1 besides those given in the paradigm (§ **23**), as *šikin, šakun.*[b]

Illustrations of the permansive: *ašbâ* 52⁹ they dwell, *šapuḫ* 52¹¹ it is spread, *ṣabtû* 15¹⁵ they held, *šitkunu* 15¹⁴ it was situated, *muššurâ* 16²⁴ they were left, *purrukû* 26³¹ they were barred, *išâku* I R 9, 58 I had.

A similar formation to the permansive[c] is the union of pronoun with noun or adjective, as *šarraku, bilaku, ḳarradaku, dannaku* I R 17, 32. 33 I am king, I am lord, I am strong, I am mighty.

---

a. Some students call the first impf. a present, a future, a second aorist, while they name the second impf. a preterite, an imperfect, a first aorist. The terms present, future, preterite, aorist, are all objectionable. The terms first and second impf., applied here to the Assyrian verb, so far as I am aware, for the first time, may be somewhat long, but they recognize the essential unity of the two forms. I have called that form first impf. which I suppose to have been first developed.

b. Cf. two papers on the permansive by Mr. T. G. Pinches in the Proceedings of the Society of Biblical Archæology for Nov. 1882 and Jan. 1884.

c. This is possibly identical with the permansive, a subject which I leave here without discussion.

§ 23. **Inflection of the strong verb, šakânu, to establish.**

			I 1 Pe'al.	**II 1 Pa'el.**	**III 1 Shafel.**	**IV 1 Nifal.**
1st Impf.	SG.	3. m.	*išakan*	*ušakkan*	*ušaškan*	*iššakan*
		3. f.	*tašakan*	*tušakkan*	*tušaškan*	*taššakan*
		2. m.	*tašakan*	*tušakkan*	*tušaškan*	*taššakan*
		2. f.	*tašakanî*	*tušakkanî*	*tušaškanî*	*taššakanî*
		1. c.	*ašakan*	*ušakkan*	*ušaškan*	*aššakan*
	PL.	3. m.	*išakanû(ni)*	*ušakkanû(ni)*	*ušaškanû(ni)*	*iššakanû(ni)*
		3. f.	*išakanâ(ni)*	*ušakkanâ(ni)*	*ušaškanâ(ni)*	*iššakanâ(ni)*
		2. m.	*tašakanû*	*tušakkanû*	*tušaškanû*	*taššakanû*
		2. f.	*tašakanâ*	*tusakkanâ*	*tušaškanâ*	*taššakanâ*
		1. c.	*nišakan*	*nušakkan*	*nušaškan*	*niššakan*
2nd Impf.	SG.	3. m.	*iškun*	*ušakkin*	*ušaškin*	*iššakin*
		3. f.	*taškun*	*tušakkin*	*tušaškin*	*taššakin*
		2. m.	*taškun*	*tušakkin*	*tušaškin*	*taššakin*
		2. f.	*taškunî*	*tušakkinî*	*tušaškinî*	*taššakinî*
		1. c.	*aškun*	*ušakkin*	*ušaškin*	*aššakin*
	PL.	3. m.	*iškunû(ni)*	*ušakkinû(ni)*	*ušaškinû(ni)*	*iššakinû(ni)*
		3. f.	*iškunâ(ni)*	*ušakkinâ(ni)*	*ušaškinâ(ni)*	*iššakinâ(ni)*
		2. m.	*taškunû*	*tušakkinû*	*tušaškinû*	*taššakinû*
		2. f.	*taškunâ*	*tušakkinâ*	*tušaškinâ*	*taššakinâ*
		1. c.	*niškun*	*nušakkin*	*nušaškin*	*niššakin*
Perm.	SG.	3. m.	*šakin*	*šukkun*	*šuškun*	*naškun*
		3. f.	*šaknat(a)*	*šukkunat*	*šuškunat*	*naškunat*
		2. m.	*šaknâta*	*šukkunâta*	*šuškunâta*	*naškunâta*
		2. m.	*šaknâti*	*šukkunâti*	*šuškunâti*	*naškunâti*
		1. c.	*šaknâk(u)*	*šukkunâk(u)*	*šuškunâk(u)*	*naškunâk(u)*
	PL.	3. m.	*šaknû(ni)*	*šukkunû(ni)*	*šuškunû(ni)*	*naškunû(ni)*
		3. f.	*šaknâ*	*šukkunâ*	*šuškunâ*	*naškunâ*
		2. m.	*šaknâtunu*	*šukkuṇâtunu*	*šuškunâtunu*	*naškunâtunu*
		2. f.	*šaknâtina*(?)	*šukkunâtina*(?)	*šuškunâtina*(?)	*naškunâtina*(?)
		1. c.	*šaknâni*	*šukkunâni*	*šuškunâni*	*naškunâni*
Impv.	SG.	2. m.	*šukun*	*šukkin*	*šuškin*	*naškin*
		2. f.	*šukunî*	*šukkinî*	*šuškinî*	*naškinî*
	PL.	2. m.	*šukunû*	*šukkinû*	*šuškinû*	*naškinû*
		2. f.	*šukunâ*	*šukkinâ*	*šuškinâ*	*naškinâ*
Infin.			*šakânu*	*šukkunu*	*šuškunu*	*naškunu*

		I 1 Pe'al.	II 1 Pa'el.	III 1 Shafel.	IV 1 Nifal.
Part.	Sg. m.	*šak(i)nu*	*mušakkinu*	*mušaškinu*	*muššakinu*
	f.	*šaknatu*	*mušakkinatu*	*mušaškinatu*	*muššakinatu*
	Pl. m.	*šaknûti*	*mušakkinûti*	*mušaškinûti*	*muššakinûti*
	f.	*šaknâti*	*mušakkinâti*	*mušaškinâti*	*muššakinâti*

		I 2 Ifte'al.	II 2 Ifta'al.	III 2 Ishtafal.	I 3 Iftane'al.
1st Impf.	Sg. 3. m.	*ištakan*	*uštakkan*	*uštaškan*	*ištanakan*
	3. f.	*taštakan*	*tuštakkan*	*tuštaškan*	*taštanakan*
		etc.	etc.	etc.	etc.
2nd Impf.	Sg. 3. m.	*ištakin*	*uštakkin*	*uštaškin*	*ištanakin*
	3. f.	*taštakin*	*tuštakkin*	*tuštaškin*	*taštanakin*
		etc.	etc.	etc.	etc.
Perm.	Sg. 3. m.	*šitkun*	[*šutakkun*]	[*šutaškun*]	
		etc.			
Impv.	Sg. 2. m.	*šit(a)kan*	*šutakkan*	*šutaškin*	[*šitakkin*]
		etc.	etc.	etc.	
Infin.		*šitkunu*	*šutakkunu*	*šutaškunu*	
Part.	Sg. m.	*muštak(i)nu*	*muštakkinu*	*muštaškinu*	[*muštakkinu*]
		muštak(i)natu	*muštakkinatu*	*muštaškinatu*	
		etc.	etc.	etc.	

§ **24. Remarks on the paradigm.** 1. In stems II and III the vowel of the preformatives in the two imperfects is *u*. In stems I and IV the original *a* vowel has been thinned to *i* in the third person (except fem. sing.) and in the 1st pers. pl.

2. In the second impf. I 1 the vowel found oftenest after the second radical is *u*. The vowels *u, i, a* after the second radical are used indiscriminately with the various classes of verbs (transitive, intransitive, stative). Some verbs fluctuate between two vowels; for instance, the verb *ṣabâtu* to take, generally has *a*, as 36[32], but sometimes *u*, as *iṣbutû* I R 18, 67 var.

3. In the stems II and III one frequently finds *i* for the normal *a* (§ **8.** 1), as *lûkîrin* 2[15] (= *lû* + *ukarrin*) I heaped up. Similarly in impv. II 1 instead of the form *šukkin* one occasionally meets the form *šakkin*.

4. The termination *ûni* in the pl. sometimes appears as *ûnu*, as *iḳipûnu* 36[7] they entrusted.

5. The verb terminations *u*, *a* (rarely *i*, as 40[1]), in relative sentences (§ **11**), are perhaps a remnant of an original usage in which all verb forms had a vowel termination. Even in sentences not relative those forms of the verb which regularly end in a consonant are sometimes found with final *a*, as *ušalbina* Sargon Cyl. 59 I caused to mould bricks.

6. By constructio ad sensum a masculine form of the verb often occurs with a feminine subject, as *ḳâtî ikšud* 3[80] my hand captured.

7. Besides the form *šukun* of the impv. I 1 the forms *šakan* and *šikin* also occur.

§ **25. The weak verb.** The inflection of verbs whose stems contain ו, י, נ or a guttural (except *ḫ*), presents no differences from the inflection of the strong verb that are not easily understood by a knowledge of the phonic principles of the language; thus *ibil* 17[17] he prevailed = *ibעal* (§§ **7.** 2; **8.** 1; **22.** 1) like *iškun* (§ **23**), *ukîn* 10[28] I placed = *ukain* = *uka*וו*in* (§§ **7.** 2; **8.** 1) like *ušakkin*. Since the weak letters are lost in Assyrian, the problem in any given case is to determine what the weak letter really is. The problem becomes more difficult when the stem contains two weak letters, but the principles remain the same, as *uḳî* 1[8] I waited = *uḳa i'* = *uḳa*וו*i*ה like *ušakkin*. For the determination of weak letters reference to the cognate languages is often of prime importance.

Verbs containing *ḫ* (strong ח) and those whose second and third radicals are alike are not weak in Assyrian, as *idbub* 29[82] he planned st. *dabâbu*, *iḫsus* 14[26] he reflected st. *ḫasâsu*.

§ **26. Verbs initial** נ. The assimilation of vowelless *n* (as *abbul* 2[1] I destroyed = *anbul*) and subsequent loss of the assimilated letter (as *abul* 8[23]) have already been noted (§ **8.** 2 *d*), and also the striking peculiarity of this class of verbs, the loss of *n* in the impv. I 1 (§ **8.** 2 *d*).

§ **27. Verbs initial guttural.** Stem I 1: In the 1*st impf.* the second radical is regularly doubled, as *ikkal* 60[14] he eats = *i*א*akal*, *immar* 58[24] he sees, *innaḫ* 24[15] it shall decay, *irruba* 52[16] I shall enter, *illak* 58[16]. (The verb *alâku* to go, doubles the second radical even in the 2nd impf., as *allik* 1[22] I went.) Occasionally the vowel following the first radical is preserved, as *i-ab-ba-tu* 24[20] he will destroy. — In the 2*nd impf.* the guttural falls away, and *a* in the first syllable becomes *i*, as *írub* 58[7] I entered = *a*$א_5$*rub*, *ímid* 10[21] I placed, *ínaḫ* 6[18] it decayed. The strong preference of the guttural for the *i* vowel (§ **8**. 1) often makes a 1st and a 3rd pers. sing. indistinguishable, as *íli* 7^{26} I ascended 8^{21} he ascended.

It seems that א$_1$ and א$_2$ do not change an *a* vowel immediately before or after them to *i*, while א$_3$-א$_5$ regularly do (but not without exceptions), as א$_1$ *abut* 16^{14} I destroyed, *aḫuz* 20^{12} I took, *amur* 37^{21} I saw, *tarur* 23^{10} thou didst curse, *arâku* 41^{31} to be long, *aḫizu* V R 3, 123 seizing; א$_2$ *abuk* 17^{31} I carried off, *allik* 1^{22} and *alik* 8^{28} I went, *alik* 63^{1} go, *alâku* 13^{28} to go, *âliku* 6^{13} going; א$_3$ *íṣín* 57^{16} I collected; א$_4$ *íbir* 2^{8} I crossed, *íṭír* 3^{32} I spared, *ílî* 7^{26} I ascended, *ímid* 10^{21} I placed, *íṣir* 10^{7} I laid up; א$_5$ *ípuš* 6^{25} I made, *írub* 7^{22} I entered, *ípuš* 35^{18} make, *írub* 58^{2} enter, *íribu* 37^{6} to enter, *íribu* 52^{5} entering.

Stems I 2, I 3: *ittallaka* 40^{15} = *i*ה*talaka* he was marching (א$_2$), *itílâ* 60^{1} = *i*ע*tali*ʾ*a* it ascended (א$_4$), *itímid* 60^{2} = *a*ע*tamid* I directed (א$_4$), *ítíttiḳ* 19^{16} = *a*ע*tatiḳ* I marched (א$_4$), *ittanallakâ* 16^{24} = *i*ה*tanalakâ* they were running to and fro.

Intensive stem: *ubbit* 35^{11} = *u*א*abbit* he destroyed (א$_1$), *ubbib* 27^{1} = *u*ה*abbib* I adorned (א$_2$), *uddiš* 24^{15} = *u*ה*addiš* he renewed (א$_3$), *ullî* 24^{6} = *u*ע*alli*ʾ I made high (א$_4$), *uppiš* 63^{2} = ע*uppiš* do, make (א$_5$).

Causative stem: *ušaḫizzû* 28^{13} = *uša*א*ḫizû* they took, kindled (א$_1$), *ušakil* 26^{24} I caused to eat, *ušalik* 35^{11} he caused to go (א$_2$), *ušílî* 57^{20} = *uša*ע*li*ʾ I caused to go up (א$_4$), *ušírib* 10^{17} = *uša*ע*rib* I caused to enter (א$_5$), *šuzub* 2^{12} = *šu*ע*zub* to rescue (א$_4$), *uštílî* 57^{19} = *ušta*ע*li*ʾ I caused to go up. For other examples cf. *ušítiḳ* 2^{28}, *ušípiš* 19^{2}. The form *ušaliṣ* 10^{12} I caused to rejoice (א$_4$), instead of *ušíliṣ* is made on the analogy of verbs initial א$_{1-2}$.

Stem IV 1: *innabit* 10^{20} = *in*א*abit* he vanished (§ **8**. 2 *e*) st. *abâtu*, *innamru* 9^{13} he was seen st. אמר, *innamdu* 37^{5} they are established st. עמד.

§ **28. Verbs middle guttural.** א$_1$. *išalu* 25^{8} (written *iš-a-lu*) = *iš*א*alu* he asked, *iš'ala* 29^{28} (written *iš-'a-a-la*) = *iš*א*ala* he asked, *ištana'alûm* 32^{22} (written *iš-ta-na-'a-a-lum*) they were enquiring (the final *m* is the *mimmation*, which occurs with verbs as well as with nouns, cf. § **16**. 3), *uša'ilû* 11^{27} they called out = *uša*אא*ilû*. — א$_2$. *ir'ub* 64^{6} she raged, *ula'iṭu* Sargon Cyl. 22 (written *u-la-'i-ṭu*) he burnt = *ula*הה*iṭu*, *uma'ir* ib. 74 I sent = *uma*הה*ir*, *ušna'il* 2^{14} I cast down = *ušna*הה*il* (III–II). — א$_3$. *iramû* 40^{32} (written *ir-a-mu*) they love. — א$_4$. *iša'û* 30^{11} it seeks = *iša*ע*a*ו*u* (?) (relative sentence, § 11), *ibílu* 9^{9} he acquired possession = *ib*ע*alu*, *aši'a* 41^{8} I sought = *aš*ע*i*ו*a* (?), *iští'í* 40^{6} he sought, = *išta*ע*i*ו (?), *ištíni'í* 40^{11} he provided for = *ištana*ע*i*ו (?).

§ **29. Verbs final guttural.** $א_1$. SIMPLE STEM: *1st impf. ibâ'û* 58[19] they come = *ibaוaאû* like *išakanû, tanaša* 52[23] thou shalt lift up = *tanašaא* like *tašakan; 2nd impf. uṣi* 26[15] he went out = *iוṣiא* (§ **8.** 1) like *iškun, niḫtû* 32[25] we have sinned = *niḫtiאu, ašši* 42[14] I lifted = *anšiא*; *perm. malû* 26[31] they were full = *malאû; impv. i-ši* 35[18] carry up = *nišiא*; *part. nâbû* 5[16] naming = *nâbiאu, nâš* 1[3] (cstr.) bearing.

OTHER STEMS: *imtali* (I 2) 61[5] it was filled, like *ištakin, attabi* (I 2) 19[3] I named = *antabiא, iḳtíra* (I 2) 15[7] he invited = *iḳtariאa* (§§ **8.** 1; **24.** 5); *umalli* (II 1) 17[29] I filled = *umalliא, umdallû* (II 2) 32[2] they filled = *umtalliאû* (§ **8.** 2 *b*); *ušíṣi* (III 1) 2[17] I caused to go out = *ušaוṣiא* (cf. § **30**), *šûṣâ* (III 1 impv.) 64[11] bring out = *šuוṣiאa, multaḫṭû* (III 2) 26[15] sinner, rebel = *muštaḫṭiאu* (§ **8.** 1, 2 *a*).

$א_3$. *1st impf. tapattâ* 52[16] thou shalt open = *tapata*$א_3$*a; 2nd impf. alḳi* 2[5] = *alḳi*$א_3$, *alḳâ* 6[18] = *alḳi*$א_3$*a* I took, *àpti* 10[6] = *apti*$א_3$, *aptâ* 61[19] = *apti*$א_3$*a* I opened; *impv. pitâ* 52[14] = *piti*$א_3$*a* open.

$א_4$. SIMPLE STEM: *1st impf. iḳabbi* 52[21] he was speaking = *iḳaba*$א_4$, *išimmí* 24[18] he will hear = *išama*$א_4$; *2nd impf. aḫrî* 18[13] I dug = *aḫri*$א_4$, *idû* 2[28] he knew = *iידa*$א_4$*u* (§ **11**), *itbâ* 24[30] he advanced = *itba*$א_4$*a; perm. tíbûni* 15[11] they were advanced = *tab*$א_4$*ûni*.

OTHER STEMS: *altími* (I 2) IV R 52 No. 1, 5 I heard = *aštami*$א_4$; *uṭabi* (II 1) 6[20] I made low = *uṭabbi*$א_4$, *u'addûni* (II 1) 36[11] they made known = *uיaddi*$א_4$*ûni, uriti* (II 1) 6[27] I erected = *uratti*$א_4$ (§§ **8.** 1; **21.** 3); *utaddâ* (II 2) 58[24] they recognize one another = *uיtadda*$א_4$*â* like *uštakkanâ; ušapâ* (III 1) 34[26] I magnified = *ušaוpi*$א_4$*a, ušatbâ* (III 1) 36[3] I caused to come = *ušatbi*$א_4$*a*.

§ **30. Verbs initial ו or י.** In some cases there seems to be a mingling of forms from verbs initial ו and initial י, but in general the two classes are distinct. The vowels *u, a* or *-i* + ו give *u*, except in Shafel where *a* + ו gives *í* or *a*. Initial ו before *a* falls away without influence on the vowel. The vowel *a* before or after י regularly becomes *i*.

1. INITIAL ו. *Stem* I 1: *ûbal* 16[5] I was bringing = *aוabal; ubila* 21[7] he brought = *iוbila; bîl* Delitzsch Lesest[3] 107, 229 bring, but *urû* Haupt Nimrodepos 10, 40 take st. ורה, *ašâbu* 46[14] to dwell = *וašâbu; âlidu* 20[7] one who begets, *alittu* 59[3] = *וalidtu* one who bears. — *Stem* I 2: *ittíḫsû* 59[1] they fled = *iוtaḫisû* (§ **8.** 1, 2 *e*), *attašab* 59[23] I was seating myself = *aוtašab*. — *Stem* II 1: *ullada* 59[9] I cause to hear = *uוallada, mu'allidat* 62[7] causing to hear = *muוallidat*. — *Stem* III 1: *ušíbila* 21[9] he sent = *ušaוbila, ušíṣi* 2[17] I caused to go out = *ušaוṣiא, ušíšib* 10[27] I caused to

sit = *uša*ו*šib*, *ušapâ* 34^{26} I magnified = *uša*ו*pi*א₄*a*, *ušašib* I R 15, 35 I caused to sit = *uša*ו*šib*, *ušatír* 39^{9} I caused to abound = *uša*ו*tir*, *šûṣâ* 64^{11} bring out = *šu*ו*ṣi*א*a*, *šušib* 64^{11} cause to sit = *šu*ו*šib*, *mušíšib* 23^{19} one who causes to inhabit = *muša*ו*šib*. — *Stem* III 2: *uštíšibû* 62^{8} they caused to dwell = *ušta*ו*šibû*.

2. Initial י. *Stem* I 1: *idû* 23^{9} he knew = *i*י*da*א₄*u*, *íniḳû* 32^{19} they sucked = *i*י*niḳû*, *išî* 58^{6} I had = *a*י*šî*, *išâ* 18^{26} they had = *i*י*šâ*. — *Stem* II 1: *u'addûni* 36^{11} they made known = *u*י*addûni*. — *Stem* II 2: *utaddâ* 58^{24} they recognize one another = *u*י*tadda*א₄*â*. — *Stem* III 1: *ušíšir* 25^{22} he stroked (the ground with his beard) = *uša*י*šir*, *mušíniḳâtí* 32^{19} those who give suck. — *Stem* III 2: *uštíššíra* 24^{24} I made straight = *ušta*י*šira*, *šutíšur* 20^{28} it prospered (perm.) = *šuta*י*šur*.

§ **31. Verbs middle** ו **or** י. *Stem* I 1: *išâṭ* 11^{14} he draws = *iša*ו*aṭ*, *inârû* 20^{18} they subdue = *ina*י*arû*, *itarri* 60^{14} for *itâri* he goes to and fro (?) *ita*ו*ari*(?), *išammû* 32^{5} for *išâmû* they appoint = *iša*י*amû*; *aduk* 11^{34} I killed = *ad*ו*uk*, *iṭíbu* 7^{16} it pleased = *iṭ*ו*ibu*, *aḫiṭ* 20^{14} I saw = *aḫ*י*iṭ*, *anir* 33^{31} I subdued = *an*י*ir*, *išimû* 35^{4} they appointed = *iš*י*imû*; *ḫiša* 14^{23} hasten = *ḫi*י*iša*; *dâku* 42^{8} to kill = *da*ו*âku*. — *Stem* I 2: *imtût* 14^{3} he died = *imta*ו*ut*. — *Stem* II 1: *ukîn* 39^{4} I placed = *uka*וו*in*, *mušîm* 7^{8} one who appoints = *muša*יי*im*. — *Stem* II 2: *uktîn* 60^{17} I placed = *ukta*וו*in*, *uttîr* 64^{17} he restored = *utta*וו*ir* st. תור.

§ **32. Verbs final** ו **or** י. *Stem* I 1: *abakki* 59^{23} I was weeping = *abakî*, st. *bakû*, *ibašši* 35^{24} he shall be st. *bašû*, *atamâ* 35^{20} I was speaking st. *tamû*, *ibanna* 61^{8} he makes st. *banû*; *abnî* 6^{14} I built, *adkî* 42^{15} I mustered, *almî* 11^{17} I surrounded, *addî* 18^{19} and *addâ* 36^{2} I placed st. *nadû*, *aḳḳî* 10^{11} and *aḳḳâ* 50^{25} I sacrificed, *aršî* 36^{1} and *aršâ* 3^{31} I granted, *amnû* 6^{2} I reckoned, *aḳmû* 13^{22} I burned, *liḫdû* 63^{5} may it rejoice; *bakû* 59^{11} they weep, *nadû* 41^{23} it is established; *dikâ* 14^{22} muster (impv.); *bânû* 20^{9} maker, *râš* 14^{4} possessor (cstr.). — *Stem* I 2: *attaḳî* 60^{15} I sacrificed st. *naḳû*, *irtašî* 40^{4} he granted, *artídî* 8^{21} I pursued. — *Stem* II 1: *uṣallî* 22^{30} I besought, *uṣallâ* 25^{25} he besought, *utammî* 4^{1} I caused to swear. — *Stem* III 1: *ušabrî* 22^{11} he caused to see, *ušalmî* 33^{32} I encircled, *ušardâ* 16^{8} I caused to flow, *ušarmâ* 39^{8} I caused to inhabit, *ušaršâ* 22^{26} he granted; *šurmâ* 35^{19} cause to inhabit. — *Stem* IV 1: *ibbanû* 62^{13} they were created, *innadî* 23^{3} he was cast down.

§ **33. Quadriliteral verbs.** The quadriliteral verbs are few in number, but some of them are of frequent occurrence, as פלכת to cross, transgress, rebel, פרשד to flee, escape, שחרר to be narrow, contracted, שפרר to spread out. Illustrations: *appalkit* 1[9] I crossed (IV 1), *ippalki* 24[81] he rebelled, *ušapalkat* 52[18] I will destroy (III 1); *ipparšidû* 1[17] they fled (IV 1), *ittanapraššidu* 34[14] he fled (IV 3, relative sentence); *ušḫarir* 59[18] it contracted; *šuparruru* I R 15, 58 it was spread out.

TEXT.

I. TIGLATHPILESER I (c. 1120–1100 B.C.).

1. **Campaign against Mušku and Kummuḫ** (I R 9, 62–10, 24).

[62]I-na šur-ru šarrû-ti-ya XX M amílûti*pl* [63]*mâtu*Muš-ka-a-ya*pl* ù V šarrâ*pl*-ni-šú-nu [64]šá L šanâ*pl*-tí *mâtu*Al-zi [65]ù *mâtu*Pu-ru-kuz-zi na-a-aš bilti [66]ù ma-da-at-tí šá *ilu*A-šur bíli-ya iṣ-ba-tu-ni [67]šarru ya-um-ma i-na tam-ḫa-ri irat-su-nu [68]la-a ú-ni-ḫu[a] a-na da-na-ni-šú-nu [69]it-ka-lu-ma ur-du-ni *mâtu*Kum-mu-ḫi [70]iṣ-ba-tu. I-na tukul-ti *ilu*A-šur bíli-ya [71]*iṣu*narkabâti*pl* ù um-ma-na-tí-ya lup-tí-ḫir [72]arka-a ul ú-ḳi. *šadû*Ka-ši-ya-ra [73]íḳil nam-ra-ṣi lu-ú ap-pal-kit. [74]It-ti XX M ṣâbî*pl* muḳ-ṭab-li-šú-nu [75]ù V šarrâ*pl*-ni-šú-nu i-na *mâtu*Kum-mu-ḫi [76]lu al-ta-na-an a-bi-ik-ta-šú-nu [77]lu aš-kun šal-ma-at ḳu-ra-di-šú-nu [78]i-na mit-ḫu-uṣ tu-šá-ri ki-ma ra-ḫi-ṣi [79]lu-ki-mir dâmî*pl*-šú-nu ḫur-ri [80]ù ba-ma-a-tí šá šadi-i lu-šar-di [81]ḳaḳḳadî*pl*-šú-nu lu-na-ki-sa i-da-at [82]alâ*pl*-ni-šú-nu ki-ma ka-ri-í lu-ší-pi-ik [83]šal-la-su-nu bu-šá-a-šú-nu nam-kur-šú-nu [84]a-na la-a mi-na lu-ší-ṣa-a. VI M [85]si-tí-it um-ma-na-tí-šú-nu šá i-na pa-an [86]*iṣu*kakkî*pl*-ya ip-pár-ši-du šípî*pl*-ya [87]iṣ-ba-tu al-ḳa-šú-nu-ú-ti-ma [88]a-na niši*pl* mâ-ti-ya am-nu-šú-nu-ti.

[89]I-na û-mi-šú-ma a-na *mâtu*Kum-mu-ḫi la-a ma-gi-ri [90]šá bilta ù ma-da-ta a-na *ilu*A-šur bíli-ya [91]ik-lu-ú lu al-lik. *mâtu*Kum-mu-ḫi [92]a-na si-ḫír-ti-šá lu-ú ak-šud [93]šal-la-su-nu bu-šá-šú-nu nam-kur-šú-nu [94]ú-ší-ṣa-a alâ*pl*-

a. I R **ti**.

ni-šú-nu i-na išâti*pl* [10, 1]aš-ru-up ab-bul aḳ-ḳur. Si-tí-it [2]*mâtu*Kum-mu-ḫi šá i-na (*iṣu*[a])pa-an *iṣu*kakkî*pl*-ya [3]ip-pár-ši-du a-na *alu*Ší-ri-íš-ší [4]šá padanî*pl* am-ma-a-tí šá *nâru*Diḳlat [5]lu í-bí-ru ala a-na dan-nu-ti-šú-nu [6]lu iš-ku-nu *iṣu*narkabâti*pl* ù ḳu-ra-di-ya*pl* [7]lu al-ḳi šada-a mar-ṣa ù gir-ri-tí-šú-nu [8]pa-aš-ḳa-a[b]-tí i-na ag-gúl-lat írî*pl* [9]lu aḫ-si ḫu-la a-na mí-tí-iḳ [10]*iṣu*narkabâti*pl*-ya ù um-ma-na-tí-ya lu-ṭí-ib [11]*nâru*Diḳlat lu í-bir *alu*Ší-ri-ší [12]ali dan-nu-ti-šú-nu ak-šú-ud [13]ṣâbî*pl* muḳ-ṭab-li-šú-nu i-na ki-rib ḫur-ša-ni [14]ki-ma šut-ma-ši lu ú-mi-ṣi [15]dâmî*pl*-šú-nu *nâru*Diḳlat ù ba-mat šadi-i [16]lu-šar-di. I-na û-mi[c]-šú-ma um-ma-na-at [17]*mâtu*Kúr-ṭí-í*pl* šá a-na šú-zu-ub [18]ù ni-ra-ru-ut-tí šá *mâtu*Kum-mu-ḫi [19]il-li-ku-ú-ni it-ti um-ma-na-at [20]*mâtu*Kum-mu-ḫi-ma ki-ma šú-bí lu uš-na-il [21]pa-gar muḳ-ṭab-li-šú-nu a-na gu-ru-na-tí [22]i-na gi-šal-lat šadi-i lu-ki-ri-in [23]šal-mat ḳu-ra-a-di-šú-nu *nâru*Na-a-mí [24]a-na *nâru*Diḳlat lu ú-ší-ṣi.

2. **Campaign against the Nairi** (I R 12, 40–13, 21).

[40]*m*Tukul-ti-apal-ì-šár-ra šarru dan-nu [41]ka-šid kib-rat nakrûti*pl* šá-ni-nu [42]gi-mir kâl šarrâni*pl*.

[43]I-na û-mi-šú-ma i-na í-mu-ḳi ṣi-ra-tí [44]šá *ilu*A-šur bíli-ya i-na an-ni ki-í-ni [45]šá *ilu*Šamaš ḳu-ra-di i-na tukul-ti [46]šá ilâni*pl* rabûti*pl* šá i-na kib-rat arba'-i [47]mí-ší-riš ul-tal-li-ṭu-ma mu-ni-ḫa [48]i-na ḳabli šá-ni-na i-na taḫazi la i-šú-ú [49]a-na mâtât*pl* šarrâ*pl*-ni ni-su-tí [50]šá a-aḫ tâmti í-li-ni-tí [51]šá ka-na-šá la i-du-ú [52]*ilu*A-šur bílu ú-ma-'i-ra-ni-ma al-lik. [53]Ṭu-ud-di mar-ṣu-tí ù ni-ri-bi-tí [54]šup-šú-ḳa-a-tí šá i-na maḫ-ra [55]šarru ya-um-ma líb-ba-šú-nu la i-du-ú [56]ar-ḫi it-lu-ti du-ur-gi [57][d]la-a[d] pi-tu-tí ú-ší-ti-iḳ [58]*šadû*Í-la-ma *šadû*A-ma-da-na *šadû*Íl-ḫi-iš [59]*šadû*Ší-ra-bí-li *šadû*Tar-ḫu-na [60]*šadû*Tir-ka-ḫu-li *šadû*Ki-is-ra [61]*šadû*Tar-ḫa-

a. *iṣu* inserted by scribal error, due to presence of *iṣu* after **pa-an.** One copy correctly omits. — *b.* I R om. — *c.* I R **mí.** — *d–d.* I R erroneously **ta.**

na-bí *šadû*Í-lu-la [62]*šadû*Ḫa-aš-ta-ra-í *šadû*Šá-ḫi-šá-ra [63]*šadû*Ú-bí-ra *šadû*Mi-li-at-ru-ni [64]*šadû*Šú-li-an-zi *šadû*Nu-ba-na-a-ší [65]ù *šadû*Ší-í-ší XVI šadî*pl* dan-nu-tí [66]íḳla ṭâba i-na *iṣu*narkabti-ya ù mar-ṣa [67]i-na ag-gúl-lat írî*pl* lu aḫ-si [68]ú-ru-mi iṣî*pl* šadi-i lu ak-ki-is [69]ti-tur-ra-a-ti a-na mí-ti-iḳ [70]um-ma-na-a-tí-ya*pl* lu ú-ṭí-ib. [71]*nâru*Pu-rat-ta í-bir šar *mâtu*Nim-mí [72]šar *mâtu*Tu-nu-bí šar *mâtu*Tu-a-li [73]šar *mâtu*Ḳi-da-ri šar *mâtu*Ú-zu-la [74]šar *mâtu*Un-za-mu-ni šar *mâtu*An-di-a-bí [75]šar *mâtu*Pi-la-ḳi-ni šar *mâtu*A-ṭur-gi-ni [76]šar *mâtu*Ku-li-bar-zi-ni šar *mâtu*Pi-ni-bir-ni [77]šar *mâtu*Ḫi-mu-a šar *mâtu*Pa-i-tí-ri [78]šar *mâtu*Ú-i-ra-am šar *mâtu*Šú-ru-ri-a [79]šar *mâtu*A-ba-í-ni šar *mâtu*A-da-í-ni [80]šar *mâtu*Ki-ri-ni šar *mâtu*Al-ba-ya [81]šar *mâtu*Ú-gi-na šar *mâtu*Na-za-bi-ya [82]šar *mâtu*A-bar-si-ú-ni šar *mâtu*Da-ya-í-ni [83]napḫar XXIII šarrâni*pl* mâtâti*pl* Na-i-ri [84]i-na ki-rib mâtâti*pl*-šú-nu-ma *iṣu*narkabâti*pl*-šu-nu [85]ù um-ma-na-tí-šú-nu ul-taḳ-ṣi-ru-ma [86]a-na í-piš ḳabli ù ta-ḫa-zi [87]lu it-bu-ni. I-na šú-mur *iṣu*kakkî*pl*-ya [88]iz-zu-tí as-ni-ḳa-šú-nu-ti [89]šá-gal-ti um-ma-na-tí-šú-nu rapšâti*pl* [90]ki-ma ri-ḫi-il-ti *ilu*Ramân [91]lu aš-ku-un. Šal-ma-at ḳu-ra-di-šú-nu [92]i-na ṣíri ba-ma-at šadi-i ù i-da-at [93]alâ*pl*-ni-šú-nu ki-ma šut-ma-ší [94]lu-mi-ṣi II šú-ši *iṣu*narkabâti*pl*-šú-nu [95]ḫa-lap-ta i-na ki-rib tam-ḫa-ri [96]lu-tí-mí-iḫ I šú-ši šarrâ*pl*-ni [97]mâtâti Na-i-ri a-di šá a-na [98]ni-ra-ru-ti-šú-nu il-li-ku-ni [99]i-na mul-mul-li-ya a-di tâmti [100]í-li-ni-ti lu ar-di-šú-nu-ti [101]ma-ḫa-zi-šú-nu rabûti*pl* ak-šud [13,1]šal-la-su-nu bu-šá-šú-nu nam-kur-šú-nu [2]ú-ší-ṣa-a alâni*pl*-šú-nu i-na išâti*pl* [3]aš-ru-up ab-bul aḳ-ḳur [4]a-na tili ù kar-mi ú-tir [5]su-gúl-lat *imîru*sisî*pl* rapšû*pl*-ti [6]pa-ri-í a-ga-li*pl* ù mar-šit [7]kir-bí-tí-šú-nu a-na la ma-ni-í [8]ú-tir-ra.

Nap-ḫar šarrâ*pl*-ni [9]mâtâti Na-i-ri bal-ṭu-su-nu ḳa[a]-ti [10]ik-šud a-na šarrâ*pl*-ni šá-tu-nu [11]ri-í-ma ar-šá-šú-nu-ti-ma [12]na-piš-ta-šú-nu í-ṭí-ir šal-lu-su-nu [13]ù ka-mu-su-nu i-na ma-ḫar *ilu*Šamaš bíli-ya [14]ap-ṭu-ur-ma ma-mi-it ilâni*pl*-ya [15]rabûti*pl* a-na ar-kat ûmî*pl* a-na û-um [16]ṣa-a-tí a-na ardu-

a. Om. by error in I R.

ut-tí ú-tam-mi-šú-nu-ti [17]mârî*pl* nab-ni-it šarrû-ti-šú-nu [18]a-na li-ṭu-ut-tí aṣ-bat [19]I M II C *imiru* sisî*pl* II M alpî*pl* [20]ma-da-at-ta i-na muḫ-ḫi-šú-nu aš-kun [21]a-na mâtâti*pl*-šú-nu ú-maš-šír-šú-nu-ti.

3. **Campaign against the Ḳumani** (I R 13, 82–14, 21).

[82]I-na û-mi-šú-ma kúl-lat *mâtu*Ḳu-ma-ni-i [83]šá a-na ri-ṣu-ut[a] *mâtu*Mu-us-ri iš-ša-ak-nu [84]nap-ḫar mâtâti*pl*-šú-nu lu id-ku-ni-ma [85]a-na í-piš ḳabli ù ta-ḫa-zi [86]lu iz-zi-zu-ni-ma i-na šú-mur *iṣu*kakkî*pl*-ya [87]iz-zu-tí it-ti[b] XX M um-ma-na-tí-šú-nu [88]rapšâti*pl* i-na *šadû*Ta-la lu am-da-ḫi-iṣ [89]a-bi-ik-ta-šú-nu lu-ú aš-kun [90]ki-ṣir-šú-nu gab-šá lu-pi-ri-ir [91]a-di *šadû*Ḫa-ru-sa šá pa-an *mâtu*Mu-us-ri [92]ab-ku-su-nu lu ar-du-ud šal-ma-at [93]ḳu-ra-di-šú-nu i-na gi-šal-lat šadi-i [94]ki-ma šú-ú-bí lu ú-mi-ṣi [95]dâmî*pl*-šú-nu ḫur-ri ù ba-ma-a-tí ša šadi-i [96]lu-šar-di ma-ḫa-zi-šú-nu rabûti*pl* [97]ak-šud i-na išâti*pl* aš-ru-up [98]ab-bul aḳ-ḳur a-na tili ù kar-mí [c]ú-tir.[c]

[99]*alu*Ḫu-nu-sa ali dan-nu-ti-šú-nu [100]ki-ma til a-bu-bí aš-ḫu-up [14, 1]it-ti um-ma-na-a-tí-šu-nu gab-šá-a-tí [2]i-na ali ù šadi-í šam-riš lu am-da-ḫi-iṣ [3]a-bi-ik-ta-šú-nu lu-ú aš-kun [4]ṣâbî*pl* muḳ-ṭab-li-šú-nu i-na ki-rib ḫur-ša-ni [5]ki-ma šú-bí uš-na-il ḳaḳḳadî*pl*-šú-nu [6]ki-ma zi-ir-ḳi ú-ni-ki-is [7]dâmî*pl*-šú-nu ḫur-ri ù ba-ma-a-tí ša šadi-i [8]lu-šar-di ala šú-a-tu ak-šud [9]ilâni*pl*-šú-nu aš[d]-šá-a bu-šá-šú-nu nam-kur-šú-nu [10]ú-ší-ṣa-a ala i-na išâti*pl* aš-ru-up [11]III dûrâni*pl*-šú-nu rabûti*pl* šá i-na a-gúr-ri [12]ra-aš-bu ù si-ḫír-ti ali-šú [13]ab-bul aḳ-ḳur a-na tili ù kar-mi [14]ú-tir ù abnî*pl* ṣi-pa i-na muḫ-ḫi-šú [15]az-ru biriḳ siparri í-pu-uš [16]ki-ši-ti mâtâti šá i-na [e]ili-ya[e] bíli-ya [17]ak-šú-du ala šú-a-tu a-na la ṣa-ba-tí [18]ù dûra-šú la-a ra-ṣa-pi i-na muḫ-ḫi [19]al-ṭu-ur bîta šá a-gúr-ri i-na muḫ-ḫi-šú [20]ar-ṣip biriḳ siparri šá-a-tu-nu [21]i-na líb-bi ú-ší-ši-ib.

---

a. I R **ti.** — *b.* One copy om. — *c–c.* One copy and I R om. — *d.* I R erroneously **pa.** — *e–e.* Var. *ilu* **A-šur.**

II. ASSURNAZIRPAL (883–859 B.C.).

Standard Inscription (Layard 1).[a]

[1]Ìkal *m*Aššur-naṣir-apli šangi Aššur ni-šit *ilu*Bíl u *ilu*Adar na-ra-am *ilu*A-nim u *ilu*Da-gan ka-šú-uš ilâni*pl* rabûti*pl* šarru dan-nu šar kiššati šar *mâtu*Aššur apal Tukulti-Adar šarri rabi-í [2]šarri dan-ni šar kiššati šar *mâtu*Aššur apal Ramân-nirari šar kiššati šar *mâtu*Aššur-ma it-lu ḳar-du ša ina tukul-ti Aššur bíli-šu ittalla-ku-ma ina mal-ki*pl* ša kib-rat irbit-ta ša-nin-šu [3]la-a išu-ú *amilu*ri'i tab-ra-a-tí la a-di-ru tuḳunti í-du-ú gab-šu ša ma-ḫi-ra la-a išu-ú šarru mu-šak-niš la kan-šú-tí-šu ša nap-ḫar kiš-šat niši*pl* [4]i-pi-lu zikaru dan-nu mu-kab-bi-is kišad a-a-bi-šu da-a-iš kul-lat nakrûti*pl* mu-pa-ri-ru ki-iṣ-ri mul-tar-ḫi šarru ša ina tukul-ti ilâni*pl* rabûti*pl* [5]bílî*pl*-šu ittalla-ku-ma mâtâti*pl* kâli-ši-na ḳât-su takšu-ud ḫur-ša-ni kâli-šu-nu i-pi-lu-ma bi-lat-su-nu im-ḫu-ru ṣa-bit li-i-ṭí ša-kin li-i-tí [6]íli kâli-ši-na mâtâti*pl*.

Í-nu-ma Aššur bílu na-bu-ú šumi-ya mu-šar-bu-ú šarrû-ti-a *iṣu*kakka-šu la pa-da-a a-na i-da-at bílû-ti-a lu-ú it-muḫ [7]ummânât*pl* *mâtu*Lu-ul-lu-mí-í rapšâti*pl* ina ki-rib tam-ḫa-ri ina *iṣu*kakkî*pl* lu ú-šam-ḳít. Ina ri-ṣu-tí ša *ilu*Ša-maš [8]u *ilu*Ramân ilâni*pl* tik-li-a ummânât*pl* mâtâti Na-i-ri *mâtu*Kil-ḫi *mâtu*Šú-ba-ri-í u *mâtu*Ni-rib kîma *ilu*Ramân ra-ḫi-ṣi íli-šu-nu [9]aš-gu-um šarru ša ištu í-bir-tan *nâru*Diḳlat a-di *šadû*Lab-na-na u tâmti rabî-tí *mâtu*La-ḳi-í ana si-ḫír-ti-ša *mâtu*Su-ḫi a-di *alu*Ra-pi-ḳi ana šípî*pl*-šu ú-šik-ni-ša [10]ištu ríš í-ni *nâru*Su-ub-na-at a-di *mâtu*Ú-ra-ar-ṭí ḳât-su takšu-ud ištu *šadû*ni-rib ša *mâtu*Kír-ru-ri a-di *mâtu*Kír-za-ni ištu í-bir-tan *nâru*Za-ba šupalî a-di [11]*alu*Til-ba-a-ri ša íl-la-an *mâtu*Za-ban ištu *alu*Til-ša-ab-ta-ni a-di *alu*Til-ša-za-ab-da-ni *alu*Ḫi-ri-mu *alu*Ḫa-ru-tu *mâtu*Bi-ra-a-tí ša *mâtu*Kar-du-ni-aš ana mi-iṣ-ri [12]mâti-ya ú-tir ištu *šadû*ni-

a. From Layard and from photographs.

rib ša *mâtu* Ba-bi-tí a-di *mâtu* Ḫaš-mar a-na nišî*pl* mâti-a am-nu. Ina mâtâti*pl* ša a-pi-lu-ši-na-ni *amilu* šák-nu-tí-ya al-ta-kan ur-du-ti ú-pu-šu. *m* Aššur-naṣir-apli [13] rubu-ú na-a-du pa-líḫ ilâni*pl* rabûti*pl* ú-šúm-gal-lu ik-du ka-šid alâni u ḫur-ša-ni pad gim-ri-šu-nu šar bílî*pl*-í mu-la-iṭ iḳ-ṣu-tí a-pi-ir ša-lum-ma-tí la a-di-ru [14] tuḳunti ur-ša-nu la pa-du-ú mu-rib a-nun-tí šar ta-na-da-tí *amilu* ri'u ṣa-lu-lu kibrâti*pl* šarru ša ki-bit pî-šu uš-ḫám-ma-ṭu šadî*pl*-í u tâmâti*pl* ša ina ḳi-it-ru-ub [15] bílû-ti-šu šarrâ*pl*-ni ik-du-tí la pa-du-tí ištu ṣi-it *ilu* šam-ši a-di í-rib *ilu* šam-ši pa-a išt-ín ú-ša-aš-kin.

alu Kal-ḫu maḫ-ra-a ša *m ilu* Šúl-ma-nu-ašârid šar *mâtu* Aššur [16] rubû a-lik pa-ni-a ípu-uš alu šú-ú í-na-aḫ-ma iṣ-lal. Alu šú-ú ana íš-šu-tí ab-ni. Nišî*pl* kišit-ti ḳâti-ya ša mâtâti*pl* ša a-pi-lu-ši-na-ni ša *mâtu* Su-ḫi *mâtu* La-ḳi-í ana si-ḫír-ti-ša [17] *alu* Muš-ḳu ša ni-bir-ti *nâru* Purat *mâtu* Za-mu-a ana pad gim-ri-ša *mâtu* Bît-A-di-ni u *mâtu* Ḫat-tí u ša *m* Lu-bar-na *mâtu* Pa-ti-na-a-a al-ḳa-a ina líb-bi ú-ša-aṣ-bit. Tilu la-bi-ru lu ú-na-ki-ir a-di [18] íli mí*pl* lu ú-ša-pil I C XX tik-pi ina muš-pa-li lu ú-ṭa-bi. Ìkal *iṣu* í-ri-ni ìkal *iṣu* šurmíni ìkal *iṣu* dap-ra-ni ìkal *iṣu* urkarini*pl* ìkal *iṣu* mis-kan-ni ìkal *iṣu* bu-uṭ-ni u *iṣu* ṭar(?)-pi-'i a-na šú-bat šarrû-ti-a [19] ana mul-ta-'i-it bílû-ti-a ša da-ra-a-tí ina líb-bi ad-di. Ú-ma-am šadî*pl*-í u tâmâti*pl* ša *abnu* pi-li piṣi-í u *abnu* pa-ru-tí ípu-uš ina bâbâni*pl*-ša ú-ší-zi-iz ú-si-im-ši ú-šar-riḫ-ši si-kat kar-ri siparri*pl* [20] al-mí-ši. *iṣu* Dalâti*pl* *iṣu* í-ri-ni *iṣu* šurmíni *iṣu* dap-ra-ni *iṣu* mis-kan-ni ina bâbâni*pl*-ša ú-ri-ti. Kaspi*pl* ḫuraṣi*pl* anaki*pl* siparri*pl* parzilli*pl* kišit-ti ḳâti-ya ša mâtâti*pl* ša a-pi-lu-ši-na-ni a-na ma-'a-diš al-ḳa-a ina líb-bi ú-kin.

III. SHALMANESER II. (858–824 B.C.).

1. **Genealogy; First Campaign** (Layard 87 ff.).[a]

[1] *ilu* Aššur bílu rabu-ú šar gim-rat [2] ilâni*pl* rabûti*pl* *ilu* A-nu šar *ilu* i-gi-gi [3] ù *ilu* a-nun-na-ki *ilu* bíl mâtâti *ilu* Bíl [4] ṣi-i-ru a-bu ilâni*pl* ba-nu-ú [5] [kâla-ma *ilu*] Ì-a šar apsî mu-šim šîmâti*pl* [6] [*ilu* Sin] šar a-gi-í ša-ḳu-ú nam-ri-ri [7] [*ilu* Ramân] giš-ru šú-tu-ru bíl ḫigal-li *ilu* Ša-maš [8] dân šami-í ù irṣi-ti mu-ma-'i-ir gim-ri [9] [*ilu* Marduk] abkal ilâni*pl* bíl tí-ri-í-tí *ilu* Adar ḳar-du [10] [šar *ilu*] igigi*pl* ù *ilu* a-nun-na-ki ilu dan-dan-nu *ilu* Nírgal [11] [git]-ma-lu šar tam-ḫa-ri *ilu* Nusku na-ši *iṣu* ḫaṭṭi ílli-tí [12] ilu mul-ta-lu *ilu* Bílit ḫi-ir-ti *ilu* Bíl ummi ilâni*pl* [13] [rabûti]*pl* *ilu* Ištar riš-ti šami-í ù irṣi-tí ša paraṣ ḳar-du-tí šuk-lu-lat [14] [ilâni]*pl* rabûti*pl* mu-ši-mu šîmâti*pl* mu-šar-bu-ú šarrû-ti-ya. [15] [*m ilu*] Šúl-ma-nu-ašârid šar kiš-šat niši*pl* rubu-ú šangi Aššur šarru dan-nu [16] šar kúl-lat kib-rat irbit-ta *ilu* Šam-šú kiš-šat niši*pl* mur-tí-du-ú [17] ka-liš mâtâti apal *m* Aššur-naṣir-apli šangu-ú ṣi-i-ru ša šangût-su íli ilâni*pl* [18] i-ṭí-bu-ma mâtâti nap-ḫar-ši-na a-na šípî-šú ú-šik-ni-šú [19] nab-ni-tu ílli-tu ša *m* Tukul-ti-*ilu* Adar [20] ša kúl-lat za-i-ri-šú i-ni-ru-ma [21] iš-pu-nu a-bu-ba-ni-iš.

[22] I-na šur-rat šarrû-ti-ya ša ina *iṣu* kussi [23] šarrû-ti rabi-iš ú-ši-bu *iṣu* narkabâti*pl* [24] ummânâti-ya ad-ki ina *šadû* ni-ri-bí ša *mâtu* Si-mí-si [25] íru-ub *alu* A-ri-du ali dan-nu-ti-šú [26] ša *m* Ni-in-ni akšu-ud. I-na išt-ín pali-ya [27] [*nâru*] Purat ina mi-li-ša í-bir a-na tam-di ša šúl-mí *ilu* Šam-ši [28] al-li-ik *iṣu* kakkî*pl*-ya ina tam-di ú-lil *kirru* niḳâni*pl* [29] a-na ilâni*pl*-ya aṣ-bat. A-na šadi-í *šadû* Ḫa-ma-a-ni í-li [30] *iṣu* gu-šur*pl* *iṣu* í-ri-ni *iṣu* burâši a-kis. A-na [31] *šadû* Lal-la-ar í-li ṣa-lam šarrû-ti-ya ina líb-bi ú-ší-ziz.

---

a. Selections 1 and 2 are prepared from photographs and from a cast of the original, known as the "obelisk inscription," now in the British Museum.

2. Campaign against Damascus.[a]

[54]. . . Ina VI pali-ya a-na alâ*pl*-ni ša ši-di *nâru*Ba-li-ḫi [55]aḳ-ṭí-rib *m*Gi-am-mu ḳípa-šu-nu idu-ku [56]a-na *alu*Til-tur-a-ḫi íru-ub [57]*nâru*Purat ina mi-li-ša í-bir [58]ma-da-tu ša šarrâ*pl*-ni ša *mâtu*Ḫat-ti [59][kâli]-šu-nu am-ḫur. Ina û-mi-šu-ma *m ilu*Addu-id-ri [60][šar] *mâtu*Dimašḳi *m*Ir-ḫu-li-na *mâtu*A-mat-a-a a-di šarrâ*pl*-ni [61]ša *mâtu*Ḫat-ti ù a-ḫat tam-ti a-na ímuḳâni*pl* a-ḫa-miš [62]it-tak-lu-ma a-na í-piš ḳabli u taḫazi [63]a-na irti-ya it-bu-ni. Ina ki-bit Aššur bíli rabî bíli-ya [64]it-ti-šu-nu am-dáḫ-ḫi-iṣ abikta-šu-nu aš-kun [65]*iṣu*narkabâti*pl*-šu-nu bit-ḫal-la-šu-nu ú-nu-ut taḫazi-šu-nu í-kim-šu-nu [66]XX M VC ṣâbî*pl* ti-du-ki-šu-nu ina *iṣu*kakkî*pl* ú-šam-ḳít.

3. Western Campaign; Tribute of Jehu (III R 5, No. 6).[b]

[1]Ina XVIII palí*pl*-ya XVI šanîtu *nâru*Purat [2]í-bir. *m*Ḫa-za-'-ilu ša *mâtu*Dimašḳi [3]a-na gi-biš ummânâti*pl*-šu [4]it-ta-kil-ma ummânâti*pl*-šu [5]a-na ma-'a-diš id-ka-a. [6]*šadû*Sa-ni-ru uban šadi-í [7]ša pu-ut *šadû*Lab-na-na a-na dan-nu-ti-šu [8]iš-kun. It-ti-šu am-dáḫ-ḫi-iṣ [9]abikta-šu aš-kun XVI M [10]ṣâbî*pl* ti-du-ki-šu ina *iṣu*kakkî*pl* [11]ú-šam-ḳít IM IC XXI *iṣu*narkabâti*pl*-šu [12]IV C LXX bit-ḫal-lu-šu it-ti uš-ma-ni-šu [13]í-kim-šu a-na šú-zu-ub [14]napšâti*pl*-šu í-li arki-šu ar-tí-di [15]ina *alu*Di-maš-ḳi ali šarrû-ti-šu í-sír-šu [16]*iṣu*kirî*pl*-šu ak-kis. A-di šadi-í [17]*mâtu*Ḫa-ú-ra-ni a-lik alâ*pl*-ni [18]a-na la ma-ni a-bùl a-ḳur [19]ina išâti*pl* ašru-up šal-la-su-nu [20]a-na la ma-ni aš-lu-la. [21]A-di šadi-í *šadû*Ba-'-li-ra-'-si [22]ša ríš tam-di a-lik ṣa-lam šarrû-ti-a [23]ina líb-bi aš-ḳup. Ina û-mí-šu-ma [24]ma-da-tu ša *mâtu*Ṣur-ra-a-a [25]*mâtu*Ṣi-du-na-a-a ša *m*Ya-ú-a [26]apal Ḫu-um-ri-i am-ḫur.

---

a. See note *a*, page 7. — *b.* Also Delitzsch Assyr. Lesestücke, ed. 2, p. 98.

IV. SARGON (722–705 B.C.).

Conquests; Restoration of Calah (Layard 33).[a]

[1]Ìkal *m*Šarru-kínu ša-ak-nu *ilu*Bíl nisakku *ilu*A-šur ni-šit íni *ilu*A-nim ù *ilu*Bíl šarru dan-nu šar kiššati šar *mâtu*Aššur*ki* šar kib-rat arba'-i mi-gir ilâni*pl* rabûti*pl* [2]ri'u ki-í-nu ša *ilu*A-šur *ilu*Marduk ut-tu-šú-ma zi-kir šú-mi-šu ú-ší-ṣu-u a-na ri-ší-í-tí [3]zi-ka-ru dan-nu ḫa-lib na-mur-ra-tí šá a-na šum-ḳut na-ki-ri šú-ut-bu-u *iṣu*kakku-šú [4]it-lu ḳar-du ša ul-tu û-um bí-lu-ti-šu mal-ku gab-ri-šu la ib-šú-ma mu-ni-ḫa ša-ni-na la i-šú-ú [5]mâtâti kâli-ši-na ultu ṣi-it *ilu*šam-ši a-di í-rib *ilu*šam-ši i-bí-lu-ma ul-taš-pi-ru ba-'u-lat *ilu*Bíl [6]mu-'-a-ru bu-bu-lu šá í-mu-ḳa-an ṣi-ra-a-tí *ilu*Ìa iš-ru-ku-uš *iṣu*kakku la maḫ-ri uš-tib-bu i-du-uš-šu [7]rubû na-'i-du šá ina ri-bit Dûr-ili*ki* it-ti *m ilu*Ḫum-ba-ni-ga-aš šar *mâtu*Í-lam-ti in-nam-ru-ma iš-ku-nu táḫ-ta-šu [8]mu-šak-niš *mâtu*Ya-ú-du ša a-šar-šu ru-ú-ḳu na-si-iḫ *mâtu*Ḫa-am-ma-tí šá *m ilu*Ya-ú-bi-'i-di ma-lik-šu-nu ik-šú-du ḳâtu-šu [9]mu-ni-'i i-rat *mâtu*Ka-ak-mi-í *amílu*nakri lim-ni mu-ta-ḳi-in *mâtu*Man-na-a-a dal-ḫu-ú-tí mu-ṭib líb-bi mâti-šu mu-rap-piš mi-ṣir *mâtu*Aššur [10]mal-ku pit-ḳu-du šú-uš-kal la-a ma-gi-ri šá *m*Pi-si-ri šar *mâtu*Ḫat-ti ḳât-su ik-šú-du-ma íli *alu*Gar-ga-mis ali-šu iš-ku-nu *amílu*zikar(?)-šu [11]na-si-iḫ *alu*Ši-nu-uḫ-ti šá *m*Ki-ak-ki šar *mâtu*Ta-ba-li a-na ali-šu Aššur*ki* ub-lam-ma *mâtu*Mu-us-ki í-mid-du ab-ša-an-[šu] [12]ka-šid *mâtu*Man-na-a-a *mâtu*Kar-al-lu ù[b] *mâtu*Pad-di-ri mu-tir gi-mil-li mâti-šu mu-šim-ḳít *mâtu*Ma-da-a-a ru-ḳu-ú-tí a-di *mâtu ilu*šam-ši(?).

[13]I-na û-mi-šú-ma ìkal *iṣu*dup-ra-ni šá *alu*Kal-ḫa šá *m*Aššur-naṣir-apli rubû a-lik pa-ni-ya i-na pa-na í-pu-šú [14]šá bîti šú-a-tu uš-šú-šu ul dun-nu-nu-ú-ma íli du-un-ni ḳaḳ-ḳa-ri ki-ṣir šadi-i ul šur-šú-da iš-da-a-šu [15]i-na ra-a-di

---

a. The transliterated text is from my copy of the original, a slab in the British Museum. — *b*. Layard. My copy omits.

ti-iḳ šami-í an-ḫu-ta la-bi-ru-ta il-lik-ma ší-pit-su ip-pa-ṭir-ma ir-mu-ú rik-su-šu [16]a-šar-šu ú-ma-sí-ma lib-na-su ak-šú-ud. Íli *abnu*pi-i-li dan-ni tim-mi-in-šu ki-ma ši-pik šadi-i zaḳ-ri aš-pu-uk. [17]Ištu uš-ší-šu a-di taḫ-lu-bi-šu ar-ṣip ú-šak-lil. Bâb zi-i-ḳi a-na mul-ta-'i-ti-ya ina šumíli bâbi-šu ap-ti. [18]Ka-šad alâ*pl*-ni ša uṣûni(?) *iṣu*kakkî*pl*-ya šá íli *amilu*nakrûti*pl* aš-ku-nu ina ki-rib-šu í-ṣir-ma a-na ì-ri-í lu-li-í ú-mal-li-šu. [19]*ilu*Nírgal *ilu*Ramân ù ilâni*pl* a-ši-bu-ut *alu*Kal-ḫa a-na líb-bi aḳ-ri-ma gû-maḫ-ḫi rabûti*pl* *kirru*ardâni*pl* ma-ru-ti **kur-gi** *iṣṣuru pl* **us-tur** *iṣṣuru pl* [20]iṣṣurî*pl* šami-í mut-tap-riš-ú-tí ma-ḫar-šú-un aḳ-ḳi ni-gu-tú aš-kun-ma ka-bat-ti nišî*pl* *mâtu*Aššur*ki* ú-ša-li-iṣ.

[21]I-na û-mí-šú-ma i-na bît na-kam-tí šú-a-ti XI **gun** XXX ma-na ḫuraṣi II M I C **gun** XXIV ma-na kaspi ina rabî-ti [22]ki-šit-ti *m*Pi-si-ri šar *alu*Gar-ga-mis šá *mâtu*Ḫat-ti šá kišad *nâru*Pu-rat-ti šá ḳa-ti ik-šú-du ina líb-bi ú-ší-rib.

V. SENNACHERIB (705–682 B.C.).

1. **Syrian Campaign; Tribute of Hezekiah** (I R 38, 34–39, 41).[a]

[34]I-na šal-ši gir-ri-ya a-na *mâtu*Ḫa-at-ti lu[b] al-lik. [35]*m*Lu-li-i šar *alu*Ṣi-du-un-ni púl-ḫi mí-lam-mí [36]bí-lu-ti-ya is-ḫu-pu-šú-ma a-na ru-uk-ki [37]ḳabal tam-tim in-na-bit-ma mâta-šu í-mid. [38]*alu*Ṣi-du-un-nu rabu-ú *alu*Ṣi-du-un-nu ṣiḫru [39]*alu*Bît-zi-it-tí *alu*Za-ri-ip-tú *alu*Ma-ḫal-li-ba [40]*alu*Ú-šú-ú *alu*Ak-zi-bi *alu*Ak-ku-ú [41]alâni*pl*-šu dan-nu-ti bît-dûrâ*pl*-ni a-šar ri-i-ti [42]ù maš[c]-ki-ti bît-tuk-la[d]-ti-šu ra-šub-bat *iṣu*kakki [43]*ilu*Aššur bíli-ya is-ḫu-pu-šú-nu-ti-ma ik-nu-šú [44]ší-pu-ú-a. *m*Tu-ba-'a-lu i-na *iṣu*kussi šarrû-ti [45]íli-šu-un ú-ší-šib-ma biltu man-da-at-tu bí-lu-ti-ya [46]šat-ti-šam la ba-aṭ-lu ú-kín ṣi-ru-uš-šu.

---

a. See also Delitzsch, Assyr. Lesestücke, ed. 2, pp. 100–103. — *b.* I R **ki**. — *c.* I R **nu**. — *d.* I R **ad**.

[47]Šá *m*Mi-in-ḫi-im-mu *alu*Sam-si-mu-ru-na-a-a [48]*m*Tu-ba-’a-lu *alu*Ṣi-du-un-na-a-a [49]*m*Ab-di-li-’i-ti *alu*A-ru-da-a-a [50]*m*Ú-ru-mil-ki *alu*Gu-ub-la-a-a [51]*m*Mi-ti-in-ti *alu*As-du-da-a-a [52]*m*Pu-du-ilu *mâtu*Bît-*m*Am-ma-na-a-a [53]*m*Kam-mu-su-na-at-bi *mâtu*Ma-’a-ba-a-a [54]*m ilu*Malik-ram-mu *mâtu*Ú-du-um-ma-a-a [55]šarrâ*pl*-ni *mâtu*Aḫarrî*ki* ka-li-šu-un ši-di-i [56]šad-lu-ti ta-mar-ta-šu-nu ka-bit-tu a-di bušî [57]a-na maḫ-ri-ya iš-šú-nim-ma iš-ši-ḳu šípî-ya. [58]Ù *m*Ṣi-id-ḳa-a šar *alu*Is-ḳa-al-lu-na [59]šá la ik-nu-šu a-na ni-ri-ya ilâni*pl* bît abi-šu ša-a-šu [60]aššat-su aplî*pl*-šu binâti*pl*-šu aḫî*pl*-šu zir bît abi-šu [61]as-su-ḫa-am-ma a-na *mâtu*Aššur*ki* ú-ra-aš-šu. [62]*m*Šarru-lu-dá-ri apal *m*Ru-kib-ti šarri-šu-nu maḫ-ru-ú [63]íli niši*pl* *alu*Is-ḳa-al-lu-na aš-kun-ma na-dan bilti [64]kat-ri-í bí-lu-ti-ya í-mid-su-ma i-ša-aṭ ab-ša-a-ni. [65]I-na mí-ti-iḳ gir-ri-ya *alu*Bît-Da-gan-na [66]*alu*Ya-ap-pu-ú *alu*Ba-na-a-a-bar-ḳa *alu*A-zu-ru [67]alâ*pl*-ni šá *m*Ṣi-id-ḳa-a šá a-na[a] šípî-ya [68]ár-ḫiš la ik-nu-šu al-mí akšu-ud aš-lu-la šal-la-sun.

[69]*amílu*Šakkanakkî*pl* *amílu*rubûti*pl* ù niši*pl* *alu*Am-ḳar-ru-na [70]šá *m*Pa-di-i šarra-šu-nu bíl a-di-í ù ma-mit [71]šá *mâtu*Aššur*ki* bi-ri-tu parzilli id-du-ma a-na *m*Ḫa-za-ḳi-yà-ú [72]*mâtu*Ya-ú-da-a-a id-di-nu-šu nak-riš a-na *an*ṣil-li í-sir-šu [73]ip-laḫ lib-ba-šu-un šarrâ*pl*-ni *mâtu*Mu-ṣu-ri [74]*amílu*ṣâbî*pl* *iṣu*ḳašti *iṣu*narkabâti*pl* *imíru*sisî*pl* šá šar *mâtu*Mí-luḫ-ḫi [75]í-mu-ki la ni-bi iḳ-tí-ru-nim-ma il-li-ku [76]ri-ṣu-us-su-un. I-na ta-mir-ti *alu*Al-ta-ḳu-ú [77]íl-la-mu-ú-a si-id-ru šit-ku-nu ú-ša-’i-lu [78]*iṣu*kakkî*pl*-šu-un. I-na tukul-ti *ilu*Aššur bíli-ya it-ti-šu-un [79]am-da-ḫi-iṣ-ma aš-ta-kan abikta-šu-un [80]*amílu*bíl *iṣu*narkabâti*pl* ú aplî*pl* šarri *mâtu*mu-ṣu-ra-a-a [81]a-di *amílu*bíl *iṣu*narkabâti*pl* šá šar *mâtu*Mí-luḫ-ḫi bal-ṭu-su-un [82]i-na ḳabal tam-ḫa-ri ik-šu-da ḳâta-a-a *alu*Al-ta-ḳu-ú [83]*alu*Ta-am-na-a al-mí akšu-ud aš-lu-la šal-la-sun.

[39, 1]A-na *alu*Am-ḳar-ru-na aḳ-rib-ma *amílu*Šakkanakkî*pl* [2]*amílu*rubûti*pl* šá ḫi-iṭ-ṭu ú-šab-šú-ú a-duk-ma [3]i-na di-ma-

a. I R tú.

a-tí si-ḫir-ti ali a-lul pag-ri-šu-un [4]aplî *pl* ali í-piš an-ni ù ḫab-la-ti [5]a-na šal-la-ti am-nu si-it-tu-tí-šu-nu [6]la ba-ní ḫi-ṭi-ti ù ḳúl-lul-ti šá a-ra-an-šu-nu [7]la ib-šú-ú uš-šur-šu-un aḳ-bi. *m* Pa-di-i [8]šarra-šu-nu ul-tu ki-rib *alu* Ur-sa-li-im-mu [9]ú-ší-ṣa-am-ma i-na *iṣu* kussi bí-lu-ti íli-šu-un [10]ú-ší-šib-ma man-da-at-tu bí-lu-ti-ya [11]ú-kín ṣi-ru-uš-šu. Ŭ *m* Ḫa-za-ḳi-a-ú [12]*mâtu* Ya-ú-da-a-a šá la ik-nu-šu a-na ni-ri-ya [13]XLVI alâni *pl*-šu dan-nu-ti bît-dûrâni *pl* ù alâni *pl* ṣiḫrûti *pl* [14]šá li-mí-ti-šu-nu šá ni-ba la i-šú-ú [15]i-na šuk-bu-us a-ram-mí ù ḳít-ru-ub šú-pi-i [16]mit-ḫu-ṣu[a] zu-uḳ šípi bíl-ši nik-si u[b] lab-ban-na-tí [17]al-mí akšu-ud. II C M I C L nišî *pl* ṣiḫru rabû zikaru ù zinnišu [18]*imíru* sisî *pl* *imíru* parí *pl* imírî *pl* *imíru* gammalî *pl* alpî *pl* [19]ù ṣi-í-ni šá la ni-bi ul-tu kir-bi-šu-un ú-ší-ṣa-am-ma [20]šal-la-tiš am-nu. Ša-a-šu kîma iṣṣuri ḳu-up-pi ki-rib *alu* Ur-sa-li-im-mu [21]ali šarrû-ti-šu í-sir-šu *alu* ḫal-ṣu *pl* íli-šu [22]ú-rak-kis-ma a-ṣi-í abulli ali-šu ú-tir-ra [23]ik-ki-bu-uš. Alâni *pl*-šu šá aš-lu-la ul-tu ki-rib mâti-šu [24]ab-tuḳ-ma a-na *m* Mi-ti-in-ti šar *alu* As-du-di [25]*m* Pa-di-i šar *alu* Am-ḳar-ru-na ù *m* Ṣillu-Bíl [26]šar *alu* Ḫa-zi-ti ad-din-ma ú-ṣa-aḫ-ḫir mât-su. [27]Í-li bilti maḫ-ri-ti na-dan mâ-ti-šu-un [28]man-da-at-tu kat-ri-í bí-lu-ti-ya ú-rad-di-ma [29]ú-kín ṣi-ru-uš-šu-un.

Šú-ú *m* Ḫa-za-ḳi-a-ú [30]púl-ḫi mí-lam-mí bí-lu-ti-ya is-ḫu-pu-šú-ma [31]*amílu* Úr-bi ù *amílu* ṣâbî *pl*-šu damḳûti *pl* [32]šá a-na dun-nu-un *alu* Ur-sa-li-im-mu ali šarrû-ti-šu [33]ú-ší-ri-bu-ma ir-šú-ú bí-la-a-ti [34]it-ti XXX **gun** ḫuraṣi VIII C **gun** kaspi ni-siḳ-ti [35]gu-uḫ-li dag-gas-si *abnu* an-gug-mí rabûti *pl* [36]*iṣu* iršî *pl* šinni *iṣu* kussî *pl* ni-mí-di šinni mašak pîri [37]šin pîri *iṣu* ušû *iṣu* urkarina mimma šum-šu ni-ṣir-tú ka-bit-tú [38]ù binâti *pl*-šu *f* zikrîti *pl* ìkalli-šu *amílu* **lib** *pl* [39]*f* **lib** *pl* a-na ki-rib Ninâ *ki* ali bí-lu-ti-ya [40]arki-ya ú-ší-bi-lam-ma a-na na-dan man-da-at-ti [41]ù í-piš ardu-ú-ti iš-pu-ra rak-bu-šu.

---

a. Var. **uṣ**.—*b.* I R **bab**.

2. **Campaign against Elam** (I R 40, 43–41, 4).

[43]I-na sibi-í gir-ri-ya *ilu*Aššur în-ni ú-tâk-kil-an-ni-ma [44]a-na *mâtu*Îlamti*ki* lu al-lik. *alu*Bît-*m*Ḫa-'a-i-ri [45]*alu*Ra-ṣa-a alâ*pl*-ni šá mi-ṣir *mâtu*Aššur*ki* [46]šá i-na tar-ṣi abi-ya *amílu*Í-la-mu-ú í-ki-mu da-na-niš [47]i-na mí-ti-iḳ gir-ri-ya akšud-ma aš-lu-la šal-la-sun. [48]*amílu*Ṣâbî*pl* šú-lu-ti-ya ú-ší-rib ki-rib-šu-un [49]a-na mi-ṣir *mâtu*Aššur*ki* ú-tir-ram-ma [50]ḳâtû *amílu*rab-*alu*ḫal-ṣu Dûr-ili*ki* am-nu. [51]*alu*Bu-bi-í *alu*Dun-ni-*ilu*Šamaš *alu*Bît-*m*Ri-si-ya [52]*alu*Bît-aḫ-la-mí-í *alu*Du-ru *alu*Dan-nat[a]-*m*Su-la-a-a [53]*alu*Ši-li-ib-tu *alu*Bît-*m*A-ṣu-si *alu*Kar-*m*Mu-ba-ša [54]*alu*Bît-gi-iṣ-ṣi *alu*Bît-*m*Kat-pa-la-ni *alu*Bît-*m*Im-bi-ya [55]*alu*Ḫa-ma-nu *alu*Bît-*m*Ar-ra-bi *alu*Bu-ru-tu [56]*alu*Di-in-tu šá *m*Su-la-a-a *alu*Di-in-tu [57]šá *m ilu*Tur-bit-íṭi-ir *alu*Ḫur-ri-aš-la-ki-í *alu*Ra-ba-a-a [58]*alu*Ra-a-su *alu*Ak-ka-ba-ri-na *alu*Til-*m*Ú-ḫu-ri [59]*alu*Ḫa-am-ra-nu *alu*Na-di-tu a-di alâni*pl* ša ni-ri-bi [60]šá *alu*Bît-*m*Bu-na-ki *alu*Til-*ilu*Ḫu-um-bi *alu*Di-in-tu [61]šá *m*Du-mí-ilu *alu*Bît-*m*Ú-bi-ya *alu*Ba-al-ti-li-šir [62]*alu*Ta-gab-li-šir *alu*Ša-na-ḳi-da-a-ti [63]*alu*Ma-su-tú-šap-li-tu *alu*Sa-ar-ḫu-di-í-ri *alu*A-lum-šá-tar(?)-bit [64]*alu*Bît-*m*Aḫî*pl*-iddi-na *alu*Il-tí-ú-ba XXXIV alâni*pl* dan-nu-ti [65]a-di alâ*pl*-ni ṣiḫrûti*pl* šá li-mí-ti-šu-nu [66]šá ni-ba la i-šú-ú al-mí akšu-ud aš-lu-la šal-la-sun [67]ab-búl aḳ-ḳur i-na išâti aḳ-mu. [68]Ḳu-ṭúr na-aḳ-mu-ti-šu-nu kîma imbari kab-ti [69]pa-an šami-í rap-šú-ti ú-šak-tim. Iš-mí-ma ki-šit-ti [70]alâni*pl*-šu *m*Kudur-*ilu*Na-ḫu-un-du *amílu*Í-la-mu-ú im-ḳut-su [71]ḫa-at-tum si-it-ti alâni*pl*-šu a-na dan-na-ti ú-ší-rib. [72]Šú-ú *alu*Ma-dak-tí ali šarrû-ti-šu í-zib-ma [73]a-na *alu*Ḫa-i-da-la šá ki-rib šad-di-i rûḳûti*pl* [74]iṣ-ṣa-bat ḫar-ra-nu. A-na *alu*Ma-dak-tí ali šarrû-ti-šu [75]a-la-ku aḳ-bi araḫ tam-ṭí-ri kuṣṣu dan-nu [76]í-ru-ba-am-ma ša-mu-tum ma-at-tum ú-ša-az-ni-na [77]zunnî*pl* ša zunnî*pl* ù šal-gu na-aḫ-li na-ad-bak [78]šad-di-i a-du-ra pa-an ni-ri-ya ú-tir-ma [79]a-na Ninâ*ki* aṣ-ṣa-bat ḫar-ra-nu. I-na û-mí-šú-ma [80]i-na

---

a. I R ši.

ki-bit *ilu* Aššur bíli-ya *m* Kudur-*ilu* Na-ḫu-un-di [41,1] šar *mâtu* Ílamti *ki* III arḫu ul ú-mal-li-ma [2] i-na û-um la ši-im-ti-šu ur-ru-ḫiš im-tu-ut. [3] Arki-šu *m* Um-ma-an-mí-na-nu la ra-aš ṭì-í-mí ù mil-ki [4] aḫu-šu dub-bu-us-su-ú i-na *iṣu* kussi-šu ú-šib-ma.

3. **Campaign against Babylon** (I R 41, 5–42, 24).

[5] I-na šamni-í gir-ri-ya arka *m* Šú-zu-bi is-si-ḫu-ma [6] aplî *pl* Babili *ki* gallî *pl* lim-nu-ti abullî *pl* ali [7] ú-di-lu iḳ-pu-ud lib-ba-šu-nu a-na í-piš tuḳunti. [8] *m* Šú-zu-bu *amílu* Kal-dá-a-a [ḫab]-lum dun-na-mu-ú [9] ša la i-šú-ú bir-ki [la da]-gil pa-an *amílu* bíl piḫât [10] *alu* La-ḫi-ri *amílu* a-ra-[du pa-áš]-ḳu mun-nab-tu [11] a-mir da-mí ḫab-bi-lu ṣi-ru-uš-šu ip-ḫu-ru-ma [12] ki-rib *nâru* a-gam-mí ú-ri-du-ma ú-šab-šú-u si-ḫu [13] a-na-ku ni-tum al-mí-šú-ma nap-ša-tuš ú-si-ḳa. [14] La-pa-an ḫat-ti ù ni-ip-ri-ti a-na *mâtu* Ílamti *ki* in-na-bit. [15] Ki-i ri-kil-ti ù ḫab-la-ti ṣi-ru-uš-šu ba-ši-i [16] ul-tu *mâtu* Ílamti *ki* i-ḫi-šam-ma ki-rib Šú[a]-an-na *ki* í-ru-ub. [17] *amílu* Babili *ki pl* a-na la si-ma[b]-tí-šu i-na *iṣu* kussi [18] ú-ší-ši-bu-šu bí-lu-ut *mâtu* Šumíri ù Akkadi *ki* ú-šad-gi-lu pa-ni-šu. [19] Bît makkuri šá Ì-sag-ili ip-[tu]-ma ḫuraṣa kaspa [20] šá *ilu* Bíl *ilu* Zir-bani-tum ša [ina] íšríti *pl*-šu-nu ú-ší-ṣu-ni [21] a-na *m* Um-ma-an-mí-na-nu šar *mâtu* Ílamti *ki* šá la i-šú-ú [22] ṭì-í-mu ù mil-ki ú-ší-bi-lu-uš da-'a-tú: [23] Pu-uḫ-ḫir um-man-ka di-ka-a karaša-ka [24] a-na[c] Babili *ki* ḫi-šam-ma i-da-a-ni i-zi-iz-ma [25] tu-kul[d]-ta-ni[e] lu at-ta. Šú-ú *amílu* Í-la-mu-ú [26] šá i-na a-lak gir-ri-ya maḫ-ri-ti šá *mâtu* Ílamti *ki* [27] alâni *pl*-šu ak-šud-du-ma ú-tir-ru a-na kar-mí [28] lib-bu-uš ul iḫ-su-us da-'a-tu im-ḫur-šu-nu-ti-ma [29] ummânâti *pl*-šu karas-su ú-pa-ḫir-ma *iṣu* narkabâti *pl* *iṣu* ṣu-um-bi [30] í-šú-ra *imíru* sisî *pl* *imíru* parí *pl* is-ni-ḳa ṣi-in-di-šu. [31] *mâtu* Par-su-aš *mâtu* An-za-an *mâtu* Pa-ši-ru *mâtu* Íl-li-pi [32] *amílu* Ya-az-an *amílu* La-kab-ra[f] *amílu* Ḫa-

a. I R **ba.**—*b.* I R **ba.**—*c.* I R omits.—*d.* I R **mu.**—*e.* I R **pa.**—*f.* I R **ri.**

ar-zu-nu [33] *alu* Du-um-mu-ḳu *alu* Su-la-a-a *alu* Sa-am-ú-na [34] apal *m ilu* Marduk-apla-iddi-na *mâtu* Bît-*m* A-di-ni *mâtu* Bît-*m* A-muk-ka-na [35] *mâtu* Bît-*m* Šil-la-na *mâtu* Bît-*m* Sa-a-la-lara-ak-ki *alu* La-ḫi-ru [36] *amîlu* Pu-ḳu-du *amîlu* Gam-bu-lum *amîlu* Ḫa-la-tu *amîlu* Ru-'u-u-a [37] *amîlu* Ú-bu-lum *amîlu* Ma-la-ḫu *amîlu* Ra-pi-ḳu [38] *amîlu* Ḫi-in-da-ru *amîlu* Da-mu-nu siḫ-ru rabu-ú [39] iḳ-tí-ra it-ti-šu gi-ib-šú-su-un ú-ru-uḫ [40] *mâtu* Akkadi *ki* iṣ-ba-tu-nim-ma a-na Babili *ki* tí-bu-ni [41] a-di *m* Šú-zu-bi *amîlu* Kal-dá-a-a šar Babili *ki* [42] a-na a-ḫa-miš iḳ-ru-bu-ma pu-ḫur-šu-nu in-nin-du [43] ki-ma ti-bu-ut a-ri-bi ma-'a-di šá pa-an mâ-ti [44] mit-ḫa-riš a-na í-piš tuḳ-ma-ti tí-bu-ú-ni [45] ṣi-ru-ú-a. Iprâti šípî-šu-nu kîma imbari kab-tí [46] šá dun-ni í-ri-ya-a-ti pa-an šami-í rap-šú-ti [47] ka-ti-im íl-la-mu-ú-a i-na *alu* Ḫa-lu-li-í [48] šá ki-šad *nâru* Diḳlat šit-ku-nu si-dir-ta [49] pa-an maš-ki-ya ṣab-tu-ma ú-ša-'i-lu *iṣu* kakkî *pl*-šu-un.

[50] A-na-ku a-na *ilu* Aššur *ilu* Sin *ilu* Šamaš *ilu* Bíl *ilu* Nabû *ilu* Nírgal [51] *ilu* Ištar šá Ninâ *ki* *ilu* Ištar šá *alu* Arba'-ili ilâni *pl* ti-ik-li-ya [52] a-na ka-ša-di *amîlu* nakri dan-ni am-ḫur-šu-nu-ti-ma [53] su-pi-í-a ur-ru-ḫiš iš-mu-ú il-li-ku [54] ri-ṣu-ti. La-ab[a]-biš an-na-dir-ma at-tal-bi-ša [55] si-ri-ya-am ḫu-li-ya-am si-mat ṣi-il-tí [56] a-pi-ra ra-šú-ú-a. I-na *iṣu* narkabat taḫazi-ya ṣir-ti [57] sa-pi-na-at za-'i-i-ri i-na ug-gat lib-bi-ya [58] ar-ta-kab ḫa-an-ṭiš *iṣu* ḳaštu dan-na-tum [59] šá *ilu* Aššur ú-šat-li-ma i-na ḳâti[b]-ya aṣ-bat. [60] *iṣu* Ḳut-ta-ḫu pa-ri-'i nap-ša-tí at-muḫ rit-tu-u-a. [61] Ṣi-ir gi-mir um-ma-na-a-ti na-ki-ri lim-nu-ti [62] zar-biš láḫ-mí-iš al-sa-a kîma *ilu* Ramân aš[c]-gu-um. [63] I-na ki-bit *ilu* Aššur bíli rabî bíli-ya a-na šid-di ù pu-tí [64] kîma ti-ib mí-ḫi-í šam-ri a-na *amîlu* nakri a-zi-iḳ. [65] I-na *iṣu* kakkî *pl* *ilu* Aššur bíli-ya ù ti-ib taḫazi-ya [66] iz-źi i-rat-su-un a-ni-'i-ma suḫ-ḫur-ta-šu-nu [67] aš-kun ummânât na-ki-ri i-na uṣ-ṣi mul-mul-li [68] ú-ša-kir-ma gim-ri *amîlu* pagrî *pl*-šu-nu ú-pal-li-ša [69] tam(?)-zi-zi-iš.

m ilu Ḫu-um-ba-an-un-da-ša *amîlu* na-gi-ru [70] šá šar

a. I R **ad.** — *b*. I R **lib.** — *c*. I R **is.**

*mâtu*Ílamti*ki* it-lum pit-ḳu-du mu-ma-'i-ir ummânâti-šu [71]tu-kul[a]-ta-šu rabu-ú[b] a-di *amilu*rabûti*pl*-šu [72]šá paṭru šib-bi ḫuraṣi šit-ku-nu ù i-na šimirî*pl* [73]aṣ-pi ḫuraṣi ru-uš-ši-i ruk-ku-sa rit-ti-šu-un [74]ki-ma šú-ú-ri ma-ru-ti šá na-du-ú šum-man-nu [75]ur-ru-ḫiš ú-bal-šú-nu-ti-ma aš-ku-na táḫ-ta-šu-un. [76]Ki-ša-da-tí-šu-nu ú-nak-kis as-li-iš [77]aḳ-ra-tí nap-ša-tí-šu-nu ú-pár-ri-'i gu-'ú-iš [78]kîma míli gab-ši šá ša-mu-tum si-ma-ni ù mun-ni-šu-nu [79]ú-šar-da-a ṣi-ir ir-ṣi-ti ša-di-il-tí [80]la as-mu-ti mur-ni-is-ki ṣi-mit-ti ru-ku-pi-ya [81]i-na da-mí-šú-nu gab-šú-ti i-šal-lu-ú *ilu*Nâri-iš. [82]Šá *iṣu*narkabat taḫazi-ya sa-pi-na-at rag-gi ù ṣi-ni [83]da-mu ù par-šu ri-it-mu-ku ma-ša-ru-uš. [84]Pag-ri ḳu-ra-di-šu-nu ki-ma ur-ki-ti [85]ú-mal-la-a ṣíra sa-ap-sa-pa-tí ú-na-kis-ma [42,1]šupil-ta-šu-un a-bu-ut ki-ma bi-ni kiš-ší-í [2]si-ma-ni u-na-ak-kis ḳa-ti-šu-un [3]šimirî*pl* aṣ-pi ḫuraṣi kaspi(?) ib-bi ša rit-ti-šu-nu am-ḫur. [4]I-na nam-ṣa-ri zaḳ-tu-ti ḫu-za-an-ni-šu-nu ú-par-ri-'i [5]paṭrî*pl* šib-bi ḫuraṣi kaspi ša ḳablâti*pl*-šu-nu í-kim.

[6]Si-it-ti *amilu*rabûti*pl*-šu-nu a-di *m ilu*Nabû-šum-iš-kun [7]apal *m ilu*Marduk-apla-iddi-na šá la-pa-an ta-ḫa-zi-ya [8]ip-la-ḫu id-ku-ú i-da-šu-un bal-ṭu-su-un [9]i-na ḳabal tam-ḫa-ri it-mu-ḫa ḳâta-a-a. *iṣu*Narkabâti*pl* [10]a-di *imiru*sisî*pl*-ši-na šá ina ḳít-ru-ub ta-ḫa-zi dan-ni [11]ra-ki-bu-ši-in di-ku-ma bílu-ši-na muš-šú-ra-ma [12]ra-ma-nu-uš-šin it-ta-na-al-la-ka mit-ḫa-riš [13]ú-tir-ra. A-di II kas-bu mi-il-li-ku [14]da-ak-šú-nu ap-ru-uṣ. Šú-ú *m*Um-ma-an-mí-na-nu [15]šar *mâtu*Ílamti*ki* a-di šarrâni*pl* Babili*ki* *amilu*na-sik-ka-ni [16]šá *mâtu*Kal-di a-li-kut idi-šu mur-ba-šú taḫazi-ya kîma li-í [17]zu-mur-šú-un is-ḫu-up.[c] *iṣu*Za-ra-tí-šu-un ú-maš-ší-ru-ma [18]a-na šú-zu-ub napšâti*pl*-šu-nu pag-ri um-ma-na-tí-šu-nu ú-da-i-šu [19]i-ti-ḳu ki-i šá ad-mi summati *iṣṣuru* kúš-šú-di i-tar-ra-ku lib-bu-šu-un [20]ši-na-tí-šu-un ú-za-ra-bu ki-rib *iṣu*narkabâti*pl*-šu-nu [21]ú-maš-ší-ru ni-ṣu-šú-un. A-na ra-da-di-šu-nu [22]*iṣu*narkabâti*pl* *imiru*sisî*pl*-ya ú-ma-'i-ir ar-

a. I R **mu.** — b. I R adds **pa.** — c. I R **tur.**

ki-šu-un [23]mun-na-rib (?)-šu-nu ša a-na nap-ša-a-ti ú-ṣu-ú [24]a-šar i-kaš-ša-du ú-ra-sa-pu i-na *iṣu*kakki.

4. **Destruction of Babylon** (III R 14, 34–53).

[34]. . . I-na šatti-šam-ma it-ti ḫi[a]-ri nâri šú-a-tu šá aḫ-ru-ú it-ti *m*Um-ma-an-mí-na-nu [35]šar *mâtu*Ílamti*ki* ù šar Babili*ki* a-di šarrâ*pl*-ni ma-'a-du-ti šá šadi-i ù tam-tim šá ri-ṣu-ti-šu-nu i-na ta-mir-ti *alu*Ḫa-lu-li-í [36]aš-ta-kan si-dir-ta. I-na ki-bit Aššur bíli rabi-í bíli-ya ki-i *iṣu*ḳut-ta-ḫi šam-ri i-na líb-bi-šu-nu al-lik-ma si-kip-ti ummânâti*pl*-šu-nu [37]aš-kun pu-ḫur-šu-nu ú-sap-pi-iḫ-ma ú-par-ri-ir íl-lat-su-un. *amílu*Rabûti*pl* šar *mâtu*Ílamti*ki* a-di *m ilu*Nabû-šum-išku-un apal *m ilu*Marduk-apla-iddi-na [38]šar *mâtu*Kár-*ilu*Dun-yá-àš bal-ṭu-su-un ki-rib tam-ḫa-ri ik-šú-da ḳâta-a-a. Šar *mâtu*Ílamti*ki* ù šar Babili*ki* mur-ba-šú taḫazi-ya dan-ni [39]is-ḫup-šu-nu-ti-ma ki-rib *iṣu*narkabâti*pl*-šu-nu ú-maš-ší-ru ni-šá-a-šu-un. A-na šú-zu-ub nap-ša-tí-šu-nu ma-tu-uš-šu-un in-nab-tu-ma [40]la i-tu-ru-ni. Ar-kiš man-di-ma *m ilu*Sin-aḫî*pl*-irba šar *mâtu*Aššur*ki* ag-giš i-bìl-ma a-na *mâtu*Ílamti*ki* i-šak-ka-nu ta-a-a-ar-tú. [41]Ḫat-tu pu-luḫ-tu íli *mâtu*Ílamti*ki* ka-li-šu-un it-ta-bi-ik-ma mât-su-nu ú-maš-ší-ru-ma a-na šú-zu-ub nap-ša-tí-šu-nu ki-i našri *iṣṣuru* [42]šad-da-a mar-ṣu in-nin-du-ma ki-i šá[b] iṣ-ṣu-ri kúš-šú-di i[c]-tar-ra-[ku] lib-bu-šu-un a-di û-mi ši-tim-ti-šu-nu ṭu-du [43]la ip-tu-ma la í-pu-šú ta-ḫa-zu.

I-na šani-i ḫarrani-ya a-na Babili*ki* šá a-na ka-ša-di ú-ṣa-am-mí-ru-šú ḫi-it-mu-ṭiš [44]al-lik-ma ki-ma ti-ib mí-ḫi-í a-ziḳ-ma ki-ma im-ba-ri as-ḫu-up-šu ala ni-i-ti al-mí-ma i-na [45]bíl-ti ù na-pal-ḳa-ti ala(?) [šu-a-tu ak-]šud [ša] niší*pl*-šu ṣiḫra ù raba-a la í-zib-ma *amílu*pagrî*pl*-šu-nu ri-bit ali [46]ú-mal-li. *m*Šú-zu-bu šar Babili*ki* ga-du kim-ti-šu [aṣ-bat] bal-ṭu-su-un a-na ki-rib mâti-ya ú-bíl-šú. [47]Makkur ali šú-a-tu a-bu-uk ḫuraṣu abnî*pl* ni-siḳ-ti bušâ makkuru

a. III R ši. — *b*. III R a-na. — *c*. III R at.

a-na ḳât niši$_{\textit{pl}}$-ya am-ni-i-ma a-na i-di ra-ma-ni-šu-nu ú-tir-ru. [48] Ilâni$_{\textit{pl}}$ a-šib líb-bi-šu ḳât niši$_{\textit{pl}}$-ya ik-šú-su-nu-ti-ma ú-šab-bi-ru-ma [bušâ-šu-nu] makkur-šu-nu il-ḳu-ni. $_{\textit{ilu}}$Ramân $_{\textit{ilu}}$Šá-la ilâni$_{\textit{pl}}$ [49] šá $_{\textit{alu}}$Ìkallâti$_{\textit{pl}}$ šá $_{\textit{m ilu}}$Marduk-nadin-aḫî$_{\textit{pl}}$ šar $_{\textit{mâtu}}$Akkadi$_{\textit{ki}}$ a-na tar-ṣi $_{\textit{m}}$Tukul-ti-apal-ì-šár-ra šar $_{\textit{mâtu}}$Aššur$_{\textit{ki}}$ il-ḳu-ma a-na Babili$_{\textit{ki}}$ ú-bì-lu [50] i-na IV C XVIII šanâti$_{\textit{pl}}$ ul-tu Babili$_{\textit{ki}}$ ú-ší-ṣa-am-ma a-na $_{\textit{alu}}$Ìkallâti$_{\textit{pl}}$ a-na aš-ri-šu-nu ú-tir-šu-nu-ti.

Ala ù bîtâti$_{\textit{pl}}$ [51] ul-tu uššî-šu a-di taḫ-lu-bi-šu ab-búl aḳ-ḳur i-na išâti aḳ-mu. Dûru ù šal-ḫu-u bîtât$_{\textit{pl}}$ ilâni$_{\textit{pl}}$ ziḳ-ḳur-rat libitti u iprâti ma-la ba-šú-ú [52] as-suḫ-ma a-na $_{\textit{nâru}}$A-ra-aḫ-ti ad-di. Ina bu-ṣur ali šú-a-tu ḫi-ra[a]-a-ti aḫ-ri-í-ma ir-ṣi-is-su i-na mí$_{\textit{pl}}$ as-pu-un. Ši-kín [53] uš-ší-šu ú-ḫal-liḳ-ma íli šá a-bu-bu na-pal-ḳa-ta-šu ú-ša-tir. Aš-šú aḫ-rat û-mí ḳaḳ-ḳar ali šú-a-tu ù bîtât$_{\textit{pl}}$ ilâni$_{\textit{pl}}$ [54] la muš-ši i-na ma-a-mi uš-ḫám-miṭ-su-ma ag-da-mar ú-sal-liš.

VI. ESARHADDON (681–668 B.C.).

Campaign against Sidon (I R 45 col. I 9–53).

[9] Ka-šid $_{\textit{alu}}$Ṣi-du-un-ni ša ina ḳabal tam-tim [10] sa-pi-nu gi-mir da-ád-mí-šu [11] dûra-šu ù šú-bat-su as-suḫ-ma [12] ki-rib tam-tim ad-di-i-ma [13] a-šar maš-kán-i-šu ú-ḫal-liḳ. [14] $_{\textit{m}}$Ab-di-mil-ku-ut-ti šarra-šú [15] ša la-pa-an $_{\textit{iṣu}}$kakkî$_{\textit{pl}}$-ya [16] ina ḳabal tam-tim in-nab-tu [17] ki-ma nu-ú-ni ul-tú ki-rib tam-tim [18] a-bar-šú-ma ak-ki-sa ḳaḳ-ḳa-su. [19] Nak-mu makkur-šu ḫuraṣu kaspu abnî$_{\textit{pl}}$ a-ḳar-tu [20] mašak pîri šin pîri $_{\textit{iṣu}}$ušû $_{\textit{iṣu}}$urkarina [21] $_{\textit{ku}}$lu-búl-ti birmi u kiti mimma šum-šú [22] ni-ṣir-ti ìkalli-šu [23] a-na mu-'u-di-í aš-lu-la. [24] Niši$_{\textit{pl}}$-šu rapšâti$_{\textit{pl}}$ ša ni-ba la i-ša-a [25] alpî$_{\textit{pl}}$ ù ṣi-í-ni imírî$_{\textit{pl}}$ [26] a-bu-ka a-na ki-rib $_{\textit{mâtu}}$Aššur$_{\textit{ki}}$ [27] ú-pa-ḫir-ma

---

a. III R **šú**.

šarrâni*pl* *mâtu*Ḫat-ṭi [28]ù a-ḫi tam-tim ka-li-šu-nu [29]ina [aš-ri] ša-nim-ma ala[a] ú-ší-piš-ma [30]*alu*[Dûr-*m ilu*Aššur]-aḫî-iddi-na at-ta-bi ni-bit-su. [31]Nišî*pl* ḫu-bu-ut *išu*ḳašti-ya ša šadi-i [32]ù tam-tim ṣi-it *ilu*šam-ši [33]ina líb-bi ú-ší-ši-ib [34]*amîlu*šu-par-šaḳ-ya *amîlu*piḫâta íli-šu-nu aš-kun.

[35]Û *m*Sa-an-du-ar-ri [36]šar *alu*Kun-di *alu*Si-zu-ú [37]*amîlu*nakru aḳ-ṣu la pa-liḫ bí-lu-ti-ya [38]šá ilâni*pl* ú-maš-šír-ú-ma [39]a-na šadi-i mar-ṣu-ti it-ta-kil [40]u *m*Ab-di-mil-ku-ut-ti šar *alu*Ṣi-du-ni [41]a-na ri-ṣu-ti-šu iš-kun-ma [42]šum ilâni*pl* rabûti*pl* a-na a-ḫa-miš iz-kur-u-ma [43]a-na í-mu-ḳi-šú-un it-ták-lu. [44]A-na-ku a-na Aššur bíli-ya at-ta-kil-ma [45]ki-ma iṣ-ṣu-ri ul-tú ki-rib šadi-i [46]a-bar-šú-ma ak-ki-sa ḳaḳ-ḳa-su. [47]Aš-šu da-na-an *ilu*Aššur bíli-ya [48]nišî*pl* kul-lum[b]-mi-im-ma [49]ḳaḳḳadî*pl* *m*Sa-an-du-ar-ri [50]ù *m*Ab-di-mi-il-ku-ut-ti [51]ina ki-ša-di *amîlu*rabûti*pl*-šu-un a-lul-ma [52]it-ti *amîlu*lib*pl* zikaru(?) u zinnišu [53]ina ri-bit Ninâ*ki* í-tí-it-ti-iḳ.

VII. ASSURBANIPAL (668–c. 626 B.C.).

1. Youth and Accession to the Throne (V R 1, 1–51).

[1]A-na-ku *m ilu*Aššur-bâni-apli bi-nu-tu *ilu*Aššur u *ilu*Bílit [2]apal-šarrûti rabu-ú šá bît ri-du-u-ti [3]šá *ilu*Aššur u *ilu*Sin bíl agí ul-tu ûmî*pl* rûḳûti*pl* [4]ni-bit šum-šu iz-ku-ru a-na šarru-u-ti [5]ù ina libbi ummi-šu ib-nu-u a-na ri'u-ut *mâtu ilu*Aššur*ki*. [6]*ilu*Šamaš *ilu*Ramân u *ilu*Ištar ina purussí-šu-nu ki-í-ni [7]iḳ-bu-ú í-piš šarrû-ti-ya. [8]*m ilu*Aššur-aḫî-iddi-na šar *mâtu ilu*Aššur*ki* abu ba-nu-u-a [9]a-mat *ilu*Aššur u *ilu*Bílit ilâni*pl* ti-ik-li-í-šu it-ta-'i-id [10]šá iḳ-bu-u-šu í-piš šarrû-ti-ya. [11]Ina *arḫu*âru araḫ *ilu*Ì-a bíl tí-ni-ší-í-ti [12]ûmu XII*kam* ûmu magiru **si-gar** šá *ilu*Gu-la [13]ina í-piš pi-i mut-tal-li [14]šá *ilu*Aššur *ilu*Bílit *ilu*Sin *ilu*Šamaš *ilu*Ramân [15]*ilu*Bíl *ilu*Nabû *ilu*Ištar ša Ninâ*ki* [16]*ilu*šar-rat kid-mu-ri

---

a. I R ṣi. — *b*. Var. lu.

ilu Ištar ša *alu* Arba'-ili *ki* [17] *ilu* Adar *ilu* Nírgal *ilu* Nusku iḳ-bu-ú [18] ú-paḫ[a]-ḫir nišî *pl* *mâtu ilu* Aššur *ki* ṣiḫra u rabâ [19] šá tam-tim í-li-ti ù šap-lit [20] a-na na-ṣir apal-šarrû-ti-ya ù arkâ-nu [21] šarrû-tu *mâtu ilu* Aššur *ki* í-pi-íš a-di-í šum ilâni *pl* [22] ú-ša-aš-kĭr-šú-nu-ti ú-dan-ni-na rik-sa-a-tí. [23] Ina ḫidâti *pl* ri-ša-a-tí í-ru-ub ina bît ridu-u-ti [24] pa-ru-nak-ki[b] mar-kas šarru[c]-u-ti [25] šá *m ilu* Sin-aḫî *pl*-irba abi abi a-li-di-ya [26] apal[d]-šarrû-tú ù šarrû-tú í-pu-šu ina líb-bi-šu [27] a-šar *m ilu* Aššur-aḫî-iddina abu bânu-u-a ki-rib-šu 'a-al-du [28] ir-bu-u í-pu-šu bí-lut *mâtu ilu* Aššur *ki* [29] gi-mir ma-al-ki ir-du-u kim-tú ú-rap-pi-šu [30] iḳ-ṣu-ru ni-šú-tú u sa[e]-la-tú [31] ù a-na-ku *m ilu* Aššur-bâni-apli ki-rib-šu a-ḫu-uz ni-mí-ki[f] *ilu* Nabû [32] kul-lat dup-šar-ru-u-ti ša gi-mir um-ma-ni [33] ma-la ba-šú-ú aḫ-zi-šu-nu a-ḫi-iṭ [34] al-ma-ad ša-li-í *iṣu* ḳašti ru-kub *imíru* sisî *iṣu* narkabti ṣa-mid-su a-ša-a-tí [35] ina ki-bit ilâni *pl* rabûti *pl* ša az-ku-ra ni-bit-sun [36] a-da-bu-ba ta-nit-ta-šu-un iḳ-bu-u í-piš šarrû-ti-ya [37] za-nin íš-ri-í-ti-šu-un ú-šad-gi-lu pa-nu-u-a [38] ki[g]-mu-u-a í-tap-pa-lu ín-ni-ti-ya i-na[h]-ru ga-ri-ya [39] zi-ka-ru ḳar-du na-ram *ilu* Aššur u *ilu* Ištar [40] [i]li-ib-li-pi[i] šarru-u-ti a-na-ku. [41] Ul-tu *ilu* Aššur *ilu* Sin *ilu* Šamaš *ilu* Ramân *ilu* Bíl *ilu* Nabû [42] *ilu* Iš-tar ša Ninâ *ki* *ilu* Šar-rat kid-mu-ri [43] *ilu* Iš-tar ša Arba'-ili *ki* *ilu* Adar *ilu* Nírgal *ilu* Nusku [44] ṭa-biš ú-ší-ši-bu-in-ni ina *iṣu* kussi abi bâni-ya [45] *ilu* Ramân zunnî *pl*-šu ú-maš-ší-ra *ilu* Ì-a ú-paṭ-ṭi-ra naḳbî *pl*-šu [46] V ana[j] ammati ší-am iš-ḳu ina **ab-nam**-ni-šu [47] í-ri-ik šú-búl-tu parab ana[j] ammati [48] išâr (?) dišu (?) na-pa-aš *an* nirba [49] ka-a-a-an ú-šaḫ-na-pu gi-pa-ru [50] ṣip-pa-a-ti šú-um-mu-ḫa in-bu bûlu šú-tí-šur ina ta-lit-ti [51] ina pali-ya šûḳu (?) duḫ-du ina šanâti *pl*-ya ku-um-mu-ru ḫigal-lum.

---

a. Var. **pa.** — *b.* V R **lu.** — *c.* V R **in.** — *d.* V R **muk.** — *e.* Var. **sal.** *f.* Var. **ḳi.** — *g.* Var. adds **í.** — *h.* Var. **ni.** — *i–i.* Var. **li-id-da-tú.** — *j.* Var. omits.

2. **Campaign against Tyre; Submission of Gyges of Lydia**
(V R 2, 49–125).

[49]Ina šal-ši gir-ri-ya íli $_{m}$Ba-'a-li[a] šar $_{m\hat{a}tu}$Ṣur-ri [50]a-šib ḳabal tam-tim lu-u al-lik[b] [51]šá[c] a-mat šarrû-ti-ya la iṣ-ṣu-ru la iš-mu-u zi-kir [d]šap-tí[d]-ya. [52]$_{alu}$Ḫal-ṣu[e]$_{pl}$ í-li-šu ú-rak-kis [53]ina tam-tim ù na-ba-li gir-ri-í-ti-šu ú-ṣab-bit [54]nap-šat-su-nu ú-si-iḳ ú-kar-ri [55]a-na $_{iṣu}$nîri-ya ú-šak-ni-is[f]-su-nu-ti. [56]Bintu ṣi-it líb-bi-šu ù binât$_{pl}$ aḫî$_{pl}$-šu [57]a-na í-piš $_{f}$ittu-ú-ti ú-bi-la a-di maḫ-ri-ya. [58]$_{m}$Ya-ḫi-mil-ki apal-šu ša ma-tí-ma ti-amat la í-bi-ra [59]iš-tí-niš ú-ší-bi-la a-na í-piš ardû-ti-ya [60]binat-su ù binât$_{pl}$ aḫî$_{pl}$-šu [61]it-ti tir-ḫa-ti ma-'a-as-si am-ḫur-šu [62]ri-í-mu ar-ši-šu-ma apla ṣi-it líb-bi-šu ú-tir-ma a[g]-din-šu. [63]$_{m}$Ya-ki-in-lu-u šar $_{m\hat{a}tu}$A-ru-ad-da a-šib ḳabal tam-tim [64]šá a-na šarrâni$_{pl}$ abî$_{pl}$-ya la kan-šu ik-nu-ša a-na $_{iṣu}$nîri-ya [65]binat-su it-ti nu-dun-ni-í ma-'a-di [66]a-na í-piš $_{f}$ittu-u-ti a-na Ninâ$_{ki}$ [67]ú-bíl-am-ma ú-na-aš-ši-ḳa šípî-ya.

[68]$_{m}$Mu-gal-lu šar $_{m\hat{a}tu}$Tab-ali ša it-ti šarrâni$_{pl}$ abî$_{pl}$-ya [69]id-bu-bu da-za-a-ti [70]bi-in-tú ṣi-it líb-bi-šu it-ti tir-ḫa-ti [71]ma-'a-as-si a-na í-piš $_{f}$ittu-u-ti a-na Ninâ$_{ki}$ [72]ú-bíl-am-ma ú-na-aš-šíḳ šípî-ya. [73]Íli[h] $_{m}$Mu-gal-li $_{imíru}$sisî$_{pl}$ rabûti$_{pl}$ [74]man-da-at-tú šat-ti-šam-ma ú-kín ṣîr-uš-šu. [75]$_{m}$Sa-an-da-šar-mí $_{m\hat{a}tu}$Ḫi-lak-ka-a-a [76]šá a-na šarrâni$_{pl}$ abî$_{pl}$-ya la ik-nu-šu [77]la i-šú-ṭu ab-ša-an-šu-un [78]bintu ṣi-it líb-bi-šu it-ti nu-dun-ni-í ma-'a-di [79]a-na í-piš $_{f}$ittu-u-ti a-na Ninâ$_{ki}$ [80]ú-bíl-am-ma ú-na-aš-šíḳ šípî-ya.[i]

[81]Ul-tú $_{m}$Ya-ki-in-lu-u šar $_{m\hat{a}tu}$A-ru-ad-da í-mí-du mâta-šu [82]$_{m}$A-zi-ba-'a[j]-al $_{m}$A-bi-ba-'a[j]-al $_{m}$A-du-ni-ba-'a[j]-al [83]$_{m}$Sa-pa-ṭi-ba-al $_{m}$Pu-di-ba-al $_{m}$Ba-'a[j]-al-ya-šú-bu [84]$_{m}$Ba-'a-al-ḫa-nu-nu $_{m}$Ba-'a[j]-al-ma-lu-ku $_{m}$A-bi-mil-ki $_{m}$Aḫi[k]-mil-ki [85]aplî$_{pl}$ $_{m}$Ya-ki-in-lu-u a-šib ḳabal tam-tim [86]ul-tú ḳabal

---

a. Var. **al**. — *b*. V R **lak**. — *c*. Var. **aš-šu**. — *d–d*. Var. **šaptí**. — *e*. Not **nin** (V R). — *f*. Var. omits. — *g*. Var. **ad**. — *h*. Var. **í-li**. — *i*. V R has one wedge too many. — *j*. Var. omits. — *k*. Var. **A-ḫi**.

tam-tim í-lu-nim-ma it-ti ta-mar-ti-šu-nu ka-bit-ti [87]il-li-ku-ú-nim-ma ú-na-aš-ši-ḳu šípî-ya. [88]*m*A-zi-ba-'a-al ḫa-diš ap-pa-lis-ma [89]a-na šarru-u-ti *mâtu*A-ru-ad-da aš-kun-šu. [90]*m*A-bi-ba-'a[a]-al *m*A-du-ni-ba-al *m*Sa-pa-ṭi-ba-al [91]*m*Pu-di-ba-al *m*Ba-'a-al-ya-šú-bu *m*Ba-'a-al-ḫa-nu-nu [92]*m*Ba-'a[a]-al-ma-lu-ku *m*A-bi-mil-ki *m*A-ḫi-mil-ki [93]lu-búl-ti bir-mí ú-lab-biš šimir*pl* ḫuraṣi ú-rak-ki-sa [94]rit-tí-í-šu-un ina maḫ-ri-ya ul-ziz-su-nu-ti.

[95]*m*Gu-ug[a]-gu šar *mâtu*Lu-ud-di na-gu-u ša ni-bir-ti tâmti [96]aš-ru ru-u-ḳu šá šarrâni*pl* abî*pl*-ya la iš-mu-ú [b]zi-kir[b] šum-šu [97]ni-bit [c]šumi-ya[c] ina šutti ú-šab-ri-šu-ma *ilu*Aššur ilu ba-nu-u-a [98]um-ma šípî *m ilu*Aššur-bâni-apli šar *mâtu ilu*Aššur*ki* ṣa-bat-ma [99]ina zi-kir šum-šu ku-šú-ud *amîlu*nakrûti*pl*-ka. [100]Û-mu šutta an-ni-tú í-mu-ru *amîlu*[d]rak-bu[d]-šu iš-pu-ru[e] [101]a-na ša-'a-al šul-mí-ya šutta an-ni-tú ša í-mu-ru [102]ina ḳâti *amîlu*allaki-šu iš-pur-am-ma ú-ša-an-na-a ya-a-ti. [103]Ul-tú líb-bi û-mí ša iṣ-ba-tú šípî šarrû-ti-ya [104]*amîlu*Gi-mir-ra-a-a mu-dal[f]-li-pu nišî*pl* mâti-šu [105]ša la ip-tal-la-ḫu abî*pl*-ya ù at-tu-u-a la iṣ-ba-tú [106]šípî šarrû-ti-ya ik-šú-ud. [107]Ina tukul-ti *ilu*Aššur u *ilu*Ištar ilâni*pl* bílî*pl*-ya ultu[g] líb-bi *amîlu*ḳípâni*pl* [108]šá *amîlu*Gi-mir-ra-a-a ša ik-šú-du II *amîlu*ḳípâni*pl* [109]ina *iṣu*ṣi-iṣ-ṣi iš-ḳa-ti parzilli bi-ri-ti parzilli ú-tam-mí-iḫ-ma [110]it-ti ta-mar-ti-šu ka-bit-tú[h] ú-ší-bi-la a-di maḫ-ri-ya.

[111]*amîlu*Rak-bu-šu ša a-na ša-'a-al šul-mí-ya ka-a-a-an iš-ta-nap-pa-ra [112]ú-šar-ša-a ba-ṭi-il-tú [i]aš-šu[i] ša a-mat *ilu*Aššur ili bâni-ya [113]la iṣ-ṣu-ru a-na í-muḳ ra-man-i-šu it-ta-kil-ma ig-bu-uš líb-bu. [114]Í-mu-ki[j]-í-šu a-na kit-ri *m*Tu[k]-ša-mí-il-ki šar *mâtu*Mu-ṣur [115]šá is-lu-ú *iṣu*nîr bílû-ti-ya iš-pur-ma. A-na-ku aš-mí-í-ma [116]ú-ṣal-li *ilu*Aššur u *ilu*Ištar um-ma pa-an *amîlu*nakri-šu pa-gar-šu

---

a. Var. omits. — *b–b*. Var. **zik-ri.** — *c–c*. Var. **šarrû-ti-ya kab-ti.** — *d–d*. Var. **ra-káb-ú** (III R 19, 12). — *e*. III R 19, 12 **ra.** — *f*. Var. **da-al.** — *g*. Var. **ul-tu.** — *h*. Var. **ti.** — *i–i*. Var. omits. — *j*. Var. **ḳi.** — *k*. Var. **Tù.**

li[a]-na-di-ma [117]liš-šú-u-ni nír-pad-du[b] *pl*-šu. Ki-i ša a-na *ilu*Aššur am-ḫu-ru[c] iš-lim[d]-ma [118]pa-an *amilu*nakri-šu pa-gar-šu in-na-di-ma iš-šu-u-ni nír-pad-du[b] *pl*-šu [119]*amilu*Gi-mir-a-a ša ina ni-bit šumi-ya ša-pal-šu ik-bu-su [120]it-bu-nim-ma is-pu-nu gi-mir mâti-šu.

Arki-šu apal-šu ú-šib ina *iṣu*kussi-šu [121]ip-šit *f*limut-tim ša ina ni-iš ḳâti-ya ilâni*pl* tik-li-ya [122]ina pa-an abi bâni-šu ú-šab-ri-ku ina ḳâti *amilu*allaki-šu iš-pur-am-ma [123]iṣ-ba-ta[e] šípî šarrû-ti-ya um-ma šarru ša ilu i-du-u-šu at-ta [124]abu-u-a ta-ru-ur-ma *f*limuttu iš-ša-kín ina pa-ni-šu [125]ya-a-ti ardu pa-lìḫ-ka kur-ban-ni-i-ma la-šú-ṭa ab-ša-an-ka.

3. **Account of Temple Restorations** (V R 62).

[1]*m ilu*Aššur-bâni-apli šarru rabû šarru dan-nu šar kiššati šar *mâtu*Aššur šar kib-rat irbit-ti [2]šar šarrâni*pl* rubû la ša-na-an ša ina a-mat ilâni*pl* ti-ik-li-šu ul-tu tam-tim í-lit [3]a-di tam-tim šap-lit i-bí-lu-ma gi-mir ma-lik ú-šak-niš ší-pu-uš-šu [4]apal *m ilu*Aššur-aḫî-iddi-na šarru rabû šarru dan-nu šar kiššati šar *mâtu*Aššur šakkanakku Tin-tir*ki* [5]šar *mâtu*Šumíri u Akkadi*ki* mu-ší-šib Tin-tir*ki* í-piš Ì-sag-ili [6]mu-ud-diš íš-ri-í-ti kul-lat ma-ḫa-zi ša ina ki-rib-ši-na iš-ták-kan si-ma-ti [7]ù sat-tuk-ki-ši-na baṭ-lu-tu ú-ki-nu bin-bini *m ilu*Sin-aḫî*pl*-irba šarru rabû [8]šarru dan-nu šar kiššati šar *mâtu*Aššur a-na-ku-ma.

Ina pali-í-a bílu rabû *ilu*Marduk ina ri-ša-a-ti [9]a-na Tin-tir*ki* i-ru-um-ma ina Ì-sag-ili ša da-ra-ti šú-bat-su ir-mí. [10]Sat-tuk-ki Ì-sag-ili u ilâni*pl* Tin-tir*ki* ú-kín. Ki-tin-nu-tu Tin-tir*ki* [11]aḳ-ṣur aš-šu dan-nu a-na ínši la ḫa-ba-li *m ilu*Šamaš-šum-ukin aḫu ta-li-mí [12]a-na šarru-ú-ut Tin-tir*ki* ap-ḳíd ù ši-pìr Ì-sag-ili la ḳa-ta-a [13]ú-šak-lil. Ina kaspi ḫuraṣi ni-siḳ-ti abnî*pl* Ì-sag-ili az-nun-ma [14]ki-ma ši-ṭir bu-ru-mu ú-nam-mir Ì-ku-a ù ša iš-

a. Var. adds **in.** — *b.* Var. **da.** — *c.* Var. **ra.** — *d.* Var. **li.** — *e.* Var. **tu.**

ri-í-ti ka-li-ši-na [15]ḫi-bíl-ta-ši-na ú-šal-lim í-li kul-lat ma-ḫa-zi ú-šat-ri-ṣi ṣalu(?)-lum.

[16]Ina û-mí-šu-ma Ì-babbar-ra ša ki-rib Sippar*ki* bît *ilu*Šamaš bílu rabû bíli-ya ša la-ba-riš [17]il-lik-u-ma i-ḳu-pu in-nab-tu aš-ra-ti-šu aš-tí-'i ina ši-pìr *ilu*[Ìa(?)] [18]íš-šiš ú-ší-piš-ma ki-ma šadi-i ri-í-ši-i-šu ul-li a-na šat(?)-ti [ ] [19]dânu rabû ilâni*pl* bílu rabû bíli-yá ip-ší-ti-ya dam-ḳa-a-ti ḫa-diš lip-[pa-lis-ma] [20]a-na ya-a-ši *m ilu*Aššur-bâni-apli šar *mâtu*Aššur rubû pa-lìḫ-šu balâṭ û-mí rûḳûti*pl* ší-bi-í [lit-tu-ti] [21]ṭu-ub šîri u ḫu-ud líb-bi li-šim ši-ma-ti u ša *m ilu*Šamaš-šum-ukin [22]šar Tin-tir*ki* aḫi ta-lim-ya û-mí-šu li-ri-ku liš-bi bu-'a-a-ri-ma [ ].

[23]Ina aḫ-rat û-mí rubû ar-ku-ú ša ina û-mí pali-šu ši-pìr šú-a-ti in-na-ḫu-ma [24]an-ḫu-us-su lu-ud-diš šú-mí it-ti šum-šu liš-ṭur mu-sar-u-a li-mur-[ma] [25]kisalla lip-šú-uš *kirru*niḳa liḳ-ḳí it-ti mu-sar-í-šu liš-kun iḳ-ri-bi[-šu] [26]*ilu*Šamaš i-šim-mí. Ša šú-mí šaṭ-ru ù šum ta-lim-ya ina ši-pìr ni-kil-ti [27]i-pa-aš-ši-ṭu šú-mí it-ti šum-šu la i-šaṭ-ṭa-ru mu-sar-ú-a [28]i-ab-ba-tu-ma it-ti mu-sar-í-šu la i-šak-ka-nu *ilu*Šamaš bíl í-la-ti u šap-la-ti [29]ag-gi-iš lik-rim-mí-šu-ma šum-šu zir-šu ina mâtâti li-ḫal-liḳ.

4. **War against Šamaššumukin of Babylon** (V R 3, 128–4, 109).

[128]Ina šiš-ši gir-ri-ya ad-ki ummânâti-ya. [129]Ṣîr *m ilu*Šamaš-šum-ukin uš-tí-íš-ší-ra ḫar-ra-nu. [130]Ki-rib Sippar*ki* Babili*ki* Bàr-sip*ki* Kûtí*ki* [131]ša-a-šu ga-du mun-dáḫ-ṣi-í-šu í-si-ir-ma [132]ú-ṣab-[a]bi-ta[a] mu-uṣ-ṣa-šu-un. [133]Ki-rib ali u ṣîri ina la mí-ni aš-ták-ka-na abikta-šu. [134]Si-it-tu-u-ti ina lipi-it *ilu*Dibba-ra [135]su-un-ḳu bu-bu-ti iš-ku-nu na-piš-tu. [136]*m*Um-man-i-gaš šar *mâtu*Ílamti*ki* ši-kín ḳâti-ya [137]ša da-'a-a-tu im-ḫu-ru-šu-ma [138]it-ba-a a-na kit-ri-šu [4, 1]*m*Tam-ma-ri-tú ṣîr-uš-šu ip-pal-kit-ma

a–a. Var. bit.

[2]ša-a-šu ga-du kim-ti-šu ú-ras[a]-sip ina *iṣu*kakkî*pl*. [3]Arka *m*Tam-ma-ri-tú ša arki *m*Um-man-i-gaš [4]ú-ši-bu ina *iṣu*kussi *mâtu*Ílamti*ki* [5]la iš-[b]a-lu[b] šú-lum šarrû-ti-ya [6]a-na ri-ṣu-tú *m ilu*Šamaš-šum-ukin aḫi [c]nak-ri[c] [7]il-lik-am-ma a-na mit-ḫu-ṣi ummânâti-ya [8]ur-ri-ḫa *iṣu*kakkî*pl*-šu.

[9]Ina su-up-pi-í ša *ilu*Aššur u *ilu*Ištar ú-sap-pu-u [10]un[d]-nin-ni-ya il-ḳu-u iš-mu-ú zi-kir šaptí-ya. [11]*m*In-da-bi-gaš arad-su ṣîr-uš-šu ip-pal-kit[e]-ma [12]ina taḫazi ṣíri iš-ku-na abikta-šu. *m*Tam-ma-ri-tu [13]šar *mâtu*Ílamti*ki* ša íli ni-kis ḳaḳḳadi *m*Tí-um-man [14]mi-ri[f]-iḫ-tu iḳ-bu-ú [15]šá ik-ki-su a-ḫu-ur[g]-ru-u ummânâti-ya [16]um-ma i-nak-ki-su-u ḳaḳḳadi šar *mâtu*Ílamti*ki* [17]ki-rib mâti-šu ina puḫur ummânâti-šu [18]ša-ni-ya[h]-a-nu iḳ-bi ù *m*Um-man-i-gaš [19]ki-í[i] ú-na-aš-šíḳ ḳaḳ-ḳa-ru [20]ina pa-an *amílu*allakî*pl* ša *m ilu*Aššur-bâni-apli šar *mâtu ilu*Aššur *ki*.

[21]Íli a-ma-a-ti an-na-a-tí ša il-zi-nu [22]*ilu*Aššur u *ilu*Ištar í[i]-ri-ḫu-šu-ma [23]*m*Tam-ma-ri-tú aḫî*pl*-šu ḳin-nu-šu zir bît abi-šu [24]it-ti LXXXV rubûti*pl* a-li-kut i-di-í-šu [25]la-pa-an *m*In-da-bi-gaš in-nab-tú-nim-ma [26]mi-ra-nu-uš-šu-un ina íli libbî*pl*-šu-nu [27]ib-ši-lu-nim-ma il-lik-u-ni a-di Ninâ*ki*. [28]*m*Tam-ma-ri-tu šípî šarrû-ti-ya ú-na-aš-šíḳ-ma [29]ḳaḳ-ḳa-ru ú-ší-šir ina ziḳ-ni-šu. [30]Man[j]-za-az *iṣu*ma[k]-ša-ri-ya iṣ-bat-ma [31]a-na í-piš ardû-ti-ya ra-ṃan-šu im-nu-ma [32]aš-šu í-piš di-ni-šu a-lak ri-ṣu-ti-šu [33]ina ki-bit *ilu*Aššur u *ilu*Ištar ú-ṣal-la-a bílu-u-ti. [34]Ina maḫ-ri-ya i-zi-zu-u-ma [35]i-dal-la-lu ḳur-di ilâni*pl*-ya dan-nu-ti [36]šá il-li-ku ri-ṣu-ú-ti. [37]A-na-ku *m ilu*Aššur-bâni-apli líb-bu rap-šu [38]la ka-ṣir ik-ki-mu pa-si-su ḫi-ṭa-a-tí [39]a-na *m*Tam-ma-ri-tú ri-í-mu ar-ši-šu-ma [40]ša-a-šu ga-du zir bît abi-šu ki-rib ìkalli-ya [41]ul-ziz-su-nu-ti.

Ina û-mí-šu nišî*pl* Akkadi*ki* [42]šá it-ti *m ilu*Šamaš-šum-ukin iš-šak-nu [43]iḳ-pu-du limut-tú ni-ip-ri-í-tú iṣ-bat-su-

a. Var. **ra.** — *b–b.* Var. **al.** — *c–c.* Var. **la ki-í-nu.** — *d.* Not **dan** (V R). — *e.* V. **ki-tu.** — *f.* Not **ik** (V R). — *g.* Var. omits. — *h.* Var. **'a.** — *i.* Var. **i.** — *j.* Var. **ma.** — *k.* Var. **man.**

nu-ti. [44]A-na bu-ri-šu-nu šîrî*pl* aplî*pl*[a]-šu-nu binâti*pl*-šu-nu [45]í-ku-lu ik-su-su ku-ru-us-su. [46]*ilu*Aššur *ilu*Šamaš *ilu*Ramân *ilu*Bíl *ilu*Nabû [47]*ilu*Ištar ša Ninâ*ki* *ilu*Šar-rat kid-mu-ri [48]*ilu*Ištar ša *alu*Arba'-ili *ilu*Adar *ilu*Nírgal *ilu*Nusku [49]šá ina maḫ-ri-ya il-li-ku i-na-ru ga-ri-ya [50]*m ilu*Šamaš-šum-ukin aḫu nak-ri ša i-gi-ra-an-ni [51]ina mi-ḳít išâti a-ri-ri id-du-šu-ma [52]ú-ḫal-li-ḳu nap-šat-su.

[53]Û nišî*pl* ša a-na *m ilu*Šamaš-šum-ukin [54]aḫi nak-ri ú-šaḳ-pi-du [55]ip-ší-í-tú an-ni-tú limut-tú í-pu-šu [56]šá mi-tu-tu ip-la-ḫu nap-šat-su-un pa-nu-uš-šu-un [57]tí-kir(?)-u-ma it-ti *m ilu*Šamaš-šum-ukin [58]bíli-šu-nu la im-ḳu-tú ina išâti [59]šá la-pa-an ni-kis paṭar parzilli su-un-ḳí[b] bu-bu-ti[c] [60]išâti a-ri-ri i-ší-tu-u-ni í-ḫu-zu mar-ki[d]-i-tú [61]sa-par ilâni*pl* rabûti*pl* bílî*pl*-ya ša la na-par-šú-di [62]is-ḫu-up-šu-nu-ti í-du ul ip-par-šid [63]mul-táḫ-ṭu ul ú-ṣi ina ḳâti-ya im-nu-u ḳâtu[e]-u-a [64]*iṣu*narkabâti*pl* *iṣu*ša-ša-da-di *iṣu*ša-ṣil-li [f]zik-ri-í-ti-šu [65]makkur ìkalli-šu ú-bíl-u-ni a-di maḫ-ri-ya. [66]*amílu*Ṣâbî*pl* ša-a-tú-nu šil-la-tú pi-i-šu-nu [67]ša ina íli *ilu*Aššur ili-ya šil-la-tú iḳ-bu-u [68]ù ya-a-ti rubû pa-lìḫ-šu iḳ-pu-du-u-ni limut-tú [69][f]pi-i[f]-šu-nu aš-lu-uḳ abikta-šu-nu aš-kun. [70]Si-it-ti nišî*pl* bal-ṭu-sun ina *ilu*šídi *ilu*lamassi [71]šá *m ilu*Sin-aḫî*pl*-irba abi abi bâni-ya ina líb-bi is-pu-nu [72]í-nin-na a-na-ku ina ki-is-pi-šu [73]nišî*pl* ša-a-tu-nu ina líb-bi as-pu-un. [74]Šîrî*pl*-šu-nu nu-uk-ku-su-u-ti [75]ú-ša-kil kalbâni*pl* šaḫî*pl* zi-i-bi *iṣṣuru* [76]našrî *iṣṣuru pl* iṣṣurî*pl* šami-í nûnî*pl* ap-si-í[g].

[77]Ul-tú ip-ší-í-ti an-na-a-ti í[g]-tí-ip-pu-šu [78]ú-ni-iḫ-ḫu líb-bi ilâni*pl* rabûti*pl* bílî*pl*-ya [79]*amílu*pagrî*pl* nišî*pl* ša *ilu*Dibba-ra ú-šam-ḳí-tú [80]ù ša ina su-un-ḳí[h] bu-bu-ti iš-ku-nu na-piš-tú [81]ri-ḫi-it ú-kul-ti kalbâni*pl* šaḫî*pl* [82]šá sûḳî*pl* pur-ru-ku ma-lu-u ri-ba-a-ti [83]nír-pad-du*pl*-šu-nu-ti ul-tú ki-rib Babili*ki* [84]Kûtí*ki* Sippar*ki* ú-ší-ṣi-ma [85]at-ta-ad[i]-di a-na na-ka-ma-a-ti. [86]Ina ši-pìr i-šib-bu-ti parakkî*pl*-

---

a. V R omits *pl.* — *b.* Var. **ḳu.** — *c.* Var. **tú.** — *d.* Not **ku** (V R). *e.* Var. **ḳa-tu.** — *f-f.* Var. **lišan.** — *g.* Var. **i.** — *h.* Var. **ḳi.** — *i.* Var. omits.

šu-nu ub-bi-ib [87] ul-li-la su-ul-li-í-šu-nu lu-'u-u-ti. [88] Ilâni*pl*-šu-nu zi-nu-u-ti *ilu*ištarâti*pl*-šu-nu sab-sa-a-tí [89] ú-ni-iḫ ina tâḳ-rib-ti u šigû libbi **ku-mal.** [90] Sat-tuk-ki-šu-un ša i-mí-ṣu ki-ma ša û-mí ul-lu-u-ti [91] ina šal-mí ú-tir-ma ú-kín. Si-it-ti aplî*pl* Babili*ki* Kûtí*ki* Sippar*ki* [93] šá ina šib-ṭi šak-bi-ti ù ni-ip-ri-í-ti [94] i-ší-tu-u-ni ri-í-mu ar-ši-šu-nu-ti [95] ba-laṭ na-piš-ti-šu-nu aḳ-bi [96] ki-rib Babili*ki* ú-ší-šib-šú-nu-ti. [97] Nišî*pl* *mâtu*Akkadi*ki* ga-du *mâtu*Kal-du[a] *mâtu*A-ra[b]-mu mât tam-tim [98] šá *m ilu*Šamaš-šum-ukin iḳ-tir-u-ma [99] a-na išt-ín pi-i ú-tir-ru [100] a-na pa-[c]ra-as[c] ra-ma-ni-šu-nu ik-ki-ru it-ti-ya [101] ina ki[d]-bit *ilu*Aššur u *ilu*Bílit u ilâni*pl* rabûti*pl* tik-li-ya [102] a-na pad gim-ri-šu-nu ak-bu-us [103] *iṣu*nîr *ilu*Aššur ša is-lu-u í-mid-su-nu-ti. [104] *amîlu*šaknûti*pl* *amílu***bí-gid-da***pl* ši-kín ḳâti-ya [105] aš-ták-ka-na í-li-šu-un. [106] **di-ka***pl* gi-[e]ni-í[e] ríšî(?)*pl* *ilu*Aššur u *ilu*Bílit [107] ù ilâni*pl* *mâtu ilu*Aššur*ki* ú-kín ṣîr-uš-šu-un. [108] Bíl-tu man-da-at-tú bílû-ti-ya [109] šat-ti-šam-ma la na-par-ka-a í-mid-su-nu-ti.

5. **Arabian Campaign** (V R 7, 82–10, 39).

Cause of the War.—[82] Ina IX-í gir-ri-ya ad-ki ummânâti-ya. [83] Ṣîr *m*Ú-a-a-tí-'i šar *mâtu*A-ri-bi [84] uš-tí-íš-ší-ra ḫar-ra-nu [85] šá ina a-di-ya iḫ-ṭu-ú [86] ṭâbtu í-pu-šú-uš la iṣ-ṣur-ú-ma [87] is-la-a *iṣu*nîr bílu-ú-ti-ya [88] šá *ilu*Aššur í-mí-du-uš[f] i-šú-ṭu ab-ša-a-ni. [89] A-na ša-'a-al šul-mí-ya šípî-šu ip-ru-us-ma [90] ik-la-a ta-mar-ti man-da-at-ta-šu ka-bit-tú. [91] Ki-i *mâtu*Ílamti*ki*-ma da-bab sur-ra-a-tí [92] *mâtu*Akkadi*ki* iš-mí-í-ma [93] la iṣ-ṣu-ra a-di-ya. [94] Ya-a-ti *m ilu*Aššur-bâni-apli šarru šangu íllu [95] ri-í-šu mut-nin-nu-ú [96] bi-nu-ut ḳâtî *ilu*Aššur ú-maš-šir-an-ni-ma [97] a-na *m*A-bi-ya-tí-'i *m*A-a-mu aplî *m*Tí-í[g]-ri [98] í-mu-ki id-din-šú-nu-ti [99] a-na ri-ṣu-tu *m ilu*Šamaš-šum-ukin [100] aḫi nak-ri iš-pur-am-ma [101] iš-ta-kan pi-i-šu. [102] Nišî*pl* *mâtu*A-ri-bi it-ti-šu ú-šam-kĭr-ma [103] iḫ-ta-nab-ba-ta

---

a. Var. **di.** — *b.* Var. **ru.** — *c–c.* Var. **ras.** — *d.* Not **ku** (V R). — *e–e.* Var. **nu-u.** — *f.* Var. **šu.** — *g.* Var. **'i.**

ḫu-bu-ut nišî *pl* [104]šá *ilu*Aššur *ilu*Ištar u ilâni *pl* rabûti *pl* [105]id-din-u-ni ri'û-si-na í-pi-ši[a] [106]ù ú-mal-lu-ú ḳâtu[b]-u-a.

Flight of Uâti, son of Bir-Dadda, to the Nabatheans.—[107]Ina ki-bit *ilu*Aššur u *ilu*Ištar ummânâti-ya [108]ina gi-ra-a *alu*A-ṣa-ar-an [109]*alu*Ḫi-ra-ta-a-ḳa-za-a-a ina *alu*Ú-du-mí [110]ina ni-rib *alu*Ya-ab-ru-du ina *alu*Bît-*m*Am-ma-ni [111]ina na-gi-í ša *alu*Ḫa-ú-ri-i-na [112]ina *alu*Mu-'a-a-ba ina *alu*Sa-'a-ar-ri [113]ina *alu*Ḫa-ar-gi-í ina na-gi-í [114]šá *alu*Ṣu-bi-ti di-ik-ta-šu [115]ma-'a-at-tu a-duk. [116]Ina la mí-ni aš-kun abikta-šu. [117]Nišî *pl* *mâtu*A-ri-bi ma-la it-ti-šu it-bu-u-ni [118]ú-ra-as-sip ina *iṣu*kakkî *pl*. [119]Ù šú-ú la-pa-an *iṣu*kakkî *pl* *ilu*Aššur dan-nu-ti [120]ip-par-šid-ma in-na-bit a-na ru-ki-í-ti. [121]Bît-ṣíri zir-ta-ra-a-tí mu-ša-bi-šu-nu [122]išâti ú-ša-ḫi-iz-zu iḳ-mu-u ina išâti. [123]*m*Ú-a-a-tí-'i ma-ru-uš-tú im-ḫur-šu-u-ma [124]í-diš-ši-šu in-na-bit a-na *mâtu*Na-ba-a-a-tí.

Capture of Uâti, son of Hazael.—[8,1]*m*Ú-a-a-tí-'i apal *m*Ḫa-za-ilu [2]apal aḫi abi ša *m*Ú-a-a-tí-'i apal *m*Bir-*ilu*Dadda [3]šá ra-man-šu iš-ku-nu [4]a-na šarru-u-ti *mâtu*A-ri-bi [5]*ilu*Aššur šar ilâni *pl* šadu-ú rabu-ú [6]ṭì-ín-šu ú-ša-an-ni-ma [7]il-li-ka a-di maḫ-ri-ya. [8]A-na kul-lum ta-nit-ti *ilu*Aššur [9]ù ilâni *pl* rabûti *pl* bílî *pl*-ya [10]an-nu kab-tu í-mid-su-ma [11]*iṣu*ši-ga-ru aš-kun-šú-ma [12]it-ti **a-si** kalbi ar-ku-us-šu-ma [13]ú-ša-an-ṣir-šu abulli ḳabal *alu*Ninâ *ki* [14]ni-rib maš-nak-ti ad-na-a-ti.

Capture of Ammuladi, the Kedarene.—[15]Ù šú-u *m*Am-mu-la-di šar *mâtu*Ki-id-ri [16]it-ba-am-ma a-na mit-ḫu-uṣ-ṣi šarrâni *pl* *mâtu*Aḫarrî *ki* [17]šá *ilu*Aššur *ilu*Ištar u ilâni *pl* rabûti *pl* [18]ú-šad-gi-lu pa-nu-u-a. [19]Ina tukul-ti *ilu*Aššur *ilu*Sin *ilu*Šamaš *ilu*Ramân [20]*ilu*Bíl *ilu*Nabû *ilu*Ištar ša Ninâ *ki* [21]*ilu*Šarrat[c] kid-mu-ri *ilu*Ištar šá *alu*Arba'-ili [22]*ilu*Adar *ilu*Nírgal *ilu*Nusku [23]abikta-šu aš-kun. [24]Ša-a-šu bal-ṭu-us-su it-ti *f*A-di-ya-a [25]aššat *m*Ú-a-a-tí-'i šar *mâtu*A-ri-bi [26]iṣ-ba-tu-nim-ma ú-bíl-u-ni a-di maḫ-ri-ya. [27]Ina ki-bit ilâni *pl* rabûti *pl* bílî *pl*-ya [28]ul-li kalbi aš-kun-šu-ma [29]ú-ša-an-ṣir-šu *iṣu*ši-ga-ru.

---

a. Var. **šu.** — *d.* Var. **ḳa-tu.** — *c.* Var. **šar-rat.**

Submission of Arabian generals, Abiyati and Âmu.—[30]Ina ki-bit *ilu* Aššur *ilu* Ištar u ilâni *pl* rabûti *pl* bílî *pl*-ya [31]šá *m* A-bi-ya-tí-'i *m* A-a-mu aplî *m* Tí-'i-ri [32]šá a-na ri-ṣu-u-tu *m ilu* Šamaš-šum-ukin aḫi nak-ri [33]a-na í-rib Babili *ki* il-li-ku [34]ri-ṣi-í-šu a-duk abikta-šu aš-kun. [35]Si-it-tu-ti ša ki-rib Babili *ki* í-ru-bu [36]ina su-un-ḳí ḫu-šaḫ-ḫi [37]í-ku-lu šîr a-ḫa-miš. [38]A-na šú-zu-ub napiš-tim-šu-nu [39]ul-tú ki-rib Babili *ki* ú-ṣu-nim-ma [40]*amílu* í-mu-ki-ya ša ina íli *m ilu* Šamaš-šum-ukin šak-nu [41]ša-ni-ya-a-nu abikta-šu iš-ku-nu-ma [42]šú-ú í-diš ip-par-šid-ma [43]a-na šú-zu-ub napiš-tim-šu iṣ-ba-tú šípî-ya.

Abiyati appointed king of Arabia.—[44]Ri-í-mu ar-ši-šú-u-ma [45]a-di-í ni-iš ilâni *pl* rabûti *pl* ú-ša-as-kir-šu-ma [46]ku-um *m* Û-a-a-tí-'i apal *m* Ḫa-za-ilu [47]a-na šarru-u-ti *mâtu* A-ri-bi aš-kun-šu.

Abiyati's conspiracy with the Nabatheans.—[48]Û šú-u it-ti *mâtu* Na-ba-a-a-ta-a-a [49]pi-i-šu iš-kun-ma [50]ni-iš ilâni *pl* rabûti *pl* la ip-laḫ-ma [51]iḫ-tab[a]-ba-ta ḫu-bu-ut mi-ṣir mâti-ya.

Submission of Nathan the Nabathean.—[52]Ina tukul-ti *ilu* Aššur *ilu* Sin *ilu* Šamaš *ilu* Ramân [53]*ilu* Bíl *ilu* Nabû *ilu* Ištar šá Ninâ *ki* [54]*ilu* Šar-rat kid-mu-ri *ilu* Ištar šá *alu* Arba'-ili [55]*ilu* Adar *ilu* Nírgal *ilu* Nusku [56]*m* Na-at-nu šar *mâtu* Na-ba-a-a-ti [57]šá a-šar-šu ru-ú-ḳu [58]šá *m* Û-a-a-tí-'i ina maḫ-ri-šu in-nab-tu [59]iš-mi-í-ma da-na-an *ilu* Aššur šá ú-ták-kil-an[b]-ni [60]šá ma-tí-í-ma a-na šarrâni *pl* abî *pl*-ya [61]*amílu* allak-šu la iš-pu-ra [62]la iš-'a-a-lu šú-lum šarrû-ti-šu-un [63]ina pu-luḫ-ti *iṣu* kakkî *pl* *ilu* Aššur ka-ši-du-u-ti [64]is-sa-an-ḳa-am-ma iš-'a-a-la šú-lum šarrû-ti-ya.

Revolt of Abiyati and Nathan.—[65]Û *m* A-bi-ya-tí-'i apal *m* Tí-'i-í-ri [66]la ḫa-sis ṭa-ab-ti [67]la na-ṣir ma-mit ilâni *pl* rabûti *pl* [68]da-bab sur-ra-a-tí it-ti-ya id-bu-ub-ma [69]pi-i-šu it-ti *m* Na-at-ni [70]šar *mâtu* Na-ba-a-a-ti iš-kun-ma [71]*amílu* í-mu-ki-šu-nu id-ku-u-ni [72]a-na ti-ib limut-tim a-na mi-ṣir-ya.

---

a. Var. ta-nab.—*b.* Var. a.

March of Assyrian army from Nineveh.—[73]Ina ki-bit *ilu*Aššur *ilu*Sin *ilu*Šamaš *ilu*Ramân [74]*ilu*Bíl *ilu*Nabû *ilu*Ištar šá Ninâ*ki* [75]*ilu*Šar-rat kid-mu-ri *ilu*Ištar šá Arba'-ili*ki* [76]*ilu*Adar *ilu*Nírgal *ilu*Nusku [77]ummânâti-ya ad-ki. Ṣîr *m*A-bi-ya-tí-'i [78]uš-tí-íš-ší-ra ḫar-ra-nu. [79]*nâru*Diḳlat u *nâru*Puratta [80]ina míli-ši-na gab-ši šal-míš lu-u í-bi-ru. [81]Ir-du-ú ur-ḫi ru-ḳu-u-ti [82]í-til-lu-ú ḫur-ša-a-ni ša-ḳu-u-ti [83]iḫ-tal-lu-bu *iṣu*kišâti*pl* ša ṣu-lul-ši-na rap-šu [84]bi-rit iṣî*pl* rabûti*pl* gi-iṣ-ṣi [85]*iṣu***gištin-gir**(?)*pl* ḫar-ra-an *iṣu*id-di-í-ti [86]í-tí-it-ti-ḳu šal-mi-iš. [87]*mâtu*Maš a-šar ṣu-um-mí ḳàl-ḳàl-ti [88]šá iṣṣur šami-í la i-ša-'a-u ki-rib-šu [89]*imíru*purimî*pl* ṣabîti*pl* [90]la ir-tí-'i-ú ina líb-bi [91]I C kas-bu ḳaḳ-ḳa-ru ultu Ninâ*ki* [92]ali na-ram *ilu*Iš-tar ḫi-raṭ *ilu*Bíl [93]arki[a] *m*Ú-a-a-tí-'i šar *mâtu*A-ri-bi [94]ù *m*A-bi-ya-tí-'i ša it-ti *amílu*í-mu-ki [95]*mâtu*Na-ba-a-a-ta-a-a il-li-ka [96]ir-du-u il-li-ku.

Ina *arḫu*simâni araḫ *ilu*Sin [97]apli riš-[b]tu-u[b] a-ša-ri-du šá *ilu*Bíl [98]ûmu XXV*kam* ša da-ḫu ša *ilu*Bí-lit Babili*ki* [99]ka-bit-ti ilâni*pl* rabûti*pl* [100]ul-tú *alu*Ḫa-da-at-ta-a at-tu-muš. [101]Ina *alu*La-ri-ib-da bît-dûri šá *abnu***šit***pl* [102]ina íli gu-ub-ba-a-ni ša mí*pl* [103]at-ta-ad-di uš-man-ni. [104]Ummânâti-ya mí*pl* a-na maš-ti-ti-šu-nu iḫ-pu-ma [105]ir-du-ú il-li-ku [106]ḳaḳ-ḳar ṣu-um-mí a-šar ḳàl-ḳàl-ti [107]a-di *alu*Ḫu-ra-ri-na bi-rit *alu*Ya-ar-ki [108]ù *alu*A-za-al-la ina *mâtu*Maš aš-ru ru-u-ḳu [109]a-šar ú-ma-am ṣíri la ib-ba-aš-šú-u [110]ù iṣṣur šami-í la i-šak-ka-nu ḳin-nu. [111]Abikti *amílu*I-sa-am-mí-'i [112]*amílu***iz-da** ša *ilu*A-tar-sa-ma-a-a-in [113]ù *mâtu*Na-ba-a-a-ta-a-a aš-kun. [114]Nišî*pl* imírî*pl* *imíru*gammalî*pl* ù ṣínî [115]ḫu-bu-us-su-nu ina la mí-ni aḫ-bu-ta.

[116]VIII kas-bu ḳaḳ-ḳa-ru [117]ummânâti-ya lu-u it-tal-la-ku šal-ṭiš [118]šal-mí-iš lu i-tu-ru-nim-ma [119]ina *alu*A-za-al-li lu iš-tu-u mí*pl* niš-bi-í. [120]Ultu líb-bi *alu*A-za-al-la [121]a-di *alu*Ḳu-ra-ṣi-ti [122]VI kas-bu ḳaḳ-ḳa-ru a-šar ṣu-um-mí [123]ḳàl-ḳàl-ti ir-du-u il-li-ku. [124]*amílu*'A-lu ša *ilu*A-tar-sa-

---

a. Var. **ṣír**.—*b*–*b*. Var. **ti-í**.

ma-a-in [9,1]ù *amílu*Ḳíd-ra-a-a ša *m*Ú-a-a-tí-'i [2]apal *m*Bir-*ilu*Dadda[a] šar *mâtu*A-ri-bi al-mí. [3]Ilâni*pl*-šu umma-šu bílta-šu aššat-su [4]ḳin-nu-šu niší*pl*-šu *mâtu*Ki-id-ri ka-la-mu [5]imírî*pl* *imíru*gammalí*pl* u ṣi-í-ni [6]ma-la ina tukul-ti *ilu*Aššur u *ilu*Ištar [7]bílî*pl*-ya ik-šú-da ḳâta-a-a [8]ḫar-ra-an *mâtu*[b]Di-maš-ḳa ú-ša-aš-ki-na ší-pu-uš-šu-un.

[9]Ina *arḫu*abi araḫ kakkab ḳašti [10]ma-rat *ilu*Sin ḳa-rit-tu [11]ûmu III*kam* nu-bat-tú ša šar ilâni*pl* *ilu*Marduk [12]ul-tú *alu*Di-maš-ḳa at-tu-muš. [13]VI kas-bu ḳaḳ-ḳa-ru mu-ši-tu ka-la-ša [14]ar-di-í-ma al-lik a-di *alu*Ḫul-ḫu-li-ti. [15]Ina *šadû*Ḫu-uk-ku-ri-na šadu-ú mar-ṣu [16]*amílu*'a-lu šá *m*A-bi-ya-tí-'i apal *m*Tí-'i-ri [17]*mâtu*Ḳíd-ra-a-a ak-šú-ud [18]abikta-šu aš-kun aš-lu-la šal-lat-su.

Capture of Abiyati and Âmu. — [19]*m*A-bi-ya-tí-'i *m*A-a-am-mu [20]aplî *m*Tí-'i-ri ina ki-bit *ilu*Aššur u *ilu*Ištar bílî*pl*-ya [21]ina ḳabal tam-ḫa-ri bal-ṭu-us-su-un ú-ṣab-bit ḳâti[c]. [22]Ḳâtî u šípî bi-ri-tú parzilli ad-di-šu-nu-ti. [23]It-ti šal-lat mâti-šu-un [24]al-ḳa-aš-šu-nu-ti a-na *mâtu ilu*Aššur*ki*.

Flight of the Rebels. — [25]Mun-nab-ti šá la-pa-an *iṣu*kakkî*pl*-ya in-nab-tu [26]ip-la-ḫu-ma iṣ-ba-tú *šadû*Ḫu-uk-ku-ru-na šadu-ú mar-ṣu. [27]Ina *alu*Ma-an-ḫa-ab-bi *alu*Ap-pa-ru [28]*alu*Tí-nu-ḳu-ri *alu*Ṣa-a-a-ú-ra-an [29]*alu*Mar-ḳa-na-a *alu*Sa-da-tí-in [30]*alu*Ín-zi-kar-mí *alu*Ta-'a-na-a *alu*Ir-ra-a-na [31]a-šar kup-pi nam-ba-'i ša mí*pl* ma-la ba-šu-u [32]maṣarâti*pl* ina muḫ-ḫi u-ša-an-ṣir-ma [33]mí*pl* balâṭ napiš-tim-šu-nu ak-šú(?) [34]maš-ti-tu ú-ša-kir a-na pi-i-šu-un [35]ina ṣu-um-mí ḳàl-ḳàl-ti iš-ku-nu na-piš-tí.

[36]Si-it-tu-u-ti *imíru*gammalî*pl* ru-ku-ši-šu-nu ú-šal-li-ḳu [37]a-na ṣu-um-mí-šu-nu iš-ta-at-tu-u dâmî*pl* u mí*pl* par(?)-šu. [38]Šá ki-rib šadi-í í-lu-ú [39]í-ru-bu í-ḫu-zu mar-ki-tu [40]í-du ul ip-par-šid mul-táḫ-ṭu ul ú-ṣi ina ḳâti-ya [41]a-šar mar-ki-ti-šu-nu ḳâti ik-šú-us-su-nu-ti. [42]Niší*pl* zikaru u zinnišu imírî*pl* *imíru*gammalî*pl* alpî*pl* u ṣi-í-ni [43]ina la mí-ni aš-lu-la a-na *mâtu ilu*Aššur*ki*.

---

a. Var. **Da-ad-da.** — *b.* Var. *alu.* — *c.* Var. **ina ḳa-ti.**

Sale of booty and slaves in Assyria. — [44]Nap-ḫ̮ar mâti-ya ša *ilu*Aššur id-di-na ka-la-mu [45]a-na si-ḫ̮ir-ti-ša um-dal-lu-u a-na pad gim-ri-ša. [46]*imíru*Gammalî*pl* ki-ma ṣi-í-ni ú-par-ri-is [47]ú-za-'i-iz a-na nišî*pl* *mâtu ilu*Aššur*ki*. [48]Ina ḳa-bal-ti mâti-ya *imíru*gammalî*pl* ana ½ ṭu ½ ṭu kas-pi [49]i-šam-mu ina bâb ma-ḫ̮i-ri. [50]Ṣu-ut(?)-mu ina ni-id-ni *amílu*x[a] ina ḫ̮a-pi-í [51]*amílu*zikar-*iṣu*kirî ina ki-ši-šu ša ú-kin [52]im-da-na-ḫ̮a-ru *imíru*gammalî*pl* ù a-mí-lu-ti.

Flight of Uâti, son of Bir-Dadda, and his army. — [53]*m*Ú-a-a-tí-'i a-di *amílu*ummânâti-šu [54]šá a-di-ya la iṣ-ṣu-ru [55]šá la-pa-an *iṣu*kakki *ilu*Aššur bíli-ya [56]ip-par-ši-du-ma in-nab-tu-ni ma-ḫ̮ar-šu-nu [57]ú-šam-ḳít-su-nu-ti *ilu*Dibba-ra ḳar-du. [58]Su-un-ḳu ina bi-ri-šu-nu iš-ša-kín-ma [59]a-na bu-ri-šu-nu í-ku-lu šîr aplî*pl*-šu-nu. [60]Ina ar-ra-a'-ti ma-la ina a-di-í-šu-nu šaṭ-ra [61]ina bit-ti i-ši-mu-šu-nu-ti *ilu*Aššur *ilu*Sin *ilu*Šamaš [62]*ilu*Ramân *ilu*Bíl *ilu*Nabû *ilu*Ištar šá Ninâ*ki* [63]*ilu*šar-rat kid-mu-ri *ilu*Ištar šá Arba'-ili*ki* [64]*ilu*Adar *ilu*Nírgal *ilu*Nusku. [65]Ba-ak-ru su-ḫ̮i-ru **gû-ṣur lu-num** [66]ina íli VII*ta-a-an* mu-ší-ni-ḳa-a-tí í-ni-ḳu-u-ma [67]ši-is-pu la ú-šab-bu-u ka-ra-ši-šu-nu.

Lament of the Arabian fugitives. — [68]Nišî*pl* *mâtu*A-ri-bi išt-ín a-na išt-ín [69]iš-ta-na-'a-a-lum a-ḫ̮a-miš [70]um-ma ina íli mi-ni-í ki-i ip-ší-í-tú an-ni-tú limut-tú [71]im-ḫ̮u-ru *mâtu*A-[b]ru-bu[b] [72]um-ma aš-šu a-di-í rabûti*pl* šá *ilu*Aššur la ni-iṣ-ṣu-ru [73]ni-iḫ̮-ṭu-ú ina ṭâbti *m ilu*Aššur-bâni-apli [74]šarri na-ram líb-bi *ilu*Bíl.

Assyrian army aided by the gods. — [75]*ilu*Bílit ri-im-tú *ilu*Bíl mí-i-tu[c] [76]ka-dir(?)-ti i-lą-a-ti [77]šá it-ti *ilu*A-nim u *ilu*Bíl šit-lu-ṭa-at man-za-zu [78]ú-na-ḳib *amílu*nakrûti*pl*-ya ina ḳarnâti*pl*-ša gaš-ra-a-tí [79]*ilu*Ištar a-ši-bat *alu*Arba'-ili [80]išâti lit-bu-šat mí-lam-mí na-ša-[d]a-ta[d] [81]íli *mâtu*A-ri-bi i-za-an-nun nab-li [82]*ilu*Dibba-ra ḳar-du a-nun-tu ku-uṣ-ṣur-ma [83]ú-ra-as-si-pa ga-ri-ya [84]*ilu*Adar ḳut-ta-ḫ̮u ḳar-ra-du

---

a. An unknown ideogram. — *b–b.* Var. **ri-bi.** — *c.* Var. **ti.** — *d–d.* Var. **at.**

rabu-u apal *ilu*Bíl [85]ina uṣ-ṣi-šu zaḳ-ti ú-par-ri-'i napiš-tim *amilu*nakrûti*pl*-ya [86]*ilu*Nusku sukkallu na-'i-du mu-ša-pu-u bílu-u-ti [87]šá ina ki-bit *ilu*Aššur *ilu*Bílit ḳa-rit-tú *ilu*bí-lit [taḫazi] [88]idi-a-a il-lik-ma iṣ-ṣu-ra šarru-u-ti [89]mi-iḫ-rit ummânâti-ya iṣ-bat-ma ú-šam-ḳí-ta ga-ri-ya.

Revolt of the Arabians against Uâti, son of Bir-Dadda. — [90]Ti-bu-ut *iṣu*kakkî*pl* *ilu*Aššur u *ilu*Ištar [91]ilâni*pl* rabûti*pl* bílî*pl*-ya [92]šá· ina í-piš taḫazi il-li-ku ri-ṣu-ti [93]ummânâti*pl* šá *m*Ú-a-a-tí-'i [94]iš-mu-u-ma íli-šu ip-pal-ki-tu. [95]Šú-ú ip-laḫ-ma [96]ul-tu bîti in-nab-tu ú-ṣa-am-ma.

Capture of Uâti.—[97]Ina tukul-ti *ilu*Aššur *ilu*Sin *ilu*Šamaš *ilu*Ramân [98]*ilu*Bíl *ilu*Nabû *ilu*Ištar ša Ninâ*ki* [99]*ilu*Šar-rat kid-mu-ri *ilu*Ištar ša *alu*Arba'-ili [100]*ilu*Adar *ilu*Nírgal *ilu*Nusku [101]ḳâtu ik-šú-us-su-ma [102]ú-ra-aš[a]-šu a-na *mâtu ilu* Aššur *ki*.

[103]Ina ni-iš ḳâtî-ya ša a-na ka-šad *amilu*nakrûti*pl*-ya [104]am-da-aḫ-ḫa-ru ina ki-bit *ilu*Aššur u *ilu*Bílit [105]ina *iṣu*ḫu-ut-ni-í ma-ší-ri ṣi-bit ḳâtî-ya [106]šîra(?) mí-ṣi-šu ap-lu-uš [107]ina la-aḫ íni-šu at-ta-di ṣir-ri-tú. [108]Ul-li kalbi ad-di-šu-ma [109]ina abulli ṣi-it *ilu*šam-ši ša ḳabal *alu*Ninâ*ki* [110]šá ni-rib maš-nak-ti ad-na-a-tí na-bu-u zi-kir-ša [111]ú-ša-an-ṣir-šu *iṣu*ši-ga-ru. [112]A-na da-lál ta-nit-ti *ilu*Aššur *ilu*Ištar [113]ù ilâni*pl* rabûti*pl* bílî*pl*-ya [114]ri-í-mu ar-ši-šú-ma ú-bal-liṭ nap-šat-su.

Return march to Nineveh.—[115]Ina ta-a-a-ar-ti-ya *alu*Ú-šú-ú [116]šá ina a-ḫi tam-tim na-da-ta šú-bat-su ak-šú-ud. [117]Nišî*pl* *alu*Ú-šú-u ša a-na *amilu*piḫâti*pl*-šu-nu la sa-an-ḳu [118]la i-nam-di-nu man-da-at-tú [119]na-dan mâ-ti-šu-un a-duk. [120]Ina líb-bi nišî*pl* la kan-šú-u-ti šib-ṭu aš-kun. [121]Ilâni*pl*-šu-nu nišî*pl*-šu-nu aš-lu-la a-na *mâtu ilu* Aššur *ki*. [122]Nišî*pl* *alu*Ak-ku-u la kan-šú-ti a-nir. *amilu*Pagrî*pl*-šu-nu ina *iṣu*ga-ši-ši a-lul [124]si-ḫir-ti ali ú-šal-mi. [125]Si-it-tu-ti-šu-nu al-ḳa-a a-na *mâtu ilu*Aššur *ki*. [126]A-na ḳí[b]-ṣir aḳ-ṣur-ma

---

a. Var. **a**.—*b*. Not **ku** (V R).

[127]íli ummânâti-ya ma-'a-da-a-ti [128]ša *ilu* Aššur i-ki-ša ú-rad-di.

Flaying of Âmu, brother of Abiyati. —[10,1]*m* A-a-mu apal *m* Tí-í-ri [2]it-ti *m* A-bi-ya-tí-'i aḫi-šu [3]i-zi-zu-ma it-ti ummânâti-ya í-pu-šu taḫazu[a] [4]ina ḳabal tam-ḫa-ri bal-ṭu-us-su ina ḳâtî aṣ-bat [5]ina Ninâ *ki* ali-bílu-ú-ti-ya mašak[b]-šu aš-ḫu-uṭ.

Grand demonstration in the temples of Nineveh.—[6]*m* Umman-al-das šar *mâtu* Ílamti *ki* [7]šá ul-tú ul-la *ilu* Aššur u *ilu* Ištar bílî *pl*-ya [8]iḳ-bu-ú a-na í-piš ardu-ú-ti-ya [9]ina ki-bit ilû-ti-šu-nu ṣir-tu[c] ša la in-nin-nu-u [10]arkâ-nu mât-su íli-šu ip-pal-kit-ma [11]la-pa-an kit(?)-bar-ti ardâni *pl*-šu šá ú-šab-šu-u íli-šu [12]í-diš-ši-šu ip-par-šid-ma iṣ-ba-ta šadu-ú. [13]Ultu šadi-í bît mar-ki-ti-šu [14]a-šar it-ta-nap-raš-ši-du [15]ki-ma surdû *iṣṣuru* a-bar-šú-ma [16]bal-ṭu-us-su al-ḳa-aš-šu a-na *mâtu ilu* Aššur *ki*. [17]*m* Tam-ma-ri-tú *m* Pa-'a-í *m* Um-man-al-das [18]šá arki a-ḫa-miš í-pu-šu bí-lút *mâtu* Ílamti *ki* [19]šá ina í-mu-ki *ilu* Aššur u *ilu* Ištar bílî *pl*-ya [20]ú-šak-ni-ša a-na *iṣu* nîri-ya [21]*m* Ú-a-a-tí-'i šar *mâtu* A-ri-bi [22]šá ina ki-bit *ilu* Aššur u *ilu* Ištar abikta-šu aš-ku-nu [23]ul-tu mâti-šu al-ḳa-šú a-na *mâtu* Aššur *ki* [24]ul-tu a-na na-dan(?)[d] *kirru* nikâni *pl* í-lú-u [25]ina Ì-bar-bar šú-bat bílû-ti-šu-un [26]ma-ḫar *ilu* Bílit ummi ilâni *pl* rabûti *pl* [27]ḫi-ir-tu na-ram-ti *ilu* Aššur [28]í-pu-šú a-di ilâni *pl* Ì-id-ki-id [29]*iṣu* nîr *iṣu* ša-ša[e]-da[f]-di ú-ša-aṣ-bit-su-nu-ti [30]a-di bâb ì-kur iš-du-du ina šapliti-ya [31]al-bi-in ap-pi at-ta-'i-id ilû-us-su-un [32]ú-ša-pa-a dan-nu-us-su-un ina puḫur ummânâti-ya [33]šá *ilu* Aššur *ilu* Sin *ilu* Šamaš *ilu* Ramân [34]*ilu* Bíl *ilu* Nabû *ilu* Ištar šá Ninâ *ki* [35]*ilu* Šar-rat kid-mu-ri *ilu* Ištar šá Arba'-ili *ki* [36]*ilu* Adar *ilu* Nírgal *ilu* Nusku šá la kan-šú-ti-ya [37]ú-šak-ni-šu a-na *iṣu* nîri-ya [38]ina li-i-ti ù da-na-a-ni [39]ú-ša-zi-zu-in-ni ṣîr *amílu* nakrûti *pl*-ya.

---

a. Var. **ta-ḫa-zu.** —*b*. Var. **ma-šak.** —*c*. Var. **ti.** —*d*. V R **saḫ.** — *e*. Var. **šad.** —*f*. Not **šá** (V R).

VIII. NABONIDUS (555–538 B.C.).

Temple Restorations in Haran and Sippar (V R 64).

Col. I. [1]A-na-ku *ilu* Na-bi-um-na-'i-id šarru ra-bu-ú šarru dan-nu [2]šar kiš-ša-ti šar Tin-tir *ki* šar kib-ra-a-ti ir-bit-ti [3]za-ni-in Ì-sag-ili ù Ì-zi-da [4]šá *ilu* Sin ù *ilu* Nin-gal i-na libbi um-mi-šú [5]a-na ši-ma-at šarru-ú-tu i-ši-mu ši-ma-at-su [6]apal *m ilu* Nabû-balaṭ-su-iḳ-bi rubû í-im-ḳu pa-li-iḫ ilâni rabûti [7]a-na-ku.

[8]Ì-ḫul-ḫul bît *ilu* Sin šá ki-rib *alu* Ḫar-ra-nu [9]šá ul-tu û-mu ṣa-a-ti *ilu* Sin bílu ra-bu-ú [10]šú-ba-at ṭu-ub líb-bi-šú ra-mu-ú ki-ri-ib-šu [11]í-li ali ù bîti ša-a-šú líb-bu-uš i-zu-uz-ma [12]*amílu* Ṣab-man-da ú-šat-ba-am-ma bîta šú-a-tim ub-bi-it-ma [13]ú-šá-lik-šú kar-mu-tu. I-na pa-li-í-a ki-i-nim [14]*ilu* Bíl bílu rabu-ú i-na na-ra-am šarru-ú-ti-ya [15]a-na ali ù bîti ša-a-šú is-li-mu ir-šú-ú ta-a-a-ri.

[16]I-na ri-íš šarru-ú-ti-ya dârâ-ti ú-šab-ru-'-in-ni [17]šú-ut-ti. [18]*ilu* Marduk bílu rabû ù *ilu* Sin na-an-na-ri šami-í ù irṣi-tim [19]iz-zi-zu ki-lal-la-an. *ilu* Marduk i-ta-ma-a it-ti-ya: [20]*ilu* Nabû-nâ'id šar Tin-tir *ki* i-na *imíru* sisî ru-kụ-bi-ka [21]i-ši libnâti *pl* Ì-ḫul-ḫul í-pu-uš-ma *ilu* Sin bílu rabu-ú [22]i-na ki-ir-bi-šú šú-ur-ma-a šú-ba-at-su. [23]Pa-al-ḫi-iš a-ta-ma-a a-na *ilu* bíl ilâni *pl* *ilu* Marduk: [24]Bîta šú-a-tim šá táḳ-bu-ú í-pi-šú [25]*amílu* Ṣab-man-da sa-ḫi-ir-šum-ma pu-ug-gu-lu í-mu-ga-a-šú. [26]*ilu* Marduk-ma i-ta-ma-a it-ti-ya: *amílu* Ṣab-man-da ša táḳ-bu-ú [27]šá-a-šú mâtu-šú ù šarrâni *pl* a-lik i-di-šú ul i-ba-aš-ši.

[28]I-na šá-lu-ul-ti šatti i-na ka-ša-du [29]ú-šat-bu-niš-šum-ma *m* Ku-ra-aš šar *mâtu* An-za-an arad-su ṣa-aḫ-ri [30]i-na um-ma-ni-sú i-ṣu-tu *amílu* Ṣab-man-da rap-ša-a-ti [31]ú-sap-pi-iḫ. [32]*m* Iš-tu-mí-gu šar *amílu* Ṣab-man-da iṣ-bat-ma ka-mu-ut-su a-na mâti-šú [33]il-ḳí.

[34]A-mat *ilu* bílu rabu-ú *ilu* Marduk ù *ilu* Sin na-an-na-ri šami-í ù irṣi-tim [35]ša ki-bi-it-su-nu la in-nin-nu-ú a-na

ki-bi-ti-šu-nu ṣir-ti [36]ap-la-aḫ ak-ku-ud na-kut-ti ar-ší-í-ma tul-lu-ḫu [37]pa-nu-ú-a. [38]La í-gi la a-ší-it a-ḫi la ad-da ú-šat-ba-am-ma [39]um-ma-ni-ya rap-ša-a-ti ul-tu *mâtu* Ḫa-az-za-ti [40]pa-ad *mâtu* Mi-ṣir [41]tam-tim í-li-ti a-bar-ti *nâru* Puratti a-di tam-tim [42]šap-li-ti [43]šarrâni *pl* rubûti *pl* šakkanakkî *pl* ù um-ma-ni-ya rap-ša-a-ti [44]šá *ilu* Sin *ilu* Šamaš ù *ilu* Iš-tar bílî *pl*-í-a ya-ti [45]i-ki-pu-nu [46]a-na í-pi-šú Ì-ḫul-ḫul bît *ilu* Sin bíli-ya a-lik i-di-ya [47]šá ki-rib *alu* Ḫar-ra-nu ša *m ilu* Aššur-ba-an-apli šar *mâtu* Aššur *ki* [48]apal *m ilu* Aššur-aḫî-iddina šar *mâtu* Aššur *ki* rubû a-lik maḫ-ri-ya [49]i-pú-šú.

[50]I-na arḫi ša-al-mu i-na û-mi nâdi ša i-na bi-ri [51]ú-ad-du-ni *ilu* Šamaš ù *ilu* Ramân [52]i-na ni-mí-ḳu *ilu* Ì-a ù *ilu* Marduk ina pî ílli iḳ-ú-tu [53]i-na ši-ip-ri *ilu* Libittu bíl uš-šú ù libnâti *pl* Col. II. [1]i-na kaspi ḫuraṣi abni ni-siḳ-ti šú-ḳu-ru-tu ḫi-biš-ti *iṣu* kišti [2]riḳḳî *pl* *iṣu* írini i-na ḫi-da-a-ti ù ri-ša-a-ti [3]í-li tí-mí-ín-na šá *m ilu* Aššur-ba-an-apli šar *mâtu* Aššur *ki* [4]šá tí-mí-ín-na *m* Šul-man-ašârid apal *m ilu* Aššur-na-ṣir-apli i-mu-ru [5]uš-šú-šú ad-di-ma ú-kín lib-na-at-su. I-na kurunni karani šamni dišpi [6]šal-la-ar-šú am-ḫa-aṣ-ma ab-lu-ul ta-ra-aḫ-ḫu-uš. [7]Í-li ša šarrâni *pl* ab-bi-í-a íp-ší-ti-šú ú-dan-nin-ma [8]ú-nak-ki-lu ši-bi-ir-šu. Ì-kur šú-a-tim ul-tu tí-mí-ín-šu [9]a-di taḫ-lu-bi-šu í-íš-ši-iš ab-ni-ma ú-ša-ak-li-il ši-bi-ir-šu. [10]*iṣu* Gušur *iṣu* írini ṣi-ru-tu ta-ar-bi-it *šadû* Ḫa-ma-na[a] [11]ú-šá-at-ri-iṣ ṣi-ru-uš-šú. *iṣu* Dalâti *pl* *iṣu* írini [12]šá i-ri-is-si-na ṭa-a-bi ú-ra-at-ta-a i-na bâbî *pl*-šu. [13]Kaspu ḫuraṣu igarâti *pl*-šú ú-šal-biš-ma ú-ša-an-bi-iṭ ša-aš-ša-ni-iš. [14]Ri-i-mu za-ḫa-li-í ib-bi mu-naḳ-ḳib ga-ri-ya [15]ka-at-ri-iš uš-zi-iz i-na ad-ma-ni-šú. [16]II *ilu* laḫ-mu íš-ma-ru-ú sa-pi-in a-a-bi-ya [17]i-na bâb ṣi-it *ilu* šam-ši imittu ù šumílu ú-šar-ši-id.

[18]Ga-tim *ilu* Sin *ilu* Nin-gal *ilu* Nusku ù *ilu* Sa-dar-nun-na [19]bílî-*pl*-í-a ul-tu Šú-an-na *ki* ali šarru-ú-ti-ya [20]aṣ-ba-at-ma i-na ḫi-da-a-ti ù ri-ša-a-ti [21]šú-ba-at ṭu-ub líb-bi ki-ir-ba-šú ú-ší-ši-ib. [22]*kirru* Niḳâni taš-ri-iḫ-ti ib-bi ma-ḫar-

---

a. V R tú.

šu-nu aḳ-ḳí-ma [23]ú-šam-ḫi-ir kad-ra-a-a. Ì-ḫul-ḫul ri-iš-tum ú-mal-li-ma [24]*alu* Ḫar-ra-an a-na pa-ad gi-im-ri-šú [25]ki-ma ṣi-it arḫi ú-nam-mi-ir šá-ru-ru-šú.

[26]*ilu* Sin šar ilâni*pl* ša šami-í ù irṣi-tim ša ul-la-nu-uš-šú [27]alu ù mâtu la in-nam-du-ú la i-tur-ru aš-ru-uš-šú [28]a-na Ì-ḫul-ḫul bît šú-bat la-li-í-ka i-na í-ri-bi-ka [29]damiḳ-tim ali ù bîti ša-a-šú liš-ša-ki-in šap-tu-uk-ka. [30]Ilâni*pl* a-ši-bu-tu šá šami-í ù irṣi-tim [31]li-ik-ta-ra-bu bît *ilu* Sin a-bi ba-ni-šú-un. [32]Ya-ti *ilu* Nabû-nâ'id šar Tin-tir *ki* mu-šak-lil bîti šú-a-tim [33]*ilu* Sin šar ilâni*pl* ša šami-í ù irṣi-tim i-na ni-iš i-ni-šu damḳâti*pl* [34]ḫa-di-iš lip-pal-sa-an-ni-ma ár-ḫi-šam-ma i-na ni-ip-ḫi ù ri-ba [35]li-dam-mi-iḳ it-ta-tu-ú-a ûmî*pl*-ya li-ša-ri-ik [36]šanâti*pl*-ya li-ša-an-ṭi-il lu-ki-in pa-lu-ú-a [37]*amilu* na-ak-ru-ti-ya lik-šú-ud *amilu* za-ma-ni-ya li-ša-am-ḳít [38]li-is-pu-un ga-ri-ya. *ilu* Nin-gal ummi ilâni rabûti [39]i-na ma-ḫar *ilu* Sin na-ra-mi-šu li-iḳ-ba-a ba-ni-ti. [40]*ilu* Šamaš ù *ilu* Iš-tar ṣi-it libbi-šu na-am-ra [41]a-na *ilu* Sin a-bi ba-ni-šú-nu li-iḳ-bu-ú damiḳ-tim. [42]*ilu* Nusku sukkallu ṣi-i-ri su-pi-í-a li-iš-mí-í-ma [43]li-iṣ-ba-at a-bu-tu.

Mu-sa-ru-ú ši-ṭi-ir šú-um [44]ša *m ilu* Aššur-ba-an-apli šar *mâtu* Aššur *ki* a-mu-ur-ma [45]la ú-nak-ki-ir kisalla[a] ap-šú-uš *kirru* niḳâni aḳ-ḳí [46]it-ti mu-sa-ri-í-a aš-kun-ma ú-tí-ir aš-ru-uš-šú.

[47]A-na *ilu* Šamaš da-a-a-nu šá šami-í ù irṣi-tim [48]Ì-babbar-ra bît-su ša ki-rib Sippar *ki* [49]ša *m* Nabû-kudurri-uṣur šarru maḫ-ri i-pu-šú-ma [50]tí-mí-ín-šú la-ba-ri ú-ba-'i-ú la i-mu-ru [51]bîta šú-a-tim i-pu-uš-ma i-na XLV šanâti*pl* [52]šá bîti šú-a-tim i-ḳu-pu i-ga-ru-šú ak-ku-ud aš-hu-ut [53]na-kut-ti ar-ší-í-ma tul-lu-ḫu pa-nu-ú-a. [54]A-di *ilu* Šamaš ul-tu ki-ir-bi-šú ú-ší-ṣu-ú [55]ú-ší-ši-bu i-na bîti ša-nim-ma bîta šú-a-tim ad-ki-í-ma [56]tí-mí-ín-šú la-bi-ri ú-ba-'i-ma XVIII ammat ga-ga-ri [57]ú-šap-pi-il-ma tí-mí-ín-na *m* Na-ram-*ilu* Sin apal *m* Šarru-kínu [58]šá III M II C šanâti*pl* ma-na-ma šarru a-lik maḫ-ri-ya la i-mu-ru [59]*ilu* Šamaš bílu rabu-ú

a. Or šamni.

Ì-babbar-ra bît šú-bat ṭu-ub libbi-šu [60]ú-kal-lim-an-ni ya-a-ši i-na *arḫu*tišrîti i-na arḫi šal-mu i-na ûmi magiri [61]šá i-na bi-ri ú-ad-du-ni *ilu*Šamaš ù *ilu*Ramân [62]i-na kaspi ḫuraṣi abni ni-siḳ-ti šú-ḳu-ru-tu ḫi-biš-ti *iṣu*kišti [63]riḳḳî*pl* *iṣu*írini ina ḫi-da-a-ti ù ri-ša-a-ti [64]í-li tí-mí-ín-na *m*Na-ra-am-*ilu*Sin apal *m*Šarru-kínu [65]ubanu la a-ṣi-i ubanu la í-ri-bi[a] ú-kín lib-na-at-su.

Col. III. [1]V M *iṣu*írini dan-nu-tu a-na ṣu-lu-li-šu ú-šat-ri-iṣ [2]*iṣu*dalâti*pl* *iṣu*írini ṣi-ra-a-ti as-kup-pu ù nu-ku-ší-í [3]i-na bâbî*pl*-šú ú-ra-at-ti. [4]Ì-babbar-ra a-di Ì-i-lu-an-azag-ga ziḳ-ḳur-ra-ti-šu [5]í-ís-ši-iš í-pu-uš-ma ú-šak-lil ši-bi-ir-šú. [6]Ga-tim *ilu*Šamaš bíli-ya aṣ-bat-ma i-na ḫi-da-a-ti ù ri-ša-a-ti [7]šú-ba-at ṭu-ub líb-bi ki-ir-ba-šú ú-ší-ši-ib. [8]Ši-ṭi-ir šú-um ša *m*Na-ra-am-*ilu*Sin[b] apal *m*Šarru-kínu a-mu-ur-ma [9]la ú-nak-ki-ir kisalla ap-šú-uš *kirru*niḳâni aḳ-ḳí [10]it-ti mu-sar-ri-í-a aš-ku-un-ma ú-tí-ir aš-ru-uš-šú.

[11]*ilu*Šamaš bílu rabu-ú ša šami-í ù irṣi-tim nu-úr ilâni*pl* ab-bi-í-šú[c] [12]ṣi-it líb-bi šá *ilu*Sin ù *ilu*Nin-gal [13]a-na Ì-babbar-ra bît na-ra-mi-ka i-na í-ri-bi-ka [14]parakku-ka da-ru-ú i-na ra-mi-í-ka [15]ya-ti *ilu*Nabû-nâ'id šar Tin-tir*ki* rubû za-ni-in-ka [16]mu-ṭi-ib líb-bi-ka í-bi-iš ku-um-mi-ka ṣi-i-ri [17]íp-ší-tu-ú-a damḳâti*pl* ḫa-di-iš na-ap-li-is[d]-ma [18]û-mi-šam-ma i-na ni-ip-ḫi ù ri-ba i-na ša-ma-mi ù ga-ga-ri [19]du-um-mi-iḳ it-ta-tu-ú-a un-nin-ni-ya li-ḳí-í-ma [20]mu-gu-ur ta-aṣ-li-ti *iṣu*ḫaṭṭi ù ši-bir-ri ki-i-nim [21]ša tu-šat-mi-ḫu ḳa-tu-ú-a lu-bi-íl a-na du-ú-ri da-a-ri.

[22]A-na *ilu*A-nu-ni-tum bílit taḫazi na-ša-ta *iṣu*ḳašti ù iš-pa-ti [23]mu-šal-li-ma-at ki-bi-it *ilu*Bíl[e] a-bi-šú [24]sa-pi-na-at *amílu*na-ak-ru mu-ḫal-li-ḳa-at ra-ag-gu [25]a-li-ka-at maḫ-ri šá ilâni [26]šá i-na ṣît šamši ù írib šamši ú-dam-ma-ḳu it-ta-tu-ú-a [27]Ì-ul-bar bît-su ša i-na Sippar*ki* *ilu*A-nu-ni-tum ša VIII C[f] šanâti*pl* [28]ul-tu pa-ni *m*Šà-ga-šal-ti-bur-

---

a. Var. **bu.** — *b.* Sign for **Sin** omitted in V R. — *c.* Scribal error for **ka**? — *d.* V R **ma,** scribal error. — *e.* Scribal error for **Sin**? — *f.* In PSBA. 1882, p. 9, Pinches seems to have read V C.

ya-àš šar Tin-tir *ki* [29]apal *m*Kudurri-*ilu*Bíl šarru ma-na-ma la i-pu-šú [30]tí-mí-ín-šú la-bi-ri aḫ-ṭu-uṭ-ma a-ḫi-iṭ ab-ri-í-ma [31]í-li tí-mí-ín-na *m*Šà-ga-šal-ti-bur-ya-aš apal *m*Kudurri-*ilu*Bíl [32]uš-šú-šú ad-di[a]-ma ú-ki-in lib-na-at-su [33]bîta ša-a-šú íš-šiš í-pu-uš ú-šak-lil ši-bi-ir-šu.

[34]*ilu*A-nu-ni-tum bílit taḫazi mu-šal-li-mat ki-bit *ilu*Bíl[b] a-bi-šú [35]sa-pi-na-at *amílu*na-ak-ru mu-ḫal-li-ḳa-at rag-gu [36]a-li-ka-at maḫ-ri ša ilâni*pl* ú-šar-ma-a šú-ba-at-su [37]sat-tuk-ku ù nin-da-bi-í í-li ša maḫ-ri ú-ša-tí-ir-ma [38]ú-kín ma-ḫar-šu. At-ta *ilu*A-nu-ni-tum bílti rabî-ti [39]a-na bîti šú-a-tim ḫa-di-iš i-na í-ri-bi-ka [40]íp-ší-tu-ú-a damḳâti*pl* ḫa-di-iš na-ap-li-si-ma [41]âr-ḫi-šam-ma i-na ṣît šamši ù írib šamši [42]a-na *ilu*Sin a-bi a-li-di-ka šú-uḳ-ri-ba damiḳ-tim.

[43]Man-nu at-ta ša *ilu*Sin ù *ilu*Šamaš a-na šarru-ú-tu i-nam-bu-šú-ma [44]i-na pa-li-í-šu bîtu šú-a-tim in-na-ḫu-ma íš-šiš ib-bu-šú [45]mu-sa-ru-ú ši-ṭir šú-mi-ya li-mur-ma la ú-nak-ka-ar [46]kisalla lip-šú-uš *kirru*niḳâni li-iḳ-ḳí [47]it-ti mu-sa-ru-ú ši-ṭir šú-mi-šu liš-kun-ma lu-tir aš-ru-uš-šú [48]*ilu*Šamaš ù *ilu*A-nu-ni-tum su-pu-ú-šú li-iš-mu-ú [49]li-im-gu-ra ki-bit-su i-da-a-šu lil-li-ku [50]li-ša-am-ḳí-ta ga[c]-ri-šu û-mi-šam-ma a-na *ilu*Sin [51]a-bi ba-ni-šú-un da-mi-iḳ-ta-šu li-iḳ-bu-ú.

IX. CYRUS (KING OF BABYLON, 538 B.C.).

Capture of Babylon, Restoration of Gods to their Temples (V R 35).[d]

[7]Sat-tuk-ku ú-šab-ṭi-li ú-la- ....[e][iš]-ták-ka-an ki-rib ma-ḫa-zi pa-la-ḫa *ilu*Marduk šar ilâni*pl* .. -ší-a ḳâtu-uš-šú [8]li-mu-ut-ti ali-šú .. -nu(?) ip-pu-uš û-mi-šá-am ....*pl*-šu i-na ab-šá-a-ni la ta-ab-šú-tu šal-ḫu-tim ú-ḫal-li-iḳ kul-lat-si-in [9]a-na ta-zi-im-ti-ši-na *ilu*bíl ilâni*pl* iz-zi-iš i-gu-ug-ma(?) .... ki-su-úr-šú-un. Ilâni*pl* a-ši-ib líb-bi-šú-nu i-zi-bu

---

a. V R **ki.** — *b.* Scribal error for **Sin?** — *c.* V R **ta.** — *d.* From a barrel-cylinder found at Babylon. The first six lines and the last ten (36–45), as published in V R, are so fragmentary as to be unintelligible. — *e.* The dots mark lacunæ in the text.

ad-ma-an-šú-un [10]i-na ug-ga-ti šá ú-ší-ri-bi a-na ki-rib Šú-an-na*ki* *ilu*Marduk .... li sa-aḫ-ra a-na nap-ḫar da-ád-mi šá in-na-du-ú šú-bat-su-un. [11]Ŭ niši*pl* *matu*Šú-mí-ri ù Akkadi*ki* šá i-mu-ú šá-lam-ta-aš ú-sa-ḫi-ir ka- ... -pi ir-ta-ši ta-a-a-ra kul-lat ma-ta-a-ta ka-li-ši-na i-ḫi-iṭ ib-ri-í-šu-[ma] [12]iš-tí-'i-í-ma ma-al-ki i-ša-ru bi-bíl líb-bi šá it-ta-ma-aḫ ḳa-tu-uš-šú *m*Ku-ra-aš šar *alu*An-šá-an it-ta-bi ni-bi-it-su a-na ma-li-ku-tim kul-la-ta nap-ḫar iz-zak-ra ḳat-su(?) [13]*matu*Ḳu-ti-i gi-mir um-man man-da ú-ka-an-ni-šá a-na ší-pi-šú. Niši*pl* ṣal-mat ḳaḳḳadi šá ú-šá-ak-ši-du ḳa-ta-a-šu [14]i-na ki-it-tim ù mi-ša-ru iš-tí-ni-'i-í-ši-na-a-tim. *ilu*Marduk bílu rabû ta-ru-ú niši*pl*-šu ip-ší-í-ti šá-nin-šu ḳa-a-ta ù líb-ba-šú i-šá-ra ḫa-di-iš ip-pa-li-is.

[15]A-na ali-šú Babili*pl ki* a-la-ak-šú iḳ-bi ú-šá-aṣ-bi-it-su-ma ḫar-ra-nu Tin-tir*ki*. Ki-ma ib-ri ù tap-pi-í it-tal-la-ka i-da-a-šú. [16]Um-ma-ni-šú rap-šá-a-tim šá ki-ma mí-í nâri la ú-ta-ad-du-ú ni-ba-šú-un *iṣu*kakki*pl*-šú-nu ṣa-an-du-ma i-šá-aṭ-ṭi-ḫa i-da-a-šú. [17]Ba-lu ḳab-li ù ta-ḫa-zi ú-ší-ri-ba-aš ki-rib Šú-an-na*ki* ala-šú Babili*pl ki* i-ṭi-ir i-na Šap-šá*ki* *m ilu*Nabû-nâ'id šarru la pa-li-ḫi-šú ú-ma-al-la-a ḳa-tu-uš-šu. [18]Niši*pl* Tin-tir*ki* ka-li-šú-nu nap-ḫar *matu*Šú-mí-ri u Akkadi*ki* ru-bi-í ù šak-kan-nak-ka šá-pal-šú · ik-mi-sa ú-na-aš-ši-ḳu ší-pu-uš-šú iḫ-du-ú a-na šarru-ú-ti-šu im-mi-ru pa-nu-uš-šu-un. [19]Bí-lu šá i-na tu-kul-ti šá ú-bal-li-ṭu mi-tu-ta-an i-na pu-uš[a]-ḳu ù pa-ki-í ig-mi-lu kul-la-ta-an ṭa-bi-iš ik-ta-ar-ra-bu-šú iš-tam-ma-ru zi-ki-ir-šú.

[20]A-na-ku *m*Ku-ra-aš šar kiš-šat šarru rabû šarru dan-nu šar Tin-tir*ki* šar *matu*Šú-mí-ri ù Ak-ka-di-i šar kib-ra-a-ti ir-bi-it-tim [21]apal *m*Ka-am-bu-zi-ya šarru rabû šar *alu*An-šá-an bin-bini *m*Ku-ra-aš šarru rabû šar *alu*An-šá-an líb-bal-bal *m*Ši-iš-pi-iš šarru rabû šar *alu*An-šá-an [22]ziru da-ru-ú šá šarru-ú-tu šá *ilu*Bíl u *ilu*Nabû ir-a-mu pa-la-a-šú a-na ṭu-ub líb-bi-šu-nu iḫ-ši-ḫa [ri'u]-ut-su.

Í-nu-ma a-[na ki-]rib[b] Tin-tir*ki* í-ru-bu sa-li-mi-iš [23]i-na

a. V R ta. — b. V R 1.

ul-ṣi[a] ù ri-šá-a-tim i-na ìkal ma-al-ki ar-ma-a šú-bat bí-lu-tim *ilu*Marduk bílu rabû líb-bi ri-it-pa-šú šá aplî[*pl* ša] Tin-tir*ki* ù ... -an-ni-ma û-mi-šam a-ší-'i-a pa-la-aḫ(?)-šu [24]um-ma-ni-ya rap-šá-a-tim i-na ki-rib Tin-tir*ki* i-šá-aṭ-ṭi-ḫa šú-ul-ma-niš nap-ḫar [*mâtu*Šumíri u] Akkadi*ki* dim(?)-gal .... -tim ul ú-šar-ši [25]ki-rib Babili*ki* ù kul-lat ma-ḫa-zi-šú i-na šá-li-im-tim aš-tí-'i-í aplî*pl* Tin-tir[*ki*] ...*ki* ma-la líb ... -ma ab-ša-a-ni la si-ma-ti-šu-nu šú-bat-su(?) [26]an-ḫu-ut-su-un ú-pa-aš-ši-ḫa ú-šá-ap-ṭi-ir sa-ar-ma-šú-nu.

A-na ip-ší-í-ti [an-na-ti] *ilu*Marduk bílu rabu-ú iḫ-di-í-ma [27]a-na ya-a-ti *m*Ku-ra-aš šarri pa-li-iḫ-šú ù *m*Ka-am-bu-zi-ya apli ṣi-it líb-bi[-ya ù] ana(?) nap-[ḫar(?)] um-ma-ni-ya [28]da-am-ḳí-iš ik-ru-ub-ma i-na ša-lim-tim ma-ḫar-šú[b](?) ṭa-bi-iš ni-it-ta[-at-ti-iḳ. I-na kibîti-šu] ṣir-ti nap-ḫar šarrâni a-ši-ib parakkî*pl* [29]šá ka-li-iš kib-ra-a-ta iš-tu tam-tim í-li-tim a-di tam-tim šap-li-tim a-ši-ib kul[-lat mâtâti] šarrâni*pl* *mâtu*A-ḫar-ri-i a-ši-ib su-ta-ri ka-li-šu-un [30]bi-lat-su-nu ka-bi-it-tim ú-bi-lu-nim-ma ki-ir-ba Šú-an-na*ki* ú-na-aš-ši-ḳu ší-pu-ú-a.

Iš-tu ....-a*ki* *alu*Aššur*ki* ù Ištar-x[c]*ki* [31]A-ga-dí*ki* *mâtu*Ab-nu-nak *alu*Za-am-ba-an *alu*Mí-tùr-nu Dûr-ilu*ki* a-di pa-ad *mâtu*Ḳu-ti-i ma-ḫa[-zi ša í-bir-]ti *nâru*Diḳlat šá iš-tu ab-na-ma na-du-ú šú-bat-su-un [32]ilâni*pl* a-ši-ib líb-bi-šu-nu a-na aš-ri-šú-nu ú-tir-ma ú-šar-ma-a šú-bat dâra-a-ta. Kul-lat niší*pl*-šu-nu ú-pa-aḫ-ḫi-ra-am-ma ú-tí-ir da-ád-mi-šu-un. [33]Ù ilâni*pl* *mâtu*Šú-mí-ri ù Akkadi*ki* šá *m ilu*Nabû-nâ'id a-na ug-ga-tim bíl ilâni*pl* ú-ší-ri-bi a-na ki-rib Šú-an-na*ki* i-na ki-bi-ti *ilu*Marduk bílu rabû i-na šá-li-im-tim [34]i-na maš-ta-ki-šú-nu ú-ší-ši-ib šú-ba-at ṭu-ub líb-bi. Kul-la-ta ilâni*pl* šá ú-ší-ri-bi a-na ki-ir-bi ma-ḫa-zi-šú-un [35]û-mi-šá-am ma-ḫar *ilu*Bíl ù *ilu*Nabû šá a-ra-ku ûmî*pl*-ya li-ta-mu-ú lit-taz-ka-ru a-ma-a-ta du-un-ḳí-ya ù a-na *ilu*Marduk bíli-ya li-iḳ-bu-ú šá *m*Ku-ra-aš šarru pa-li-ḫi-ka u *m*Ka-am-bu-zi-ya aplu-šu.

---

a. V R **ad.** — *b.* V R **šá.** — *c.* An unknown ideogram.

X. ASSURBANIPAL.

1. **First Egyptian Campaign** (V R 1, 52–2, 27).

[52]I-na maḫ-ri-í gir-ri-ya a-na *mâtu*Ma-kan u *mâtu*Mí-luḫ-ḫa lu-u al-lik. [53]*m*Tar-ḳu-ú šar *mâtu*Mu-ṣur u *mâtu*Ku-ú-si [54]šá *m ilu*Aššur-aḫî-iddina šar *mâtu ilu*Aššur*ki* abu ba-nu-u-a [55]abikta-šu iš-ku-nu-ma i-bí-lu mât-su ù šú-u *m*Tar-ḳu-u [56]da-na-an *ilu*Aššur *ilu*Ištar u ilâni*pl* rabûti*pl* bílî*pl*-ya im-ši-ma [57]it-ta-kil a-na í-muḳ ra-man-i-šu. Í-li šarrâni*pl* [58]*amílu*ki-í-pa-a-ni ša ki-rib *mâtu*Mu-ṣur ú-pa-ki-du abu bânu-u-a [59]a-na da-a-ki ḫa-ba-a-tí ù í-kim[a] *mâtu*Mu-ṣur il-li-ka. [60]Ṣîr-uš-šu-un í-ru-um-ma ú-šib ki-rib *alu*Mí-im-pi [61]ali ša abu bânu-u-a ik-šú-du-ma a-na mi-ṣir *mâtu ilu*Aššur*ki* ú-tir-ru[b]. [62]Al-la-ku ḫa-an-ṭu ina ki-rib Ninâ*ki* il-lik-am-ma [63]ú-ša-an-na-a ya-a-ti.

Íli ip-ší-í-ti an-na-a-ti [64]líb-bi í-gug-ma iṣ-ṣa-ru-uḫ ka-bit-ti. [65]Aš-ši ḳâtî-ya ú-ṣal-li *ilu*Aššur u *ilu*Ištar aššur-i-tú. [66]Ad-ki-í *amílu*í-mu-ki-ya ṣi-ra-a-tí[c] ša *ilu*Aššur u *ilu*Ištar [67]ú-mal-lu-u ḳâtu[d]-u-a. A-na *mâtu*Mu-ṣur u *mâtu*Ku-u-si [68]uš-tí-íš-ší-ra ḫar-ra-nu.

Ina mí-ti-iḳ gir-ri-ya [69]XX*a-an*II šarrâni*pl* ša a-ḫi tam-tim ḳabal tam-tim u na-ba-li [70]ardâni*pl* da-gil pa-ni-ya ta-mar-ta-šu-nu ka-bit-tú [71]ina maḫ-ri-ya iš-šú-nim-ma ú-na-aš-ši-ḳu šípî-ya. [72]Šarrâni*pl* ša-a-tú-nu a-di í-mu-ki-šu-nu *iṣu*ílippî*pl*-šu-nu [73]ina tam-tim u na-ba-li it-ti ummânâti-ya [74]ur-ḫu pa-da-nu ú-ša-aṣ-bit-su-nu-ti. [75]A-na na-ra-ru-u-ti [e]ḫa-mat[e] (?) ša šarrâni*pl* *amílu*ki-pa-a-ni [76]ša ki-rib *mâtu*Mu-ṣur ardâ*pl*-ni da-gil pa-ni-ya [77]ur-ru-ḫi-iš ar-di-í-ma al-lik a-di *alu*Kar-*ilu*Bâni[f]-ti.

---

a. Var. **ki-mu**. — *b*. Var. **ra**. — *c*. Var. **ti**. — *d*. Var. **ḳa-tu**. — *e–e*. Var. omits. — *f*. Var. **Ba-ni**.

X. ASSURBANIPAL.

1. **First Egyptian Campaign** (V R 1, 52–2, 27).

[52]In my first expedition (lit. the first my expedition) to Makan and Miluḫḫa I went. [53]Tarḳû king of Egypt and of Cush [54]who Esarhaddon, king of Assyria, my father (lit. the father my begetter) [55]his overthrow accomplished and took possession of his country, and he Tarḳû [56]the might of Aššur, of Ištar and of the gods great my lords forgot and [57]trusted to the power of himself. Against the kings, [58]governors, whom within Egypt appointed my father (lit. the father my begetter), [59]to kill, to plunder and to seize Egypt he came. [60]Against them he entered and dwelt in Memphis, [61]a city which my father had captured and to the territory of Assyria had added. [62]A courier swift into the midst of Nineveh came and [63]informed me.

At (lit. upon) deeds these [64]my heart was enraged and was angry my liver. [65]I lifted my hands, I besought Aššur and Ištar of Assyria (lit. the Assyrian). [66]I mustered my forces noble [with] which Aššur and Ištar [67]had filled my hand. To Egypt and Cush [68]I directed (lit. made straight) the way.

In the progress of my expedition [69]twenty two kings of the side of the sea, the midst of the sea and the land, [70]servants subject to me (lit. beholding my face) their present heavy [71]into my presence brought (lit. bore) and kissed my feet. [72]Kings these together with their forces, their ships, [73]by sea and by land with my troops [74]the road, the way, I caused them to take (i.e. to march). [75]For the help, the aid of the kings, the governors, [76]who [were] in Egypt, servants subject to me (lit. beholding my face) [77]quickly I set out and came to Kar-Banit.

[78] *m* Tar-ḳu-ú šar *mâtu* Mu-ṣur u *mâtu* Ku-u-si ki[a]-rib *alu* Mí-im-pi [79] a-lak gir-ri-ya iš-mí-í-ma a-na í-piš ḳabli *iṣu* kakkî *pl* [80] ù taḫazi ina[b] maḫ-ri-ya id-ka-a *amilu* ṣâbî *pl* taḫazi-šu. [81] Ina tukul-ti *ilu* Aššur *ilu* Bíl *ilu* Nabû ilâni *pl* rabûti *pl* bílî *pl*-ya [82] a-li-kut idî-ya ina taḫazi ṣíri rap-ši aš-ku-na abikti ummânâti-šu. [83] *m* Tar-ḳu-u ina ki-rib *alu* Mí-im-pi iš-ma-a táḫ-tí-í ummânâti-šu [84] nam-ri-ri *ilu* Aššur u *ilu* Ištar is-ḫu-pu-šu-ma il-li-ka[c] maḫ-[d]ḫu-ur[d] [85] mí-lam-mí šarru-u-ti-ya ik-tu-mu-šu-ma [86] šá ú-ṣa-'i-i-nu-in-ni ilâni *pl* šú-par(?) šamí irṣiti. [87] *alu* Mí-im-pi ú-maš-šir-ma a-na šú-zu-ub napiš-tim-šu [88] in-na-bit a-na ki-rib *alu* Ni-'i. [89] Ala šú-a-tú aṣ-bat ummânâti-ya ú-ší-rib ú-ší-šib i-na líb-bi.

[90] *m* Ni-ku-ú	šar *alu* Mí-im-pi u *alu* Sa-a-a
[91] *m* Šarru-lu-dá-ri	šar *alu* Ṣi-'i-nu
[92] *m* Pi-ša-an-ḫu-ru	šar *alu* Na-at-ḫu-ú
[93] *m* Pa-ak-ru-ru	šar *alu* Pi-šap-tú
[94] *m* Bu-uk-ku-na-an-ni-'i-pi	šar *alu* Ḫa-at-ḫi-ri-bi
[95] *m* Na-aḫ-ki-í	šar *alu* Ḫi-ni-in-ši
[96] *m* Pu-ṭu-biš-ti	šar *alu* Za-'a-nu
[97] *m* Ú-na-mu-nu	šar *alu* Na-at-ḫu-ú
[98] *m* Ḫar-si-ya-í-šu	šar *alu* Zab[e]-nu-ú-ti
[99] *m* Pu-u-a-a-ma	šar *alu* Pi[f]-in-di-di
[100] *m* Su-si-in-ḳu	šar *alu* Pu-ši-ru
[101] *m* Tap-na-aḫ-ti	šar *alu* Pu-nu-bu
[102] *m* Bu-uk-ku-na-an-ni-'i-pi	šar *alu* Aḫ-ni
[103] *m* Ip-ti-ḫar-di-í-šu	šar *alu* Pi-ḫa-at-ti-ḫu-ru-un-pi-ki
[104] *m* Na-aḫ-ti-ḫu-ru-an-si-ni	šar *alu* Pi-sap-di-[g]'a-a[g]
[105] *m* Bu-kur-ni-ni-ip	šar *alu* Pa-aḫ-nu-ti
[106] *m* Ṣi-ḫa-a	šar *alu* Ši-ya-a-u-tú
[107] *m* La-mí-in-tú	šar *alu* Ḫi-mu-ni
[108] *m* Iš-pi-ma-a-ṭu	šar *alu* Ta-a-a-ni
[109] *m* Ma-an-ti-mí-an-ḫi-í	šar *alu* Ni-'i

a. Not **ku** (V R). — *b.* Var. **a-na.** — *c.* Var. **ku.** — *d–d.* Var. **ri** (III R 17, 87). — *e.* So III R 17, 100. V R has **Tam.** — *f.* Var. **Bi.** — *g–g.* Var. **nu-ti.**

[78]Tarḳû, king of Egypt and of Cush, in Memphis [79][of] the march of my expedition heard and to make fight, arms [80]and battle, in front of me (lit. my front) he mustered the men of his battle (i.e. his soldiers). [81]By the help of Aššur, Bel, Nabu, the gods great, my lords, [82]marching [at] my sides, in a battle of the plain wide I accomplished the overthrow of his troops. [83]Tarḳû in the midst of Memphis heard of the defeat of his troops, [84]the brilliance of Aššur and of Ištar cast him down and he went forward, [85]the lustre of my royalty covered him [86][with] which had favored me the gods rulers(?) of heaven and earth. [87]Memphis he left and to save his life [88]he fled (lit. vanished) to the midst of Thebes. [89]That city I took, my troops I caused to enter, I caused to remain therein (lit. in the heart).

[90]Necho	king of Memphis and of Sais
[91]Šarru-ludari	king of Ṣi'nu
[92]Pišanḫuru	king of Natḫû
[93]Pakruru	king of Pišaptu
[94]Bukkunanni'pi	king of Athribis
[95]Naḫkî	king of Ḫininši
[96]Puṭubišti	king of Za'nu
[97]Unamunu	king of Natḫû
[98]Ḫarsiyaîšu	king of Zabnûti
[99]Pûâma	king of Mendes
[100]Susinḳu	king of Puširu
[101]Tapnaḫti	king of Punubu
[102]Bukkunanni'pi	king of Aḫni
[103]Iptiḫardîšu	king of Piḫattiḫurunpiki
[104]Naḫtiḫuruansini	king of Pisapdi'â
[105]Bukurninip	king of Paḫnuti
[106]Ṣiḫâ	king of Šiyâutu
[107]Lamintu	king of Ḫimuni
[108]Išpimâṭu	king of Tâni
[109]Mantimianḫî	king of Thebes

[110]šarrâni$_{pl}$ an-nu-ti $_{amîlu}$piḫâti$_{pl}$ $_{amîlu}$ki-pa-a-ni šá ki-rib $_{mâtu}$Mu-ṣur [111]ú-pa-ki-du abu ba-nu-u-a ša la-pa-an ti-bu-ut $_{m}$Tar-ḳu-u [112]pi-ḳít-ta-šu-un ú-maš-ší-ru im-lu-u ṣíra [113]ú-tir-ma a-šar pi-ḳít-ti-šu-un ina maš-kán-i-šu-un ap-ḳíd-su-nu-ti. [114]$_{mâtu}$Mu-ṣur $_{mâtu}$Ku-u-su ša abu bânu-u-a ik-šú-du a-na íš-šú-ti aṣ-bat. [115]Maṣarâti$_{pl}$ í-li ša û-mí pa-ni ú-dan-nin-ma ú-rak-ki-sa [116]rik-sa-a-tí. It-ti ḫu-ub-ti ma-'a-di šal-la-ti [117]ka-bit-ti šal-míš a-tu-ra a-na Ninâ$_{ki}$.

[118]Arkâ[a]-nu šarrâni$_{pl}$ an-nu-ti ma-la ap-ki-du ina a-di-ya iḫ-ṭu-ú [119]la iṣ-ṣu-ru ma-mit ilâni$_{pl}$ rabûti$_{pl}$ ṭâbtu í-pu-us-su-nu-ti im-šu-ma [120]líb-ba-šu-nu-ti iḳ-pu-ud $_{f}$limut-tú da-bab-ti sur-ra-a-ti id-bu-bu-ma [121]mi-lik la ku-šìr(?) im[b]-li-ku ra-man-šu-un um-ma: $_{m}$Tar-ḳu-u [122]ul-tú ki-rib $_{mâtu}$Mu-ṣur i-na-saḫ-u-ma at-tu-ni a-ša-ba-ni mí-i-nu. [123]Í-li $_{m}$Tar-ḳu-ú šar $_{mâtu}$Ku-ú-si a-na ša-kan a-di-í u sa-li-mí [124]ú-ma-'i-í-ru $_{amîlu}$rak-bi-í-šu-un um-ma: Su-lum-mu-u [125]ina bi-ri-in-ni liš-ša-kín-ma ni-in-dag[c]-ga-ra a-ḫa-míš [126]mât a-ḫi-ín-na-a ni-zu-uz-ma a-a ib-ba-ši ina bi-ri-in[d]-ni ša-nu-um-ma bí-lum. [127]A-na ummânât $_{mâtu}$ $_{ilu}$Aššur$_{ki}$ í-muḳ bílû-ti-ya ša a-na kit-ri-šu-nu uš-zi-zu [128]iš-tí-ni-'i-u a-mat limut-tim.

$_{amîlu}$Šu-par-šaḳî$_{pl}$-ya a-ma-a-tí[e] an-na-a-tí[e] [129]iš-mu-u $_{amîlu}$rak-bi-í-šu-un a-di šip-ra-a-ti-šu-nu iṣ-bat-u-nim-ma [130]í-mu-ru ip-šit sur-ra-a-tí[e]-šu-un. Šarrâni$_{pl}$ an-nu-tí[e] iṣ-bat-u-nim-ma [131]ina bi-ri-ti parzilli iš-ḳa-ti parzilli ú-tam-mí-ḫu ḳâtî u šípî. [132]Ma-mit $_{ilu}$Aššur šar ilâni$_{pl}$ ik-šú-us-su-nu-ti-ma ša iḫ-ṭu-u ina a-di-í [133]ilâni$_{pl}$ rabûti$_{pl}$ ṭâbti[f] ḳâtuš[g]-šu-ún ú-ba-'i-i-ma ša í-pu-us[h]-su-nu-ti [134]du-un-ḳu.

---

a. Var. **ar-ka-a.** — *b.* Var. **mi.** — *c.* Var. **it.** — *d.* Var. omits. — *e.* Var. **ti.** — *f.* Var. **ṭa-ab-ti.** — *g.* Var. **ḳa-tuš.** — *h.* Var. **šu.**

[110]kings these, prefects, governors, whom in Egypt [111]had appointed my father, who before the approach of Tarḳû [112]their appointment left, filled the plain, [113]I brought back and [to] the place of their appointment in their stations I appointed them. [114]Egypt, Cush, which my father had conquered, anew (lit. to newness) I seized. [115]Guards more than before (lit. upon those of the days before) I strengthened and I bound [116]bonds. With plunder much, booty [117]heavy, peacefully I returned to Nineveh.

[118]Afterwards kings these, as many as I had appointed, against my compact sinned, [119]did not keep the oath of the gods great, the good I had done them forgot and [120]their heart made a plan of evil, a device of seditions they devised and [121]a counsel not becoming(?) they counseled [with] themselves, saying: "Tarḳû [122]out of the midst of Egypt they drive (lit. wrench) and as for us our dwelling is numbered." [123]To Tarḳû king of Cush for the establishment of compacts and alliance [124]they sent their messengers, saying: "An alliance [125]between us let be established and let us favor each other, [126]the country of this side we will strengthen and not shall there be amongst us another lord." [127]Against the troops of Assyria, the force of my lordship, which for their assistance I had stationed, [128]they devised a plot (lit. word) of evil.

My generals things these [129]heard, their messengers together with their dispatches they caught and [130]saw the work of their seditions. Kings these they seized and [131]in bonds of iron, fetters of iron, bound hands and feet. [132]The oath of Aššur, king of the gods, captured them, who had sinned against the compacts [133]of the gods great, the good of whose hands I had sought and had done them [134]favor.

Û nišî*pl* *alu*Sa-a-a *alu*Pi[a]-in-di-di *alu*Ṣi[b]-'a-nu [2,1]ù si-it-ti alâni*pl* ma-la it-ti-šu-nu šak-nu iḳ-pu-du limut-tú [2]ṣiḫra u rabâ ina *iṣu*kakkî*pl* ú-šam-ḳi-tu. Í-du a-mí-lum[c] la í-zi-bu ina líb-bi. [3]*amílu*Pagrî*pl*-šu-nu i-lu-lu ina *iṣu*ga-ši-ši. [4]Mašak[-šu-nu ša iš]-ḫu-ṭu ú-ḫal-li-bu dûr ali.

[5]Šarrâni*pl* an-nu-ti ša limut[d]-tu iš-tí-ni-'i-u [6]a-na ummânât *mâtu ilu*Aššur*ki* bal-ṭu-us-su-nu [7]a-na Ninâ*ki* a-di maḫ-ri-ya ú-bíl-u-ni. [8]A-na *m*Ni-ku-u ultu bi-ri-šu-nu ri-í-mu ar-ši-šu-ma ú-bal-liṭ nap-šat-su. [9]A-di-í íli ša maḫ-ri ú-ša-tir-ma it-ti-šu aš-kun. [10]Lu-búl-tu bir-mí ú-lab-bi-su-ma al-lu ḫuraṣi [11]si-mat šarrû-ti-šu aš-kun-šu šimir*pl* ḫuraṣi ú-rak-ki-sa [12]rit-tí-í-šu. Paṭar parzilli šib-bi ša iḫ-zu-šu ḫuraṣu [13]ni-bit šumi-ya ina muḫ-ḫi aš-ṭur-ma ad[e]-din-šu. [14]*iṣu*Narkabâti*pl* *imíru*sisî*pl* *imíru*parí*pl* a-na ru-kub bílû-ti-šu a-ḳis-su. [15]*amílu*Šú-par-šaḳî*pl*-ya *amílu*piḫâti*pl* a-na kit-ri-šu it-ti-šu aš-pur. [16]A-šar abu bânu-u-a ina *alu*Sa-a-a a-na šarru-u-ti ip-ḳíd[f]-du-uš[g] [17]a-na maš-kán-i-šu ú-tir-šu. Û *m ilu*Nabû-ší-zib-an[h]-ni apal-šu [18]a-na *alu*Ḫa-at-ḫa-ri-ba ap-ḳíd. Ṭâbtum[i] damiḳ-tu [19]í-li ša abi bâni[j]-ya ú-ša-tir-ma í-pu-us-su.

[20]*m*Tar-ḳu-ú a-šar in-nab-tu ra-šub-bat *iṣu*kakki *ilu*Aššur bíli-ya [21]is-ḫu-up-šu-ma il-lik šîmat mu-ši-šu. [22]Arkâ-nu *m*Ur-da-ma-ni-í apal *m*Ša-ba-ku-u ú-šib ina *iṣu*kussi šarrû-ti-šu. [23]*alu*Ni-'i *alu*Ú-nu a-na dan-nu-ti-šu iš-kun ú-paḫ-ḫi-ra íl-lat-su. [24]A-na mit-ḫu-ṣi ummânâti-ya aplî*pl* *mâtu ilu*Aššur*ki* [25]šá ki-rib *alu*Mí-im-pi id-ka-a ḳa-bal-šu. [26]Nišî*pl* ša-a-tu-nu í-si-ir-ma iṣ-ba-ta mu-uṣ-ṣa-šu-un. [27]*amílu*Allaku ḫa-an-ṭu a-na Ninâ*ki* il-lik-am-ma iḳ-ba-a ya-a-ti.

---

a. Var. **Bi.**—*b.* Var. **Ṣa.**—*c.* Var. **lu.**—*d.* Var. **li-mut.**—*e.* Var. **a.** *f.* Var. **ki.**—*g.* Var. **šu.**—*h.* Var. **a.**—*i.* Var. **ṭa-ab-tum.**—*j.* Var. **ba-ni.**

And the people of Sais, of Mendes, of Ṣi’anu [2,1]and of the rest of the cities, as many as with them were arrayed [and] made a plan of evil, [2]small and great with weapons they overthrew. One man they did not leave therein. [3]Their corpses they hung up on stakes. [4][With their] skins [which] they stripped off they covered the wall of the city.

[5]Kings these, who evil devised [6]against the troops of Assyria, alive (lit. their life) [7]to Nineveh unto my presence they brought. [8]To Necho out of their midst favor I granted him and spared (lit. caused to live) his life. [9]Compacts more than before (lit. upon those of before) I increased and with him I established. [10][In] clothing **birmi** I clothed him and a chain of gold, [11]insignia of his royalty, I gave him (lit. made for him), rings of gold I bound [12][on] his hands. An iron girdle-dagger (lit. a dagger of iron of the girdle), which its hilt [was] of gold, [13]the naming of my name thereon I wrote and gave to him. [14]Chariots, horses, asses(?), for the riding of his lordship I presented him. [15]My generals, prefects, for his assistance with him I sent. [16]Where my father in Sais to royalty had appointed him [17]to his station I restored him. And Nabu-šizibanni, his son, [18]to Athribis I appointed. Good, favor, [19]more than that of my father, I increased and did to him.

[20]Tarḳû, where he had fled, the might of the weapon of Aššur my lord [21]cast him down and he went [to] the fate of his night. [22]Afterwards Urdamanî, son of Šabakû, sat on the throne of his royalty. [23]Thebes, On, his strength (lit. unto his might) he made, he assembled his army. [24]To fight my troops, native Assyrians (lit. sons of Assyria), [25]who [were] in Memphis, he mustered his troops. [26]People those he besieged and he seized their exit. [27]A courier swift to Nineveh came and informed me.

2. **Second Egyptian Campaign** (V R 2, 28–48).

[28]Ina II-í gir-ri-ya a-na *mâtu*Mu-ṣur u *mâtu*Ku-u-si uš-tí-íš-ší-ra ḫar-ra-nu. [29]*m*Ur-da-ma-ni-í a-lak gir-ri-ya iš-mí-ma [30]šá ak-bu-su mi-ṣir *mâtu*Mu-ṣur. *alu*Mí-im-pi ú-maš-šir-ma [31]a-na šú-zu-ub napiš-tim-šu in-na-bit a-na ki-rib *alu*Ni-'i. [32]Šarrâni*pl* *amílu*piḫâti*pl* *amílu*ki-pa-a-ni ša ki-rib *mâtu*Mu-ṣur aš-ku-nu [33]ina irti-ya il-li-ku-ú-nim-ma ú-na-aš-ši-ḳu šípî-ya. [34]Arki *m*Ur-da-ma-ni-í ḫar-ra-nu aṣ-bat [35]al-lik a-di *alu*Ni-'i ali dan-nu-ti-šu. [36]Ti-ib taḫazi-ya dan-ni í-mur-ma *alu*Ni-'i ú-maš-šir [37]in-na-bit a-na *alu*Ki-ip-ki-pi. Ala šú-a-tú a-na si-ḫir-ti-šu [38]ina tukul-ti *ilu*Aššur u *ilu*Ištar ik-šú-da ḳâta-a-a. [39]Kaspu ḫuraṣu ni-siḳ-ti abnî*pl* bušâ ìkalli-šu ma-la ba-šu-u [40]lu-búl-ti bir-mí kitû*pl* *imíru*sisî*pl* rabûti*pl* nišî*pl* zik-ru[a] u zin-niš [41]II *iṣu*dim-mí ṣîrûti*pl* pi-tiḳ[b] za-ḫa-li-í ib-bi [42]šá II M VC **gun** ki-lal-šu-nu man-za-az bâb ì-kur [43]ul-tu man-za-al-ti-šu-nu as-suḫ-ma al-ḳa-a a-na *mâtu ilu*Aššur*ki*. [44]Šal-la-tú ka-bit-tú ina la mí-ni aš-lu-la ul-tú ki-rib *alu*Ni-'i [45]í-li *mâtu*Mu-ṣur ù *mâtu*Ku-ú-si [46]*iṣu*kakkî*pl*-ya ú-šam-ri-ir-ma aš-ta-kan li-i-tu. [47]It-ti ḳa-ti ma-li-ti šal-míš a-tu-ra [48]a-na Ninâ*ki* ali bílû-ti-ya.

3. **Hunting Inscription** (I R 7, No. IX A).[c]

[1]A-na-ku *m ilu*Aššur-bâni-apli šar kiššati šar *mâtu ilu*Aššur*ki* ša *ilu*Aššur *ilu*Bílit í-mu-ki ṣi-ra-a-ti [2]ú-šat-li-mu-uš. Níšî*pl* ša ad-du-ku *iṣu*mid-pa-a-nu iz-zi-tú ša *ilu*Ištar bí-lit taḫazi [3]íli-šu-un az-ḳu-up muḫ-ḫu-ru í-li-šu-nu ú-ma-ḫir karana aḳ-ḳa-a í-li-šu-un.

---

a. Var. **ra.** — *b*. Var. **ti-iḳ.** — *c*. Accompanying a bas-relief in which the king is pouring out wine over slain lions.

2. **Second Egyptian Campaign** (V R 2, 28–48).

[28]In my second expedition to Egypt and Cush I directed the way. [29]Urdamanî the march of my expedition heard and [30]that I had trodden the territory of Egypt. Memphis he left and [31]to save his life he fled to Thebes. [32]The kings, prefects, governors, whom in Egypt I had established, [33]to meet me (lit. into my front) came and kissed my feet. [34]After Urdamanî the road I took, [35]I went to Thebes, the city of his might. [36]The approach of my mighty battle he saw and Thebes he left, [37]he fled to Kipkipi. That city to its whole extent (lit. to its circumference) [38]by the help of Aššur and of Ištar captured my hands. [39]Silver, gold, **nisiḳti**, stones, possession of his palace, as much as there was, [40]clothing **birmi**, **kitû**, horses great, people male and female, [41]two columns(?) lofty, a work of **zaḫali** metal bright, [42]which two thousand five hundred **gun** [was] their weight, stationed at (lit. seat of) the gate of a temple, [43]from their position I wrenched and took to Assyria. [44]Booty heavy without measure I carried off from the midst of Thebes. [45]Over Egypt and Cush [46]my weapons I caused to march and I established authority (lit. might). [47]With a hand full peacefully I returned [48]to Nineveh the city of my lordship.

3. **Hunting Inscription** (I R 7, No. IX A).

[1]I [am] Assurbanipal, king of hosts, king of Assyria, who Aššur, Beltis powers exalted [2]gave to him. The lions which I killed the bow strong of Ištar, queen of battle, [3]over them I erected, a prayer over them I presented, wine I poured out over them.

Ištar's Descent to Hades.

(Delitzsch Assyr. Lesest.[3] p. 110; IV R 31.)

A-na mâti lâ târat ḳaḳ-ḳa-ri i-ṭi-[i]
*ilu*Ištar binat *ilu*Sin ú-zu-un-ša [iš-kun]
iš-kun-ma binat *ilu*Sin ú-zu-un-[ša]
a-na bît [a]í-ṭi-í[a] [b]šú-bat[b] *ilu*Ir-kal-la
a-na bîti šá í-ri-bu-šu la a-ṣu-ú
a-na [c]ḫar-ra-ni[c] šá a-lak-ta-ša[d] la ta-a-a-rat
a-na bîti šá [e]í-ri-bu[e]-šu zu-um-mu-ú nu-ú-ra
a-šar iprâti[f] bu-bu-us-[g]su-nu[g] a-kal-[h]šu-nu[h] ṭi-iṭ-ṭu[i]
nu-ú-ru[j] ul[k] im-ma-ru[j] ina í-ṭu-ti aš-ba
lab-šú[l]-ma kîma [m]iṣ-ṣu-ri[m] ṣu-bat káp[n]-pi
íli *iṣu*dalti u *iṣu*sikkuri ša-pu-uḫ ip-ru.
*ilu*Ištar a-na bâb mâti lâ târat ina ka-ša-di-ša
a-na *amílu*ḳípi ba-a-bi a-ma-tum iz-zak-kar
*amílu*ḳípi mí-í pi-ta-a ba-ab-ka.
pi-ta-a ba-ab-ka-ma lu-ru-ba a-na-ku
šum-ma la ta-pat-ta-a ba-a-bu la ir-ru-ba a-na-ku
a-maḫ-ḫa-aṣ dal-tum sik-ku-ru a-šab-bir
a-maḫ-ḫa-aṣ si-ip-pu-ma ú-ša-pal-kat *iṣu*dalâti*pl*
ú-ší-íl-la-a mi-tu-ti akilûti*pl* bal-ṭu-ti
íli bal-ṭu-ti i-ma-'a-du mi-tu-ti.
*amílu*Ḳípu pa-a-šu i-pu-uš-ma i-ḳab-bi
iz-zak-ka-ra a-na rabî-ti *ilu*Iš-tar
i-zi-zi bí-íl-ti la ta-na-šá-aš-ši
lu-ul-lik šum-ki lu-ša-an-ni a-na šar-ra-ti *ilu*Nin-ki-gal.

---

a–a. Var. **iḳ-li-ti.** — *b–b*. Var. **mu-šab.** — *c–c*. Var. **ḫarrani.** — *d*. Var. **šu.** — *e–e*. Var. **a-ši-bu.** — *f*. Var. **ip-ru.** — *g–g*. Var. **si-na-ma.** — *h–h*. Var. **ši-na.** — *i*. Var. **ṭi.** — *j*. Var. **ra.** — *k*. Var. **la.** — *l*. Var. **ša.** — *m–m*. Var. **iṣṣuri.** — *n*. Var. **kap.**

Assurbanipal's First Egyptian Campaign.

(V R 1^{52}-2^{27}. Transliterated & translated p. 42-49.)

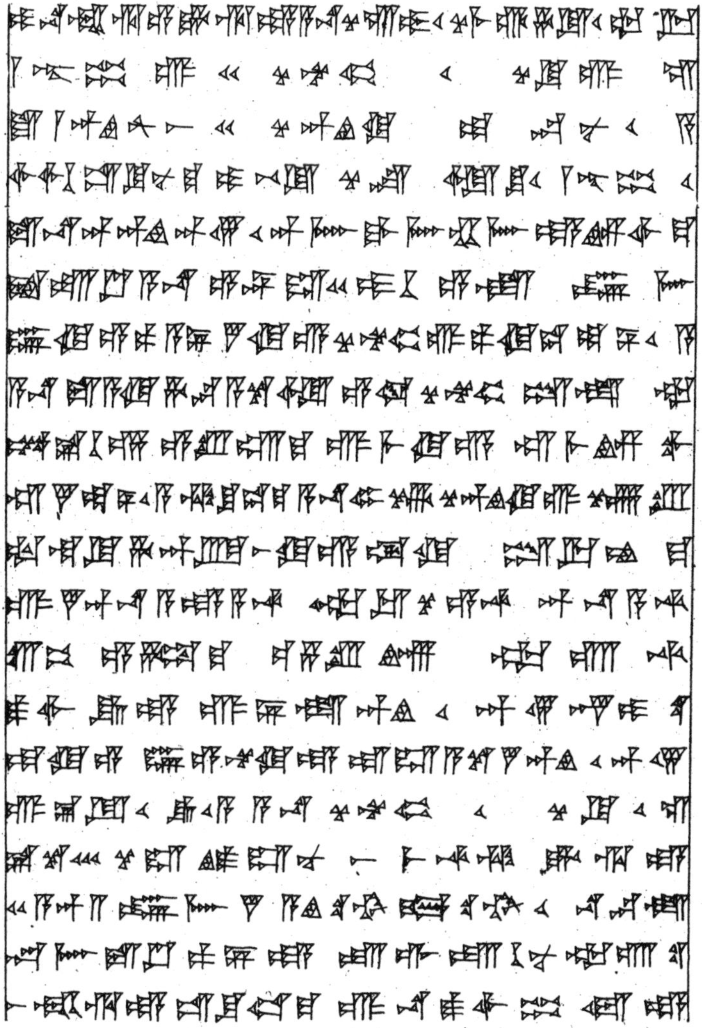

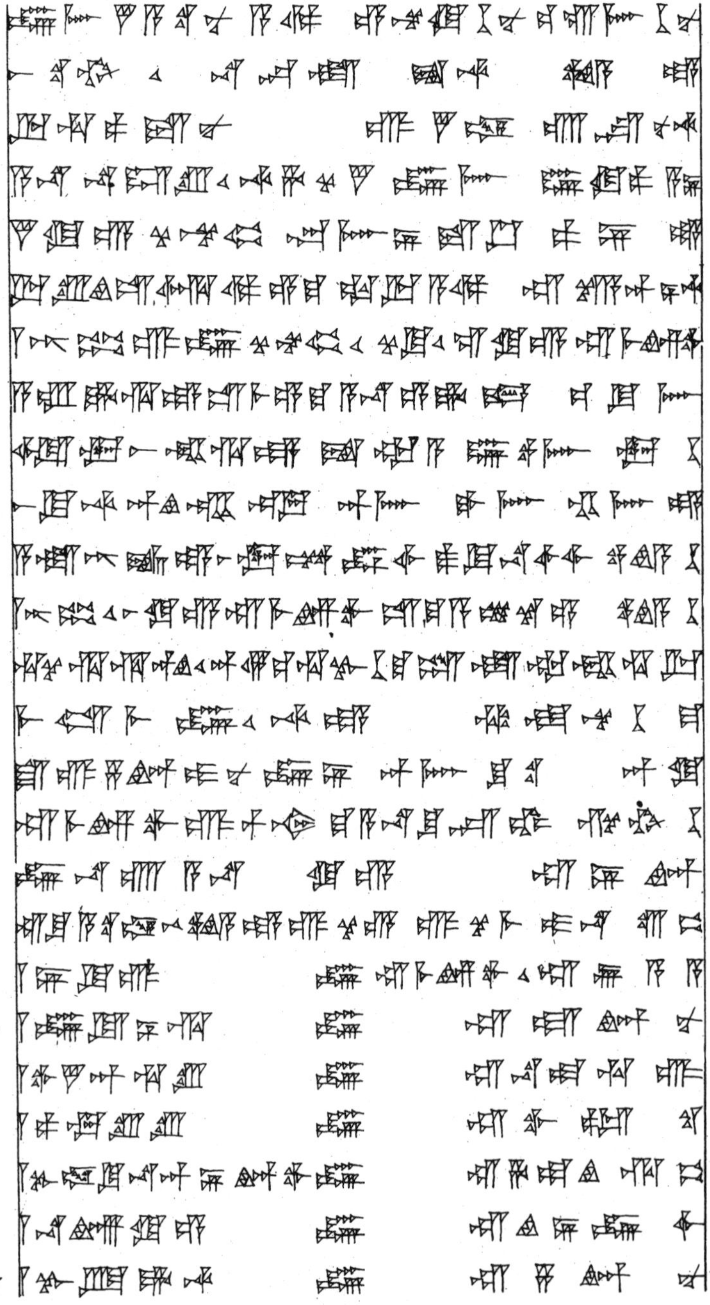

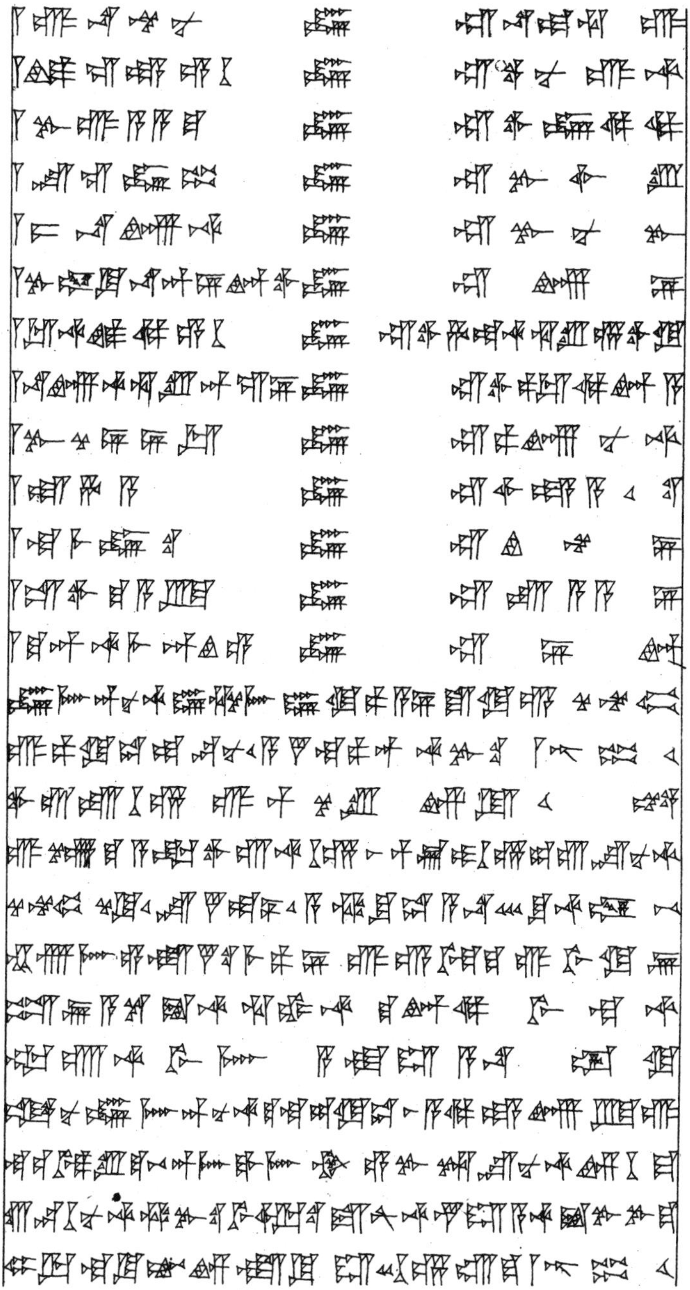

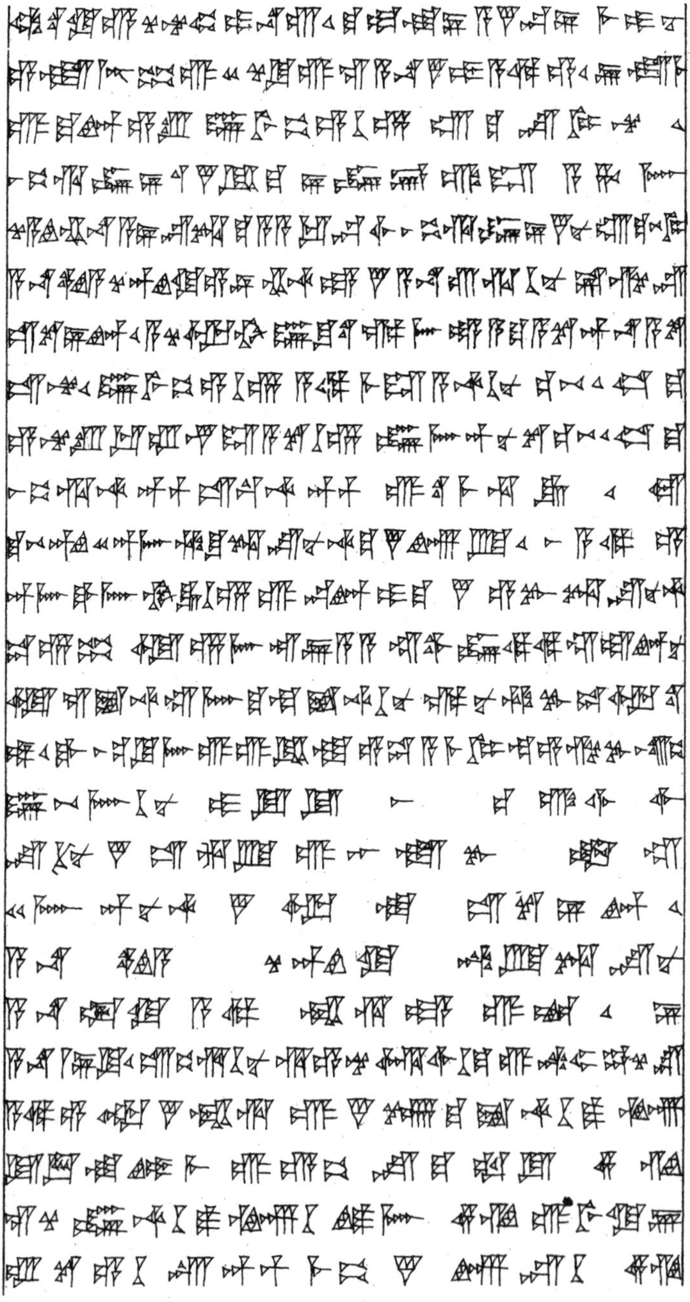

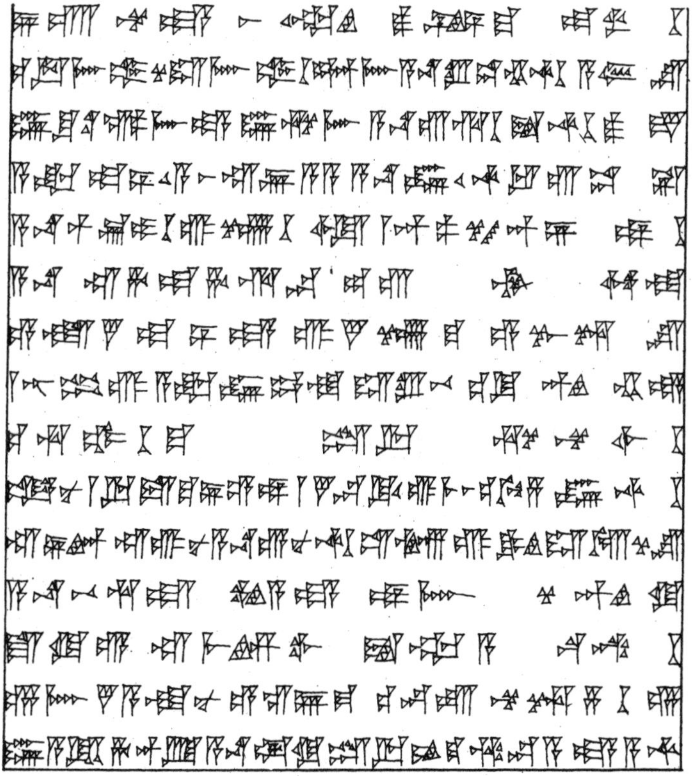

Account of the Deluge.

(Delitzsch, Assyr. Lesest.^{3} 103^{77}–106^{185}; IV R 50 col. 2^{25} – 51 col. 4^{30}.)

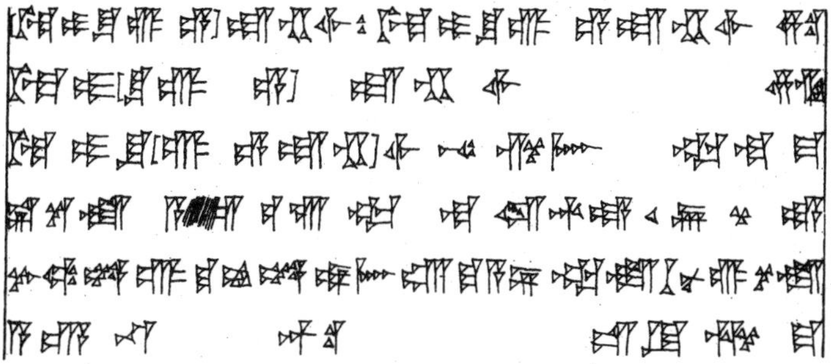

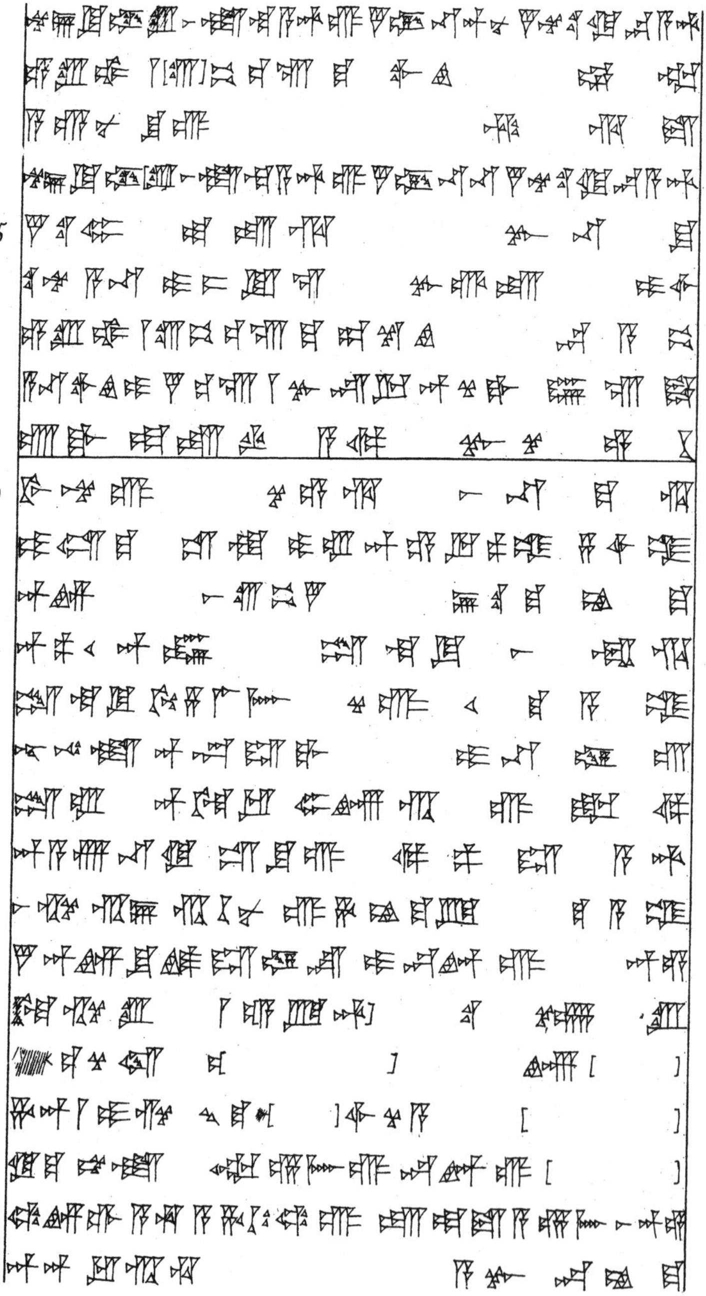

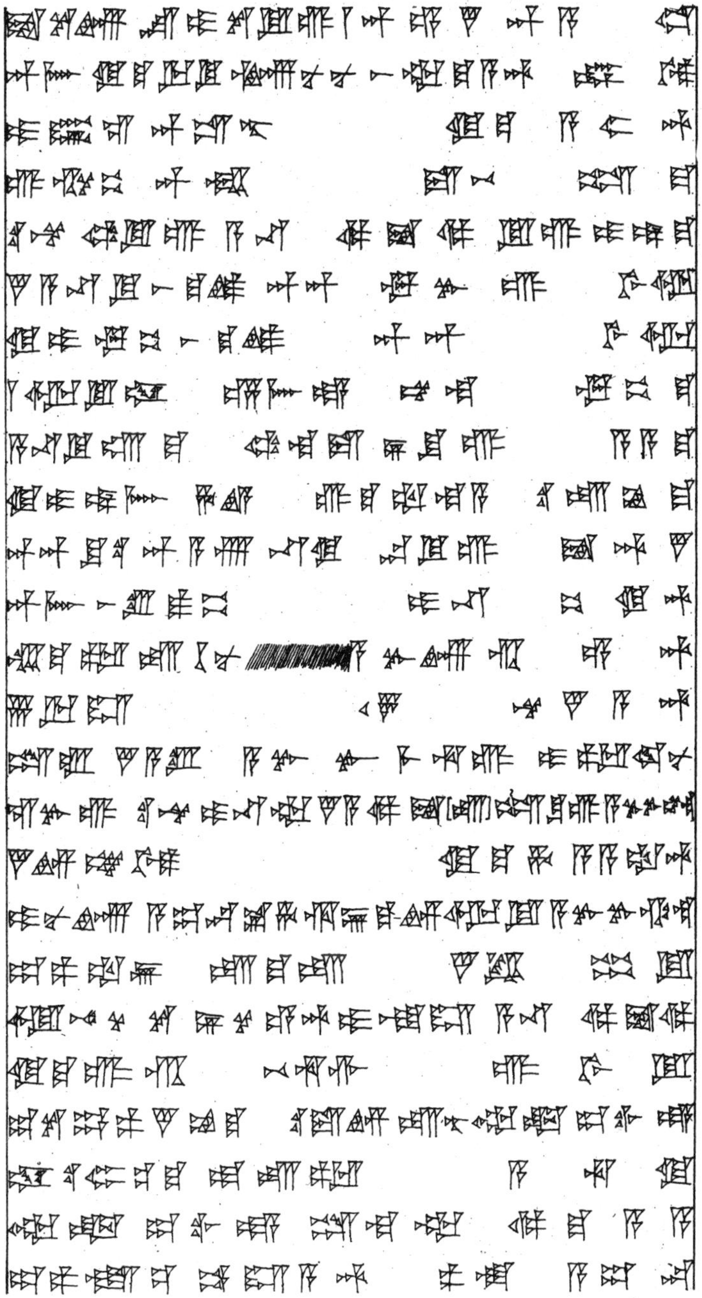

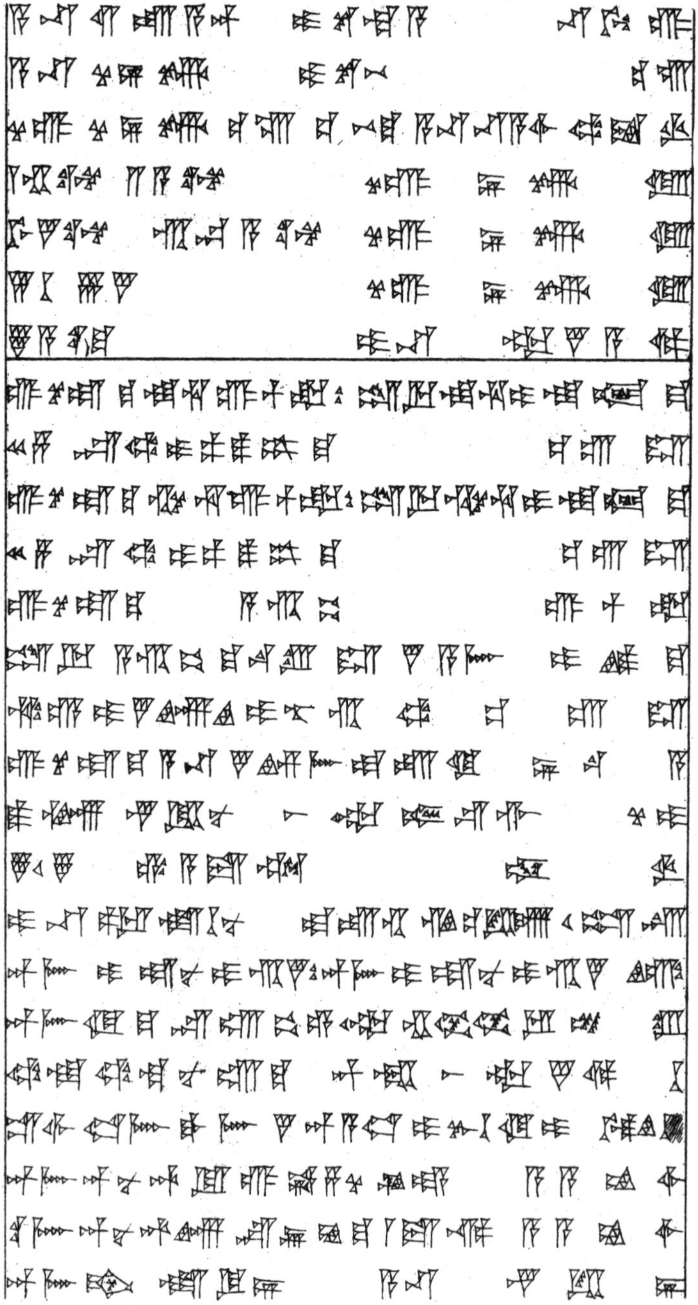

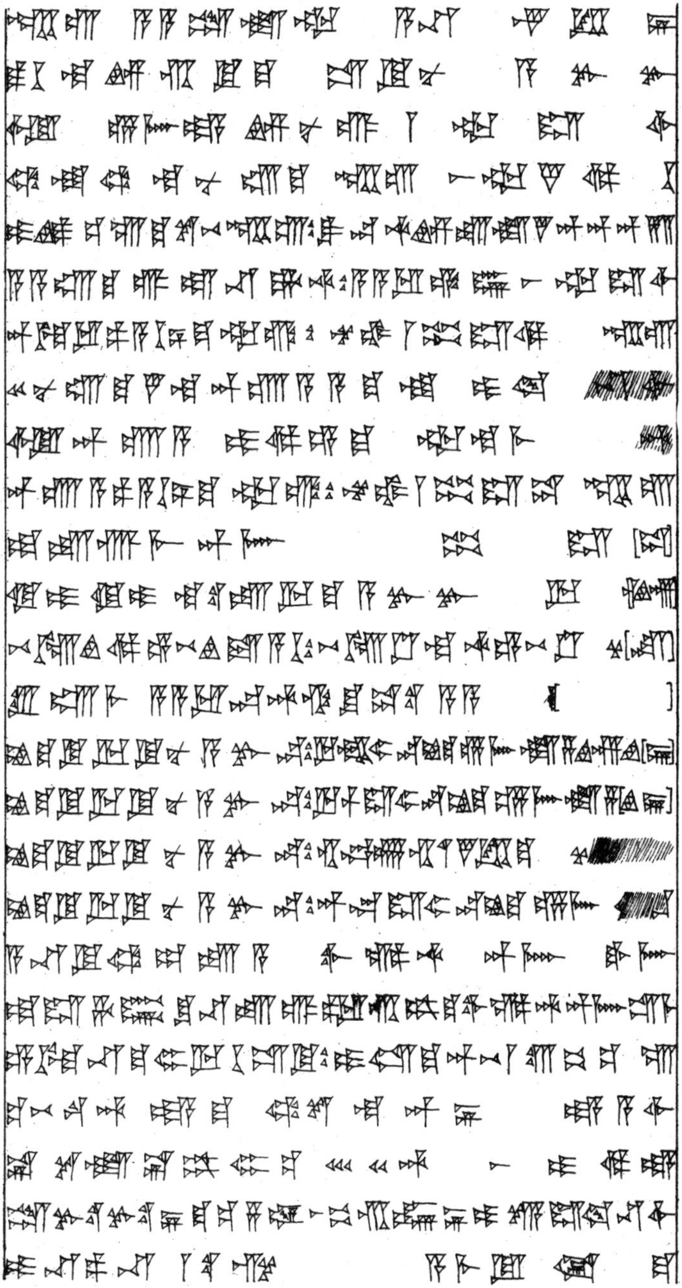

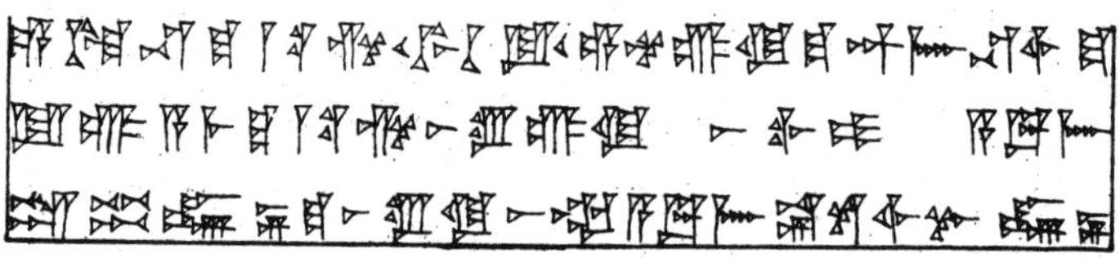

Fragment of a Creation Tablet.

(From my collation of the original, in the British Museum.)

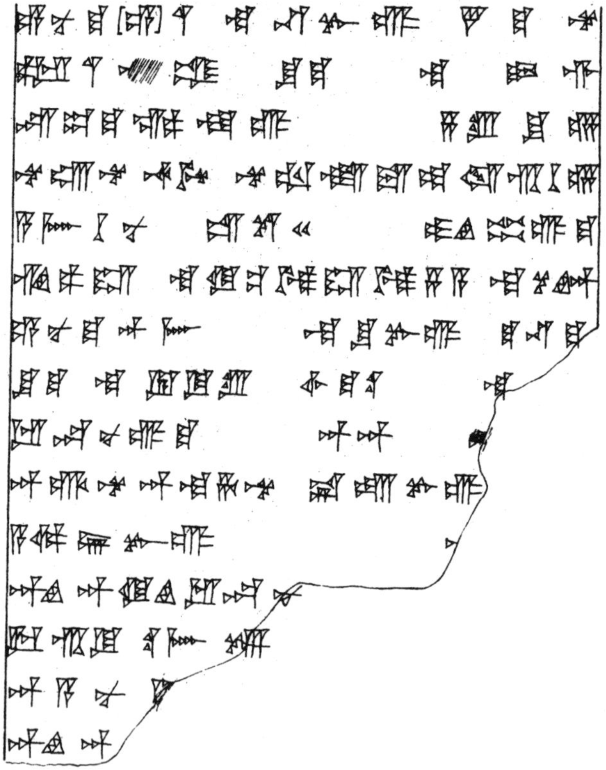

From Ištar's Descent to Hades.

a. Passing the Gates (IV R 31 col. I$^{37-64}$)

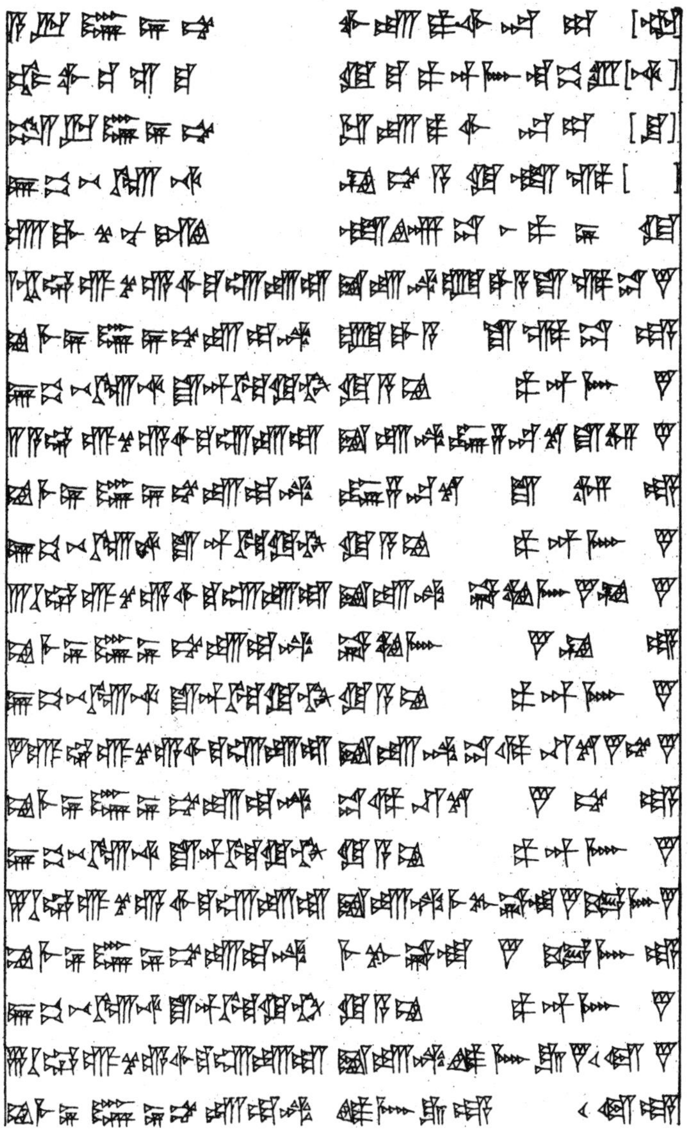

b. The Return (IV R 31 col. 2^{24-45}).

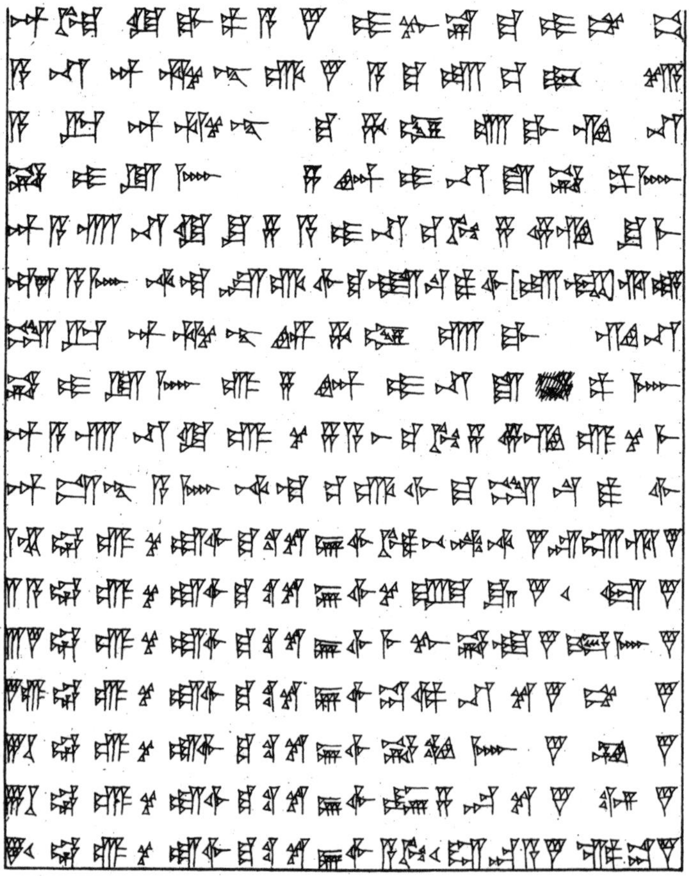

NOTES.

1, 1. *šurru,* st. *šarû,* inf. II 1, whence the final *u* although cstr., like *šukkun.* — *Muškâya* and *šarrâni* are subjects of *itkalû, urdûni* (= *uridûni* §§ **8**. 1; **30**) and *iṣbatû; ša* l. 2 is subj. of *iṣbatûni; Alzi* and *Purukuzzi* are objects of *iṣbatûni; nâš* is part. I 1 referring to A. and P. The clause beginning with *šarru* l. 4 is parallel to the one beginning with *ša* l. 2; translate: whose breast no king had overcome in battle. — 7. *ummânâtíya.* The suff. belongs also to *narkabâti.* When the same suff. belongs to several words it is generally expressed only with the last word, cf. 2^{5}. — *lûptíḫir* = *lû* + *uptaḫḫir* § **24**. 3. — 8. *uḳî* § **25**. — 9. *muḳtablî* part. I 1 st. *ḳabâlu* § **8**. 2 *b*. — 10. *altanan* st. *šanânu* § **8**. 2 *a*. — 12. *râḫiṣi* part. I 1, the destroyer, from *raḫâṣu* to overflow, either *Ramân* as storm-god, or the storm itself. — *lûkimir* = *lû* + *ukammir* st. *kamâru* to cast down. — *dâmî* is the direct obj. and *ḫurrî* and *bamâtí* are indirect obj. of *lûšardî.* The sign for *dâmu* represents also *pagru* a corpse Heb. פֶּגֶר and so Lotz renders here, but that makes unnecessary tautology in this passage, and does not give so good a meaning in other places in this inscription where the id. occurs. — 15. *šallasunu* § **8**. 2 *a, b*. — 16. *lûšíṣâ* §§ **29**; **30**. — 17. *ipparšidû* § **33**. — 20. *ûmišuma* that day, time, *ûmi* + demon. *šu* + *ma* § **18**. — 21. *mâdâta* = *mandanta,* st. *nadânu.*

2, 1. *sitít,* etc., render: the rest of K., who . . . had fled, crossed over to S., etc. — 3. *padanî* pl. of *padanu* cf. on 42^{23}. — *ammâtí* fem. pl., opposite of *annâti* these; *padanî ammâti* those regions, the other side. — 4. *dannûti* strength, stronghold, abstr. noun. — 5. *ḳurâdîya;* cf. on 1^{7}. — 7. *aḫsî* 1st pers. sing. second impf. I 1 of a verb with weak 3rd radical. — *ḫula* bad, supply *šadâ.* — 8. *lûṭîb* = *lû* + *uṭawwib.* — 10. *umiṣi,* form like *ukimir* 1^{12}. — 12. *šuzub* § 27. — 14. *ušna'il* § **28**. — *pagar* cstr. of *pagru,* used collectively. — 15. *ana gurunâtí lûkirin* (= *lû* + *ukarrin*). The syllables *gu* and *ki* have also the values *ḳu* and *ḳi,* and the stem in both these words may be קרן to heap up; *gurunâtí* from *guruntu* is like *tuḳmâti* from *tuḳuntu* battle, or *libnâti* from *libittu* brick. —— 18. *kibrât* § **16.** 2. —— *ša* l. 20, 21, 22 (before *ilâni*) is in each case gen. sign § **11,** *ša* before *ina* l. 22 refers to Tiglathpileser rather than to the gods. —— 23. *muniḫa* (part. II 1 st. נוח), *šânina* are objects of *išû*. —— 25. *ílînitu* fem. of *ílînu* upper, formation like *surkînu* 60^{16} libation, the same as the formation in *ân* § **15.** 3 *c*. —— Translate l. 22–25: (me) who . . . ruled righteously . . . Aššur the lord sent me and I went. —— 28. *ušítiḳ* III. 1 § **27.**

3, 4. *marṣa,* supply *íḳla*. —— 5. *urumî,* either a part of a tree or a species of tree. —— 18. *šagalti, riḫilti* §§ **8.** 2 *a;* **16.** 4. —— 21. *ḫalapta* fem. acc., in appos. with *narkabâti,* may also be read *ḫalabta,* st. *ḫalâbu* to be covered. —— 28. *kirbîtí* the interior (of the cities), fem. pl. —— 29. *utirra* = *utîra* = *utawwira*. —— 30. *ḳa-ti* = *ḳâtî* § **9.** 2. —— 34. *ardutti* = *ardûtí*.

4, 2. *lîṭûtí,* abstr. noun from *lîṭu* hostage. —— 24. *rašbû* perm. I 1. —— 26. *azru* I scattered (stones over the devastated cities), cf. 2 Kings 3, 19. —— *biriḳ*. The double id. here is so rendered IV R 3, 3. 4; *biriḳ siparri* may be an emblem of victory, composed of copper plates, engraved with symbols of lightning. The *šâtunu* l. 29 treats the *biriḳ siparri* as a plural. After destroying the city the king makes a *biriḳ siparri,* whereon he writes a decree never to build the city nor to construct its wall again (cf. Jos. 6, 26), and places the *biriḳ siparri* in a house made for the purpose on the old ruins.

5, 1. *šangi* priest. For the reading cf. S^b 243. Cf. 7^{15} where the son of our king applies the title to his father, and V R 6, 46 where we find the pl. written *ša-an-gi-í* = *šangî*. —— 2. *kašuš* favorite title of this king, I R 17, 21 *bíl bílî kašušu šar šarrâni;* cf. also I R 26, 127. —— 5. *itlu;* the titles here return to Assurnazirpal. —— 6. *ittallaku* § **27.** —— 7. *ri'i tabrâti* shepherd (= king) of *t.* A word written the same way occurs in accounts of building operations, as Sargon St. 79 *ana tabrâti ušalik* I caused it to advance to *t.* —— 11. *multarḫî* = *muštariḫî* § **8.** 2 *a,* name for the enemies of the king. —— 14. *ṣâbit lîṭî* receiver of hostages. —— 16. *ínuma* = *ínu* time (masc.) + *ma,* st. אן$_4$, whence Heb. עת = ענת. —— 17. *itmuḫ* he caused to hold, he presented. The verb *tamâḫu* means generally *simply* to hold, seize. —— 22. *ílišunu,* construction according to real gender, though the grammatical gender of *ummânât* is fem. —— *ašgum;* cf. Isa. 5, 29, where the Assyrians are represented as a lion roaring over its prey; cf. also 15^{27}. —— *šarru* refers to Assurnazirpal. —— 27. *íbirtân,* formation in *ân* from *íbirtu.*

6, 3. *urdûti* obeisance, or *urdûtî* obeisance unto me. The usual form for obeisance is *ardûtu*, as 21^9; cf. *urḫu* 42^{23} and *arḫu* 2^{28} way. — *upušû*, an unusual form for *ípušû* § **27**; on the expression cf. 21^9 *ípiš ardûti.* — 4. *ušumgallu*, composed of *ušu* or *ušum* + *gallu* the large *ušu*, apparently a loan word S^b 125, like *íkallu* (i.e. *í* + *gallu*) the large house, palace. From such passages as II R 19, 62 the *u.* appears to be some wild beast: *kakku ša kîma u. šalamta ikkalu* weapon which devours a corpse like an *u.;* cf. also IV R 20 No. 3, 15. — 6. *âpir* part. I 1 cstr., may be intrans. like *lâbiš*, *ḫâlib*, the one clothed with *š.* — *uršanu* syn. of *kašušu* Lotz Tiglathpileser p. 89, 21. — 7. *tanâdâtí* pl. of *tanittu* st. נאר. — *ṣalulu* for *ṣalul* cstr. shadow, protection. — 8. *ša kibit*, etc., the command of whose mouth causes mountains and countries to tremble. — 10. *pâ ištín šuškunu* to establish one word, to bring into agreement, *pâ šakânu* to enter into an agreement, as $29^{17,32}$. Cf. Sargontexte p. 78. — 12. On *Šulmânu-ašârid* = Šulman is leader, Heb. שַׁלְמַנְאֶסֶר, cf. Schrader in ZKF. II 197. — 13. *ípuš* without the usual final *u* in rel. sentence § **11**; so also l. 11 *ušaškin.* — 18. *ušaṣbit* I caused to work. — 20. *íkal;* the repetition of this word is peculiar, for there seems to have been but one palace built, l. 25. — 25. *ušíziz* III 1, st. *nazâzu.* — 26. I surrounded it with a *sikat karri* of copper. Cf. *sikkat kaspi ibbi* a *sikkat* of bright silver I R 47 col. VI 8.

7, 2. *igigi* the spirits of heaven. — *bíl mâtâti* is a title applied to various deities, as II R 57, 21 to Adar. Here it belongs to Bíl and so also I R 9, 4. — 3. *abu ilâni* is likewise applied to various gods. — *kâlama*, supplied from I R 27, 9. — 4. *Sin*, supplied from I R 27, 4, where the Moon-god is called *iršu bíl agî* the wise, the lord of the crown, cf. also I R 9, 5. — *Ramân*, supplied from I R 27, 6, where R. is called *gišru kaškaššî ilâni* the mighty, the all-powerful one of the gods (*kaškaššu* like *dandannu* § **15**. 2). — 5. *bíl ḫigalli*, title of R. as god of the weather; *ḫigalli* a loan-word. — 6. *Marduk*, supplied from I R 27, 5 *Marduk ab-ak-lu bíl tirîtí.* — *abkal* cstr. of *abkallu;* so one may read from the similarity of id. here and in V R 13, 35; *abaklu* I R 27, 5 would then be only orthographically different from *abkallu.* — *bíl tírîtí* lord of laws(?), syn. of *mûdû* wise, *ḫassu* wise, etc., V R 13, 38–42. — 7. *šar igigi;* Adar is called *ḳardu* in I R 27, 6 but not *šar igigi.* The reading *igigi* for the id. *nun-gal* comes from a comparison of l. 2 above, where Anu is called *šar i-gi-gi*, with III R 7, 1, where the same god is called *šar nun-gal.* — 8. *gitmalu*, so I R 27, 8. On the formation cf. § **15**. 3 *b.* — 9. *multalu* for *muštalu.* The latter form occurs I R 59, 7 a; 65, 4 a as a title of Nebuchadnezzar, IV R 26, 31 as title of a deity, and the feminine *muštaltu* is applied to a goddess IV R 7, 13. In the last two cases the word renders a double id., whose signs may mean heart + strength. Instead of *multalu* the parallel passage I R 27, 7 reads *mutallu* (= *mutalu*), as does also I R 17, 5. *muštalu, multalu, mutallu* seem to come from the same stem, perhaps from a stem אלה to be strong (?); *mutalû* (?) = *mu*א*tali*ה*u* would be part. I 2 and *muštalû* (*multalû*) = *mušta*א*li*ה*u* part. III 2 from this stem. Another possibility is to regard *mutallu* as coming from a different st. and to derive *muštalu, multalu* from שׁא₁ל, as I have done in the glossary. — 11. *ilâni*, supplied from I R 27, 11. — *mušîmû* pl. in *û*, part. II 1. — 14. *šamšu* the sun of all peoples, title of Shalmaneser. — 22. *dannûti-šu ša Ninni* his stronghold, namely of N., the suff. *šu* anticipating the name N., a usage so familiar in Aramaic. — 24. *tâmdi ša šúlmí šamši* = the Mediterranean sea. — 25. *ulil*, 27[1] *ullil* = *u*ה*allil*, I made bright, caused to shine. — 27. *ílî* § **27**. — 28. *ušíziz* cf. on 6^{25}.

8. 2. *idukû*. In the fuller record III R 8, 79 we read: *ina kakki ramânišunu Giammu bílašunu i-du-ku* with their own weapons they killed G. their lord. Lines 1–4 are only brief notes of the campaign, and G. was murdered by his own subjects. — 6. *Amatâ* § **15**. 3 *c*. — 9. *amdaḫḫiṣ* = *amtaḫiṣ*. — 21. *ílî* § **27**. — 22. *ísiršu* § **27**. — 26. *Ṣurrâ* the Tyrian.

9. 4. *ša . . . uttûšu* whom they appointed; *uttû* = *u*א*atti*ה*û*. — *zikir šumi* = fame. — 6. *ša . . . šutbû kakkušu* whose weapon was caused to advance; *šutbû* perm III 1. — 7. *ûm bílûti* = day of accession to the throne. — *ibšû*, subj. is *malku*. — 8. *išû*, subj. is *ša* l. 7. — 9. *mu'aru*, noun of the form *ḳurâdu*, perhaps from st. כא₂ר. — 10. *ša . . . Ìa išrukuš* to whom Ìa gave. — 11. adorned (?) his hand with an irresistible weapon, *uštibbu* = *ušta*א₂*bibu* III 2 with loss of short *i*. — 13. *innamru* IV 1 he was seen = he contended st. א₁מר. — 16. *mutaḳin* part. II 1. — 20. *ali-šu*, the suff. refers to Pisiri. — *zikar-šu*, the suff. refers to *ša* l. 19. For *zikar*, cstr. of *zikaru*, the original has the sign *uš*, well known as an id. for man, male. Perhaps the sign had also the value *šaknu* or *piḫâtu*, one of which we should expect here. — 22. *ubla* = *ubila* §§ **8**. 1; **30**. — *ímiddu* = *ímidu* § **27** has two acc., Muski the indirect and *abšân* the direct acc. — 23. *mutîr gimilli*, cf. I R 17, 21 *mutîr gimilli abîšu*, III R 3, 19 *mutîr gimil Aššur*, I R 22, 118 *ana târi gimilli* (var. *gimílim*) *ša·Ammíba'la alik*. The verb *gamâlu* means to finish, to reward, to give, and the noun *gimillu* completion, recompense, gift; *gimillu turru* (II 1 from תור) means to return recompense, to avenge. — 25. *šamši*, doubtful reading owing to damaged condition of the slab. Perhaps we should read *mâtu An-di-a*, a country elsewhere mentioned by Sargon, cf. Delitzsch Paradies p. 100. — 27. *ípušu,* cf. 6^{12-30}. — 28. *dunnunû* perm. II 1 they were made strong. — 29. *šuršudâ* perm. III. 1 they were established.

10, 1. It went to decay (and) ruin. — 2. *ašaršu*, etc., cf. I R 15, 76 *ḳaḳḳaršu umísi libnasu akšud; libnasu* or *libnâsu* may stand for *libnatsu, libnâtsu* its bricks; *libnasu akšud* I reached its *libnatu*, (the old foundation (?)). — 5. *bâb zîḳi* a gate of *zîḳi*, private entrance (?). — 6. The booty of the cities to which my weapons went forth (?). *uṣûni* is written by the id. which is explained S^b 84 as *aṣû* to go out, inf. I 1. — 8. *ìrî* might also be read *bitrî*, which might be gen. from a noun *bitrû* fulness, completion, made with formative *t*, like *gitmalu, šitmuru*, etc. An adjective *bitrû* large, fatted, from the same stem we meet in the pl. form *bitrûti* I R 65, 27 *b;* Khors. 168, in both cases applied to animals offered in sacrifice. — *lulî* pearls (?), jewels (?), Arab. *lu'lu'*. *lulî* or *lalî* 37^6 is often mentioned in accounts of embellishing palaces and temples. — *Nírgal*, god of war and of the chase. The name is frequently written with the same ids. as here; as I R 20, 25. 27; 24, 52; III R 7 col. I 44; 8, 70. 96. — 9. *ana líbbi aḳri* I invoked therein. We should expect *ina líbbi*. The meaning is I went in and invoked. — *gûmaḫḫî* oxen; composed of *gû* = *alpu* ox S^b 96 and *maḫḫu* syn. of *rabû*. — 10. *ardâni*. The meaning tame sheep for the double id. here, composed of the sign for sheep *kirru* + the sign for servant *ardu*, is clear. But how to read the name is uncertain. In the very similar passage Khors. 168 Sargon offers in sacrifice *gûmaḫḫî bitrûti šu-'-í marûti kurgi ustur* fatted oxen, fatted *šu'í*, etc. It will thus be seen that *šu'î* corresponds to the signs for tame sheep, and perhaps we should read in our passage *šu'î*, i.e. Heb. שֶׂה.

11, 1. *ša*. We expect in l. 7 *tamarta amḫur* of (= from) *Minḫimmu*, etc., I received tribute, a sentence like that on p. 8^{26-28}, or III R 7, 41. This is perhaps the form which the sentence had in the writer's mind when he began it and his change to the expression *tamarta iššûni* was the more easy because of the many intervening names. — 5. *Malikrammu*. The reading *Malik* for the name of the deity represented by the signs *a-a* is very doubtful. This deity occurs frequently associated with *Šamaš*. — 6. *šidî šadlûti*, in appos. with *šarrâni* or with *Aḫarrî*. — 11. *uraššu* §§ **25**; **30**; **32**; **9**. 2. — 14. *katrî*. The dental might also be read *d*. With Schrader KAT.[2] 295 I regard the *t* as formative and the st. as כרע to bow, bend, the *katrû* thus being a token of submission. — 19. *Šakkanakkî*, cf. Sargontexte p. 79. — 20. *adî*, cf. on 46^{15}. — *mamît ša*. The gen. relation is doubly indicated, by the cstr. form and by *ša*. — 22. *nakriš . . . ísiršu*, a parenthetical clause, he (i.e. Hezekiah) in a hostile manner confined him (i.e. Padî) in a dungeon. — *ana ṣilli*, literally: into a dungeon. *ṣillu* = shadow, darkness; and *an* may be cstr. of *anu* receptacle, vessel, so that *an ṣilli* = vessel of darkness = dungeon, cf. Delitzsch Lesest.[3] XVI. — 23. *libbašun*, nom. § **16.** 3, the suff. referring to the names in l. 19. — 25. *iḳtírûni* I 2 they invited. The subj. is the people of Ekron, and the obj. the kings of Egypt. — *riṣussun* = *ana riṣûtišun* § **20.** — 29. *šarri muṣurâ* the Egyptian king, not the king of Egypt.

12, 1. *siḫirti ali* around the city. — 3. *ša*, etc., whose sin had no existence, i.e. who had not sinned. — 9–11. Difficult military terms describing the means by which the cities were taken; *labbanâtí* might be read *kalbanâti*. — 11. *almî*. Obj. is *alâni*, etc., l. 8. — 16. *aṣî* the one coming out, part I 1. — 24. *Urbî*, etc. It is not certain whether *Urbî* is subj. of *iršû* l. 26 (so apparently Delitzsch Lesest.[3] XV) or obj. of *ušíbila* l. 31. In the latter case, which seems to me more probable, we must construe: The Arabians . . . whom . . . he brought into Jerusalem and (to whom) he gave wages (?), he sent behind me to Nineveh l. 31, along with gold, etc. l. 26, and his daughters, etc. l. 30.

13, 4. *Ílamû* the Elamite, subj. of *íkimu*. — 5. *šulûti* has perhaps the same meaning as *šalûtu* which in V R 11, 11 is the reading for the signs meaning royalty. — 7. *ḳâtû* = *ina ḳâti*. — 25. *imḳutsu; su* = *šu* is indirect obj. of *imḳut;* subject of the verb is *ḫattum*. — 28. I commanded the march, a month of rain, a mighty hurricane (?) took place, the heavens rained greatly, rains upon rains and snow, I avoided the streams, the outflow (?) of the mountains.

14, 6. After Šuzub had revolted, the Babylonians, wicked demons, bolted the city gates, etc. *issiḫu* = *istaḫu* I 2, the *ma* not connective. — 8–11. *Šuzubu . . . ṣîruššu ipḫurû* = *ṣîr Š. ipḫurû* they assembled about *Š*. The epithets between *Šuzubu* l. 8 and *ṣîruššu* l. 11 are all descriptive of *Šuzub*. — 13. *nîtum*. For this reading, not *ṣaltum*, I am indebted to a note by Prof. Haupt in the Andover Review V 545, who renders "cordon (of warriors)." In 17^{26} we have *ala nîti almî* I surrounded the city with *nîti*, and in V R 19, 21 *nîtum ša lamî*, i.e. *nîtum* used of surrounding, besieging. I know neither the etymology nor the meaning of *nîtu*. It may be a feminine word from a stem whose 2nd and 3rd radicals are weak (like *lîtu* 50^{18}, *mîtu* 32^{28}), perhaps from the same st. as the verb forms *a-ni-'-i* 15^{31}, *mu-ni-'i* 9^{15}, so that *nîtu* would mean destruction (?), destructive warfare (?). — 14. When slander . . . arose, he hastened from Elam, etc. — 22. *da'âtu* bribe. Cf. Khors. 39:

twenty two fortresses *kî da'tûti iddinšu* as a bribe (abstr.) he gave him.

15, 7. *gibšûsun* = *gibšûtšun* their mass = they united. — 9. To Š. the Chaldean, king of B., they came together and their masses were arranged. *innindû*, IV 1 st. אמר$_4$, is pl. because *puḫru* is a collective noun. — 10. Like the advance of numerous locusts over the face of the land. — 12. *imbari* heavy wind, storm; *i. ša dunni íriyâti* a wind storm of powerful heavy clouds (?). *dunni* cstr. before *íriyâti*, or the latter an adj. agreeing with the former. With the use of *dunni* for clouds we might compare the use of Heb. שַׁחַק. — 13. The face of the broad heavens was covered with the dust from their feet, etc. — 14. *šitkunu*, perm. I 2. The subj. is *ša*; translate: which was situated on the bank of the Tigris. Cf. Sargon St. 29: *ša . . . šitkunat šubatsun* whose abode was situated. — 15. They had taken position in battle array (immediately) in front of me. *maški* skin, then self, analogous to Heb. גֶּרֶם, עֶצֶם. — 20. *labbiš*, etc.; cf. Khors. 40: *ina uggat libbiya ummânât Aššur gabšâti adkîma lab-biš an-na-dir-ma ana kašâd mâtâti šatina aštakan paniya*. — 21. *si-ri-ya-am hu-li-ya-am*. The meaning of both words is clear from the connection and that of *si-ri-ya-am* from the Heb. סִרְיוֹן. The *ya* seems to be in each case the pronom. suff. The *am* might be an id., but its well-known value *rîmu* wild ox seems well nigh impossible here. The most plausible explanation seems to me to be that *m* (shortened from *ma*) is the mimmation. We meet both forms *ma* and *m* after nouns, as *Aššur-ma* 5^{5}, *tâmtim* 42^{19}, and *ma* is not rare after verbal pronom. suffixes, as *ušabrišuma Aššur* 22^{11} Aššur showed to him. In such petrified forms as *šattišam* 10^{27} we have the mimmation attached to a nominal suffix, and the words under examination seem to be of the same class. If this conjecture be correct, the words for coat of mail and helmet would be *siru* and *ḫulu* respectively. — 25. *ḳuttaḫu* or *tartaḫu*; meaning uncertain, most probably spear, javelin. — 26. *rittû'a* = *ina rittîya*. — 28. *ana šiddi ù putí* "on flank and front" (Haupt). — 32. *ušakir*; form II 1 defectively written from *šakâru* or III 1 from a st. initial weak, like *ušakil* I fed, *ušašib* I caused to dwell. Possibly we should read *ušaḳir*, III 1 from st. וקר. — 33. *tamziziš*. The syllable *tam* may also be read *par*, *bár*, etc. — 34. *nagiru* guide, leader. Cf. Zeitschr. f. Aegypt. Spr. 1878 p. 59.

16, 2. *tukultašu rabû* his chief support, reliance. — *ša paṭru*, etc., whose golden girdle-daggers were put in place. — 3. *aṣpi* seems to be a pl. adj. belonging to *šimirî*. It may come from אצף$_4$ meaning to be double, to join, though we should expect *iṣpu* instead of *aṣpu* on account of the guttural. — 4. *ša*, etc., which were placed in bonds. — 8. *munnî* utensils, weapons, pl. of *munnu*, probably for *mu*$ℵ_1$*nu*, like *puḫru*, Aram. מָאן. Translate: their banners and weapons I caused to flow over the broad land. — 9. *lâ asmûti*. The sibilant may be *s*, *z* or *ṣ*. Render: my horses swam without *asmûti* (?), etc. *asmûti* is most probably an abstract noun. — 10. *Nâriš* like the river god, adv. from a proper name. — 10–12. *ša . . . mašaruš* = *ina mašari ša narkabat* on the *m*. of the chariot clave (lit. were poured out) blood and filth. The var. *manšaru* 25²² indicates that the st. is *našâru*. — 14. *simânî*, etc., as trophies I cut off their hands. — 23. *ša . . . râkibušin* whose riders; the suff. here, in *bílušina* and in *ramânuššin* refers to *narkabâti*. — 25. As far as two *kasbu* I commanded to kill them. A *kasbu* was as measure of time two hours and also as measure of distance the space travelled in two hours. — 31. *kî ša*, etc., just like a young dove captured, cf. 17²¹.

17, 1. *munnaribšunu* their fugitives, those of them who were concealing themselves. The st. may be ארב$_1$, whence Heb. אוֹרֵב ambush. In form *m*. is part. IV 1, like *munnabtu* a fugitive. — 3. In the same year with the digging, etc. — 6. *aštakan sidirta* I placed the battle array = I fought. — 15. *nišâ;* mistake (?) for *niṣâ*, cf. 16³³. — *mâtuššun* § **20**. — 16. *man-di-ma*. It is not clear whether these signs are to be taken as syllables or as ids. But the connection seems to demand a meaning like: it was reported (i.e. in Elam). The report follows: S. king of A. has mightily prevailed and they will return to Elam. — 27. *bílti* is perhaps a scribal error for *bílši* 12¹¹. *napalḳati* may be divided *napal ḳati*. With these obscure terms we must compare I R 24, 53: *ina bíl-ší na-pi-li ṣa-a-bi-ti ala aktašad* and I R 26, 111: *ina bíl-ši iṣu ṣa-pi-tí ù ni-pi-ší ala akšud*.

18, 1. They turned into their own hands = they took for themselves. — 5. *ana tarṣi* in the time of. — 12. *buṣur*, cstr. of *buṣru* interior, secret place. Cf. III R 4, 57: she bore me *ina buṣri* in secret; Khors. 41: He fled from his city and dwelt *ina buṣrât šadî marṣi* in the secret places of the steep mountain. — 15. *muššî*, inf. II 1. Cf. 4²⁷⁻³⁰. — 16. *agdamar* = *agtamar*, a change similar to that of *t* to *ṭ* after *ḳ*. — *usallis* completely (?), or like an *usallu*. — 17. *kâšid* agrees with Esarhaddon, whose name occurs in an earlier line. — 27. *upaḫirma* I collected also. The obj. follows.

19, 13. In order to show the peoples the might of Aššur my lord, I bound the heads of S. and A. about the necks of their chiefs, and with male and female musicians I marched through the streets of

Nineveh. Cf. 28[20]. — 17. *binûtu.* The usual form in such a connection would be *binût.* — 18. *ša . . . šumšu* whose name A., etc. named for royalty. — 26. *ina ípiš pî muttalli* in executing the exalted command.

20, 3. for my confirmation as prince regent and afterwards as king over Assyria. — 6. *parunakki* and *markas šarrûti* are in appos. to *bît ridûti.* — 7. *ša . . . ina líbbišu* wherein. — 9. *'aldu* he was born, perm. I 1, st. ילד. Cf. Khors. 156, where the same form of the word is used of the gods. — 10. *gimir*, etc., begat all the princes, enlarged the family. — 13. *dup-šarrûti* tablet of writing, tablet-writing, science. — *ummâni* means both people and art. — 14. *aḫzi* contents. Initial vowel may be *a*, *i*, or *u*. — 15–20. By the command of the great gods whose name I mentioned, whose majesty I meditate on, etc., I am the manly, the bold, etc. — 25. Five ells the grain grew in its stalk (?), the length of the ear (was) five sixths of an ell, with abundant grass (?) and thriving (?) corn the fields (?) flourished (?) continually, the *ṣippat*-reeds thrived, there was fruit, the cattle prospered in bearing, during my reign there was plenty, excess, in my years abundance was spread abroad.

21, 7. *ittûti* (?) concubinage. The meaning of the sign rendered here by *ittu* is established, and the sign frequently has the value *ittu*, as V R 50, 63. 65, but it is uncertain how the word for concubine was pronounced. — 10. *tirḫati ma-'a-as-si* means apparently the same as *nudunnî ma'di* a large dowry; cf. l. 14, 17, 23. *ma-'a-as-si* may stand for *ma'âsi* from a st. מאס. *tirhati* has the form of a feminine noun. — 14. *nudunnî*, gen. of *nudunnû*, also written *nudunû.* — 25. After I had subdued the land of Y., etc.

22, 8. *ulziz*, st. *nazâzu* § **8.** 2 *a.* — 11. *ušabrišuma; ma* not connective; subj. is *Aššur.* — 13. *ṣabat* § **24.** 7. — 14. *ûmu* = *ina ûmi ša* on the day when. — 15. *išpuru* is in the rel. sentence. — *šutta* is obj. of *ušannâ.* — 17. From the very day when. — 19. *attû* st. אנת (?). — 22. *ṣiṣṣi* seems to be a general term for bond; cf. also V R 3, 59; Khors. 112. — 25. *ša'âl šulmí* to ask after the peace = to salute. — 26. *ušaršâ* he granted. The indirect obj. is *rakbu*, and the direct *baṭiltu* cessation, leisure. The sense is, he did not send his messenger. — *aššu ša* because.

23, 1. *lînadî* var. *lînnadî* = *lî* + *innadî* IV 1. — *lîššûni*, st. *našû.* — *nírpaddu.* The pronunciation is uncertain but the meaning bones, skeleton, is assured; cf. 26[31]; V R 3, 64. According to V R 6, 70–74 Assurbanipal destroys the graves of the kings of Elam and carries the skeletons to Assyria. — 2. *išlim* it was accomplished, it happened. — 6. *ipšit limuttim* = (the account of) the evil work, obj. of *išpura.* —

7. *ina pan* in the face of = on the person of (?). — 8. *ušabrikû* III 1. The stem may have initial *b* or *p*, final *k* or *ḳ*. From *barâḳu* we should have the meaning: they caused to lighten. Perhaps we should read *ušapriḳû* and compare Heb. פָּרַק to break, to act violently. — 10. My father thou didst curse. — 11. *kurbannîma* = *kurub-anni-ma* §§ **9.** 2; **18.** — 11. *lâšuṭa abšânka* let me bear thy yoke, cf. 11^{14} 27^{22}. *lâšuṭa* = *lû* or *lî* + *ašuṭa* st. שׁוט. The contraction to *lâ* is unusual. Cf. *lûllik* 52^{24} = *lû* + *allik*. — 13. This passage has a good translation in Hebraica for Jan., 1886. — 18. *Tin-tir*. These two signs, meaning life S^b 153 and forest V R 26, 11, form a double id. for Babylon. — 19. *mušíšib* one who caused to be inhabited. Esarhaddon is so called because he rebuilt Babylon I R 50 after its destruction by his predecessor 18^{9-16}. — 25. *irumma* § **8.** 2 *c*. — 27. *kitinnûtu* law (?) st. כון, formative *t*. Cf. Sargon Cyl. 5: *ḳâṣir kitinnûtu Aššur baṭiltu*. The clause beginning with *aššu* may close the sentence or may begin the new sentence. Translate: in order that the strong might not do injury to the weak. Cf. Sargon Cyl. 50: *ana naṣâr kitti ù mîšari šutíšur lâ li'î lâ ḫabâl înšî* to preserve justice and right, to lead the powerless, not to injure the weak. — 31. like *šiṭir burumu* I made (it) bright. The comparison of the adornments in the shrines with the brilliancy of the heavenly bodies is very common, as 37^3; I R 15, 93. 100; 54 col. III 12–14. In 36^{15} *šaššâniš* is used, which may mean like marble or like suns (for *šamšâniš* (?), cf. *šaššiš* I R 52 No. 3 col. I 29). We hence look for some name for the heavens or stars in *šiṭir burumu* = the variegated writing (?), figures (?). Delitzsch Lesest.[3] glossary renders *šiṭru* by Zodiac. — *Ì-ku-a* might be taken as obj. of *unammir*, though it more probably goes with what follows. Render: I restored the damages of *Ìkua* and of all the shrines.

24, 1. Over all the cities I cast my protection (?). Cf. Sargon Cyl. 6: *ša íli Ḫarrana ṣalûlašu itruṣu*. — 3. *Ì-babbarra . . . ašrâtišu* = *ašrât Ì*. — 6. *ullî* II 1 §§ **27**; **32**. — *ana šatti*; cf. II R 66, 17: *ana šat-ti* (var. *ša-at-ti*) *Bílit*. This citation confirms the correctness of the reading *šat-ti* in our passage. In the brackets the name of the Sun-god is to be supplied. — 7. *dânu rabû* one of the most frequent titles of Šamaš, whose name has here been lost. It is rare that an adj. comes immediately after a noun in the cstr. Perhaps the scribe by mistake omitted *ša* before *ilâni*. — 9. *balâṭ*, *šíbî*, *ṭûb* and *ḫud* are all objects of *lîšîm* l. 11. — 11. *lîšîm šîmati* may he appoint as my portion, fate. — 12. May his days be long, may he be satisfied with joys. — 16. *kisalla*. For this reading of the id. cf. S^a 5. col. IV 15; II R 66, 16. 17: *kisal* (var. *ki-sal*) *bît Ištar . . . urabbî*. Cf. also III R 2, 56; I R 44, 82. From these passages the *k.* is evidently some part or appurtenance of a temple or palace. It has been variously rendered, floor, platform, altar. The sign corresponding to the word *k.* occurs in the passages transliterated in this book five times, four times with *pašâšu* and one time 36^{19} as an id. for oil *šamnu*. With *pašâšu* it frequently occurs elsewhere in the same connection as here, in directions to future princes who should find inscribed documents during temple and palace restorations, as Lay. 64, 64; I R 42, 69; 47, 68 (*pušuš* impv.). Instead of the sign under examination we find in similar connection with *pašâšu* in I R 16, 48. 57 the sign *ni*, which is an id. for *šamnu* oil, e.g. IV R 26, 47. 48. The Assyrian translation of this last passage is: with oil (*šaman*) of the *kurkî* bird . . . anoint (*pušuš*) for seven times the body of that man. A comparison of all these passages makes it probable that one should read this id. as *šamnu* whenever it occurs with *pašâšu* and that we should always render *šamnu pašâšu* to anoint with oil. — 18. *ša šumí šaṭru* whoever my name (which is) written. — 22. *lîḫalliḳ* = *lî* + *uḫalliḳ*. — 25. *mundaḫṣî* § **8**. 2 *b*, *c*. — 29. *iškunû napištu* they accomplished (their) life = they perished.

25, 10. *miriḫtu*, obj. of *iḳbû*, seems to be from the same st. as *íriḫu* l. 17. — 11. *aḫûrû*; unknown to me except here. It may be a prep. or the subj. of *ikkisu*. If the st. be אחר, the *aḫûrû* might be the rear, the stragglers, the camp-followers. The sense seems to be as follows: Tam., . . . who concerning the decapitation of T. had spoken in blame (?) (which the *aḫûrû* of my armies had cut off) saying: They cut off the head of T. . . ., within his country in the midst of his troops; a second time said: And U. surely kissed the ground, etc. For the understanding of this obscure passage, it must be observed that Ummanigaš and Tammaritu were brothers, sons of a former king of Elam, and that they fled before Tiumman to Assyria. On the subjection of Elam and decapitation of Tí., Assurbanipal appointed Um. as king of the land and made Tam. ruler over another district V R 3, 36–49. Um. was induced, however, by Assurbanipal's brother, who was governor at Babylon 23^{28}, to join in a general insurrection against Assyria 24^{29}; V R 3, 97–105. Tam. rebelled against his brother Um., killed him, succeeded to the throne of Elam $25^{1.2}$ and then likewise joined in the great coalition against Assurbanipal 25^{4}. His subject, Indabigaš, defeated him in battle 25^{8}, whereupon he fled again with all his family to Nineveh $25^{16\text{-}20}$. — 16. *ilzinu* st. *šazânu* (?). — 19. *mirânuššun* = *ina mirânišun* in their fear (?). *mirânu* from ירא would be made like *mišaru*

40[11] righteousness from ישר, with addition of the formative termination *ân*. Cf. V R 5, 112: Ummanaldas king of Elam *mi-ra-nu-uš-šu innabitma iṣbata šadû*. In Lay. 63, 14 the *mirânu* is some kind of an animal: *ša kima mi-ra-a-ni ṣaḫri kirib ikalliya irbû*, but this must be a different word. Perhaps *m.* should be construed in our passage with *innabtunimma* as in V R 5, 112, quoted above, the *ma* being taken here not as a connective, *ina* . . . *ibšilûni* being then regarded as parenthetical, describing the state of the fugitives' mind. —— 23. *aššu*, etc., to espouse his cause (lit. to do his judgment), to come to his aid, etc. —— 25. *izizû* st. *nazâzu*, subj. is Tam., his brothers, etc. —— 27. *lâ kâṣir* (or *ḳâṣir*) *ikkimu;* either *lâ kâṣir* is one title and *ikkimu* another, or *ik.* is obj. of *kâṣir*. If the latter, the expression may mean not binding the captive, st. *íkímu* to seize.

26, 2. *iksusû kurussu*. *ik(g, ḳ)susû*, 3rd pers. pl. of the second impf. *kurussu*, occurs V R 32, 56. 57 as part of a canal (*narṭabi*) and of a door (*dalti*). —— 8. The people whom I had entrusted to Š. . . ., (who) committed these evil deeds, who feared death (their lives being precious in their sight) and (who) . . . did not fall into the fire, who before the dagger . . . fled (and) took refuge, the net . . . cast them down. —— 10. *tíkiru* or *tíḳiru* st. וקר (?), whose lives were precious in their sight (?). —— 16. *imnû ḳâtû'a* they delivered into my hand; subj. seems to be the gods mentioned in l. 2–5. *ša-ša-da-di* and *ša-ṣil-li* are two kinds of vehicles or chariots, but the reading of the signs is uncertain. With this passage cf. I R 8 No. 1, where a similar list of objects of booty taken from Šamaššumukin is given. —— 18. *šillatu*, cf. Heb. שָׁלָל. —— 22. Cf. 18[2-16].

27, 3. We have here two terms from the Assyrian cultus, names of two acts of devotion or two kinds of hymn or of prayer. The two occur together in V R 22, 42–49 along with words for sighing, weeping, wailing, etc. The id. which I have rendered by *šigû* is composed of the sign for water + the sign for eye. The signs following *šigû* are a part of the description of the *šigû;* cf. Zimmern Busspsalmen p. 1. —— 10. for the separation of themselves (= for their independence from my yoke (?)). —— 14. *bí-gid-da*, id. for some official. Reading of the name unknown, perhaps *piḫâtu* satrap. Delitzsch suggests *nasîku* prince Lesest.[3] p. 8. —— 23. Like Elam, he heard of the seditious device of Akkad. —— 26. *mutninnu*, frequent title applied by the kings to themselves, meaning unknown. Cf. Lay. 63, 2: I R 59 col. I 18. —— 30. *ušamkir* § **8**. 2 *d*.

28, 1. *ša* . . . *ri'ûsina ípiši* = the exercise of whose dominion, obj. of *iddinûni*. *ri'ûsina* = *ri'ût-šina* § **8**. 2 *a*, *b*. —— 4. *ummânâti*. This word is without government as the sentence stands. The scribe perhaps intended to say the soldiers killed, but he changed his construction and wrote *aduk* l. 9. — 13. *zirtarâtí* might also be read *kultarâtí*, and is written with the other sign *kul* in Botta *Monument de Ninive* IV 89, 10. The verbs in l. 13 are perhaps impersonal, they kindled a fire, etc., i.e., the Assyrian troops. — 19. *šar ilâni* cf. 31^{8}. — *ṭínšu ušanni* he (Aššur) changed his (Uâti's) *ṭímu*. The word *ṭímu* st. טעם means counsel, wisdom, understanding $14^{4,21}$, and also information, news. The meaning here seems to be that the deity defeated the counsel, design of U. So also in the account of the war between Marduk and the dragon: *Ti-amat annita ina šímiša . . . ušanni ṭínša* Ti'amat when she heard this . . . changed her plan, Delitzsch Lesest.[3] 98, 4. 5. It is not impossible that the verb *šanû* in our passage is to be taken in the same sense as in 42^{12}. Cf. also Khors. 152: Mita who had not submitted to the kings, my predecessors, and *lâ ušannû ṭínšu* had not reported news of himself. The expression in our passage may mean that Aššur made known U.'s design. — *illika* he came, perhaps as a captive. — 20. *ana kullum*, etc., in order to manifest the majesty of A., etc., cf. 19^{13}. — 21. *annu* st. אנן, made like *dannu*. — 22. *a-si* is most likely an id. for some kind of beast. I R 45, 4. 5 *b* names *asi* along with dogs and *šaḫî* (another kind of beast). — *ušanṣiršu* I caused to keep him, had him kept. — 23. *nirib mašnakti adnâti* entrance to *m. a.*, name of one of the gates of Nineveh, cf. 33^{21}. The reading *maš* is assured by a fragment of a cylinder in the Wolfe Expedition collection.

29, 3. *ša Ab. . . . riṣišu* of Ab. his helpers = the troops of Ab. The singular suff. is used with *riṣî* because Abiyati was the chief of the two generals. — 24. Cf. 28^{15}. Translate: into whose presence, etc. — 25. *ma* not connective. — 26. *ša* refers to Natnu.

30, 7. *ítillû* they ascended, 2nd impf. I 2, st. *ílû*. — *iḫtallubu* = *iḫtalubu*, st. *ḫalâbu*, they were covered (by the forests). — 18. *attumuš* I set out = *a*א*tumuš* (?). — 19. *bît-dûri* fortress. It was made of some kind of stone represented by the sign *šit*. — 21. *iḫpû* or *iḫbu*. The meaning depends on whether *šunu* refers to the Assyrians or to the Arabians. If to the former, then *iḫpu* must mean they drew, provided themselves with; if to the latter, then it must mean that the Assyrians destroyed the cisterns, so that the Arabians might have no water left, cf. 31^{21-27}. — 24. *ašar* = *ašru ša*. — 33. *'a-lu*, an id. or possibly a tribal name.

31, 3. *bílta*. The id. so rendered has according to V R 39, 64 also the value *aḫattu* = *aḫâtu* sister. That meaning would suit very well here. —— 7. *kakkab ḳašti* star of the bow, Sagittarius, name for the goddess of war or of the planet which represented this goddess. —— 9. *mušitu.* The night was chosen for the march, because of the mid-summer heat. —— 12. *akšud* I reached, encountered. —— 26. *akšu.* If the reading be correct, the form is like *amnû, aḳmû,* and seems to mean I cut off. —— *ušakir* or *ušaḳir* I made costly, caused to be scarce (?), st. יקר, like *ušašib* from ושב. —— 29. *mí paršu,* the water in the entrails, cf. Heb. פֶּרֶשׁ.

32, 2. *umdallû* = *umtallû* they filled; subj. is the people and animals. —— 3. *ana,* etc., may be connected with what follows rather than with what precedes. —— 5. *ana,* etc., by half shekels. The id. *ṭu,* = *šiḳlu,* is repeated to express the distributive idea. —— *išammu* = *išayamu* they appointed, priced; impersonal use of the verb. —— 6. *bâb maḫîri* gate of sale, market-place. —— The difficult lines 6–8 record the sale of camels and slaves. The same account is given from two other inscriptions in Smith Asb. 275 and 286ᶜ. Both of these passages omit *-šu ša u-kin* and the second has before *ḫabî* (written *ḫa-bi-í*) the sign for vessel, pot *karpatu.* We seem thus to have here three classes of purchasers, the *ṣutmu, x* and the gardener, who pay for camels and men in different ways, one with a *nidnu,* one with a *ḫapu* and the gardener with his *kîšu.* For the id. for gardener or forester, lit. servant of the forest, cf. also III R 48, 49 *b*; IV R 48, 20 *b*. *ša ukin* = as I appointed. —— 15. *bitti* = *bîti* (?) house. With one perpendicular wedge less the word would be *kitti* righteousness, *ina kitti* righteously. In favor of *bit-ti* is 33¹⁰. —— *išimûšunûti* they put upon them (their fate). The subj. is the gods following. —— 18. *bakru,* perhaps the young camel, Arab. *bukr.* —— *gû-ṣur* is a double id., *gû* being used as det. = *alpu* ox Sᵇ 96, while *ṣur* is id. for *pûru* Sᵇ 157; V R 51, 53 *b*, according to Delitzsch a young buffalo, Lesest.[3] 29. —— *lu-num* is likewise a double id., *lu* representing *kirru* lamb II R 6, 1, while *lu* + *num* also = *kirru* II R 6, 3; cf. II R 44, 12, *lu* being used as determ. The meaning seems to be that these young animals sucked (*íniḳû*) their dams (*mušíniḳâtí*) more than seven times without finding milk enough to satisfy themselves. So Haupt. This is intended to give a picture of the extremity in which the Arabians found themselves, an extremity so great that the starving animals gave no milk. If this be the correct view of the passage, *karaši* l. 20 must be taken as meaning stomach, as in Delitzsch Lesest.[3] 98, 16, Heb. כָּרֵשׂ, Arab. *kirš.* The young animals could not satisfy their stomachs with milk. —— 23. Wherefore have the Arabians received such a hard fate? So the fugitives ask one another. With *umma* the response is introduced, *aššu* because, etc. Cf. Jer. 22, 8. 9. — 28. *mîtu* = *mâ'tu;* cf. the masc. form *mâ'* Sargon Cyl. 30. — *kadirti ilâti, k.* of the goddesses. A similar title is *garitti* (= *ḳaridti*) *ilâti* warrior of the goddesses, applied to Ištar V R 33, col. I 9; cf. 33[3]. Is *dir* in our passage not a scribal error for the similar sign *rid, rit?* — 29. *šitluṭat manzazu* she rules enthroned, subj. is *ša; šitluṭat* perm. I 2, *manzazu* seat, adverbial acc. Cf. in the account of creation *manzaz Bíl u Ìa ukîn ittišu* Delitzsch Lesest.[3] 94, 8. — 31. (who) is clothed in fire and raised aloft in brilliance. — 32. *anuntu kuṣṣur* who destroys (?) opposition. *kuṣṣur* or *ḳuṣṣur* perm. II 1 from *ḳaṣâru* to collect, bind, then to remove, destroy, a usage like Heb. אָסַף to collect, and also to take away. — 33. *ḳuttaẖu*, cf. on 15[25].

33, 9. *išmû.* Subj. is *ummânâti* and obj. is *tibût.* — 10. *bîti*, cf. 32[15]. After *bîti* the relative *ša* is to be understood. — 16. *ša . . . amdaẖẖaru* when I prayed. A variant omits *ina kibit* l. 17. With this omission Aššur and Bílit are the direct obj. of *amdaẖẖaru.* — 18. The obscure lines 18, 19 seem to record the mutilation of Uâti's body. The means used is a *ẖutnû*, which is described by the adj. or part. *mašíri; ṣibit ḳâtíya* the holding of my hands = held by my hands = with my own hands. The verb is *apluš*, the obj. being the two words before it. The sign rendered *šíra* is a common id. for flesh, Heb. שְׁאֵר. *míṣu* seems to be some part of the body. The sign before *míṣi* may be in the cstr. relation, the flesh of his *míṣu*, or it may be a det. and *míṣi* may be pl. — 19. *ina laẖ*, etc., into the *laẖ* of his eye I cast *ṣirritu*, apparently putting out of the eyes; *laẖ íni* eye-ball (?). Instead of *laẖ ínišu* we might read *laẖšišu.* — 22. *ana*, etc., to manifest the majesty of A., etc. — 28. *inamdinû* § **8**. 2 *c.* — 29. Among the unsubmissive inhabitants (of Ušû) *šibṭu aškun* I made a slaughter. — 32. I caused (the corpses) to encircle the whole city.

34, 1. *ikîša* st. קיש. — 4. Before *itti* supply *ša*, which is subj. of *izizu* and *ípušu.* — 6. *aṣbat.* This capture is recorded 31[14-16]. — 8–16. The capture of Ummanaldas took place at an earlier time. — 16. Tam., Pa'aí and Um. here and U. l. 19 are objects of *ušaṣbit* l. 24. After offering sacrifices 21, and performing the ordinances 23, Assurbanipal harnesses these captive kings to his triumphal car 24, is drawn by them to the temple door 25, there prostrates himself 25, exalts the divinity and magnifies the might of the gods 26–29, who had subdued the unsubmissive to his yoke 30, and had established him in authority and power above his enemies 31.

35. This inscription gives accounts of three restorations of temples, as follows: 1) temple of Sin **35–37**, 23; 2) temple of Šamaš **37**, 24–**38**,

26; 3) temple of Anunit **38**, 27–**39**, 13. In detail the contents are: royal titles 1–6, destruction of temple of Sin 7–13, direction in a vision to rebuild it 14–24, capture of Astyages 25–29, collection of workmen 30–**36**, 10, account of the restoration 11–30, return of the gods 31–**37**, 3, prayer to Sin and other gods 4–19, discovery of a record of Assurbanipal 20–23; restoration of temple of Šamaš, including the discovery of a very ancient document 24–**38**, 16, prayer to Šamaš 17–26; restoration of temple of Anunit 27–**39**, 5, re-establishment of the sacrifices 6–9, prayer to Anunit 10–13; appeal to royal successors 16–22. A good translation and commentary are given by Johannes Latrille in ZKF. II 231–262, 335–359, III 25–38. —— 9. *izuz* st. middle ו, like *aduk* 11[34]. The word *zâzu* means to be in commotion, to be enraged. Latrille makes the st. initial guttural. The form would be the same. —— 10. *Ṣab-manda*. One may also read *Ummân-manda* which has the same meaning, the nation or troops of the Medes. In 40[9] the name occurs written *um-man man-da* without the det. *amílu*. *Ṣab* is cstr. of *ṣabu* warrior, soldier. —— 13. *islimû iršû*. The name of Sin may be omitted by scribal oversight. Or more probably the name of Marduk is omitted, and the sign here for Bíl ought to be Sin. —— 13. *târi* return = forgiveness. —— 18. *iši* impv. I 1, § **26**. —— 21. *saḫir* perm. or part. I 1, the Ṣ. surround it. —— *puggulû* perm. II 1. —— 24. *ul ibašši* he shall be no more. —— 25. They (Marduk and Sin (?), or impersonally, the people, courtiers) caused him (= the Median people) to advance (= make an expedition) and Cyrus, king of Anzan, his small (= unimportant) servant, etc. This makes Cyrus subject to the Medes, which seems to me more likely than to suppose *arad-su* a scribal mistake for *arad-sunu* and understand that Cyrus was a worshipper of Marduk and Sin. —— 27. *iṣûtu*, masc. pl. of *iṣu*. The meaning small, few is assured by V R 11, 50, where the id. for small is read *i-ṣu*. Delitzsch thinks that חַיִץ wall is from the same st. as *iṣu*, Baer's *Liber Ezechielis* xi. —— 28. *Ištumígu* = Astyages. —— *kamûtsu* = him bound.

36, 1. *akkud*. Cf. 37[28]. The inf. *nakâdu* occurs II R 25, 73; V R 16, 77, part of the sign which it explains being in both cases the id. which represents the idea of lying down. In V R 7, 31 we read: *ikkud libbašu irsâ nakuttu*, Asb. Sm. 293: *Nadnu iplaḫma iršâ nakuttu* and V R 55, 23: *ma'diš aplaḫ nikitti arší*. A comparison of these passages shows that *ikkud*, *ikkud libbu* and *iplaḫ* are expressions of similar import. Latrille believes the st. to be *maḳâtu* to fall, and reads *aḳḳut* for *amḳut* like *attaḫar* for *amtaḫar* § **8**. 2 *c*. —— *nakutti arší* seems to mean about the same as *akkud*. —— 2. *tulluḫu panû'a* my face was *t*., perm. II 1. Latrille reads *dulluḫu* from st. *dalâḫu* to disturb, and this is perhaps to be preferred. With l. 1, 2 cf. Dan. 4, 19; 5, 6. — *ígi;* cf. Arab. *'aga'a* to flee. — *aḫî lâ addâ* I did not lay my side (= myself) down; expression of great activity. So I R 16, 20 *ana ípiši aḫî lâ addû* (rel. sentence). — 5. *rubûti.* Instead of this reading, with pl. in *ûti*, it is better to read *rubî;* cf. 40^{22} *ru-bi-í.* — 11. *nâdi*, gen. of *nâdu* exalted. For this ideographic value of the sign *i* cf. S^{c} 126. *ûmi nâdi*, a high day, is perhaps a festival day; cf. 38^{2} *ûmi magiri.* — 13. *ina pî ílli iḳûtû* by the brilliant command (which) they gave; cf. 19^{26} *ina ípiš pî muttalli.* The signs here are *ka* = *pû* mouth, word, command II R 39, 1, *azag* = *íllu* brilliant S^{b} 110. Latrille combines the signs differently and perhaps better. Comparing V R 51, 44. 45 *b*, where the signs *ka azag ik* are rendered by *a-ši-pu* (or *bu*), he regards these signs in our passage as forming one id., the *u-tu* being phon. compl. He reads *ina ašipûtu* and renders "by the aid of priests." — 19. *amḫaṣ.* The connection seems to demand for this verb the meaning to sprinkle or smear. So also V R 10, 84. Perhaps it is the same st. which we meet in Ps. 68, 24. The verb seems to be the same as the very common verb *maḫâṣu* to strike, smite. — 21. *unakkilu* I constructed skilfully. A final *u* in the sing., even outside of rel. sent., occasionally occurs. — 22. *íššiš* = *ídšiš* st. ארשׁ$_{3}$. — 25. *iris-sina* = *iriš-šina.* — 26. *igarâti.* For the id. *igaru* cf. V R 25, 38; for making the pl. in *âti* cf. I R 15, 99. The two signs mean house + brick, and are the common id. for wall, side, also called *lânu* V R 11, 50. Cf. 1 Kings 6, 22. — 28. *íšmarû* = Heb. חַשְׁמַל (?); cf. Baer's *Liber Ezechielis* p. XII. — 34. *tašriḫti* st. *šarâḫu; niḳâni t.* large sacrificial lambs, or sacrificial lambs in abundance.

37, 1. *ríštûm;* adj. with mimmation, made from the fem. *rištu*, like *maḫrû* former from *maḫru*, st. ראשׁ. *Ì-ḫulḫul ríštûm* = Ì. the former, i.e. as it formerly was. — 3. *ṣît arḫi* the beginning of the month, the new moon. Possibly *arḫi* is here used figuratively for moon. — 4. *ullânuššu* = *ina ullânišu* (?), during his separation (?) i.e. during the period of Sin's anger. — 5. during whose separation (from the city) the city and land were not established (and who) had not returned to his place. *ullânu* is formation in *ân* from *ullû; innamdû* seems to be IV 1 from עָמַד. Latrille renders *ša*, etc., "who since eternity (?) had not taken his abode in city and land, nor turned to his place." He seems to derive *innamdû* from *nadû*, the *m* being taken as "compensation for the sharpening" of the syllable. — 7. *šaptukka* § **20.** — 12. *ittâtû.* In I R 61, 25 a Sin is called *mudammiḳ idâtiya* the one who favors my hands. Hence it appears that the two expressions *dummuḳu ittâtû* and *dummuḳu idâti* have the same meaning.—13. *lîšanṭil* § **8.** 2 *c*, st. *maṭâlu.* The verb might also be read *lîšandil* and be derived from *šadâlu* to be broad, extensive, whence the adj. *šadlu* 11^7 16^9. The form would then be II 1 with dissolution of the doubling.—16. *banîti.* The st. is *banû* to shine; cf. Zimmern's Bab. Busspsalmen 37. *banîti* means brilliant, gracious words, like *damiḳtim* l. 18.—19. *lîṣbat abûtu* may he accept (my) wish, petition.—25. *šarru maḫrî* a former king, final *î* for *û*, or we may read *šar maḫri* king of the former times.—27. *ipuš* I constructed, here = restored.—*ina* in the space of.—*ša bîti*, etc., the walls of that house had decayed.—28. *akkud*, etc.; cf. on 36^1.—29. *adi* while.—31. *labiri*, acc. in *i.*—34. *ša* is omitted after *rabû* as in 24^7.

38, 2. *yâši* may be regarded as introducing a new sentence or as repeating the pronom. suffix for the sake of emphasis.—*tišrîti*, name of the seventh month. The id. is *ku* in Babylonian. A calendar in the collection of the Wolfe expedition leaves no doubt that we are to read *tišrîti.* In that calendar the *ku* corresponds to the seventh month, the other months being indicated by the same ids. as in Delitzsch Lesest.[3] p. 92.—6. *ubanu*, etc., a finger's (width) not projecting, a finger's (width) not being depressed = exactly level.—9. *askuppu* st. *sakâpu.*—17–26. Prayer to Šamaš. O Šamaš, . . . when thou enterest into Ì., . . . when thou inhabitest thy lasting sanctuary, joyfully favor (l. 22) me (l. 20), Nabonidus, etc.—24. *liḳî*, impv. I 1.—31. *bît-su*, masc. suff., though referring to a goddess. Such usage is not rare in the later literature.

39, 9. *nindabî*, cf. Heb. נְדָבָה.—23. The outline of the Cyrus passage is as follows: (Nabonidus) neglects the worship of Marduk, which enrages this deity **39**, 23–28; he gathers the gods into Babylon **40**, 1; Marduk in seeking a righteous prince for a ruler, finds Cyrus, to whom he causes the nations to submit 5–13; march of Cyrus against Babylon 14–18; entry into the city and capture of Nabonidus 18–20; rejoicings in Babylon at the overthrow of N. 21–24; genealogy of Cyrus 27–33; Cyrus restores the worship of Marduk (?) **41**, 3; Marduk in his joy blesses Cyrus 10–13; Western kings bring tribute to Babylon and kiss the feet of Cyrus 14–19; restoration to their homes of the gods which N. had brought to Babylon 20–24; restoration of captive peoples 25; restoration of the gods of Sumer and Akkad 26–29; desire that the gods who had been restored might daily pray for Cyrus before Bíl and Nabû and might speak to Marduk in behalf of Cyrus and Cambyses his son 30–34.—*ušabṭili* § **24**, 5. The subject is evidently Nabonidus, who was more favorable to the worship of the sun and the moon than to the worship of Marduk, cf. pages 35–39. — 24. *palaḫa* the reverence (?) of Marduk. — 25. *ippuš*, first impf., subj. apparently Nabonidus. — 26. *abšâni*. The usual meaning yoke, as 11^{14}, does not seem to suit here. *tabšûtu* is perhaps from the same st. — *uḫallik*, subj. still Nabonidus (?). — *kullatsin* all of them. The antecedent of the suffix is lost. It seems to have been people or countries. — 27. *ana* at their lamentation. — *bîl ilâni* = Marduk.

40, 1. in anger that he had brought (them) into Šuanna. This was a part of Babylon. — 4. *imû* they spoke (?), st. אמה; or perhaps the st. is עמה and the meaning they resembled. This verb עמה to resemble and to cause to resemble is discussed by Zimmern Busspsalmen, p. 69, and takes after it regularly an adverb in *iš* or the prep. *kîma*. — *irtaši târa* he granted return. — 5. *iḫîṭ ibrî* cf. 39^{2}. The *šu* after *ibrî* seems to me doubtful. If certainly in the original, it refers most likely to Cyrus by anticipation. — 6. *malki išaru*, a title of Cyrus; cf. Isa. 41, 2. The translation of the Isaiah passage is doubtful. — *bibîl libbi* wish of the heart = one who corresponds to the wish of another, one who is after another's own heart. — *ša*, etc., whose hand he holds. *ittamaḫ* might be in form first impf. of I 2 or IV 1. Cf. Isa. 45, 1. — 7. *ittabi nibîtsu*, cf. Isa. 45, 3. 4. — 8. *ana*, etc., cf. Isa. 41, 2. — *izzakra* = *iztakira* he named, appointed. Instead of *ḳat-su* perhaps we should read *šú-[um-šu]*, cf. 19^{19}. The only sign which is distinct is the first one and that has both values *ḳat* and *šú*. — 9. *ummân manda*, best to be taken as a proper name or as a title of the Medes, cf. 35^{10} and note. — *ukanniša*, subj. is Marduk; suff. in *šîpišu* refers to Cyrus, cf. Isa. 45, 1. — 11. *ištîni'î* he looked after, provided for. On suff. cf. § **9**. 2. — 12. *tarû*. This word seems to be a part. of a st. with final radical weak and to be a title of Marduk. — *nišî-šu*. The suff. may refer to M. or to Cyrus. — *šá-nin-šu*. The sign read *šá* may be resolved into *šú* + *ut* (*uṭ*, *ud*) and it is possible that we should read *ipšîti-šú ut*(*uṭ-ud*)-*nin-šu*, but the connection is obscure to me. — 13. The subj. of *ippalis* is Marduk; *išara* belongs perhaps to *ḳâta* as well as to *lîbba*. — 17. *utaddû* they know (impers.), st. II 2 from *idû*. — *ṣandû*, perm. I 1, their weapons were arranged. — *išaṭṭiḫâ*, cf. also 41^{4}, meaning uncertain, to march (?), to spread out (?). — 18. Subj. of *ušîriba* is Marduk. — 20. N. who did not reverence him (= Marduk) he delivered into his hand (i.e. hand of Cyrus). — 22. *šapalšu* under him, i.e. under Cyrus. — 23. *immiru* st. *namâru*; for a similar figure cf. Ps. 34, 6. — 24–26. This sentence is an ascription of praise to Marduk, who is the *bîlu*, lord. After *tukulti* we expect *šu* not *ša*, who by his aid caused the dead to live, (who) helps (?) all (?) in difficulty and fear (?), who blesses him greatly and makes his name powerful (i.e. the name of Cyrus).

41, 3. I looked after his worship (?), i.e. the worship of Marduk. The narration is made in the first person after 40^{34}.——15. *ša kâliš kibrâta* = *ša kâli ša kibrâta.*——20. *ištu* from; the correlative is *adi* l. 21. ——22. *ša . . . šubatsun* is a parenthetical sentence.——23. *abnama* seems to mean olden time.——25. The restoration of the Jews (Ezra 1) was one act in a general policy of Cyrus.——27. Cf. 40^{1}.——29. May all of the gods whom I caused to enter into their cities, etc.——31. *ša*, etc., in behalf of long life for me.——33. *ša* either introduces the oratio recta here or is anticipative of a suffix to a noun which is lost. The sentence does not stop at *aplušu*, but what follows in the next line is too mutilated to be read. A few signs and words are preserved at the end of ten other lines, but there is too little to be of value. For the sake of completeness these signs may here be added. L. 36 (V R 35): *mâtâti* (?) *ka-li-ši-na šú-ub-ti ni-iḫ-tim ú-ší-ši-ib;* l. 37: *us* (?)*-tur iṣṣurî$_{pl}$ ù tu-ta-ri$_{pl}$;* l. 38: *-na-šu du-un-nu-nim aš-tí-'-í-ma;* l. 39: *ù ši-pi-ir-šú;* l. 40: *-un Šu-an-na ki;* l. 41: *-in* (?); l. 42: *-na;* l. 43: *-ri-ì* (?); l. 44: *-tim;* l. 45: *ma* (?)*-a-tim.* L. 37 in this addition contains perhaps a reference to sacrifices; cf. 10^{10} and with *tutarî* Heb. תור turtle-dove.

42, 1. *Maḫrî* first, gen. §§ **16**. 3; **17**, st. *maḫâru* to be in front of. The usual place of the ordinal numeral is before its noun in Assyrian. When, however, *maḫrû* is a simple adj., meaning the former, it follows its noun, as 6^{12} 14^{25}.——*girriya* my expedition, gen. (§ **16**. 3) + pronom. suffix *ya* § **9**. 2, st. *garâru* to run; in gender both m. and f.——2. *lû*, particle of asseveration, § **18**.——*allik* I went = *a*ח*lik* § **27**, 2nd impf. § **22**. 1.——*šar*, cstr. of *šarru* king, § **16**. 4, Heb. שַׂר.——3. *ša . . . abiktašu* whose defeat, § **11**.——*bânû'a* my begetter, part. I 1 (§ **21**) of *banû*, = *bâni'u* §§ **7**. 2; **8**. 1; **32**, + pronom. suffix § **9**. 2.——4. *abiktašu* his overthrow, fem., acc. of *abiktu* § **16**. 1, 3, + pron. suf. § **9**. 2, st. *abâku* to turn, cf. Heb. הָפַךְ.——*iškunu* he accomplished, 2nd impf. § **22** from *šakânu*, final *u* in relative sentence § **11**.——*ma*, connective of verbs and sentences § **18**.——*ibílu* he took possession, = *ibyalu* §§ **7**. 2; **28**, relative sentence § **11**.——*mât-su* his country § **8**. 2 *a*, obj. of *ibílu*, = *mâta-šu* § **16**. 4.——*û* and, now § **18**, Heb. וְ.——*šû* § **9**. 1 *a*, Heb. הוּא.—— 5. *danân* might, cstr. of *danânu* § **16**. 4, obj. of *imšî*.——*ilâni* pl. of *ilu* § **16**. 2, Heb. אֵל.——*rabûti* pl. of *rabû* § **16**. 2.——*bílî* pl. of *bílu* § **16**. 2 = *bayalu* § **7**. 2; on *ya* cf. § **9**. 2.——6. *imšî* he forgot, 2nd impf., st. *mašû* § **32**.——*ittakil* he trusted, st. *takâlu*. The form is 1st impf. of

I 2 or IV 1 (§§ **21**; **23**), more probably the latter, cf. *natkil* I R 35 No. 2. 12, impv. IV 1. The verb *takâlu* is construed with the prepositions *ana*, *íli* or with the simple acc. —— *ímuḳ* power, st. אמק₄ to be deep, profound, cstr. of *ímuḳu* § **16**. 3, 4. —— *ramâni-šu* himself, gen. § **16**. 3 of the reflexive pronoun § **14**, + pron. suff.; *ímuḳ ramânišu* = his own power. —— *šarrâni* § **16**. 2. —— 7. *kipâni* governors, pl. of *kípu* § **16**. 2, st. *ḳâpu* = *ḳa*ʾ*âpu* to entrust, appoint, in appos. with *šarrâni*. —— *ša* § **11**, obj. of *upakidu*. —— *kirib*, cstr. of *kirbu* midst § **20**, Heb. קֶרֶב. —— *upakidu* he appointed, = *upakkidu* II 1 § **21**. 3, st. *paḳâdu*, rel. sentence § **11**. —— 8. *ana* in order to § **20**, used like Heb. לְ. —— *dâki*, gen. of the inf. *dâku* to kill, st. דוך § **31**. —— *ḫabâtí*, gen. of the inf. *ḫabâtu*. —— *íkim*, cstr. of the inf. *íkimu* to seize, = *'akâmu* st. אכם₄ § **27**. —— 9. *illika* he came, cf. *allik* l. 2; on final *a* cf. § **24**. 5. —— *ṣiruššun* against them = *íli ṣirišun* § **20**, st. צאר₂. —— *írumma* he entered and = *írubma* §§ **8**. 2 *c*; **27**. —— *ušib* he dwelt § **30**, st. ושב, Heb. יָשַׁב. —— 10. *ali* city, Heb. אֹהֶל, in appos. with Mimpi. —— *miṣir* cstr. of *miṣru* territory § **16**. 4. —— 11. *utirru* he added = *utîru*, the *r* doubled to mark the preceding vowel as long, = *utawwiru*, st. תור to turn (intrans.), II 1 to turn back, restore, add, § **31**. —— *allaku* courier = *'allaku*, § **15**. 2, st. *alâku* to go. —— *ḫanṭu* swift = *ḫamṭu* § **8**. 2 *c*, st. *ḫamâṭu* to quiver, be swift. —— *illikamma* he came and = *illika-ma*; when the connective *ma* or a pronominal suffix beginning with a consonant is appended to a word ending in a vowel the *m* or the consonant of the suffix is very often doubled, cf. § **9**. 2. —— 12. *ušannâ* he related, informed = *ušanni*ʾ*a*, st. שנה to be double, II 1 to make double, repeat. —— *yâti* me § **9**. 1 *b*. —— 13. *ipšîti* deeds, pl. of *ipištu* § **16**. 2, st. *ipíšu* to do, make § **27**. —— *annâti* these § **10**. 1. —— *líbbî* my heart § **9**. 2. —— *igug* it was enraged, st. *agâgu* § **27**. —— *iṣṣaruḫ* it was angry = *inṣaruḫ* IV 1 st. *ṣarâḫu*. —— *kabittî* my liver § **9**. 2, st. *kabâtu*, cf. Heb. כָּבֵד liver. The liver as well as the heart was regarded as a seat of the emotions. —— 14. *ašši* = *anši*א₁ §§ **26**; **29**, Heb. נשׂא. —— *ḳâtî* hands, pl. of *ḳâtu* fem. § **16**. 2. Prof. Delitzsch regards the st. as קות Lesest.[3] p. 145. If this etymology be correct, *ḳâtu* may be part. I 1 = *ḳâ*ʾ*itu* the dispenser. Lifting up the hands is frequently mentioned in connection with praying. —— *uṣallî* I besought, II 1, st. *ṣalû* § **32**, Aram. צְלָא. —— *aššuritu*, fem. adj. agreeing with Ištar, § **16**. 3, may mean of Assyria, or of the city Aššur, or it may mean the one who brings prosperity, cf. Heb. אָשַׁר, אַשְׁרֵי. —— 15. *adkî* I mustered § **32**. —— *ímuḳî ṣirâtí* § **16**. 2. —— 16. *umallû* = *umalli*א₁*û* II 1, st. *malû* to be full; to fill one's hands = to deliver to one, cf. Heb. מִלֵּא אֶת־יָד. —— *ḳâtû-a*, pl. in *û* § **16**. 2, + pron. suff. § **9**. 2. —— 17. *uštíššira* = *ušta*ʾ*šíra*, 2nd impf. III 2 from ישר

to be straight § **30**; on final vowel cf. § **24**. 5.——*ḫarranu*, form in *u* used as acc. § **16**. 3.——18. *mítiḳ*, cstr., formative *m* § **15**. 3, st. א$_4$תק.——*a-an* (= *ân*), determinative after numbers and measures. When there are tens and units, *ân* is placed between them, as here.——*ša*, genitive sign § **11**.——*aḫi* side, form in *i* used as cstr. § **16**. 4; cf. *aḫ* 2^{24}.——*tâmtim* sea, fem., genitive, with mimmation § **16**. 3, st. תא$_2$ם, Heb. תְּהוֹם. The forms *ti'amat*, *tâmdu* § **8**. 2 *b* also occur, pl. *tâmâti*.——19. *ḳabal tâmtim* the midst of the sea, i.e. the islands; *ḳabal*, cstr. of *ḳablu*.——*ardâni*, pl. of *ardu* st. ורד, Heb. ירד.——*dâgil*, cstr., part. I 1 st. *dagâlu* to see, whence Heb. דֶּגֶל a banner. Participles referring to a preceding pl. noun are often used in the sing.——*panî*, gen. of *panû*, Heb. פָּנִים. *dagâlu panâ* = to be subject to, III 1 to make subject to, to commit to a person.——20. *tamarta* present, obj. of *iššûni*; cf. on the formation § **15**. 3, st. כא$_2$ר, II 1 to send.——*iššûnimma* = *inši*א$_1$*ûni-ma* § **25**; cf. on *illikamma* l. 11.——21. *šâtunu* § **10**. 3.——22. *ílippî*, pl. of *ílippu* ship, Aram. אִלְפָא.——*itti*, gen. of *ittu* side, used as prep., Heb. אֵת.——23. *ummânâti*, pl. of *ummânu* people, army, troops, written *um-ma-na-a-ti* 15^{26}. The pl. *ummânî* also occurs; st. א$_2$מן.——*urḫu* road, acc. in *u*, secondary obj. of *ušaṣbit*, Heb. אֹרַח.——*padanu* way, road, region, same government as *urḫu*, written as an. id. 2^{8}; cf. II R 38, 28 c. d.——*ušaṣbit-sunûti*, III 1 from *ṣabâtu* to take, seize, whence צְבָתִים bundles Ruth 2, 16; the meaning to work, as 6^{18}, is secondary; on *sunûti* for *šunûti* cf. §§ **8**. 2 *a*; **9**. 2.——24. *nararûti* help, abstract noun § **15**. 3 *c*, st. *narâru*.——*ḫa-mat* (?), may also be read *ḫa-lat*, *ḫa-nat*, etc., or the two signs may be an id. They occur in II R 39, 4 e. f. in a list of apparent synonyms which includes *ḫatânu* to help (whence חתן father-in-law), *narâru* to help, *rîṣu* a helper, and *âlik tappûti* a helper.——25. *urruḫiš* swiftly § **19**. 1, st. *arâḫu* to be swift, whence II 1 *urriḫa* 25^{5} I caused to hasten.——26. *ardî* I set out, marched = *ardi*' § **32**.

44, 2. *alâk*, cstr. of inf. *alâku* § **27**.——*išmî* = *išma*א$_4$ §§ **8**. 1; **29**.——*ípîš*, cstr. inf. § **27** = א*apâšu* § **8**. 1.——*ḳabli*, *kakkî*, *taḫazi* are genitives after *ípîš*.——3. *idkâ* = *idki*'*a*.——*ṣâbî*, pl. of *ṣâbu*, cf. Heb. צָבָא.——4. *tukulti*, form in *i* instead of the vowelless form for the cstr. § **16**. 4.——5. *alikût*, cstr. pl. of the part. I 1 of *alâku* § **16**. 2.——*idî* hands, sides, gen. after *alikût*, cf. Heb. יָד.——7. *išmâ* = *išma*א$_4$*a* §§ **7**. 2; **24**. 5.——*taḫtî*, formative *t* § **15**. 3 *a*.——*namriri* st. *namâru* to shine § **15**. 2, subj. of *isḫupu*. If the word is pl., as it seems to be, we should read *namrirî*.——8. *maḫḫur*. Zimmern, Busspsalmen, p. 70, suggests the reading *maḫḫutiš*, the sign *ur* having also the value *tiš*. This would give a regular adverbial formation § **19**, though the meaning of *maḫḫu* or *maḫḫutu* is unknown. The var.

ri III R 17, 87 is not in the way of Zimmern's reading, for the text is evidently damaged. In reading *maḫḫur* and translating forward, I have connected the word with the st. *maḫâru* to be in front of. — 9. *iktumû*, second impf. pl. of *katâmu* to cover, overwhelm. The subj. *mílammí* is treated as pl., as is also often the case with the words for fire *išâti*, joy *ḫidâti*, and the metals. — *ša* may have as antecedent *mílammí* or *šarrûti*, or the first personal pronoun understood. In the latter case the construction would be the same as 2^{22} where *ša . . . ultalliṭu* means (me) who ruled. *ša* + the suffixal *inni* in our passage would then mean me whom. — *uṣa'inû*, 3rd pl. of second impf. II 1 of צא₁ן § **28.** — *šupar* (?) might also be read *šupir*, *šu-ut*, etc. It is of frequent occurrence and seems in many places to be a preposition. — 10. *umaššir* II 1 is used both in the sense of leaving, abandoning, as here, and in the sense of releasing 4^4 sending away 60^8. I have not observed any cases of the form I 1. — *šuzub* to cause to remain, to restore, inf. cstr. III 1, st. א₄זב to leave, form *šuškunu* § **25.** — 10. *napištim*, on mimmation cf. § **16.** 3. — *innabit* = *in*א₁*abit* § **8.** 2 *e.* — 12. *ušírib*, form *ušaškin*, st. א₆רב § **27**; *ušíšib*, same form, st. ושב § **30.** — *ina libbi* therein. — 13. *Mimpi*. On the list of cities following cf. Delitzsch's Paradies, p. 314.

46, 1. *annûti* § **10.** 1. — *piḫâti*, pl. of *piḫâtu*, lord of a district (originally the district itself, as seen in the expression *bíl piḫâti* 14^{10}), Heb. פֶּחָה cstr. פַּחַת, st. פחא to close, enclose. — 2. *upaḳidu* = *upaḳḳidu* §§ **11**; **21.** 3. — *lapan* = לִפְנֵי, the only form in which the preposition *la* is preserved in Assyr. — *tibût*, cstr. of abstr. noun, st. *tibû* to advance. — 3. *piḳitta* = *piḳidta* § **8.** 2 *b.* — *imlû* like *umašširû* has as subj. *ša* in l. 2. — *utîr* = *utawwir*, obj. is *šarrâni*. — 4. *maškani* § **15.** 3 *a.* — *apḳidsunûti* = *apḳidšunûti*. — 6. *iššûti* = *'ídšûti* st. א₈דש. — *maṣarâti*, st. *naṣâru*. — *ûmî*, pl. of *ûmu*, Heb. יוֹם. — 7. *ma'di*, gen. of adj. *ma'du*, also written *mâdu*, cf. Heb. מְאֹד. — 8. *šalmíš* § **19.** 1. — *atura* = *atwura*. — 9. *mala* as many as, lit. fulness, st. מלא₁, takes verbal form in *u* like the relative *ša*. — *adî* pl. of *adû*, noun of the form *arḫu*, *ardu*, st. perhaps *idû* to know or *adû* to appoint. In 32^{15} the *adî* are written documents. — 10. *iṣṣurû* § **26.** — *ípussunûti* = *ípuš-šunûti* § **8.** 2 *a.* — 11. *iḳpud* it planned, devised. Note the parallelism between *iḳpud limuttu* and *dababti surrâti idbubu*. — 12. The reading *ku-šir* is very doubtful. — 14. *inasaḫû*, 3rd pl. of first impf. I 1, they drive or were driving, cf. 44^{1-12}. *nasâḫu* is the regular word for violently removing a people and transporting them to another country. — *attûni* is composed of the stem *attû* and the pronom. suffix *ni*. — *ašabâni* our dwelling, our continuance, inf. I 1 + pronom. suff. *ni*. — *mînu*. In translating numbered, I have connected this word with the stem מנה to count, number.—15. *uma'irû* § **28.**—16. *rakbî*, pl. in *î* § **16.** 2.—*birinni* = *birî-ni* between us st. ברה to bind, whence *birîtu* pl. *birîti* 46^{25} bond, Heb. בְּרִית, and *birtu* midst, as prep. *birit* 30^{8} between.—17. *liššakin* = *linšakin* = *lî* + *inšakin* §§ **18**; **22.** 2.—*nindaggara* = *nimtagara* st. *magâru* §§ **8.** 2 *b*, *c*; **21.** 3; **24.** 5.—*aḫamíš*, a frequent word denoting the reciprocal relation, as 8^{7} *ímuḳâni aḫamiš* each other's forces, *ana aḫamiš* 15^{9} unto each other § **19.**—*aḫínna* = *aḫi* side + *anna* § **10.** 1.—18. *nizuz* § **27.**—*â*, Heb. אִי, § **19.** 1.—*ibbaši*, only orthographically different from *ibaššî* 35^{24} he shall be, first impf. I 1 from *bašû*.—*šanumma* = *šanû* + *ma* § **18.**—20. *ḳitri*. The first syllable might also be read *ḳiṭ*, *siḫ*, etc. Some such meaning as aid or alliance is demanded by the connection in which the word often occurs, cf. 22^{18} 24^{31}. If we should read *ḳiṭru* we might compare the Aram. קְטַר to bind.—*ušzizu* = *ušanzizu*, with assimilation and loss of *n* and the vowel before it, cf. §§ **8.** 2 *d*; **8.** 1; **11.**—*ištíni'û* = *ištanayi'û* like *ištanakinû*, § **21.** 1, *tín* for *tan* under the influence of the guttural ע.—*amât*, cstr. of *amâtu* st. אמה, used like Heb. דָּבָר for thing, as 46^{22}.—21. *limuttim*, gen. with mimmation of *limuttu* = *limuntu*.—22. *Šupar-šaḳî*: the explanation of the word is doubtful, but the meaning generals is assured; cf. Khors. 120: *VII šupar-šaḳî-ya adi ummânâtišunu* ... *ašpur* seven of my generals with their armies I sent. The *šupar-šaḳu* is also often appointed as governor of a conquered province, as 19^{5}.—23. *rakbîšun* their riders, messengers, i.e. the messengers of the conspiring vassals.—*šiprâtišunu* their missives, i.e. either of the vassals or of the couriers.—24. *surrâtí*, cf. Heb. סָרַר to be obstinate.—25. *išḳâti*, pl. of a sing. *išḳatu* like *šarratu*, or *išiḳtu* like *nipištu*, st. $אשק_3$ to bind, cf. Heb. חָשַׁק.—26. *mamîtu* = *ma*א*ma*י*tu* word, oath, ban, malediction.—*ikšus* for *ikšud* § **8.** 2 *b*. The verb *kašâdu* means first to reach, overtake, and then to capture. We might render here the ban of Aššur ... overtook them. The construction of lines 27 and 28 is obscure. *ma* in l. 27 is emphatic and *ša* refers back to *sunûti*. We may also render, into whose hands I had brought good and unto whom I had done favor. *ḳâtuššun* would then stand for *ina ḳâtî-šun*, *ša* would be understood before *ṭâbti*, *uba'i* would be II 1 for *uba*וו*i*א. The translation: I had sought, connects *uba'i* with the verb $בא_4ה$.—28. *dunḳu* § **8.** 2 *c*.

48, 2. *ittišunu*: the suffix refers either to the vassals or to the cities Sais, etc.—*šaknû*, perm. I 1.—3. *ušamḳitû*: the subject is my generals.—*ídu*, cf. Heb. אֶחָד.—4. *ilulû* § **27.**—The sentence l. 5 would read as well without the *ša*, their skins they stripped off, they covered the city wall, cf. 34[7].—6. *ištíni'û*, cf. on 46[20].—7. *balṭûssunu* = *balṭûtšunu* their life, i.e. them alive § **8.** 2 *b.*—8. *ubilûni* I 1 st. *abâlu* § **30.**—10. *ušatir* = *uša*ו*tir* § **30.**—*lubultu* § **8.** 2 *a.*—*birmí*, cf. Heb. בְּרוֹמִים.—11. *ulabbisu* = *ulabbiš-šu* § **8.** 2 *a.*—12. *šimir*. For the reading *šimir* cf. 63[21] with 64[18]. These passages show that the *šimirî* were worn on the hands and the feet. The ideogram means to bind. The ring may be called *šimiru* from some stone with which it was ornamented, cf. Heb. שָׁמִיר diamond.—*rittî;* etymology obscure. Meaning hand or some part of the hand clear from many passages.—13. *ša iḫzušu* whose hilt, st. אחז₁ to seize. The syl. *iḫ* might also be read *aḫ* or *uḫ*.—*nibît šumi-ya* means no more than *šumi-ya*.—15. *rukub bílûti* lordly equipage.—*aḳissu* = *aḳiš-šu* st. קיש.—16. *ašar*, cstr. of *ašru* place, = *ina ašri ša*. So also in l. 21.—21. *innabtu* = *in*א₁*abitu* IV 1, relative sentence.—22. *šîmat muši* fate of night, dark fate, death; cf. 7[11] *mušîmû šîmâti* fixers of destinies.—24. *dannûti*, abstr., gen.—25. *íllatsu* = *íllat-šu*, cf. Heb. חַיִל.—26. *ḳabal*, cstr. of *ḳablu* face to face, opposite and so middle, fight, etc. By a figure of speech the word for fight is here applied to the troops.—27. *ísir* st. אסר₁.—*muṣṣa*, acc., st. יצא₁.

50, 8. *tib*, cstr. of *tibu* = *tib'u* st. תבא₄, like *pit* from *pitu* st. פתא₃ and *ḫiṭ* from *ḫiṭu* st. חטא₁.—11. *ikšudâ*, pl. fem. I 1.—*ḳâta-a-a* pronounced *ḳatâ'a*, dual + suffix § **9.** 2. The first *a* is phonetic complement § **5.** Cf. *i-da-a-a* var. *i-da-a-šu* my (his) hands Delitzsch Lesest.[3] 109, 275.—12. *kitû:* so this id. is read, II R 44, 7. The *kitû* is often mentioned as a kind of garment, possibly the Heb. כְּתֹנֶת.—13. *dimmî*, pl. of *dimmu;* often occurs meaning column, cf. Sargontexte p. 81. According to V R 10, 101 Assurbanipal erected lofty *dimmî* in front of his palace. Here the meaning may be obelisk.—14. *Zaḫalî*, gen. of *zaḫalû*, some metal much used in architecture, etc., for ornamental purposes; as I R 54, 59 *rîmî dalât bâbí ina zaḫalî namriš abannim* the bulls of the entrances of the gates I made in a brilliant manner of *zaḫali* metal; also II R 67, 79 *ina mísir zaḫalî* with a covering of *zaḫalî;* and V R 6, 23.—*ibbi*, gen. of *ibbu* = *'ibbu*, adj. of the form *gišru* strong.—*gun;* so the id. is read S[b] 369, but the Assyrian word for talent is broken away in this syllabary.—15. *ì-kur* is a double ideogram meaning house (*ì*) of the mountain (*kur*), so called because temples were constructed on elevations.—*manzalti* § **8.** 2 *a.*—18. *ušamrir* III 1 from *marâru* to pass over, Arabic *marra*. Cf. V R 3, 50 *ultu kakkî Aššur u Ištar íli Îlamti ušamriru aštakkanu danânu u lîtu* after I had caused the weapons of A. and of I. to march over Elam and had established might and authority.—*lîtu*, fem. noun from לאה₁.—21. *kiššatu*, noun of doubtful etymology. I have regarded it as a collective noun from st. *kanâšu* to assemble. Delitzsch Lesest.^{3} derives it from *kašâšu* and renders it by might.—22. *níšî*, for this reading of the id. cf. Delitzsch Lesest.^{3} 135, 13. 14.—23. *adduku* = *adwuku* §§ **11**; **31**.—24. *muḫḫuru*, something presented, an offering or prayer st. *maḫâru*. — *umaḫir* § **21**. 3.

52, 1. *mâti lâ târat* land without return, Hades.—2. *uzna šakânu* = to direct one's attention.—12. *ina kašâdiša* on her arrival, cf. 60^7. —13. *izzakkar* = *iztakar* §§ **8**. 2 *b*; **21**. 3.—15. *lûruba* = *lû* + *íruba*, second impf. I 1, let me enter. *anâku* is emphatic.—16. *irruba* for *a*$\aleph_5$*aruba* like *ašakana*.—18. *ušapalkat* § **33**.—19. *ušíllâ* = *uša* $\aleph_4$ *la'a*, like *ušaškan*.—*mitûti* the dead.—*akilûti;* the ideogram here means to eat. Translate: eating (and) living.—20. *ima'adû* they shall be numerous.—23. *izizî* for *nizizî*, impv. I 1.—*tanašašši* = *tanaša-ši* §§ **22**. 2; **9**. 2. The suffix refers to *daltu* l. 17 as its antecedent.—24. *lûllik* = *lû* + *allik* § **22**. 2.—*lûšannî* = *lû* + *ušannî* like *ušaškin*.

57, 16. Translations of the story of the Deluge may be found in Smith's Chaldean Account of Genesis and in Schrader's Keilinschriften und das Alte Testament, ed. 2. Lines 57^{16}–58^{9} record the entrance into the ship.—*i-šú-ú* I had, cf. Heb. יֵשׁ.—*í-ṣi-ín-ši* I collected it, st. אצן$_3$; on *ši* cf. § **9**. 2.—18. *zir*, cstr. of *ziru* = *zir'u* seed, Heb. זֶרַע.—19. *uš-tí-li* § **27**.—*a-*(?). We expect *a-na*, or *a-na libbi* and one of these expressions, no doubt, stood in the text.—*kimti* family, immediate kinsmen st. *kamû*.—*sa-lat*. The reading *lat* and not *mat*, *nat*, etc., is made certain by many passages in which the word is written *sa-la-tu* (or *ti*). In the contract-tablets *kimtu* is often associated with *nisutu* and *salatu;* cf. also 20^{11}, where *nišutu* is perhaps scribal error for *nisutu*. The etymology of *salatu* is uncertain, but it perhaps means near, near kinsmen.—20. *bul* cattle, cstr. The st. may be middle ו or final guttural. —*aplî um-ma-a-ni* the artists, mechanics who had built the ship, lit. sons of art. So also II R 67, 70 in an account of building a palace: *gimir aplî ummâni ḫassûti*. In V R 13, 36–42 *apal um-ma-ni* is represented by the same ids. as *imḳu* wise, *mudû* knowing, *ḫassu* reflective, etc.—21. *a-dan-na*, obj. of *iš-ku-na*. The connection here, but especially 58^3, seems to me to favor the meaning decree, command. The st. may be ויעד to appoint, define, and *adannu* or *adânu* may be that which is appointed, therefore either a decree or a set time. Cf. Khors. 117: *uṣurât a-dan-ni ikšudaššumma illika uruḫ mûti* the ban of *adanni* overtook him and he went the road of death.

58, 1. *izzakir* = *iztakir* § **8**. 2 *b*. *mu* is id. for *zakâru* and *ir* is phon. compl.—*ina* introduces what the *kukru* said, without the usual *umma;*

so also l. 4. —— *ušaznannu* (l. 4 *ušaznana*); the subj. is *šamûtu* and the obj. *kibâti.* —— 2. *pi-ḫi,* impv. I 1. —— 3. *iḳ-ri-da.* Cf. Haupt's Nimrodepos 10, 47: *ina šalši. ûmí ina íḳli a-dan-ni iḳ-ri-du-ni* on the third day in the appointed (?) field they arrived (?). It is doubtful whether the st. begins with *g, k,* or *ḳ,* and also whether in our passage the word means the set time arrived, or the command became strong, loud. —— 5. The first sign is the numeral four. —— *mi* is phon. compl. to *ûmi.* —— *at-ta-ṭal* I 2 st. *naṭâlu* to look, here to look in entreaty. —— The suff. *šu* refers to the Sun-god 57[21]. —— 6. *ûmu* a day = *one* day. The *mu* is phon. compl. —— *i-tap-lu-si,* inf. IV 2 st. *palâsu.* The peculiarity of inf. IV 2 is the loss of the *n,* as in impv. I 1 of verbs initial *n*; cf. § **26.** —— 8. *ana,* a var. has *a-na.* —— The pilot's name is *Bu-zu-ur-kur-gal,* the sign *ilu* before *kur-gal* being a determinative. The signs *kur-gal* may mean great mountain, Assyr. *šadû rabû,* a title applied to Aššur 28[19]. —— *malaḫi* seaman, pilot, i.e. the man who has to do with the motion of the ship, composed of the sign *mâ* = ship S[b] 283 + the sign *laḫ* (= *du* + *du, du* = *alâku* to go V R 11, 1) Delitzsch Lesest.[3] p. 17. Cf. Heb. מַלָּח. —— 9. *íkalla* or *bîta rabâ,* the large house, structure = the ship. —— Lines 58[10]–60[7] record the progress of the Deluge and the landing of the ship. —— 10. *mû-šíri-ina-namâri* water of dawn at break of day, name of a mythological female character. —— 11. *i-šid,* cstr. of *išdu.* —— *ṣa-lim-tum,* fem. adj. with mimmation. —— 12. *líb-bi-ša.* The suff. refers to *ur-pa-tum.* —— *ir-tam-ma-am-ma* = *irtamamma* st. *ramâmu.* —— 14. *gu-za-lal-míš* = *guzalalî* throne bearers; *guza* = *kussu* throne II R 16, 9, and *lal* = *našû* to lift, bear V R 11, 48. The *míš* is pl. sign. —— *mâtum* land, valley, here in contrast to *šadû.* —— *tar-gul-li,* or *gug-gul-li.* The first sign seems according to II R 30, 21 to have also the value *gug.* The same word occurs S[b] 284. *tar-gul-li* is cstr. to *Dibbara* and subj. of *i-na-as-saḫ.* —— 16. *mi-iḫ-ri,* read *miḫrî* streams, canals. The st. may be *ḫirû* to dig. Pl. of *miḫru* is *miḫrâti,* as *mi-iḫ-ra-at mí-í* canals of water I R 62 col. VI 1; 63 col. VII 61. —— 17. *di-pa-ra-a-ti,* pl. of *dipâru* flame, torch (?). In II R 44, 6. 7 the word *di-pa-a-rum,* whose id. is partly effaced, follows the word *nu-mu-rum,* which explains the id. for fire. —— 19. *i-ba-'-u* they come in, attain unto; subj. is *šumurrâssu* his violence = *šumurrâti-šu.* —— 20. *í-ṭu-ti,* cf. 52[9]. —— 22. *i-zi-ḳam* (?)-*ma* it (they) blew st. זיק (?); subj. is lost. —— 23. *ḳab-li* battle or troop. —— 24. *im-mar* § **27.** —— *u-ta-ad-da-a* II 2 st. ידע, used reciprocally of recognizing one another; subj. is *nišî.* A new sentence begins with *ina.* —— 25. *ilâni,* pl. expressed by repeating the id. —— *ip-tal-ḫu* I 2.

59, 1. *it-tí-iḫ-su* = *ittaḫsû* § **8.** 2 *e.* —— The heavens of Anu are the heavens where Anu reigns. With this line compare IV R 28 No. 2, where it is said that at the fury and thundering of Ramân *ilâni ša šamî ana šamî itílû, ilâni ša irṣitim ana irṣitim itírbû.* — 2. *ḳun-nu-nu* and *rab-ṣu* are perm. pl. — 3. *i-šis-si* = *išasî*, 1st. impf., st. *šasû* to speak, cry out. — 4. *u-nam-bi* = *u-nab-bi* II 1. — *iltu ṣîrtu* or *iltu rabîtu*, title of Ištar, cf. 60[21]. — *ṭa-bat rig-ma* good of word, kind. — 5. *ud* (?)-*mu* race (?). — 6. *limuttu.* The fem. det. is often used, as here, before fem. nouns. — 8. *ana ḫul-lu-uḳ* with reference to the destruction of. — 9. *ul-la-da* = *uwallada*, first impf. II 1; cf. *mu-al-li-da-at* 62[7]; *ni-šú-ú* is obj. — 12. *aš-ru* st. ושר. — *aš-bi* st. ושב. — 13. *kat-ma*, fem. pl. perm. I 1. — 14. *ur-ra* = *ûra* st. אור. — 16. *i-na ka-ša-a-di* on (its) arrival, at its dawn; cf. 60[7]. — *it-ta-rik* st. *tarâku.* — *šú-ú a-bu-bu*, subj. of *i-nu-uḫ* l. 18. — 17. *ḫa-a-a-al-ti*, cf. Heb. חִיל. — 18. *im-ḫul-lu* storm, evil (*ḫul*) wind (*im*). — 19. *ap-pa-al-sa* IV 1 st. *palâsu.* — *ša-kín ḳu-lu* making a voice, crying aloud. — 20. *kul-lat* all of. — 21. *ki-ma ú-ri-bí pag-rat ú-šal-lu* like beams of wood (?) the corpses floated about. — 22. *ud-da*, id. for *urru* light II R 47, 60. — *dûr ap-pi* wall of the face = cheek. — 23. *uḳ-tam-mi-iṣ* II 2 st. *ḳamâṣu.* — *a-bak-ki* = *abakî.* — 25. *ḫat-tu* fear, something fearful, in appos. with following *tâmdu* (?).

60, 1. Twelve measures high a district arose. — 2. *i-tí-mid* he (I) placed, directed (the course of the ship). — 4. The last sign in lines 4, 5, 6 is the sign for repetition and repeats here all of l. 3 after *Ni-ṣir.* — 8. Lines 8–14 narrate the sending out of the birds, 15–20 the sacrifice, 21, 22 the rainbow (?), **61**, 1–21 Bíl's anger and pacification, 21–**62**, 3 translation of the hero and his wife. — *u-ší-ṣi* III 1 st. *aṣû.* — *summatu*, with post-determinative for bird. — *u-maš-šir* I released, sent forth. — 9. *i-pa-aš-šum-ma* = *ibašu-ma.* — *is-saḫ-ra* = *istaḫra* = *istaḫira* § **8.** 2 *b.* — 14. *ik-kal* he eats. — *i-ša-aḫ-ḫi*, first impf. I 1, cf. Heb. שָׂחָה. — *i-tar-ri* = *itâri* (?) st. תור (?). — 15. *ú-ší-ṣi*; obj. is the animals, etc., which were in the ship. — *at-ta-ḳí ni-ḳa-a* I sacrificed a sacrifice. — 16. *sur-ḳi-nu* libation, st. *sarâḳu*; cf. Sargon Cyl. 60: *sirḳu as-ru-ḳu.* — 17. 7 and 7 = by sevens. — *karpatu* pot, is determinative; *a-da-gur* is here the name of the vessels used in sacrifice. — *uk-tin* II 2 st. *kânu.* — 18. *at-ta-bak* I poured out, arranged. — 20. *zu-um-bi-í* = *zubbî*, cf. Heb. זְבוּב. — *bíl niḳâni* lord of sacrifices, priest. — 21. *ul-tu ul-la-nu-um-ma* from afar, *ma* emphatic. — *ka-ša-di-šu* her approach; the reference is to Ištar, although the suffix is masc. — 22. *ḳašâti* (?) bows, arches (?). The sign *nim* is so much like the sign *ban*, which represents *ḳaštu* a bow, that one may suppose that a scribal error has occurred. — *ṣu-ḫi-šu* (?). — 23. *ilâni an-nu-ti*, obj. of *am-ši.* — *lu-u* = *lû* by, particle of swearing; by the *uknu* stone of my neck, I will not forget.

61, 5. *ṭí-bí* he drew near, subject follows. KAT.[2] p. 60 says that the original has *i* before *ṭí*. In this case we might read *i-ṭí-mid* st. עמד or *i-ṭí-ziz* st. *nazâzu*. —— *lib-ba-ti*, etc., he was filled with *libbâti* against the gods (and) the *igigi*. The meaning of *libbâti* is uncertain. Cf. V R 7, 25–27 my messenger . . . *ina ma-li-í lib-ba-a-ti ú-ma-'-ir* with fulness of *libbâti* I sent. —— 6. Has anyone come out alive? Let not a man escape (live) from the destruction. —— 7. *ka-ga*, read *iḳabbi*, cf. 64[7]. —— 8. Who except Ìa?, etc. —— *a-ma-tu* word, thing, obj. of *i-ba-na*. The obj. is repeated for emphasis in *ši*. —— 9. and Ìa knows also all magic *ka-la šip-ti*. —— 11. *abkal*, cf. V R 51, 41, where the signs *nun-mí* are read *ab-kal-lu*, and note on 7[6]. —— 12. *ki-i ki-i* = *kî kî* when, since, repetition for emphasis. —— 13. The sinner bore his sin, the wrong-doer bore his wrong-doing. *bí-íl ḫi-ṭi-í* possessor of sin, sinner. —— 14. *ru-um-mí* may be impv. II 1 from *ramû* to release, obj. being those who had not been destroyed; cf. Zimmern's Busspsalmen p. 91. —— 15. *níšu* lion, composed of the signs for dog and large, cf. Delitzsch's Lesest.[3] 135, 13. 14. —— 16. *barbaru*, *ib.* 11. 12. The four plagues which are to take the place of the Deluge in diminishing the human race are lions, jackals, famine and pestilence. —— 19. The god Ìa seems here to equivocate. —— 20. *Ad-ra-ḫa-sis;* apparently the name or a title of an attendant on Ìa. Or it may be a title of the hero of the Deluge, whose name is to be read most probably *Pir-napištim* scion of life 61[25]; cf. Zimmern's Busspsalmen p. 26. —— 21. *mi-lik-šu mil-ku* his understanding (became) understanding = he became appeased, i.e. the god Bíl. —— 22. *ul-ṭí-la-an-ni* he lifted me up, st. *ílû*. —— 23. *uš-taḳ-mi-iṣ* he pressed; obj. follows, subj. is Bíl. —— 24. *pu-ut-ni* our side, st. *pitû*. —— *i-kar-ra-ban-na-ši* = *ikarab-annaši* § **9**. 2. —— 25. *i-na pa-na*, etc., before, in past time, Pir-napištim (was) a man (= was human).

62, 1. *í-mu-ú*, st. עמה to be like and to cause to be like, cf. note on 40[4]. Translate: they shall be like the gods, exalted. —— 3. *il-ḳû* they took, st. *liḳû*. —— 5. read [*irṣí*]-*tum*. —— 8. *mî-šu-nu* their waters, i.e. of Apsû and Ti-amat. —— 10. *šú-pu-ú*, perm. III 1 st. יפע (?). —— 11. *zuk-ku-ru*, perm. II 1, subj. *ilâni* l. 10. —— *ši-ma-tu* is obj. of a verb broken away, whose form was perhaps perm. I 1 or II 1 of *šâmu*, cf. 7[8.11] 35[4]. —— 15. The gods are Šar and Ki-šar. —— 18. The god is Aššur.

63, 1. *a-lik*, impv. I 1 of *alâku*. Between the part of this story transliterated on p. 52 and the part given here are twelve mutilated lines, in which the porter reports Ištar's arrival, and the answer of the queen of the underworld begins. —— *pi-ta-aš-ši* open for her. —— 2. *up-pi-is-si* = *uppiš-ši* § **8**. 2 *a* do unto her. —— 4. *ir-bi*, fem. sing. impv. I 1, st.

iríbu. — *Kûtu,* a famous burial-city, seems here to have its name applied to the underworld. The word is subj. of the following verb, part of which is lost. — 5. Palace of the land without return = the occupants of that palace, or its attendants. — 6. *um-ta-ṣi,* II 2 for *um-taṣ-ṣi,* from a st. *maṣû;* meaning uncertain, perhaps to come upon, to approach, Heb. קָצָא. — 7. *am-mí-ni* wherefore. — 8. Of *Bílit-irṣi-tim* thus are her commands = such are the commands of B. — 18. *šib-bu* belt, girdle.

64, 2. *ṣu-bat šupil-ti* is the garment of the pudenda, the garment worn next to the person. — 5. *iš-tu ul-la-nu-um-ma* = from that (very time), from the very time when, so soon as. — 6. Between this meeting of Ištar with Nin-ki-gal and the return l. 7–23, the original relates that Ninkigal ordered her servant Nam-tar to take Ištar and plague her with diseases; that owing to Ištar's absence from her throne the sexes, both man and beast, lost interest in each other; and that the god Ìa sent a special messenger to the underworld in order to secure the release of Ištar. After a curse against this special messenger, Ninkigal orders Namtar to take Ištar out of the underworld. — 9. *ma-ḫa-aṣ ìkal kitti* destroy the palace of justice. The *gi-na* might also be taken as an adj. *kitta* = *kinta,* lasting, eternal, agreeing with *ìkalla.* — 10. Before *za* IV R has *ú,* which I suppose to be due to scribal error. The verb in this line is evidently impv., like *maḫaṣ* l. 9, *šú-ṣa-a, šú-šib* l. 11, *su-luḫ* and *li-ḳa* l. 12. With l. 13 comes the change of construction to the imperfect, *il-lik, im-ḫa-aṣ, u-za-'-i,* etc. I do not know what the st. is nor where the word ends; it may end with the guttural sign, with *i* or with *na.* *za(ṣa)-'-i-na, ú-za(ṣa)-'-i-na* might be respectively impv. and second impf. II 1, § **24**. 3. 5, from a st. זאן or צאן. If the final letter of the st. be *n,* l. 10 would read *za(ṣa)-'-i-na* the threshold of *pa* stones. *i-lu* is id. for *askuppu* and the *abnu* before it is determinative. — 12. *Ištar mî balâṭi su-luḫ-ši-ma li-ḳa-aš-ši* [*ištu maḫ*]*-ri-ya* sprinkle I. with the waters of life and take her [from] my [presence].

GLOSSARY.

א$_1$ = heb. א, א$_2$ = ה, א$_3$ = ח$_1$ (weak ח), א$_4$ = ע$_1$, א$_5$ = ע$_2$, א without a number may be any one of these five gutturals.—Final ה represents a ו or י, or in some cases perhaps א$_1$.—Some of the words not defined are ideograms.

א

א$_1$א$_3$ד **ídu** one *í-du* 26^{15} 31^{30} 48^{3}; **ídiš** alone *í-diš* 29^{10} *-ši-šu* he alone 28^{15} 34^{13}; **ídû** a royal title, the one, the first *í-du-u* 5^{8}.

א$_1$א$_2$ל **alu** city 6^{13} *ali* 2^{8} *-šu* 4^{24} *ala* 2^{4} *-šu* 40^{19} *alâni* 6^{5} *alâni$_{pl}$* 12^{8} *-šu* 10^{23} *-šu-nu* 3^{26} *alâ$_{pl}$-ni* 8^{1} *-šu-nu* 1^{23}.

א$_1$ב **abu** father 19^{23} 20^{9} $42^{3,7,10}$ $46^{2,5}$ 48^{16} *a-bu* 7^{3} (cstr.) *abu-u-a* 23^{10} *abi* $20^{7,23}$ 23^{7} 26^{22} 28^{17} 48^{20} *-ya* 13^{3} *-šu* $11^{10,11}$ $25^{18,29}$ *a-bi* $37^{8,17}$ $39^{13,21}$ *-šu* 38^{28} 39^{7} *abî$_{pl}$-ya* $21^{13,16,21}$ $22^{10,19}$ 29^{26} *ab-bi-í-a* 36^{20} *-šu* 38^{18}; **abu** name of the fifth month of the Babylonian-Assyrian year *arḫu abi* 31^{7}.

א$_1$בת **abûtu** wish *a-bu-tu* 37^{19}.

א$_1$בב **abubu** deluge *a-bu-bu* 18^{14} $59^{15,16,18}$ $61^{2,12}$ *a-bu-bí* 4^{16} *a-bu-ba* 61^{15-18} *-am-ma* 58^{25} *-ni-iš* 7^{19}.

א$_2$בב **abâbu** to be bright, brilliant II 1 *ub-bi-ib* (= *u-'ab-bi-ib*) I made bright, adorned 27^{1}; *uš-tib-bu* (III 2) 9^{11}; **íbbu** bright, pure *ib-bi* 16^{15} $36^{27,34}$ 50^{14}.

א$_2$בך **abâku** to turn, defeat, carry off, drive off *a-bu-uk* 17^{31} *a-bu-ka* 18^{27}; **abiktu** defeat *-ti* 30^{25} 44^{6} *-ta-šu* 8^{17} 24^{27} 25^{9} $28^{9,30}$ $29^{5,9}$ 31^{12} 34^{20} 42^{4} *-ta-šu-un* 11^{28} *-ta-šu-nu* 8^{9} 26^{20} *a-bi-ik-ta-šu-nu* 1^{11} $4^{9,18}$; **abkûtu** defeat *ab-ku-su-nu* (= *abkût-šunu*) 4^{11}.

אבכל **abkallu** leader *abkal* 7^{6} 61^{11}.

א$_1$בל **abullu** city gate *abulli* 12^{16} 28^{23} 33^{20} *abullî$_{pl}$* 14^{7}.

א$_1$בן **abnu** stone *abni* 36^{14} 38^{4} *abnî$_{pl}$* 4^{25} 17^{31} 18^{23} 23^{30} 50^{12}; **ubanu** tip, finger, peak $38^{6\ bis}$ *uban* 8^{16}.

אבן **ab-na-ma** . . . . . 41^{23}.

אבן **ab-nam-ni-šu** . . . . . 20^{25}.

א$_3$בר **ibru** friend *ib-ri* 40^{15}.

א$_4$בר **íbíru** to cross *í-bi-ra* he crossed 21^{8} *í-bir* 2^{8} 3^{6} 7^{24} $8^{3,13}$ *í-bí-ru* 2^{4} *í-bi-ru* 30^{6}; **abartu, íbirtu** passage, beyond (?) *a-bar-ti* 36^{4} [*í-bir-*]*ti* 41^{22} *í-bir-tan* $5^{22,27}$; **nibirtu** passage *ni-bir-ti* 6^{16} 22^{9}.

אבש$_8$ **abšânu** yoke *ab-ša-a-ni* 11^{14} 27^{22} 39^{26} 41^{8} *ab-ša-an-ka* 23^{11} -[*šu*] 9^{22} -*šu-un* 21^{22}; **tabšûtu** . . . . . *ta-ab-šu-tu* 39^{26}.

אבש$_5$ **íbíšu** Babylonian for *ípíšu* to do, make.

אבת$_1$ **abâtu** to perish, destroy II I destroy IV I to vanish, flee *i-ab-ba-tu* 24^{20} *a-bu-ut* 16^{14}; *ub-bi-it* (= *u-'ab-bit*) 35^{11}; *in-na-bit* (= *in-'a-bit*) 10^{20} 14^{14} 28^{12,15} 44^{11} 50^{4,9} *in-nab-tu* 17^{16} 18^{21} 24^{5} 29^{25} 31^{20} 33^{10} 48^{21} *in-nab-tu-ni* 32^{12} -*nim-ma* 25^{19} *mun-nab-tu* 14^{11} -*ti* (pl.) 31^{19}.

אג$_1$א$_1$ to flee (?), decline (?) *í-gi* 36^{2}.

אגג **agâgu** to be powerful, angry *i-gu-ug* 39^{27} *í-gug* 42^{13}; **uggatu** anger *ug-gat* 15^{23} *ug-ga-ti* 40^{1} -*tim* 41^{27}; *ag-giš* 17^{17} *ag-gi-iš* 24^{21}.

אגג *ilu* **igigi** 61^{5} *ilu igigi$_{pl}$* 7^{7} *ilu i-gi-gi* 7^{2}.

אגו **agû** crown *a-gu-u* (acc.) 64^{23} *agí* 19^{19} *a-gi-í* 7^{4} *agâ* 63^{6,7}.

אגל$_4$ **agalu** calf *a-ga-li$_{pl}$* 3^{28}.

אגל **aggullatu** axe (?) *ag-gul-lat* 2^{6} 3^{4}.

אגם$_1$ **agammu** pond, marsh *nâru a-gam-mí* 14^{12}.

אגר **agurru** fire-baked brick *a-gur-ri* 4^{24,29}.

אגר$_8$ **ígíru** (?) to enclose **igaru** a wall *i-ga-ru-šu* 37^{28} *igarâti$_{pl}$-šu* 36^{26}.

אדגר **a-da-gur** 60^{17} name or kind of sacrificial vessel.

אדד *iṣu* **iddîti** . . . . . *id-di-í-ti* 30^{9}.

אדי$_4$ **adi** as far as, while, together with *a-di* 3^{24} 11^{30} 37^{29} 58^{9} 62^{14}.

אדל **ídílu** to bar, bolt *u-di-lu* (II I) 14^{7}.

אדם$_1$ **admu** the young, offspring *ad-mi* 16^{31}.

אדם **ud** (?)-**mu** race (?), generation (?) 59^{5}.

אדם **admânu** dwelling-place *ad-ma-ni-šu* 36^{28} *ad-ma-an-šu-un* 40^{1}.

אדן **adannu** command *a-dan-nu* 58^{3} -*na* 57^{21}.

אדן **adnâti** . . . . . (fem. pl.) *ad-na-a-ti* 28^{23} -*tí* 33^{21}.

אדר **adâru** to fear, shun *a-du-ra* 13^{31} *a-di-ru* 5^{7} 6^{6}.

אדש$_8$ **adâšu** to be new *lu-ud-diš* (II I) 24^{15} *mu-ud-diš* 23^{19}; **íššûtu** newness *íš-šu-tí* 6^{14} -*ti* 46^{6}; *í-íš-ši-iš* 36^{22} 38^{11} *íš-šiš* 24^{5} 39^{5,16}.

אור$_1$ **urru** day 59^{22} *ur-ra* 59^{14}.

אזב$_4$ **ízíbu** to leave, to cause to remain *í-zib* 17^{28} (1st pers.) 13^{26} (3rd pers.) *i-zi-bu* 39^{28} *í-zi-bu* 48^{3}; *šu-zu-ub* (III I inf.) 2^{12} 8^{20} 16^{30} 17^{15,20} 29^{7,10} 44^{10} 50^{4}.

אזד *imílu* **iz-da** . . . . . 30^{26}.

אזז$_4$ **ízízu** to be strong, make strong *ni-zu-uz* 46^{18} *i-zi-iz* (impv.) 14^{23}; **izzu** strong *iz-zi* 15^{30} *iz-zu-tí* 3^{17} 4^{8} *iz-zi-tu* 50^{23}; *iz-zi-iš* 39^{27}.

אזן$_1$ **uznu** ear, design, intention *u-zu-un-ša* 52^{2,3} *uznî-ya* 63^{10} -*ša* 63^{9} 64^{22}.

אח$_1$ **aḫu** brother 23^{28} 26^{6} -*šu* 14^{4} *a-ḫu* 58^{24} *aḫi* 24^{12} 25^{4} 26^{8} 27^{29} 28^{17} 29^{4} -*šu* 34^{4} *a-ḫa-šu* 58^{24} *aḫî$_{pl}$-šu* 11^{10} 21^{6,9} 25^{17}; **a-ḫa-miš** one another 8^{7} 15^{9} 19^{10} 29^{7} 32^{22} 34^{17} 46^{17}.

אח$_1$ **aḫu,** fem. *aḫatu* side *a-aḫ* 2^{24} *a-ḫi* 19^{1} 33^{26} 36^{2} 42^{18} *a-ḫat* 8^{6}; **a-ḫi-ín-na-a** this side 46^{17}.

אחז$_1$ **aḫâzu** to seize, take, acquire *a-ḫu-uz* 20^{12} *í-ḫu-zu* 26^{13} 31^{30}; *u-ša-ḫi-iz-zu* 28^{13}; **aḫzu** contents *aḫ-zi-šu-nu* 20^{14}; **iḫzu** hilt *iḫ-zu-šu* 48^{13}; **taḫazu** battle 34^{5} *ta-ḫa-zu* 17^{23} *taḫazi* 2^{23} 8^{8} 25^{8} $33^{4,8}$ 38^{27} 39^{6} $44^{3,5}$ 50^{23} *-ya* $15^{22,30}$ $16^{11,28}$ 17^{13} 50^{8} *-šu* 44^{3} *-šu-nu* 8^{10} *ta-ḫa-zi* 3^{16} 4^{7} 16^{23} 40^{18} *-ya* 16^{20}.

אחם **aḫamiš** cf. אח$_1$.

אחן **aḫínnâ** cf. אח$_1$.

אחר **aḫûrû** in front of (?) *a-ḫu-ur-ru-u* 25^{11}; **aḫratu** the future *aḫ-rat* 18^{15} 24^{14}.

אטח$_5$ **íṭû, íṭûtu** darkness *i-ṭi-*[*i*] 52^{1} *í-ṭi-í* 52^{4} *í-ṭu-ti* 52^{9} [58^{20}].

אטר$_4$ **íṭíru** to spare *í-ṭí-ir* 3^{32} *i-ṭi-ir* 40^{19}.

אי$_1$ **â** not *a-a* 46^{18} $60^{23,24}$ $61^{1,6,14\ bis}$ *a-a-ma* 59^{9}.

אי$_1$ **a-a-um-ma** (= *â'u* + *ma*) anyone? interrogative 61^{6}.

איב$_1$ **âbu** enemy *a-a-bi-ya* 36^{29} *-šu* 5^{10}.

איכל$_2$ **ìkallu** palace *ìkal* 5^{1} 41^{1} 63^{5} $64^{9,13}$ *ìkalli-ya* 25^{30} *-šu* 12^{30} 50^{12} *ìkalla* 58^{9}.

איל$_3$ **íllatu** power, army *íl-lat-su* 48^{25} *-su-un* 17^{9}.

אין$_4$ **ínu** eye, fountain *íni* 9^{2} *-šu* 33^{19} *í-ni* 5^{25} *i-ni-šu* 37^{11}.

איר$_1$ **âru** second month of the Babylonian-Assyrian year *arḫu âru* 19^{25}.

אכב **ikkibu** . . . . . *ik-ki-bu-uš* 12^{17}.

אכד **ikdu** strong (?) *ik-du* 6^{4} *ik-du-tí* 6^{9}.

אכל$_1$ **akâlu** to eat *ik-kal* (= *i-'a-kal*) 60^{14} *í-ku-lu* 26^{2} 29^{6} 32^{14} *akilûti$_{pl}$* 52^{19}; *u-ša-kil* 26^{24}; **akâlu, ukultu** food *a-kal-šu-nu* 52^{8} *u-kul-ti* 26^{30}.

אכם$_3$ **ikkimu** wise (?) *ik-ki-mu* 25^{28}.

אכם$_4$ **íkímu** to seize, rob *í-kim* 16^{18} (1st pers.) 42^{8} (inf. cstr.) *-šu* 8^{20} *-šu-nu* 8^{11} *í-ki-mu* 13^{4}.

אכן **uknû** crystal *abnu uknû* 60^{23}.

אכר **ì-kur** temple *ì-kur* 34^{25} 36^{21} 50^{15}.

אל *amílu* **'a-lu** a class of attendants, or a tribal name, *'a-lu* 30^{33} 31^{11}.

אל$_1$ **ilu** god $7^{8,9}$ 22^{12} 23^{9} *ili* 22^{27} *-ya* 4^{27} *ilâni* 58^{25} $59^{6,7,11}$ *ilâni$_{pl}$* 2^{22} $59^{2,12}$ $60^{19\ bis}$ *-ya* 3^{33} *-šu* 31^{2} *-šu-nu* 4^{22}; **iltu** goddess *i-la-a-ti* 32^{28}; **ilûtu** divinity *ilû-ti-šu-nu* 34^{11} *ilû-us-su-un* 34^{26}.

אלה$_4$ **ílû** to be high, ascend *í-li* $7^{26,27}$ (1st sing.) 8^{21} (3rd sing.) *í-lu-u* 34^{21} (1. s.) 31^{30} (3. p.) *i-lam-ma* 58^{11} 61^{21} (3. s.) *í-lu-nim-ma* 22^{1}; *i-tí-la-a* 60^{1} *i-tí-lu-u* 59^{1} *í-til-lu-u* 30^{7} *mut-tal-li* 19^{27}; *ul-li* (II I) 24^{6}; *u-ší-li* (III I) 57^{20} *u-ší-íl-la-a* 52^{19}; *uš-tí-li* 57^{19} (1. s.) 61^{23} (3. s.) *ul-tí-la-an-ni* 61^{22}; **ílû** fem. **ílîtu** upper *í-lit* 23^{15} *í-li-ti* 20^{3} 36^{4} *-tim* 41^{15} *í-la-ti* things in heaven 24^{21}; **ílînitu** upper *í-li-ni-tí* 2^{25} *-ti* 3^{24}; **íl-la-an** above 5^{28}; [**í**]**-liš** above 62^{4}; **íli** over, above, upon, more than, to, at, against 6^{19} 7^{16} 58^{23} $59^{22,24}$ $60^{16,20}$ *-šu* 12^{16} 33^{9} $34^{11,13}$ *-šu-un* 10^{27} *-šu-nu* 5^{22} *í-li* $46^{6,14}$ *-šu* 21^{3} *-šu-un* 27^{14} *-šu-nu* 50^{24}.

אלו **ullû** that, distant *ul-lu-u* 59^{5} *ul-lu-u-ti* 27^{4} *ul-la* 34^{9} *-nu-um-ma* 60^{21} 61^{4} 64^{5} *ul-la-nu-uš-šu* 37^{4}.

אלך$_2$ **alâku** to go *il-lak* (= *i-ha-lak*) 58^{16} 59^{15} *il-la-ka* 59^{24} *il-la-ku* $58^{13,14}$ *al-lik* 1^{22} 2^{26} 50^{8} *al-li-ik* 7^{24} *a-lik* (= *al-lik*) $8^{23,25}$ *il-lik* 10^{1} 48^{22} $60^{8,10,13}$ 63^{3} 64^{13} *il-li-ka* 28^{19} 30^{15} 42^{9} 44^{8} 61^{1} *il-lik-am-ma* 25^{4} 42^{11} 48^{28} *il-lik-u* 24^{4} (3rd sing.) *il-li-ku* 11^{25} 15^{20} *-ni* 3^{23} *-u-ni* 2^{13} *-u-nim-ma* 22^{1} 50^{6} *lil-li-ku* 39^{20} *-ni* 60^{25} *lu-ul-lik* 52^{24} *a-lik* (impv.) 63^{1} 64^{9} *a-lik* (part.) 6^{13} 35^{24} *a-li-kut* 16^{28} 25^{18} 44^{5} *a-li-ka-at* (fem. sing.) 38^{29} 39^{7} *alâku* (inf.) *a-la-ku* 13^{28} *a-lak* 14^{24} 44^{2} 50^{2} *a-la-ak-šu* 40^{14}; *ittalla-ku* (I 2) $5^{6,12}$ *it-tal-la-ka* 40^{15} *-ku* 30^{29}; *it-ta-na-al-la-ka* (I 3) 16^{24}; *u-ša-lik-šu* (III 1) 35^{11}; **allaku** a courier 48^{28} *al-la-ku* 42^{11} *allak-šu* 29^{26} *allaki-šu* 22^{16} 23^{8} *allakî*$_{pl}$ 25^{14}; **alaktu** a way *a-lak-ta-ša* 52^{6}; **milliku** distance *mi-il-li-ku* 16^{25}.

אלל$_1$ **ul** not 1^{8} $9^{28,29}$ $14^{2,26}$ $26^{15\ bis}$ $31^{31\ bis}$ 35^{24} 41^{6} 52^{9} $58^{24\ bis}$ $60^{3,9,11,14}$ 61^{19}.

אלל$_1$ **alâlu** to bind, hang up *a-lul* 12^{1} 19^{15} 33^{32} *i-lu-lu* 48^{4}; **ullu** a collar *ul-li* 28^{33} 33^{19}; **allu** a chain *al-lu* 48^{11}.

אלל$_2$ **alâlu** to be bright, clean II 1 to make bright *u-lil* 7^{25} *ul-li-la* 27^{1}; **íllu** fem. *íllitu* brilliant *íllu* 27^{26} *ílli* 36^{13} *ílli-tu* 7^{17} *ílli-tí* 7^{9}.

אלם$_1$ **íllamu** before, in front of *íl-la-mu-u-a* 11^{26} 15^{13}.

אלף$_1$ **alpu** ox *alpî*$_{pl}$ 4^{2} 12^{13}.

אלף$_1$ **íllippu** ship 60^{2} *ílippi* 57^{19} $58^{2,7,8}$ 61^{21} *ílippa* 60^{3} 61^{5} *ílippî*$_{pl}$*-šu-nu* 42^{22}.

אלץ$_4$ **ílíṣu** to rejoice, exult *u-ša-li-iṣ* 10^{12}; **ulṣu** joy *ul-ṣi* 41^{1}.

אלת **ultu** out of, from, after, since 9^{8} 22^{21} 64^{12} *ul-tu* 9^{7} 60^{21} 61^{4}.

אמה to speak *i-mu-u* 40^{4}; **amâtu** word, command, affair, thing *a-ma-tu* 61^{8} *-tum* 52^{13} *-ta* 64^{8} *a-mat* 19^{23} 23^{15} 35^{30} 46^{20} *a-ma-a-ti* 25^{16} *-tí* 46^{22} *-ta* 41^{32}; **mamîtu** oath *ma-mit* 11^{20} 29^{31} $46^{10,26}$ *ma-mi-it* 3^{33}.

אמה **um-ma** saying, as follows $22^{12,31}$ 23^{9} 25^{11} $32^{22,24}$ $46^{13,16}$.

אמה$_4$ **ímû** to be like, to equal *í-mu-u* 62^{1}.

אמבר **imbaru** black cloud, storm *imbari* 13^{22} 15^{12} *im-ba-ri* 17^{26}.

אמד$_4$ **ímídu** to place, subdue *í-mid* 10^{21} $61^{13\ bis}$ *-su* 11^{14} 28^{21} *-su-nu-ti* $27^{13,17}$ *í-mí-du* 21^{25} *-uš* 27^{21} *í-mid-du* 9^{22}; *i-tí-mid* (I 2) 60^{2}; *in-nin-du* (= *in-'im-du* IV 1) 15^{10} 17^{21} *in-nam-du-u* 37^{5}; **nimídu** station *ni-mí-di* 12^{28} (*kussi nimídi* stationary throne).

אמחל **imḫullu** evil wind, storm *im-ḫul-lu* 59^{18}.

אמך **ammaku** instead of, in place of *am-ma-ku* 61^{15-18}.

אמל **amílu** man, human being, officer, tribe 61^{6} *a-mí-lum* 48^{3} *amílûti*$_{pl}$ 1^{1} *a-mí-lu-ti* 32^{8} *-túm* 61^{25}.

אמם **ammâti** yon side *am-ma-a-tí* 2^{3}.

אמם **umâmu** beast, cattle *u-ma-am* 6^{23} 30^{24} 57^{20}.

אמם$_1$ **ummu** mother *ummi* 7[10] 34[22] 37[15] *-šu* 19[20] *um-mi-šu* 35[4] *umma-šu* 31[2]; **ammatu** cubit *ammati* 20[25,26] *ammat* 37[32].

אמן **ammíni** cf. אן.

אמן$_2$ **ummânu** pl. *ummânî*, *ummânâti* people, army *um-man* 40[9] *-ka* 14[22] *um-ma-ni* 20[13] *-ya* 36[3,6] 41[4,12] *-šu* 35[27] 40[16] *um-ma-a-ni* 57[20] *ummânâti-ya* 7[21] *-šu* 16[1] *ummânâti*$_{pl}$ 33[9] *-šu* 8[14,15] *ummânât* 15[31] *ummânât*$_{pl}$ 5[18] *um-ma-na-tí-ya* 1[7] *-šu-nu* 1[16] *um-ma-na-a-ti* 15[26] *-tí-ya*$_{pl}$ 3[6] *-tí-šu-nu* 4[17] *um-ma-na-at* 2[12,13].

אמק$_4$ **ímíḳu** to be deep **ímuḳu** depth, power, army *í-muḳ* 22[27] 42[6] 46[19] *í-mu-ḳi* 2[20] *-šu-un* 19[10] *-ki* 11[25] 27[28] 34[17] 50[22] *-šu-nu* 42[21] *amílu í-mu-ki* 30[14] *-ya* 29[8] 42[15] *-šu-nu* 29[33] *í-mu-ki-í-šu* 22[28] *í-mu-ga-a-šu* 35[22] *ímuḳâni*$_{pl}$ 8[7] *í-mu-ḳa-an* 9[10]; **nimíḳu** wisdom *ni-mí-ḳu* 36[12] *-ki* 20[12]; **ímḳu** wise *í-im-ḳu* 35[5].

אמר$_1$ **amâru** to see *im-mar* (= *i-'a-mar*) 58[24] *im-ma-ru* 52[9] *a-mu-ur* 37[21] 38[15] *i-mur* 60[13] 61[5] *-ši* 64[6] *í-mur* 50[9] *i-mu-ru* 36[18] 37[26,34] *í-mu-ru* 22[14,16] 46[24] *li-mur* 24[16] 39[16]; *in-nam-ru* (IV I = *in-'am-ru*) 9[13]; **tâmirtu** environs *ta-mir-ti* 11[26] 17[6].

אמר$_2$ **amâru** to be full *a-mir* 14[11].

אמר$_3$ **imíru** ass *imírî*$_{pl}$ 12[13] 18[27] 30[27] 31[4,33].

אמש **amâšu** (?) to set out, depart *at-tu-muš* 30[18] 31[9].

אן **a-an** determinative after numbers and measures 42[18] (cf. *ta-a-an*).

אן **înnu** lord *în-ni* 13[1]; **înnitu** lordship (?) *ín-ni-ti-ya* 20[18].

אן **ana** to, unto, in order to, at, for, on account of, against 32[5] 59[8] *a-na* 29[34] 41[10] 42[8] 60[1]; **ammíni** (= *ana míni*) why? 63[7,10,13,16,19,22] 64[3]; **aššu** (= *ana šu*) in order to, because *aš-šu* 18[14] 19[13] 22[26] 23[27] 25[23] 32[24] 61[2].

אן **ina** in, with, by, at the time of, during 21[4] 58[1] *i-na* 1[1].

אן$_4$ **ínu** time *í-nu-ma* at the time when 5[16] 40[34] 62[4,10].

אנה$_1$ **unûtu** utensils *u-nu-ut* 8[10].

אנב$_1$ **inbu** fruit *in-bu* 20[28].

אנגגם *abnu* **an-gug-mí** a kind of stone 12[27].

אנזב **inzabtu** (?) ear-ring *in-za-ba-tí* 63[9,10] 64[22].

אנח$_1$ **anâḫu** to decay *in-na-ḫu* 24[15] 39[15] *í-na-aḫ* 6[13]; **anḫûtu** decay *an-ḫu-ta* 10[1] *an-ḫu-ut-su-un* 41[8] *an-ḫu-us-su* 24[15].

אנך$_1$ **anâku** I (personal pronoun) *a-na-ku* 14[12] *-ma* 23[23] *-um-ma* 59[9].

אנך$_1$ **anaku** lead *anaki*$_{pl}$ 6[28].

אן **annû** fem. *annîtu* this *an-nu-ti* (pl.) 46[1] 60[23,24] *-tí* 46[24] *an-ni-tu* 22[14,16] 26[9] 32[23] [*an-na-ti*] 41[10] *an-na-a-ti* 26[27] 42[13] *-tí* 25[16] 46[22].

אן **íninna** now *í-nin-na* 26[23] *-ma* 61[21] 62[1].

אנן to resist *in-nin-nu-u* 34[11] 35[31]; **anuntu** resistance *a-nun-tu* 32[32] *-tí* 6[7].

אנן$_1$ **unninnu** a sigh *un-nin-ni-ya* 25^{6} 38^{24}.

אנן **annu** guilt, punishment *an-nu* 28^{21} *an-ni* 12^{1}.

אנן$_3$ **annu** favor *an-ni* 2^{21}.

אננך **anunnaki** the spirits of earth (contrasted with *igigi*, spirits of heaven) *a-nun-na-ki* 7^{2,7} 58^{17} 59^{11} 64^{11,15}.

אנף$_1$ **appu** face *ap-pi* 34^{25} *-ya* 59^{22,24}.

אנש$_1$ **nišû** people, mankind *ni-šu-u* 59^{9} *nišî pl* 1^{18} 61^{15,16,18} *-ya* 18^{1,2} 59^{8} 61^{3} *-šu* 17^{27} 18^{26} 31^{3} 40^{12} *-šu-nu* 33^{30} 41^{25}; **tínišítu** the human race, mankind *tí-ni-ší-í-ti* 19^{25} 59^{20}; **aššatu** woman, wife *-šu* 62^{1} *aššat* 28^{31} *-su* 11^{10} 31^{3}.

אנש$_1$ **ínšu** weak *ínši* 23^{27}.

אנת$_1$ **atta** thou 14^{24} 23^{10} 39^{10,14} 61^{11}.

אנת (?) **attû** (a stem to which the pronominal suffixes are attached in order to express the pronoun as the object of thought) *at-tu-u-a* as for me 22^{19} *at-tu-ni* as for us 46^{14}.

אס **a-si** . . . . . 28^{22}.

אסל **aslu** a lamb (?) *as-li-iš* (adv.) 16^{6}.

אסל **usallu** . . . . . adv. *u-sal-liš* 18^{16}.

אסמ **asmûti** . . . . . (adj. mas. pl. or abstract gen.) *as-mu-ti* 16^{9}.

אסר **asâru** (?) to surround, besiege, overlay *í-si-ir* 24^{26} 48^{27} *í-sir-šu* 11^{22} 12^{16} *í-sír-šu* 8^{22}.

אסתר **us-tur** *iṣṣuru pl* . . . . . 10^{10}.

אפל **aplu** son *apal* 5^{3} *-šu* 21^{8} *apli* 30^{16} *apla* 21^{11} *aplî* 27^{27} *aplî pl* 57^{20} 59^{10} *-šu* 11^{10} *-šu-nu* 26^{1}; **apal-šarrûtu** prince regent, regency *apal-šarrûti* 19^{18} *apal-šarrû-tu* 20^{8} *-ti-ya* 20^{8}.

אפל **apâlu** to subdue *i-pi-lu* 5^{9,13} *a-pi-lu-ši-na-ni* 6^{2,15,29}; *í-tap-pa-lu* 20^{13}.

אפסו **apsû** ocean, abyss 62^{6} *apsî* 7^{3} *ap-si-í* 26^{26}.

אפף **appu** cf. אנף$_1$.

אפר$_1$ **apâru** to cover, clothe *a-pi-ir* (part.) 6^{6} *a-pi-ra* 15^{22}.

אפר$_4$ **ipru** dust *ip-ru* 52^{11} pl. *iprâti* 15^{12} 18^{11} 52^{8}.

אפש **ípíšu** to do, make, exercise *ib-bu-šu* (1st impf.) 39^{16}; *ípu-uš* (1st pers.) 6^{25} *í-pu-uš* 4^{26} *-us-su* (= *uš-šu*) 48^{20} *-us-su-nu-ti* 46^{10} *í-pu-šu* 34^{23} *-uš* 27^{20} *ípuš* (3rd pers.) 61^{7,10} *ípu-uš* 6^{13} *i-pu-uš* 37^{27} 64^{7} *ip-pu-uš* 39^{25} *í-pu-šu* 9^{27} 20^{8} *i-pu-šu* 60^{22} *í-pu-šu* (pl.) 17^{23} *í-pu-us*(var. *šu*)*-su-nu-ti* 46^{28} *u-pu-šu* (= *í-pu-šu*) 6^{3} *í-pu-uš* (impv.) 35^{18}; *í-pi-šu* (inf.) 35^{21} *-ši* 28^{2} *í-piš* 3^{16} *í-pi-íš* 20^{4}; *í-piš* (part.) 12^{1} 23^{19} *í-bi-iš* 38^{21}; *í-tí-ip-pu-šu* (I 2) 26^{27}; *up-pi-is-si* (= *up-pi-iš-ši* do unto her II I impv.) 63^{2}; *u-ší-piš* (III I) 19^{2} 24^{6}; **ipšítu** deed *ip-ší-í-tu* 26^{9} 32^{23} *-ti* 26^{27} 40^{12} 41^{10} 42^{13} *ip-ší-ti-ya* 24^{8} *íp-ší-ti-šu* 36^{20} *íp-ší-tu-u-a* 38^{22} 39^{11} *ip-šit* 23^{6} 46^{24}.

אץ **iṣu** pl. *iṣûtu* few, small *i-ṣu-tu* 35^{27}.

אץ$_4$ **iṣu** wood, tree *iṣî*$_{pl}$ 3^{5} 30^{8}.

אצן$_3$ **íṣínu** to collect, take, seize, inhale *í-ṣi-ín-ši* $57^{16\,bis}$ $57^{17,18}$ *i-ṣi-nu* $60^{19\,bis}$.

אצף **aṣpu** ..... *aṣ-pi* $16^{3,15}$.

אצץ$_3$ **uṣṣu** arrow *uṣ-ṣi* 15^{32} *-šu* 33^{1}.

אצר$_4$ **íṣíru** to enclose, lay up *í-ṣir* 10^{7}.

אצר (?) **iṣṣuru** bird *iṣṣuri* 12^{15} *iṣ-ṣu-ri* 17^{21} *iṣṣur* 30^{10} *iṣṣurî*$_{pl}$ 10^{10} 26^{25}.

אקל$_3$ **íḳlu** field, territory *íḳla* 3^{3} *íḳil* 1^{8}.

אקץ **aḳṣu, iḳṣu** strong *aḳ-ṣu* 19^{7} *iḳ-ṣu-tí* 6^{6}.

אקרב **iḳribu** cf. קרב.

אר **urru** cf. אור$_1$.

א$_4$רא$_1$ **irtu** breast *irti-ya* 8^{8} 50^{6} 63^{16} *-ša* 63^{15} 64^{20} *i-rat* 9^{16} *-su-un* 15^{31} *-su-nu* 1^{5}.

ארה **írû** bronze *írî*$_{pl}$ 2^{6} 3^{4} *ì-ri-í* 10^{8}.

ארה$_2$ (?) **íriyâti** heavy clouds *í-ri-ya-a-ti* 15^{13}.

ארב$_1$ **aribu** locust *a-ri-bi* 15^{10}.

ארב$_5$ **íríbu** to enter *ir-ru-ba* 52^{16} *lu-ru-bu* 52^{15}; *íru-ub* (1st pers.) 7^{22} *í-ru-ub* 58^{7} *í-ru-um-ma* 42^{9} *i-ru-um-ma* 23^{25} *í-ru-bu* 40^{34} *í-ru-ba-am-ma* 13^{29}; *í-ru-ub* (3rd sing.) 14^{16}; *í-ru-bu* (pl.) 29^{6}; *í-ru-ub* (impv.) 58^{2} *ir-bi* 63^{4} 64^{1}; *í-ri-bu-šu* (part.) $52^{5,7}$; *íríbu* (inf.) entrance *í-ri-bi* 38^{7} *-ka* 37^{6} 38^{19} 39^{11} *í-rib* 6^{10} (*írib šamši* = sunset) 9^{9}; *u-ší-rib* (1st pers.) 10^{17} 13^{5} *-ri-bi* 41^{30} *u-ší-rib* (3rd pers.) 13^{26} *-ši* $63^{6,9,12}$ 64^{2} *-ri-bi* 40^{1} *-bu* 12^{25} *-ba-aš* 40^{18}; **niribu** entrance, pass *ni-ri-bi* 13^{15} *ni-rib* 5^{26} 28^{23} 33^{21} *ni-ri-bí* 7^{21} *ni-ri-bi-tí* 2^{26} (fem. pl.).

ארב$_5$ **aribu** raven *a-ri-bi* $60^{12,13}$.

ארב **uribu** beam of wood (?) *u-ri-bi* 59^{21}.

ארב **arba'u, irbittu** cf. רבא$_4$.

ארח **íríḫu** ..... *í-ri-ḫu-šu* 25^{17}; **miriḫtu** ..... *mi-ri-iḫ-tu* 25^{10}.

ארח$_1$ **arâḫu** to hasten *ur-ri-ḫa* (II I) 25^{5}; **ar-ḫiš** hastily, promptly 11^{17}; **ur-ru-ḫiš** hastily 14^{3} 15^{20} *ur-ru-ḫi-iš* 42^{25}.

ארח$_1$ **urḫu, arḫu** way, road *ur-ḫu* 42^{23} *ur-ḫi* 30^{6} *u-ru-uḫ* 15^{7} *ar-ḫi* 2^{28} (pl.).

ארך$_1$ **arâku** to be long *a-ra-ku* 41^{31} (inf.) *í-ri-ik* 20^{25} *li-ri-ku* 24^{12}; *ur-ri-ku* (II I) 62^{16}; *li-ša-ri-ik* (III I) 37^{13}.

ארכרן **urkarina** a species of tree 12^{29} 18^{24} *urkarini*$_{pl}$ 6^{21}.

ארם **arammu** wall (?) *a-ram-mí* 12^{10}.

ארם **urumu** trunk of a tree (?) *u-ru-mi* 3^{5}.

ארן$_1$ **írinu** cedar *írini* 36^{15} *í-ri-ni* 6^{20} *írina* 60^{18}.

ארן **arnu** sin, wrong *a-ra-an-šu-nu* 12^{3}.

ארף$_4$ **urpatu** cloud *ur-pa-tum* 58^{11}.

ארץ$_1$ **irṣitu** earth *irṣi-tum* [62^{5}] *irṣiti* 44^{10} *irṣi-ti* 7^{5} *-tí* 7^{10} *-tim* 35^{15} 63^{8} 64^{1} *ir-ṣi-ti* 16^{8} *ir-ṣi-is-su* (its site) 18^{13}.

ארר$_1$ **arâru** to curse *ta-ru-ur* 23[10]; **arratu** a curse *ar-ra-a-ti* 32[14]; **ariru** consuming (?) *a-ri-ri* 26[7,13].

ארש$_4$ **iršu** bed *irši*$_{pl}$ 12[28].

ארש **irišu** odor *i̥-ri-ša* 60[19 bis] *i-ri-is-si-na* (= *i-ri-iš-ši-na*) 36[25].

ארש **uršânu** strong, mighty *ur-ša-nu* 6[6].

אש$_1$ **išâti** fire 13[22] *išâti*$_{pl}$ 2[1].

אשב **išibbûtu** princehood, royalty *i-šib-bu-ti* 26[33].

אשד$_1$ **išdu** foundation, horizon *i-šid* 58[11] *iš-da-a-šu* 9[29].

אשו **ušû** a kind of tree 12[29] 18[24].

אשם$_3$ **ušmânu** camp *uš-man-ni* 30[20] *uš-ma-ni-šu* 8[20].

אשמגל **ušum-gallu** . . . . . *u-šum-gal-lu* 6[4].

אשמר$_3$ **îšmarû** a kind of metal *îš-ma-ru-ú* 36[28].

אשף$_1$ **šiptu** conjuring, magical power *šip-ti* 61[9].

אשף$_1$ **išpatu** quiver *iš-pa-ti* 38[28].

אשק$_3$ **iškatu** bond *iš-ḳa-ti* 22[23].

אשר$_1$ **aššuritu** of Aššur (title of Ištar) *aššur-i-tu* 42[14].

אשר$_1$ **ašru** place *aš-ru* 22[10] 30[23] (on 59[12] cf. ושר) *-uš-šu* (= *ina ašrišu*) 37[5,22] 38[16] 39[18] *aš-ri* [19[2]] *-šu-nu* 18[8] 41[24] *a-šar* 10[24] 17[2] 18[19] 20[8] 30[10,22,24,32] 31[24,31] 34[14] 46[4] 48[16,21] 52[8] *-šu* 9[14] 10[2] 29[24].

אשר$_3$ **îšîru** to collect *î-šu-ra* 14[28].

אשר **îširtu** pl. *îšrîti* shrine *iš-ri-î-ti* 23[31] *îš-ri-î-ti* 23[20] *-šu-un* 20[17] *îšrîti*$_{pl}$-*šu-nu* 14[20].

אשר **aširtu** pl. *ašrâti* shrine *aš-ra-ti-šu* 24[5].

אשרד$_1$ **ašaridu** leader *a-ša-ri-du* 30[16].

אשש **îššûtu** cf. ארש$_3$; **aššatu** cf. אנש$_1$.

אשש$_1$ **uššû** foundation *uš-šu* 36[13] *-šu* 9[28] 36[18] 39[4] *uššî-šu* 18[9] *uš-šî-šu* 10[4] 18[13].

אשת **ištu** out of, from 5[22] *iš-tu* 58[11] 64[5].

אשת (?) **ašâtî** . . . . . *a-ša-a-tî* 20[15].

אשתן$_4$ **ištîn** one *išt-în* 6[11] 7[23] 27[10] 32[22 bis] 60[4] 63[6] 64[17]; *iš-tî-niš* together, quickly 21[8] 62[8].

אשתר$_4$ **ištar** goddess $_{ilu}$*ištarâti*$_{pl}$-*šu-nu* 27[2].

את **atta** cf. אנת$_1$; **attû** cf. אנת.

אתה **uttû** (II 1) to appoint *ut-tu-šu* 9[4]; **ittu** side *it-ti* with, against (= at the side of) 1[9] *-ya* 27[11] *-šu* 8[17] *-ša* 59[11] *-šu-un* 11[28] *-šu-nu* 8[9]; **ittûtu** concubinage *ittu-u-ti* 21[7,14,18,23].

אתל$_4$ **itlu** high, exalted *it-lu* 5[5] 9[6] *it-lum* 16[1] *it-lu-ti* 2[28].

אתק$_4$ **îtîḳu** to march, walk *i-ti-ḳu* 16[31]; *ni-it-ta*[*-at-ti-iḳ*] (I 2) 41[14] *î-tî-it-ti-iḳ* 19[16] *î-tî-it-ti-ḳu* 30[9]; *u-šî-ti-iḳ* 2[28]; **mîtîḳu** march, progress *mî-ti-iḳ* 3[5] 11[15] 13[4] 42[18] *mî-tî-iḳ* 2[7].

אתת **ittu** pl. *ittâtu* work (?), possession (?) *it-ta-tu-u-a* 37[12] 38[24,31].

ב

בא$_4$ה to seek *u-ba-'i* 37[31] *-u* 37[26] *-i* 46[28].

בא$_4$ל **bílu** to prevail, take possession of, rule *i-bìl* 17[17] *i-bí-lu* 9[9] 23[16] 42[4] *lu-bi-íl* 38[26]; **bílu** lord 2[25] *-ši-na* 16[24] $_{ilu}$*bílu* 35[30] *bí-lu* 40[24] *bí-lum* 46[19] *bíli* 8[8] *-ya* 1[4] 24[7] *-šu* 5[6] *-šu-nu* 26[11] *bíl* 7[5] 60[20] $_{amílu}$*bíl* 11[29,30] 14[10] $_{ilu}$*bíl* 7[2] 35[20] 39[27] *bí-íl* 61[13 bis] *bílî*$_{pl}$*-í* 6[5] *-a* 36[7,32] *bílî*$_{pl}$*-ya* 22[21] *-šu* 5[12]; **bíltu** lady *bílti* 39[10] *bílta-šu* 31[3] *bílit* 38[27] 39[6] *bí-lit* 50[23] $_{ilu}$*bí-lit* 33[3] *bí-íl-ti* 52[23] 63[4] 64[1]; **bílûtu** dominion *bílû-ti-a* 5[17] 6[23] *-ya* 22[30] *-šu* 6[9] *-šu-un* 34[22] *bílu-u-ti* 25[25] 33[3] *-ya* 27[21] 34[6] *bí-lu-ti* 12[5] *-ya* 10[19] *-šu* 9[7] *bí-lu-tim* 41[1] *bí-lut* 20[10] *bí-lu-ut* 14[17]; **ba'ulâti** subjects *ba-'u-lat* 9[9].

באר **bâru** to seize, draw out *a-bar-šu* 18[22] 19[12] 34[15].

בא$_2$ר **bu'âru** pride, joy *bu-'a-a-ri* 24[12].

בב **bâbu** gate, door *ba-a-bu* 52[16] *-bi* 52[13] 58[7] *bâbi-šu* 10[6] *bâba* 63[6] *bâb* 10[5] *-ka* 58[2] *ba-ab-ka* 52[14] 63[1] *-šu* 63[3] *bâbî*$_{pl}$*-šu* 36[25] *bâbâni*$_{pl}$*-ša* 6[25,27].

בב **bubutu** hunger, food *bu-bu-ti* 24[28] 26[12,29] *bu-bu-us-su-nu* 52[8].

בבל **biblu** wish *bi-bíl* 40[6]; **bubulu** . . . . . *bu-bu-lu* 9[10].

בגד $_{amílu}$**bí-gid-da**$_{pl}$ ideogram for some high official 27[14].

בוא$_1$ **bâ'u** to come *i-ba-'a-u* 58[19]; *u-ba-'a-u* 58[23].

בול **bûlu** cattle 20[28] *bu-ul* 57[20].

בחל **bitḫallu** riding-horse *bit-ḫal-lu-šu* 8[19] *-la-šu-nu* 8[10].

בטל **baṭâlu** to cease *u-šab-ṭi-li* 39[23]; **baṭlu** cessation (as adj. stopped) *ba-aṭ-lu* 10[28] *baṭ-lu-tu* 23[21]; **baṭiltu** cessation *ba-ṭi-il-tu* 22[26].

בטן **buṭnu** pistacia tree *bu-uṭ-ni* 6[22].

בית **bîtu** house 39[15] *bîti* 9[28] *bit-ti* 32[15] *bîta* 4[28] *bît* 10[13] *bît makkuri* treasure house 14[18] *bît ridûti* harem 19[18] *bît-su* 37[25] *bîtâti*$_{pl}$ 18[9] *bîtât*$_{pl}$ 18[10,15]; *bît-dûri* stronghold 30[19] *bît-dûrâ*$_{pl}$*-ni* 10[23] *bît-dûrâni*$_{pl}$ 12[8]; *bît-ṣíri* tent 28[12]; *bît-tuklâti* barracks (?) *bît-tuk-la-ti-šu* 10[24].

בכה **bakû** to weep *a-bak-ki* 59[23] *ba-ku-u* 59[11]; **bikîtu** weeping *bi-ki-ti* 59[12].

בכר **bakru** . . . . . *ba-ak-ru* 32[18].

בלה **balû** without *ba-lu* 40[18].

בלט **balâṭu** to live *ib-luṭ* 61[6]; *u-bal-liṭ* 33[24] 48[9] *-li-ṭu* 40[24]; **balâṭu** life *balâṭi* 64[12,16] *balâṭ* 24[9] 31[25] *ba-laṭ* 27[7]; **balṭûtu** life *bal-ṭu-us-su* 28[31] 34[5,15] *-un* 31[16] *-nu* 48[7] *bal-ṭu-sun* 26[21] *-su-un* 11[30] 16[21] 17[12,30] *-su-nu* 3[30]; **balṭu** alive, living *bal-ṭu-ti* 52[19,20].

בלל **balâlu** to pour over (?) *ab-lu-ul* 36[19].

בלש **bílšu** some instrument or method of attack *bíl-ši* 12[11].

בלת **biltu, bilâti** cf. ובל.

בלת **biltu** some weapon of offense (?) *bíl-ti* 17[27].

במה **bamâtu** height *ba-mat* 2[11] *ba-ma-at* 3[20] *ba-ma-a-tí* 1[13] 4[13,21].

בן **binu** a son *bin-bini* grandson 23^{21} 40^{30} *bi-ni* sons (=seeds) 16^{14}; **bintu** daughter $21^{6,22}$ *bi-in-tu* 21^{17} *binat* $52^{2,3}$ *-su* $21^{9,13}$ *binâti*$_{pl}$*-šu* 11^{10} 12^{30} *-šu-nu* 26^{1} *binât*$_{pl}$ $21^{6,9}$.

בנה **banû** to do, make, build, create, beget *i-ban-na-ši* 61^{8} *ab-ni* 6^{14} 36^{22} *ib-nu-u* 19^{20} *bânu-u-a* 20^{9} *ba-nu-u* 7^{3} *-a* 19^{23} *bâni-ya* 20^{23} *-šu* 23^{8} *ba-ni-šu-un* 37^{9} *-šu-nu* 37^{17} *ba-ní* 12^{2}; *ib-ba-[nu]* 62^{15} *-u* 62^{12}; **binûtu** creature *bi-nu-tu* 19^{17} *bi-nu-ut* 27^{26}; **nabnîtu** offspring *nab-ni-tu* 7^{17} *-it* 4^{1}.

בנה **ba-ni-ti** . . . . . 37^{16}.

בצר **buṣru** midst (?), interior (?) *bu-ṣur* 18^{12}.

ברה **biru** midst *bi-ri-in-ni* $46^{16,18}$ 61^{24} *bi-ri-šu-nu* 32^{13} 48^{8}; **birtu** midst *bi-rit* between $30^{8,23}$; **birîtu** bond *bi-ri-tu* 11^{21} 31^{17} *-ti* 22^{23} 46^{25}.

ברה **burû** food *bu-ri-šu-nu* 26^{1} 32^{14}.

ברה **barû** to look, see *ab-ri-í* 39^{2} *ib-ri-í-šu* 40^{5}; *u-šab-ri-šum-ma* 61^{20} *-šu-ma* 22^{11} *u-šab-ru-'-in-ni* 35^{14}; **biru** a vision *bi-ri* 36^{11} 38^{3}; **tab-ra-a-tí** . . . . . 5^{7}.

ברבר **barbaru** jackal 61^{16}.

ברך **barâku** . . . . . *u-šab-ri-ku* 23^{8}.

ברך **birku** . . . . . *bir-ki* 14^{9}.

ברם **birmu** a kind of clothing *birmi* 18^{24} *bir-mí* 22^{6} 48^{10} 50^{12}; **bu-ru-mu** . . . . . 23^{31}.

ברק **birḳu** lightning *biriḳ* $4^{26,29}$.

ברש **burâšu** cypress *$_{iṣu}$ burâši* 7^{27}.

בשה **bašû** to be *i-ba-aš-ši* 35^{24} *i-pa-aš-šum-ma* $60^{9,11}$ *ib-ba-ši* 46^{18} *ib-ba-aš-šu-u* 30^{24}; *ib-šu* 9^{7} *-u* 12^{3}; *ba-ši-i* 14^{15} *ba-šu-u* 18^{11} 20^{13} 31^{24} 50^{12}; *u-šab-šu-u* 11^{34} 14^{12} 34^{12}; **bušû** possession *buší* 11^{7} *bu-ší-í-šu* 58^{9} *bušâ* 17^{31} 50^{12} [*-šu-nu* 18^{3}] *bu-ša-šu-nu* 1^{23} 3^{25} 4^{22} *bu-ša-a-šu-nu* 1^{15}.

בשל **bašâlu** to boil *ib-ši-lu-nim-ma* 25^{20}.

בתחל **bitḫallu** cf. בחל.

בתק **batâḳu** to cut off *ab-tuḳ* 12^{18}; *ib-ba-ti-iḳ* 61^{14}.

ג

גא **gu-'u-iš** . . . . . adv. 16^{7}.

גבב **gubbu** pit, cistern *gu-ub-ba-a-ni* 30^{20}.

גבר **gabru** a rival *gab-ri-šu* 9^{7}.

גבש **gabâšu** to be strong, massive *ig-bu-uš* 22^{28}; **gabšu** strong, massive *gab-šu* 5^{8} *gab-ši* 16^{7} *gab-ša* 4^{10} *gab-šu-ti* 16^{10} *gab-ša-a-tí* 4^{17}; **gibšu** mass *gi-biš* 8^{14}; **gibšûtu** mass *gi-ib-šu-su-un* 15^{7}.

גגר **gagaru** Babyl. for *ḳaḳḳaru* ground, earth *ga-ga-ri* 37^{32} 38^{23}.

גדו **gadu** with, together with *ga-du* 17^{29} 24^{25} $25^{1,29}$ 27^{8}.

גזלל **guzalalu** throne-bearer *gu-za-lalî*$_{pl}$ 58^{14}.

גחל **guḫlu** some article of tribute *gu-uḫ-li* 12^{27}.

גלל **gallu** a demon *gallî*$_{pl}$ 14^{7}.

גמח **gû-maḫḫu** large oxen *gû-maḫ-ḫi* (pl.) 10^{9}.

גמל **gamâlu** to finish, reward, give *ig-mi-lu* 40^{25}; **gimillu** gift *gi-mil-li* 9^{24} (*turru gimilli* to avenge); **gitmalu** mature, strong [*git*]-*ma-lu* 7^{8}.

גמל **gammalu** camel *gammalî*$_{pl}$ 12^{13} 30^{27} $31^{4,28,33}$ $32^{3,5,8}$.

גמר **gamâru** to be finished, to finish (trans.) *ag-da-mar* 18^{16}; **gimru** all, totality *gim-ri* 7^{6} *-ša* 6^{17} *-šu-un* 62^{7} *-šu-nu* 6^{5} *gi-im-ri-šu* 37^{2} *gi-mir* 2^{19} *gim-rat* 7^{1}.

גן **gun** ideogram for talent $10^{13,14}$ $12^{26,27}$ 50^{14}.

גן **ginu** (= *kinu*) full, proper (?) *gi-ni-í* 27^{15}.

גפר **giparu** . . . . . *gi-pa-ru* 20^{27} *-ra* 62^{9}.

גצץ **giṣṣu** a kind of tree (?) *gi-iṣ-ṣi* 30^{8}.

גצר **gû-ṣur** . . . . . 32^{18}.

גרה **garû** to be hostile, resist *i-gi-ra-an-ni* 26^{6}; **gârû** enemy *ga-ri-ya* 20^{18} 26^{5} 32^{33} 33^{5} 36^{27} 37^{15} *-šu* 39^{20}.

גרן **guruntu** a heap *gu-ru-na-tí* 2^{15}.

גרר **garâru** to go, run; **girru** way, road, expedition *gi-ra-a* 28^{4} *gir-ri-ya* 10^{18} 14^{24} *gir-ri-í-ti-šu* 21^{4} *gir-ri-tí-šu-nu* 2^{6}.

גשל **gišallatu** peak (?) *gi-šal-lat* 2^{15} 4^{12}.

גשר **gašâru** to be strong, powerful; **gašru** strong *gaš-ra-a-tí* 32^{30}; **gišru** strong *giš-ru* 7^{5}; **gušûru** beam *gu-šur*$_{pl}$ 7^{26} *gušur* (pl.) 36^{23}.

גשש **gašîšu** stake *ga-ši-ši* 33^{32} 48^{4}.

גשתן *iṣu* **gištin-gir** (?)$_{pl}$ ideogram for a kind of vine (?) 30^{9}.

גתה **gâtu** Babyl. for *ḳâtu* hand *ga-tim* 36^{31} 38^{12}.

גתמל **gitmalu** cf. גמל.

ד

דאה **da'âtu** bribe (?) *da-'a-tu* $14^{22,26}$ *da-'a-a-tu* 24^{30}.

דבב **dabâbu** to meditate, plan *a-da-bu-ba* (1st impf.) 20^{16}; *id-bu-ub* 29^{32} *id-bu-bu* 21^{17} 46^{12}; **dabâbu, dababtu** plan, device *da-bab* 27^{24} 29^{32} *da-bab-ti* 46^{11}.

דבק **nadbaku** outflow (?) *na-ad-bak* 13^{31}.

דבס **dubbusû** a younger brother (?) *dub-bu-us-su-u* 14^{4}.

דגל **dagâlu** to see *da-gil* $42^{19,25}$; III I to cause to see, commit, entrust *u-šad-gi-lu* 14^{18} 20^{17} 28^{27}.

דגס **dag-gas-si** some article of tribute 12^{27}.

דדם **dadmu** a dwelling *da-ad-mi* 40^{2} *-šu-un* 41^{25} *da-ad-mí-šu* 18^{18}.

דדן **dudinâtí** (fem. pl.) some part of attire, worn on the breast *du-di-na-tí* 63[15,16] 64[20].

דוך **dâku** to kill *a-duk* 11[34] 28[9] 29[5] 33[28] *idu-ku* (3. pl.) 8[2] *ad-du-ku* 50[23]; *da-a-ki* 42[8] *da-ak-šu-nu* 16[26]; **dîku** killed *di-ku* 16[24]; **dîktu** slaughter *di-ik-ta-šu* 28[8]; **tidûku** slaughter *ti-du-ki-šu* 8[18] *-šu-nu* 8[11].

דור **dûru** a wall 18[10] *dûra-šu* 4[28] 18[18] *dûr* 48[5] 59[22,24] (*dûr appi* = cheek) *dûrâni*$_{pl}$ 12[8] (*bît-dûrâni*$_{pl}$ = strongholds) *-šu-nu* 4[23].

דזה **dazâti** wars (?) *da-za-a-ti* 21[17].

דח **daḫu** festival (?) *da-ḫu* 30[17].

דחד **duḫdu** abundance *duḫ-du* 20[29].

דין **dânu** a judge 24[7] *da-a-a-nu* 37[24] *dân* 7[5]; **dînu** judgment *di-ni-šu* 25[24].

דיש **dâšu** to tread down *da-a-iš* 5[10] *u-da-i-šu* 16[31].

דך **di-ka**$_{pl}$ ideogram for sacrifice (?) 27[15].

דכה **dakû** to tear down, cast down *ad-ki-í* 37[31].

דכה **dakû** to collect, muster *ad-ki* 7[21] 24[23] 27[18] 30[4] *ad-ki-í* 42[15] *id-ka-a* 8[15] 44[3] 48[26] *id-ku-u* 16[21] *id-ku-ni* 4[6] *id-ku-u-ni* 29[34]; *di-ka-a* (impv.) 14[22].

דל **daltu** door *dal-tum* 52[17] *dalti* 52[11] *dalâti*$_{pl}$ 6[26] 36[24] 38[9] 52[18].

דלח **dalḫu** disturbed *dal-ḫu-u-tí* 9[17].

דלל **dalâlu** to manifest (?), exalt (?) *i-dal-la-lu* 25[26] *da-lal* 33[22].

דלף **dalâpu** II I to weaken (?) *mu-dal-li-pu* 22[18].

דמא$_4$ **dimu** a tear *di-ma-a-a* 59[24].

דמה **dâmu** blood *da-mu* 16[11] *da-mí* 14[11] *-šu-nu* 16[10] *dâmî*$_{pl}$ 31[29] *-šu-nu* 1[12].

דמה **dimmu** a column (?) *iṣu dim-mí* 50[13]; **dimtu** stake *di-ma-a-tí* 11[34].

דמגל **dim** (?)**-gal** . . . . . 41[5].

דמק **damâḳu** to favor, be gracious *u-dam-ma-ḳu* 38[30] *li-dam-mi-iḳ* 37[12]; *du-um-mi-iḳ* 38[24]; **dunḳu** (for *dumḳu*) favor *du-un-ḳu* 46[28] *-ḳí-ya* 41[32]; **damiḳtu** favor *damiḳ-tu* 48[19] *-tim* 37[6,18] 39[13] *da-mi-iḳ-ta-šu* 39[21]; **damḳu** gracious, favorable *damḳûti*$_{pl}$ 12[24] *damḳâti*$_{pl}$ 37[11] 38[22] 39[11] *dam-ḳa-a-ti* 24[8]; *da-am-ḳí-iš* graciously 41[13].

דנם **dun-na-mu-u** . . . . . 14[9].

דנן **danânu** to be strong, mighty *u-dan-nin* 36[20] 46[7] *-ni-na* 20[5]; *dun-nu-nu-u* 9[28]; *dun-nu-un* 12[25]; **danânu** might, strength *da-na-ni-šu-nu* 1[5] *da-na-a-ni* 34[30] *da-na-an* 19[13]; **dunnu** strength, mass *dun-ni* 15[13] *du-un-ni* 9[28]; **dannu** mighty *dan-nu* 2[18] 23[27] *-ni* 5[4] *dan-nu-tu* 38[8] *-ti* 10[23] *-tí* 3[3] *dan-na-tum* (fem.) 15[24]; **dannatu** strong-hold *dan-na-ti* 13[25]; **dannûtu** might *dan-nu-ti-šu* 7[22] *-šu-nu* 2[4] *dan-nu-us-su-un* 34[26]; *da-na-niš* with might 13[4]; **dan-dan-nu** almighty 7[8].

דפן **midpânu** a bow *mid-pa-a-nu* 50[23].

דפף **duppu** writing tablet *dup-šarru* tablet writer **dup-šar-ru-u-ti** tablet-writing 20[13].

דפר **dapranu, dupranu** juniper *dap-ra-ni* 6[21,27] *dup-ra-ni* 9[26].

דפר **diparu** pl. *diparâti* torch, flame *di-pa-ra-a-ti* 58[17].

דרה **dârû** everlasting *da-ru-u* 38[20] 40[31] *da-a-ri* 38[26] *dârâ-ti* 35[14] *dâra-a-ta* 41[24] *da-ra-ti* 23[25] *da-ra-a-tí* 6[23]; **dûrû** eternity *du-u-ri* 38[26]; **da-riš** forever 60[24].

דרג **durgu** way, path *du-ur-gi* 2[28].

דשא$_1$ **dišu** grass (?) 20[26].

דשף **dišpu** honey *dišpi* 36[19].

ו

ו **u** and (connecting nouns) 1[2], (connecting sentences) 61[3], now, because 11[8] 26[8] 59[20] 61[9], introducing oratio recta (like *umma*) 25[13].

ובל **abâlu** to bring *u-bal-šu-nu-ti* 16[5]; *u-bíl-šu* 17[30] *u-bi-la* 21[7] *u-bíl-am-ma* 21[15] *ub-lam-ma* 9[22] *u-bì-lu* (sing.) 18[6] *u-bíl-u-ni* 26[17] *u-bi-lu-nim-ma* 41[18]; *u-ší-bi-la* 21[9] *-lam-ma* 12[31] *u-ší-bi-lu-uš* 14[21]; **biltu** tribute 10[27] *bíl-tu* 27[16] *bilti* 1[3] *bilta* 1[21] *bi-lat-su-nu* 5[14]; **bilâti** wages (?) *bi-la-a-ti* 12[26].

וחס (?) **aḫâsu** to flee *it-tí-iḫ-su* 59[1].

ולד **alâdu** to bear, to beget *'a-al-du* 20[9] *a-li-di-ya* 20[7] *-ka* 39[13] *a-lit-ti* 59[3]; *ul-la-da* 59[9] *mu-al-li-da-at* 62[7]; **talittu** birth *ta-lit-ti* 20[28]; **littûtu** progeny [*lit-tu-ti*] 24[10].

ופא$_4$ to increase, magnify *u-ša-pa-a* 34[26] *mu-ša-pu-u* 33[2].

וצא$_1$ **aṣû** to go out *u-ṣi* 26[15] 31[31] 61[6] *u-ṣa-am-ma* 33[10] *u-ṣu-u* 17[1] *uṣûni* (?) 10[16] *u-ṣu-nim-ma*. 29[8]; *a-ṣu-u* 52[5] *a-ṣi-i* 38[6] *a-ṣi-í* 12[16]; *u-ší-ṣi* 2[17] 26[32] 60[8,10,12,15] 64[17-23] *u-ší-ṣa-a* 1[23] 3[26] 64[15] *lu-ší-ṣa-a* 1[16] *u-ší-ṣu-u* (sing.) 27[30] *u-ší-ṣa-am-ma* 12[5] *u-ší-ṣu-u* (pl.) 9[5] *u-ší-ṣu-ni* 14[20]; *šu-ṣa-a* (impv.) 64[11]; **ṣîtu** exit, (*ṣît šamši* = sunrise) *ṣît* 38[30] 39[12] *ṣi-it* 6[10] 21[6] (*ṣi-it libbi* = offspring); **ṣâtu** exit, eternity *ṣa-a-ti* 3[34] 35[8]; **mûṣu** exit *mu-uṣ-ṣa-šu-un* 24[26] 48[27]; **míṣu** . . . . . *mí-ṣi-šu* 33[18]; **nîṣu** excrement *ni-ṣu-šu-un* 16[33] (cf. *ni-ša-a* 17[15]).

וקר **aḳâru** to be costly, precious *tí-kir*(?)*-u* 26[10]; **aḳru** fem. *aḳartu* costly *a-ḳar-tu* 18[23] *aḳ-ra-tí* 16[6]; **šûḳuru** costly *šu-ḳu-ru-tu* 36[14] 38[4].

ורה **arû** to lead, carry *u-ra-aš-šu* 11[11] 33[14].

ורד **arâdu** to descend *u-ri-du* 64[5] (sing.) 14[12] *ur-du-ni* 1[6]; **ardu** servant 23[11] *arad-su* 25[8] 35[26] *ardâni*$_{pl}$ 42[19] *-šu* 34[12] *ardâ*$_{pl}$*-ni* 42[25]; **aradu** a low fellow *amílu a-ra-*[*du*] 14[10]; **ardûtu, urdûtu** servitude, obeisance *ardu-u-ti* 12[32] *-ut-tí* 3[34] *ardû-ti-ya* 21[9] *ardu-u-ti-ya* 34[10] *ur-du-ti* 6[3]; *kirru* **ardu** a tame sheep *kirru ardâni*$_{pl}$ 10[10].

ורח **arḫu** month 14[2] *arḫi* 36[11] 37[3] 38[2] *ar-ḫi-šam-ma* monthly 37[11] 39[12] *araḫ* 13[29] 19[25] 30[16] 31[7].

ורך **arkû** later, future, the rear *ar-ku-u* 24[14] *arka-a* 1[8]; **arkatu** end, future *ar-kat* 3[34]; **arki** prep. after, behind 25[2] 50[7] *-ya* 12[31] *-šu* 8[21] 14[3] *-šu-un* 16[34]; **arka, arkânu** adv. after, afterwards *arka* 14[6] 25[1] *arkâ-nu* 20[4] 34[11] 46[9] 48[22]; **ar-kiš** afterwards 17[16].

ורק **urḳitu** grass *ur-ki-ti* 16[13].

ושב **ašâbu** to sit, dwell *u-ši-bu* (1st sing.) 7[21] *u-šib* (3rd sing.) 14[5] 23[6] 42[9] 48[23] *u-ši-bu* 25[2]; *a-ša-ba-ni* (inf. + suff.) 46[14]; *a-šib* (perm.) 62[2] *aš-ba* 52[9]; *a-šib* (part.) 18[2] 21[29] *a-ši-ib* 39[28] *aš-bi* 59[12] *a-ši-bu-tu* 37[7] *a-ši-bu-ut* 10[8] *a-ši-bat* (fem. sing.) 32[30]; *at-ta-šab* 59[23]; *u-ší-šib* 10[27] 12[5] 44[12] 64[15] *-šu-nu-ti* 27[7] *u-ší-ši-ib* 4[30] 38[18] *u-ší-ši-bu* 37[30] (sing.) *-šu* 14[17] (pl.) *-in-ni* 20[23]; *šu-šib* (impv.) 64[11]; *mu-ší-šib* 23[19]; *uš-tí-ši-bu-in-ni* 62[3]; **šubtu** dwelling *šu-bat* 6[22] 34[22] *-su* 18[18] 33[26] *-su-un* 40[8] *šu-ba-at* 35[8] *-su* 35[19] 39[8]; **mûšabu** dwelling *mu-ša-bi-šu-nu* 28[18].

ושן **šunatu, šuttu** dream, vision *šu-na-ta* 61[20] *šutti* 22[11] *šu-ut-ti* 35[14] *šutta* 22[14,15].

ושר **ašru** bowed down *aš-ru* 59[12]; **tûšaru** destruction *tu-ša-ri* 1[12].

ותר **atâru** to abound *u-ša-tir* 18[14] 48[10,20] *u-šą-tí-ir* 39[9]; **šûturu** powerful *šu-tu-ru* 7[5].

ז

זאה . . . . . *u-za-'-i* 64[14] *za-'-i* 64[10].

זאב **zîbu** wolf *zi-i-bi iṣṣuru* wolf-bird, vulture 26[25].

זאז **zâzu** to be distributed (?) *u-za-'i-iz* 32[4].

זבב **zumbu** (= *zubbu*) fly *zu-um-bi-í* 60[20].

זוג **zâgu** . . . . . *i-zi-gam-ma* 58[22].

זוז **zâzu** to be agitated, enraged *i-zu-uz* 35[9].

זחל **zaḫalu** a kind of metal *za-ḫa-li-í* 36[27] 50[14].

זיק **zâḳu** to blow, storm *a-ziḳ* 17[26] *a-zi-iḳ* 15[29]; **zûḳu** storm *zu-uḳ* 12[10]; **zîḳu** ventilation (?) *zi-i-ḳi* 10[5].

זיר **zâru** to resist **za'iru** enemy *za-'i-i-ri* 15[23] *za-i-ri-šu* 7[18].

זכר **zakâru** to name, mention *az-ku-ra* 20[16] *iz-ku-ru* 19[19] *iz-kur-u* 19[10]; *zak-rat* 62[5]; *izzak-ar* 61[7,10] *iz-zak-kar* 52[18] 64[8] *-ka-ra* 52[22] *lit-taz-ka-ru* 41[32]; *izzak-ir* 58[1,4] *iz-zak-ra* 40[8]; *zuk-ku-ru* 62[11]; **zikru** name, fame, command *zi-kir* 9[4] *-ša* 33[21] *zi-ki-ir-šu* 40[26].

זכר **zikaru, zikru** male, manly, officer 12[12] *zi-ka-ru* 9[5] *amîlu zikar(?)-šu* 9[20] *amîlu zikar-iṣu kirî* gardener (?) 32[7] *zik-ru* 50[13]; **zikartu** female, woman *f zikrîti pl* 12[30] *f zik-ri-i-ti-šu* 26[17].

זמה **zummû** deprived of, bereft *zu-um-mu-u* 52[7].

זמן **zamanu** enemy *za-ma-ni-ya* 37^{14}.

זמר **zumru** body *zu-um-ri-ya* 64^{3} *-ša* 64^{2} *zu-mur-šu-un* 16^{29}.

זנא$_8$ **zinû** angry, enraged *zi-nu-u-ti* 27^{2}.

זנן **zanânu** to adorn, fill *az-nun* 23^{30}; *zaninu* adornment *za-nin* 20^{17}; *za-ni-in* (part.) 35^{3} *-ka* 38^{21}.

זנן **zanânu** to rain *i-za-an-nun* 32^{32}; *u-ša-az-na-na* 58^{4} *u-ša-az-na-an-nu* 58^{1} *u-ša-az-ni-na* 13^{30}; **zunnu** rain *zunnî*$_{pl}$ $13^{30\,bis}$ *-šu* 20^{24}.

זנש **zinnišu** female 12^{12} 19^{16} 31^{32} *zin-niš* 50^{13}; **zinništu** woman, wife *zin-niš-ti* 61^{23}.

זקן **ziḳnu** beard *ziḳ-ni-šu* 25^{22}.

זקף **zaḳâpu** to erect *az-ḳu-up* 50^{24}.

זקר **zaḳâru** to be pointed, project upwards **zaḳru** sharp, high *zaḳ-ri* 10^{4}; **ziḳḳurratu** summit, tower *ziḳ-ḳur-rat* 60^{16} (sing.) *-ra-ti-šu* 38^{11} *ziḳ-ḳur-rat* 18^{11} (pl.).

זקת **zaḳtu** sharp *zaḳ-ti* 33^{1} *zaḳ-tu-ti* 16^{16}.

זרא$_4$ **zirû** to sow, scatter, produce *az-ru* 4^{26} *za-ru-šu-un* 62^{6}; **ziru** seed 40^{31} *zir* 11^{11} 25^{17} 57^{18} *-šu* 24^{22}.

זרא **zaratu** tent *$_{iṣu}$za-ra-tí-šu-un* 16^{29}.

זרב **zarâbu** to flow *u-za-ra-bu* 16^{32}; *zar-biš* violently (?) 15^{27}.

זרק **zirḳu** heap (?) *zi-ir-ḳi* 4^{20}.

זרתר **zirtaru** tent *zir-ta-ra-a-tí* 28^{13}.

ח

חבל **ḫabâlu** to injure *ḫa-ba-li* 23^{28}; **ḫabiltu** injury, evil *ḫab-la-ti* 12^{2} 61^{13} *ḫab-lat-*[*su*] 61^{13}; **ḫibiltu** damage *ḫi-bíl-ta-ši-na* 24^{1}; **ḫabbilu, ḫablu** evil, bad *ḫab-bi-lu* 14^{11} [*ḫab*]*-lum* 14^{9}.

חבש **ḫibištu** product (?) *ḫi-biš-ti* 36^{15} 38^{4}.

חבת **ḫabâtu** to plunder, spoil *aḫ-bu-ta* 30^{28} *ḫa-ba-a-tí* 42^{8}; *iḫ-tab-ba-ta* 29^{18}; *iḫ-ta-nab-ba-ta* 27^{30}; **ḫubtu** booty *ḫu-ub-ti* 46^{7} *ḫu-bu-ut* 19^{3} 28^{1} 29^{18} *ḫu-bu-us-su-nu* 30^{27}.

חגל **ḫigallu** abundance *ḫigal-lum* 20^{29} *-li* 7^{5}.

חדה **ḫadû** to rejoice *iḫ-di-í* 41^{10} *li-iḫ-du* (sing.) 63^{5} *iḫ-du-u* 40^{23}; **ḫudu** joy *ḫu-ud* 24^{10}; **ḫidûtu** joy *ḫidâti*$_{pl}$ 20^{6} *ḫi-da-a-ti* $36^{15,33}$ $38^{5,12}$; **ḫa-diš** joyfully 22^{2} *ḫa-di-iš* 37^{11}.

חול **ḫulu** bad *ḫu-la* 2^{7}.

חוק **ḫâḳu** to embrace *i-ḫi-ḳu-u* 62^{8}.

חזן **ḫuzannu** arm *ḫu-za-an-ni-šu-nu* 16^{16}.

חטא$_1$ **ḫaṭû** to sin *iḫ-ṭu-u* 27^{20} (sing.) $46^{10,27}$ (pl.) *ni-iḫ-ṭu-u* 32^{25}; **multaḫṭu** sinner, rebel *mul-taḫ-ṭu* 26^{15} 31^{31}; **ḫiṭû, ḫiṭṭu** sin *ḫi-ṭi* 61^{13} *ḫi-ṭa-a-šu* 61^{13} *ḫi-iṭ-ṭu* 11^{34} *ḫi-ṭi-ti* 12^{3} *ḫi-ṭa-a-tí* 25^{28}.

חטט **ḫaṭâṭu** to grave, dig *aḫ-ṭu-uṭ* 39[2]; **ḫaṭṭu** style, scepter *ḫaṭṭi* 7[9] 38[25].

חיט **ḫâṭu** to look, see *a-ḫi-iṭ* 20[14] 39[2] *i-ḫi-iṭ* 40[5].

חיל **ḫâltu** army *ḫa-a-a-al-ti* 59[17].

חיר **ḫîrtu** spouse *ḫi-ir-tu* 34[23] *ḫi-ir-ti* 7[9] *ḫi-rat* 30[18].

חיש **ḫâšu** to hasten *i-ḫi-šam-ma* 14[15]; *ḫi-šam-ma* 14[23].

חלי **ḫu-li-ya-am** helmet 15[21].

חלב **ḫalâbu** to be covered *ḫa-lib* 9[5]; *iḫ-tal-lu-bu* 30[7]; *u-ḫal-li-bu* 48[5]; **taḫlubu** roof *taḫ-lu-bi-ša* 10[4] 18[9] 36[22]; **ḫa-lap-ta** . . . . . 3[21].

חלץ **ḫalṣu** fortress *ḫal-ṣu pl* 12[16] 21[3] *amilu rab-alu ḫal-ṣu* commander of a fortress 13[7].

חלק **ḫalâḳu** to perish II I to destroy *u-ḫal-liḳ* 18[14,19] *-li-iḳ* 39[26] *li-ḫal-liḳ* 24[22] *u-ḫal-li-ḳu* 26[7]; *ḫul-lu-uḳ* 59[8]; *mu-ḫal-li-ḳa-at* 38[29] 39[7].

חמט **ḫamâṭu** to quiver, hasten *u-ḫa-am-ma-ṭu* 58[18]; *uš-ḫam-ma-ṭu* 6[8] *uš-ḫam-miṭ-su* 18[16]; **ḫanṭu** (= *ḫamṭu*) swift *ḫa-an-ṭu* 42[11] 48[28] **ḫa-an-ṭiš** 15[24] 58[22] **ḫi-it-mu-ṭiš** swiftly 17[25].

חמש **ḫaššu** (= *ḫamšu*) fifth *ḫaš-šu* 60[6] 63[18] 64[21].

חמת **ḫamatu** aid *ḫa-mat* (?) 42[24].

חנף **ḫanâpu** to thrive (?) *u-šaḫ-na-pu* 20[27].

חסה **ḫasû** . . . . . *aḫ-si* 2[7] 3[4].

חסס **ḫasâsu** to reflect, plan *aḫ-su-sa-am-ma* 60[24] *iḫ-su-us* 14[26] *ḫa-sis* 29[31].

חפא₄ **ḫipû** to break, destroy *iḫ-pu* 30[21].

חפא **ḫapû** . . . . . *ḫa-pi-í* 32[7].

חרא₄ **ḫirû** to dig *aḫ-ri-í* 18[13] *aḫ-ru-u* 17[3] *ḫi-ri* (inf.) 17[3]; **ḫirîtu** ditch, canal *ḫi-ra-a-ti* 18[12].

חרן **ḫarranu** way, road *ḫar-ra-nu* 13[27] *ḫar-ra-ni* 52[6] *ḫarrani-ya* 17[24] *ḫar-ra-an* 30[9].

חרץ **ḫuraṣu** gold 17[31] *ḫuraṣi* 10[14] 64[11,15] *ḫuraṣi pl* 6[28] *ḫuraṣa* 14[19] 57[17].

חרר **ḫurru** a gorge *ḫur-ri* 1[13] 4[18,21]. For *ušḫarir* cf. שחרר.

חרש **ḫuršu** wooded mountain *ḫur-ša-ni* 2[10] 4[19] 5[13] 6[5] *ḫur-ša-a-ni* 30[7].

חשח **ḫašâḫu** to desire, need *iḫ-ši-ḫa* 40[33]; **ḫušaḫḫu** famine *ḫu-šaḫ-ḫu* 61[17] *-ḫi* 29[6].

חתת **taḫtû** defeat, destruction *taḫ-tí-í* 44[7] *taḫ-ta-šu* 9[13] *-šu-un* 16[6].

חתמט **ḫitmuṭiš** cf. חמט.

חתן *iṣu* **ḫutnû** some kind of weapon (?) *ḫu-ut-ni-í* 33[18].

חתת **ḫattu** fear *ḫat-tu* 17[18] *ḫa-at-tum* 13[25] *ḫat-ti* 14[14] *ḫat-tu* 59[25] (adj. (?) fearful).

ט

טו **ṭu** ideogram for *šiḳlu* shekel 32[5 bis].

טא₄ם **ṭîmu** understanding, news, design (?) *ṭì-í-mu* 14[21] *-mí* 14[4] *ṭì-ín-šu* 28[19].

טבא$_4$ **ṭíbû** to be low *u-ṭa-bi* (II 1) 6[20].

טוב **ṭâbu** to be good, pleasing *i-ṭí-bu* 7[16]; *u-ṭí-ib* 3[6] *lu-ṭí-ib* 2[8] *mu-ṭib* 9[17] *mu-ṭi-ib* 38[21]; **ṭûbu** good, joy *ṭu-ub* 24[10] 35[8] 36[38]; **ṭâbu** good *ṭa-a-bi* 36[25] (nom.) *ṭâba* 3[8] 60[19]; **ṭâbtu** good (noun) 27[20] 46[10] *ṭâbtum* 48[19] *ṭâbti* 32[25] 46[27] *ṭa-ab-ti* 29[31] *ṭa-bat* 59[4]; **ṭa-biš** 20[28] *ṭa-bi-iš* 40[26] 41[18].

טוד **ṭudu** way, road *ṭu-du* 17[22] *ṭu-ud-di* 2[26] (pl.).

טיט **ṭiṭṭu** clay, filth *ṭi-iṭ-ṭu* 52[8] *ṭi-iṭ-ṭi* 59[5,20].

טרף *iṣu* **ṭarpû** the ladanum tree *ṭar-pi-'i* 6[22].

י

יא **yâumma** (= *yâ'u* + *ma*) any, any one *ya-um-ma* 1[4] 2[27]; **yâši, yâti** (= *yâ* + pronominal stems *ši, ti*) me, to me, as for me *ya-a-ši* 24[8] 38[2] 61[22] *ya-ti* 36[7] 37[9] 38[20] *ya-a-ti* 22[17] 23[11] 26[19] 27[25] 41[11] 42[12] 48[29].

יד **idu** hand, side, power, might *i-du-uš-šu* 9[11] *idi-a-a* 33[4] *-šu* 16[28] *i-di* 18[1] *-ya* 36[8] *-šu* 35[24] *idî-ya* 44[5] *i-di-í-šu* 25[18] *i-da-šu-un* 16[21] *i-da-a-ni* 14[28] *i-da-a-šu* 39[20]; *i-da-at* (cstr. pl.) 1[14] 3[20] 5[17].

ידא$_4$ **idû** to know *i-di-í* 61[9] *i-du-u* 2[28] (sing.) 2[25] (pl.) *-šu* 23[9]; *u-ad-du-ni* (II 1) 36[11] 38[8]; *u-ta-ad-da-a* (II 2) 58[24] *-du-u* 40[17].

ידא$_4$ (?) **adî** compacts, agreements, ordinances *a-di* 34[23] *-ya* 32[10] *a-di-í* 11[20] *-šu-nu* 32[15] (here written agreements). The stem may be ודא$_4$.

יום **ûmu** day 19[25] *û-mu* 22[14] (= *ina ûmi ša*) 35[8] (= *û-um*) 58[6] (= *one day* (?)) 59[16] 60[4] *ûmi* 38[2] *û-mi* 17[22] 36[11] 58[5] *-šu-ma* 1[20] (= that day, then) *û-mí* 18[15] 22[17] (*líbbi ûmí* the very day) 24[10] (pl.) *-šu* 24[12] *-šu-ma* 8[26] *û-ma* 60[7] *û-um* (cstr.) 3[84] *ûmî pl* 3[84] 60[24] 62[16] *-ya* 37[18]; **û-mi-šam** daily 41[8] *-ša-am* 39[25] *-šam-ma* 38[22] 39[21].

ימן **imittu** the right (hand) 36[29].

ינק to suck *í-ni-ḳu-u* 32[19]; *mu-ší-ni-ḳa-a-tí* (III 1) 32[19].

יפא$_8$ to sprout, come into being (?) *šu-pu-u* 62[10] *uš-ta-pu-u* 62[18].

ישה **išû** to be, have *i-ši* (1st pers.) 58[6] *išu-u* 57[7,8] (3rd sing.) *i-šu-u* 57[16 bis] 57[17,18] (1st sing.) 2[24] 9[8] 14[9,21] (3rd sing.) 12[9] 13[21] *i-ša-a* 18[26].

ישר **išâru** to be straight, erect, to thrive *išâr* (?) 20[26]; *u-ší-šir* (III 1) 25[22]; *uš-tí-íš-ší-ra* (III 2) 24[24] 27[19] 30[5] 42[17] 50[1]; *šu-tí-šur* 20[28]; **uššuru** innocence *uš-šur-šu-un* 12[8]; **išaru** upright *i-ša-ru* 40[6] *i-ša-ra* 40[18]; **mîšaru** righteousness *mi-ša-ru* 40[11]; **mí-ší-riš** righteously 2[22].

כ

כאב$_1$ **kibtu** (?) ruin, destruction *ki-ba-a-ti* 58[1,4].

כבא$_4$ **kibîtu** cf. קבא$_4$.

כבס **kabâsu** to tread, tread down *ak-bu-us* 27[12] *ak-bu-su* 50[8] *ik-bu-su* 23[4]; *mu-kab-bi-is* 5[10]; *šuk-bu-us* 12[9].

כבר **kibratu** pl. *kibrâti* region *kib-rat* 2^{18} *kib-ra-a-ti* 35^{2} 59^{25} *kib-ra-a-ta* 41^{15} *kibrâti*$_{pl}$ 6^{8}.

כבר **kitbartu** . . . . . *kit*(?)-*bar-ti* 34^{12}.

כבת **kabtu** fem. *kabittu* heavy, honored *kab-tu* 28^{21} *kab-ti* 13^{23} *-tí* 15^{12} *ka-bit-tu* 11^{7} *-ti* 22^{1} *ka-bi-it-tim* 41^{17}; **kabattu, kabittu** liver *ka-bat-ti* 10^{12} *ka-bit-ti* 42^{18}.

כדמר **kidmuru** name of a temple *kid-mu-ri* 19^{28}.

כדר **kadru** a present *kad-ra-a-a* 37^{1}.

כדר **kadirtu** . . . . . *ka-dir*(?)*-ti* 32^{28}.

כום **kum** instead of, in place of *ku-um* 29^{18}.

כון **kânu** to be fixed, established *u-kín* (II I = *ukawwin*) 10^{28} 23^{26} 36^{18} *u-kin* 6^{30} *u-ki-in* 39^{4} *u-kin* 32^{7} (3rd sing.) *u-ki-nu* 23^{21} *lu-ki-in* 37^{18}; *uk-tin* (II 2 = *uktawwin*) 60^{17}; **kînu** firm, faithful *ki-í-nu* 9^{4} *-ni* 2^{21} *ki-i-nim* 35^{11} 38^{25}; **kittu** right, justice *kitti* $64^{9,18}$ *ki-it-tim* 40^{11}; **kitinnûtu** right (?), custom (?) *ki-tin-nu-tu* 23^{27}; **kân** continually, regularly *ka-a-a-an* 20^{27} 22^{25}.

כוף **kípu** cf. קוף.

כי **kî, kîma** like, according to, at the time of, when, surely *ki-i* 14^{14} 16^{31} 23^{1} 27^{23} $59^{7,10}$ 60^{22} *ki-i ki-i* 61^{12} *ki-í* 25^{13}; *kîma* 5^{21} 58^{21} *ki-ma* 1^{12} 58^{23} $59^{2,8,17,21}$ 60^{20} 62^{1} 63^{2}; **kîam** thus, so *ki-a-am* $63^{8,11,14,17,20}$ $64^{1,4}$.

כך *iṣu* **kakku** a weapon 9^{11} *-šu* 9^{6} *kakki* 10^{25} *kakka-šu* 5^{17} *kakkî*$_{pl}$ 5^{19} *-ya* 1^{17} *-šu* 25^{5} *-šu-un* 11^{27} *-šu-nu* 40^{17}.

ככב **kakkabu** star *kakkab* 31^{7}.

ככר **kukru** a voice (?) *ku-uk-ru* $58^{1,4}$.

כלא₁ **kalû** to refuse, withhold *ik-la-a* 27^{23} *ik-lu-u* 1^{21}.

כלה **kalû** to cease, be finished *ik-la* 59^{18}; **kâlu** all, totality *kâli-šu-nu* 5^{18} *-ši-na* 5^{18} *kâl* 2^{19} [*kâla-ma*] 7^{3} *ka-li-šu-un* 11^{6} *-šu-nu* 19^{1} 57^{20} *-ši-na* 24^{1} *ka-la* 57^{19} 61^{9} *-ša* 31^{10} *ka-la-mu* (= *ka-la-ma*) 31^{8} 32^{2} *ka-la-ma* 57^{18}; **ka-liš** completely 7^{15} *ka-li-iš* 41^{15} (here = *ka-li-ši-na* (?)).

כלב **ḳalbu** a dog *kalbi* $28^{22,33}$ 33^{19} 59^{2} *kalbâni*$_{pl}$ $26^{25,30}$.

כלל **kalâlu** to be complete *u-šak-lil* 10^{5} 23^{29} 38^{11} 39^{5} *u-ša-ak-li-il* 36^{22} *šuk-lu-lat* 7^{11} *mu-šak-lil* 37^{9}; **kullatu** totality *kul-lat* 4^{5} 59^{20} *-si-in* 39^{26} *kul-la-ta* (= *kullat*) 40^{8} 41^{29}; **kul-la-ta-an** all (?) 40^{25}; **kilalu** totality (of weight, value) *ki-lal-šu-nu* 50^{14}; **ki-lal-la-an** around, about 35^{16}.

כלם **kalâmu** to see II I to show *u-kal-lim-an-ni* 38^{1} *kul-lum* 28^{20} *kul-lum-mi-im-ma* 19^{13}.

כם **kam** determinative after numerals 19^{26} 30^{17}.

כמה **kamû** to bind, enclose **kummu** enclosure, dwelling place *ku-um-mi-ka* 38^{21}; **kamâtu** wall *ka-ma-a-ti* 59^{2}; **kamûtu** bondage *ka-mu-ut-su* 35^{28} *ka-mu-su-nu* 3^{32}; **kimû** . . . . . *ki-mu-u-a* 20^{18}; **kimtu** a family *kim-tu* 20^{11} *kim-ti-ya* 57^{19} *-šu* 17^{29} 25^{1}.

כמל **ku-mal** . . . . . 27^{3}.

כמס **kamâsu** to bow *ik-mi-sa* 40^{22}.

כמר **kamâru** to be cast down, spread abroad *lu-ki-mir* (= *lu* + *u-kam-mir*) 1^{12} *ku-um-mu-ru* 20^{29}.

כנף **kappu** a wing *kap-pi* 52^{10}.

כנש **kanâšu** to submit *ik-nu-ša* 21^{13} *ik-nu-šu* (sing.) 11^{9} 12^{7} 21^{22} 10^{26} (pl.) 11^{17}; *kan-šu* 21^{18} *kan-šu-ti* 33^{31} *-ya* 34^{30} *-ti-šu* 5^{9} *kan-šu-u-ti* 33^{29}; *ka-na-ša* 2^{25}; *u-ka-an-ni-ša* 40^{9}; *u-šak-niš* 23^{16} *-ni-ša* 34^{18} *-ni-is-su-nu-ti* 21^{5} *-ni-šu* 34^{30} *u-šik-ni-ša* 5^{25} *-šu* 7^{17} *mu-šak-niš* 5^{8} 9^{13}.

כנש **kiššatu** assembly, totality *kiššati* 5^{3} *kiš-ša-ti* 35^{2} *kiš-šat* 5^{9} 40^{27} (= *kiš-ša-ti*).

כסא$_1$ **kussu** throne *kussi* 7^{20} $64^{11,15}$ *-šu* 14^{5} *kussî*$_{pl}$ 12^{28}.

כסב **kasbu** a measure equal to two hours of time, or the space traveled in two hours *kas-bu* 16^{25} $30^{12,29,32}$ 31^{9}.

כסל **kisallu** floor, platform, altar (?) *kisalla* 24^{16} 37^{21} 38^{15} 39^{17}.

כסס **kasâsu** . . . . . *ik-su-su* 26^{2}.

כסף **kaspu** silver 18^{23} *kaspi* 10^{14} *kas-pi* 32^{5} *kaspa* 14^{19} 57^{16} *kaspi*$_{pl}$ 6^{28}.

כסף **kispu** . . . . . *ki-is-pi-šu* 26^{23}.

כפף **kuppu** fountain *kup-pi* 31^{24}.

כסר **kisuru** . . . . . *ki-su-ur-šu-un* 39^{28}.

כצץ **kuṣṣu** hurricane (?), waterspout (?) 13^{29}.

כצר **kaṣâru, kiṣru** cf. קצר.

כרה $_{iṣu}$**kirû** a park *kirî* 32^{7} *kirî*$_{pl}$*-šu* 8^{22}.

כרה **karû** . . . . . *ka-ri-í* 1^{14}.

כרא$_4$ **kirû** to be low, bow *u-kar-ri* 21^{5}; **katrû** submission (?) *kat-ri-í* 11^{14} 12^{21}; **ka-at-ri-iš** 36^{27}.

כרב **karâbu** to be gracious, bless *i-kar-ra-ban-na-ši* 61^{24} *ik-ru-ub* 41^{13}; *kur-ban-ni-i* 23^{11}; *ik-ta-ar-ra-bu-šu* 40^{26} *li-ik-ta-ra-bu* 37^{8}.

כרב **kirbu** cf. קרב.

כרג **kur-gi** $_{iṣṣuru\ pl}$ . . . . . 10^{10}.

כרם **karâmu** to overthrow (?) *lik-rim-mí-šu* 24^{21}; **karmu** ruin, desolation *kar-mi* 3^{27} 4^{25} *kar-mí* 4^{15} 14^{26}; **karmûtu** desolation *kar-mu-tu* 35^{11}.

כרן **karanu, kurunnu** wine *karani* 36^{19} *karana* 50^{24} *kurunni* 36^{18}.

כרן **karânu** to heap up *lu-ki-ri-in* (= *lu* + *u-kar-ri-in*) 2^{15}.

כרס **kurussu** . . . . . *ku-ru-us-su* 26^{2}.

כרף **karpatu** a pot 60[17].

כרר **karru** . . . . . *kar-ri* 6[26].

כרש **karašu** camp, host *karaša-ka* 14[22] *karas-su* 14[27] *ka-ra-ši-šu-nu* 32[20].

כרש **karašu** destruction (?) *ka-ra-ši* 61[3,6].

כשא **kiššî** encumbers (?) *kiš-ši-i* 16[14].

כשה **kašû** to cut off (?) *ak-šu* (?) 31[26]; *ki-ši-šu* . . . . . 32[7].

כשה **kištu** forest *kišti* 36[15] 38[4] *kišâti pl* 30[8].

כשד **kašâdu** to approach, reach, capture *i-kaš-ša-du* 17[2] *akšud* 13[5] *akšu-ud* 7[23] *ak-šud* 1[22] *ak-šu-ud* 2[9] 10[8] *ak-šu-du* 4[27] *ak-šud-du* 14[25] *takšu-ud* 5[18,26] *ik-šud* 3[31] *ik-šu-ud* 22[20] *ik-šu-us-su* 33[14] *-su-nu-ti* 31[32] 46[26] *ik-šu-su-nu-ti* 18[2] *ik-šu-da* 11[31] *ik-šu-du* 9[15] *lik-šu-ud* 37[14]; *ku-šu-ud* 22[13]; *ka-šid* 2[18] *ka-ši-du-u-ti* 29[28]; *ka-ša-du* 35[25] *ka-ša-di* 15[19] *-šu* 60[21] 61[4] *-ša* 52[12] *ka-ša-a-di* 59[16] 60[7] *ka-šad* 10[6] 33[16]; *u-ša-ak-ši-du* 40[10]; **kišittu** booty *kišit-ti* 6[14,28] *ki-šit-ti* 10[15] 13[23] *ki-ši-ti* 4[26]; **kuššudu** captured *kuš-šu-di* 16[32] 17[21].

כשד **kišadu** neck, bank (of a stream) *kišadi-ya* 60[23] 63[18] *-ša* 63[12] 64[21] *ki-ša-di* 19[15] *kišad* 5[10] 10[16] *ki-šad* 15[14] *ki-ša-da-tí-šu-nu* 16[6].

כשר **ku-šìr** (?) . . . . . 46[12].

כשש **kašušu** powerful *ka-šu-uš* 5[2].

כשש **kiššatu** cf. כנש.

כתה **kitu** a kind of garment *kiti* 18[24] *kitû pl* 50[12].

כתבר **kitbartu** cf. כבר.

כתם **katâmu** to cover, overwhelm *ik-tu-mu-šu* 44[9] *kat-ma* 59[13] *ka-ti-im* 15[13]; *u-šak-tim* 13[23].

כתר **kitru** aid, alliance *kit-ri* 22[28] *-šu* 24[31] 48[16] *-šu-nu* 46[20].

כתר **katrû** cf. כרא$_4$.

כתת **kittu, kitinnûtu** cf. כון.

ל

לא$_1$ **lâ** not, without *la* 8[23] 61[2] *lâ* (written *nu*) 52[1] 63[5] *la-a* 1[5].

לאה$_1$ **lu'u** strong (?) *lu-'-u-u-ti* 27[1]; **lîtu** strength, authority *li-i-tu* 50[18] *li-i-tí* 5[14] *-ti* 34[30]; **lû** a bull *li-í* 16[29]; **multa'itu** greatness, majesty *mul-ta-'i-ti-ya* 10[5] *mul-ta-'i-it* 6[23].

לאט$_2$ **lâṭu** to burn *mu-la-iṭ* 6[5].

לב *amilu* **lib** *pl* ideogram for musicians (?) 12[30] 19[16] *f* **lib** *pl* 12[31].

לבא$_1$ **labbu** a lion **la-ab-biš** like a lion 15[20].

לבב **libbu** heart, midst, womb, loins *líb-bu* 22[28] *-uš* 35[9] *lib-bu-uš* 14[26] *lib-bu-šu-un* 16[32] *libbi* 19[20] 35[8] *-šu* 37[17] *lib-bi-ya* 15[23] *líb-bi* 4[30] 41[2] (*líb-bi ritpašu* large hearted) 42[18] (my heart) [58[2]] 58[7] 61[21] [*-ya*] 41[12] *-ka* 38[21] *-šu* 18[2] *-ša* 58[12] *-šu-nu* 17[8] *lib-ba-šu-un* 11[23] *-šu-nu* 14[7] *líb-ba-šu* 40[13] *-šu-nu* 2[27] *-šu-nu-ti* 46[11] *libbî$_{pl}$-šu-nu* 25[20]; **liblibu** offspring *li-ib-li-pi* 20[19]; **líb-bal-bal** great-grandson, descendant 40[30]; **lib-ba-ti** 61[5] (fem. of *libbu*, or error for *lib-ba-šu* (?)).

לבן **labânu** to cast down (the face in devotion), to make bricks *al-bi-in* 34[25]; **libittu** (= *libin-tu*) pl. *libnâti* brick *libitti* 18[11] *libnâti$_{pl}$* 35[18] 36[14] *lib-na-at-su* 36[18] 38[7] 39[4] *lib-na-su* 10[2]; **labbannâtí** (fem. pl., or *kalbannâtí*) some kind of war engines or instruments *lab-ban-na-tí* 12[11].

לבר **labiru, labaru** old *la-bi-ru* 6[18] *-ri* 37[31] 39[2] *la-bi-ru-*[*ti*] 63[2] *la-ba-ri* 37[26] *-riš* (adv.) 24[4]; **labirûtu** old age, decay *la-bi-ru-ta* 10[1].

לבש **labâšu** to dress, be clad, put on *lab-šu* 52[10] (perm.); *at-tal-bi-ša* 15[21] *lit-bu-šat* 32[31]; *u-lab-biš* 22[6] *u-lab-bi-su* 48[11]; *u-šal-biš* 36[26]; **lubultu** (= *lubuš-tu*) clothing *lu-bul-tu* 48[10] *-ti* 18[24] 22[6] 50[12].

לו **lû** particle of wishing and asseveration *lu* 1[10] *lu-u* 1[9] 60[23] (by, in an oath?) 62[1,2].

לוט **lîṭu** hostage *li-i-ṭi* 5[14]; **lîṭûtu** hostageship *li-ṭu-ut-tí* 4[2].

לח **laḫu** front (?) *la-aḫ* 33[19] (*la-aḫ íni-šu*, or *la-aḫ-ši-šu* (?)).

לחם **laḫmu** lion **laḫ-mí-iš** like a lion 15[27]; *ilu laḫ-mu* lion colossus 36[28].

ליל **lilâti** pl. evening *li-la-a-ti* 58[1,4].

ללה **lalû, lulû** . . . . . *la-li-í-ka* 37[6] *lu-li-í* 10[8].

למה **lamû** to surround, enclose, besiege *al-mí* 11[17,32] 12[11] 13[21] 17[26] 31[2] *-šu* 14[13] *-ši* 6[26]; *u-šal-mi* 33[32]; **limîtu** environs *li-mí-ti-šu-nu* 12[9] 13[20].

למד **lamâdu** to learn *al-ma-ad* 20[14].

למן **limnu** bad, wicked *lim-ni* 9[16] *lim-nu-ti* 14[7] 15[27]; **limuttu** (= *limun-tu*) evil (fem. adj. and noun) 23[10] *limut-tu* 25[32] 26[9,20] 32[23] 46[11] 48[2,6] *li-mu-ut-ti* 39[25] *limut-tim* 23[6] 29[34] 46[21] *limutta* 59[6,7].

למס *ilu* **lamassu** bull colossus *lamassi* 26[21].

לנם **lu-num** . . . . . 32[18].

לפן **lapan** (= *la* + *pan*) before, in front of *la-pa-an* 14[13] 16[20] 18[20] 25[18] 26[12] 28[11] 31[19] 32[11] 34[12] 46[2].

לפת **lapâtu** to turn (intrans.) *il-pu-ut* 61[24]; **lipitu** overthrow *lipi-it* 24[28].

לקא$_8$ **likû** to take *al-ki* 2[5] *al-ka-a* 6[18,29] 33[33] 50[16] *al-ka-šu* 34[20] *al-ka-aš-šu* 34[15] *-šu-nu-ti* 31[18] *al-ka-šu-nu-u-ti* 1[18] *il-kí* 35[29] *il-ku* 18[6] *il-ka-aš-ši* 64[16] *il-ku-u* 25[7] *il-ku-ni* 18[8] *il-ku-in-ni* 62[3] *li-kí-í* 38[24] *li-ka-aš-ši* 64[12].

לתת **littûtu** cf. ולד.

מ

מ **ma** and 1[6], also emphatic enclitic 2[14] 3[15] 5[5] 18[27] 22[11,30] 23[23] 27[24] 35[26] 46[27].

מאה **mâ'u** fem. *mîtu* victor *mí-i-tu* 32[28].

מא$_1$ר **ma'âdû** to be numerous *i-ma-'a-du* 52[20]; **ma'adu** much, many *ma-'a-di* 15[10] 21[14,28] 46[7] *ma-'a-du-ti* 17[5] *ma-'a-at-tu* 28[9] *ma-at-tum* 13[30] *ma-'a-da-a-ti* 34[1]; **mu'udu** much *mu-'u-di-í* 18[25]; **ma-'a-diš** (adv.) 6[29] 8[15]; **ma-'a-as-si** (= *ma'âsi* (?) st. מאס (?)) 21[10,18].

מאר **mâru** son **mârtu** daughter *mârî$_{pl}$* 4[1] *ma-rat* 31[7].

מא$_2$ר **mâru** II I to send *u-ma-'i-ir* 16[34] *u-ma-'i-ra-ni* 2[25] *u-ma-'i-í-ru* 46[15]; **muma'iru** ruler, general *mu-ma-'i-ir* 7[6] 16[1]; **mu'aru** ruler (?) *mu-'-a-ru* 9[9]; **tamartu** present, gift *ta-mar-ti* 27[28] *-šu* 22[24] *-šu-nu* 22[1] *ta-mar-ta-šu-nu* 11[7] 42[20].

מגר **magâru** to be favorable, to favor *li-im-gu-ra* 39[19] *mu-gu-ur* 38[24]; *ni-in-dag-ga-ra* (= *nîmtagara*) 46[17]; **magiru** favorable 19[26] *magiri* 38[2] *ma-gi-ri* 1[20] 9[19] (masc. pl.); **migru** favorite *mi-gir* 9[8].

מדפן **midpânu** cf. דפן.

מו **mû** pl. *mî*, *mâmi* water *mí-í* 40[16] 52[14] *mí$_{pl}$* 6[19] 18[13] 30[20,21,31] 31[24,25,29] 60[18] 64[12,16] *-šu-nu* 62[8] *ma-a-mi* 18[16].

מוץ **mâṣu** to press, hinder, stop (?) *i-mí-ṣu* 27[4].

מוש **mušu, mušitu** night *mu-ši-šu* 48[22] *mu-ši-tu* 31[9] *mu-ša-a-ti* 59[14].

מות **mâtu** to die *im-tu-ut* (= *imtawut* I 2) 14[3]; **mîtu** one dead *mi-tu-ti* 52[19,20] *mi-tu-ta-an* 40[25]; **mîtûtu** death *mi-tu-tu* 26[9].

מחה **mîḫû** heavy shower, storm *mí-ḫu-u* 59[15] *mí-ḫi-í* 15[29] 17[25].

מחח **muḫḫu** the top part *muḫ-ḫi* 4[28] 31[25] 48[13] *-šu* 4[25,29] *-šu-nu* 4[3].

מחז **maḫazu** city *ma-ḫa-zi* 23[20] 24[1] 39[24] [41[22]] *-šu* 41[6] *-šu-un* 41[30] *-šu-nu* 3[24] 4[14].

מחץ **maḫâṣu** to shatter, fight *a-maḫ-ḫa-aṣ* 52[17,18] *im-ḫa-aṣ* 64[13] *ma-ḫa-aṣ* 64[9]; *am-da-ḫi-iṣ* 4[9,18] 11[28] *am-daḫ-ḫi-iṣ* 8[9,17] *im-daḫ-ṣu* 59[17]; **mundaḫ(i)ṣu** soldier *mun-daḫ-ṣi-í-šu* 24[25]; **mitḫuṣu** fight, battle *mit-ḫu-ṣu* 12[10] *-ṣi* 25[5] 48[25] *-uṣ-ṣi* 28[25] *mit-hu-uṣ* 1[12].

מחץ **maḫâṣu** . . . . . *am-ḫa-aṣ* 36[19].

מחר **maḫâru** to be in front of, to receive, to offer (prayer or sacrifice to the gods) *am-ḫur* 8[4,28] 16[16] *-šu* 21[10] *-šu-nu-ti* 15[19] *am-ḫu-ru* 23[2] *im-ḫur-šu-u-ma* 28[14] *-šu-nu-ti* 14[26] *im-ḫu-ru* 5[14] (sing.) *-šu* 24[30] *im-ḫu-ru* 32[23] (pl.); *am-da-aḫ-ḫa-ru* I prayed (I 2 = *amtaḫaru*) 33[17]; *im-da-na-ḫa-ru* (I 3) they were receiving 32[7]; *u-ma-ḫir* (II I) 50[24]; *u-šam-ḫi-ir* 37[1]; **maḫru** front *maḫri*, *maḫar* front, before *maḫ-ri* 9[11] 39[9] 58[18] *-ya* 11[8] 36[10] [64[12]] *-šu* 29[24] *ma-ḫar* 3[33] 59[6,7] *-šu* 39[9] *-šu-un* 10[11] *-šu-nu* 32[12] 36[34]; **maḫrû** fem. *maḫrîtu* former, first *maḫ-ru-u* 11[12] *maḫ-ri* 37[26] *maḫ-ri-í* 42[1] *maḫ-ra* 2[27] *maḫ-ra-a* 6[12] *maḫ-ri-ti* 12[20] 14[25]; **miḫirtu** front *mi-iḫ-rit* 33[4]; **mâḫiru** a rival *ma-ḫi-ra* 5[8]; **maḫîru** a price *ma-ḫi-ri* 32[6]; **muḫḫuru** prayer (or sacrifice (?)) *muḫ-ḫu-ru* 50[24]; **maḫ-ḫu-ur** forward 44[8]; **tamḫaru** battle *tam-ḫa-ri* 1[4] 3[22] 5[19] 7[8] 11[31] 16[21] 17[12] 31[16] 34[5]; **mitḫariš** together *mit-ḫa-riš* 15[11] 16[25].

מחר **miḫru** stream (?) *mi-iḫ-ri* 58^{16}.

מטל **maṭâlu** to extend (intrans.) *li-ša-an-ṭi-il* 37^{13}.

מטר **maṭâru** to rain **tamṭiru** rain *tam-ṭí-ri* 13^{29}.

מילם **mílammu** lustre *mí-lam-mí* 10^{19} 12^{28} 32^{31} 44^{8}.

מכר **makkuru** treasure, possession 17^{31} *makkuri* 14^{18} (*bît makkuri* treasure house) *makkur* 17^{30} 26^{17} *-šu* 18^{23} *-šu-nu* 18^{3}; **namkuru** possession *nam-kur-šu-nu* $1^{15,23}$ 3^{25} 4^{22}.

מלא$_1$ **malû** to be full, to fill (trans.) *im-lu-u* 46^{8}; *ma-lu-u* 26^{31} (perm.); *u-mal-li* 17^{29} 37^{2} *-šu* 10^{8} *u-mal-li* 14^{2} (3rd pers.) *u-mal-la-a* 16^{13} *u-ma-al-la-a* 40^{20} 59^{10} *u-mal-lu-u* 28^{2} 42^{16}; *im-ta-li* 61^{5}; *um-dal-lu-u* (II 2) 32^{2}; **mala** fulness, as many as *ma-la* 18^{11} 20^{13} 28^{10} $31^{4,24}$ 32^{14} 41^{7} 46^{9} 48^{2} 50^{12}; **mílu** overflow *míli* 16^{7} *-ši-na* 30^{6} *mi-li-ša* 7^{24} 8^{8}; **malû** fem. *malîtu* full *ma-li-ti* 50^{19}.

מלח **malaḫu** seaman, pilot *amîlu malaḫi* 58^{8}.

מלך **malâku** to take counsel *im-li-ku* 46^{12}; *im-tal-ku* 61^{2} *tam-ta-lik* 61^{12}; **milku** advice, reason, understanding *mil-ku* 61^{21} *mil-ki* $14^{4,21}$ *mi-lik* 46^{12} *-šu* 61^{21}; **malku** prince *mal-ku* $9^{7,18}$ *ma-al-ki* 40^{6} 41^{1} *ma-lik* (=*malkî* pl.) 23^{16} *ma-lik-šu-nu* 9^{15} (sing.) *mal-ki pl* 5^{6} *ma-al-ki* (pl.) 20^{10}; **malikûtu** royalty *ma-li-ku-tim* 40^{8}.

מלך **milliku** cf. אלך$_2$.

מלמל **mulmullu** spear *mul-mul-li* 15^{32} *-ya* 3^{23}.

מלת **multa'itu** cf. לאה$_1$.

מלתחט **multaḫṭu** cf. חטא$_1$.

מלתל **multâlu** cf. שאל$_1$.

מם **mummu** queen (title of Tiamat, synonym of *bíltu*) *mu-um-mu* 62^{7}.

מם **mimma** cf. מנו.

ממת **mamîtu** cf. אמה.

מנה **manû** to count, reckon *am-ni-i* 18^{1} *am-nu* 6^{2} $12^{2,14}$ 13^{7} *-šu-nu-ti* 1^{19} *im-nu* (sing.) 25^{23} *im-nu-u* 61^{3} (sing.) 26^{16} (pl.); **mînu** numbered *mí-i-nu* 46^{14}; **manû, minû** number *ma-ni* $8^{23,24}$ *ma-ni-í* 3^{29} *mí-ni* 24^{27} 28^{9} 30^{28} 31^{33} 50^{17} *mi-na* 1^{16}; **manû** mina *ma-na* $10^{14\,bis}$.

מנד **man-da** (for *madda* (?)) the Medes (?) 40^{9}.

מנד **man-di-ma** . . . . . 17^{16}.

מנד **mandattu, mâdâtu** cf. נדן.

מנו **mannu** who?, whoever *man-nu* 39^{14} *man-nu-um-ma* (= *mannu* + *ma*) 61^{8}; **minû** what? *mi-ni-í* 32^{23}; **manama** anyone *ma-na-ma* 37^{33} 39^{1} 62^{10}; **mimma** (= *minma*) anything 12^{29} 18^{24} [57^{16}] $57^{16,17,18}$ 58^{20}.

מנזז **manzazu, manzaltu** cf. נזז.

מנן **munnu** arms, utensils *mun-ni-šu-nu* 16^{8}. St. מאן$_1$ (?).

מנרב **mun-na-rib** (?)**-šu-nu** . . . . . 17^{1}.

מסא **misû** to wash, cleanse *u-ma-si* (= *umassî*) 10^{2}.

מסכן *iṣu* **miskannu** palm tree *mis-kan-ni* $6^{21,27}$.

מסר **musarû** tablet, inscription *mu-sa-ru-u* 37^{20} $39^{16,18}$ *mu-sa-ri-í-a* 37^{22} *mu-sar-u-a* $24^{16,20}$ *mu-sar-í-šu* $24^{17,20}$ *mu-sar-ri-í-a* 38^{16}.

מיץ **mûṣu, míṣu** cf. וצא.

מצה **maṣû** (?) II I to cast down (?) *u-mi-ṣi* 2^{10} 4^{18} *lu-mi-ṣi* 3^{21}; *um-ta-ṣi* (II 2) $63^{6,9,12,15,18,21}$ 64^{2}.

מצר **miṣru** region, territory *mi-iṣ-ri* 5^{30} *mi-ṣir* 9^{18} $13^{3,6}$ 29^{18} 42^{10} 50^{3} *-ya* 29^{34}.

מצר *mâtu* **muṣurâ** (adj.) Egyptian *mu-ṣu-ra-a-a* 11^{29}.

מצר **namṣaru** sword *nam-ṣa-ri* 16^{16} (pl.).

מצר **maṣartu** cf. נצר.

מקת **maḳâtu** to fall *im-ḳut-su* 13^{25} *im-ḳu-tu* 26^{11}; *im-ta-ḳut* 59^{22}; *u-šam-ḳít* 5^{19} $8^{12,18}$ *-su-nu-ti* 32^{12} *u-šam-ḳí-ta* 33^{5} *-tu* 26^{29} (sing.) 48^{3} (pl.) *li-ša-am-ḳít* 37^{14} *-ḳí-ta* 39^{20} *šum-ḳut* 9^{6} *mu-šim-ḳít* 9^{24}; **miḳtu** fall (?) *mi-ḳít* 26^{7}.

מרא₁ **marû** fat, fatted *ma-ru-ti* 10^{10} 16^{4}.

מרה **mirânu** bitterness (?) *mi-ra-nu-uš-šu-un* 25^{19}.

מרבש **murbašu** cf. רבש.

מרח **miriḫtu** cf. ארח.

מרך **markîtu** cf. רכה.

מרכס **markasu** cf. רכס.

מרנסק **murnisḳu** horse *mur-ni-is-ki* 16^{9}.

מרץ **marṣu** difficult *mar-ṣu* 17^{20} $31^{11,21}$ *mar-ṣa* 2^{6} 3^{4} *mar-ṣu-tí* 2^{26} *-ti* 19^{8}; **namraṣu** difficulty *nam-ra-ṣi* 1^{8}.

מרר **marâru** to march *u-šam-ri-ir* 50^{18}.

מרש **maruštu** ruin, destruction *ma-ru-uš-tu* 28^{14}.

מרש **maršîtu** cf. רשה.

משה **mašû** to forget *am-ši* $60^{23,24}$ *im-ši* 42^{6} *im-šu* 46^{11}.

משה **mašû** II I to feel, touch *muš-ši* 18^{15}.

משב **mûšabu** cf. ושב.

משך **mašku** skin *mašak* 12^{28} 18^{23} *-šu* 34^{6} [*-šu-nu*] 48^{5} *maš-ki-ya* 15^{15} (my skin = my self (?)).

משכן **maškanu** cf. שכן.

משנך **mašnaktu** st. שנך.

משפל **mušpalu** cf. שפל.

משק **mašḳîtu** cf. שקה.

משר **mašâru** II I to leave, release, send *u-maš-šír* $60^{8,10,12}$ *-šu-nu-ti* 4^{4} *u-maš-šir* 44^{10} $50^{3,9}$ *-an-ni* 27^{27} *u-maš-ší-ra* 20^{24} *u-maš-šír-u* 19^{7} *-ší-ru* $16^{29,33}$ $17^{14,19}$ 46^{3} *muš-šu-ra* (perm.) 16^{24}.

משר **mašaru** some part of a chariot *ma-ša-ru-uš* 16[12] *iṣu ma-ša-ri-ya* (var. *man-ša-ri-ya*) 25[22].

משר **mašíru** . . . . . *ma-ší-ri* 33[18].

משר **mîšaru, míšíriš** cf. ישר.

משת **maštîtu** cf. שתה.

משתק **maštaktu** cf. שתק.

מתא **mâtu** land, country 37[5] 58[21] *-šu* 35[23] *ma-a-tum* 58[14,18] *mâti* 52[1] 63[5] 64[5] *-a* 6[1] *-ya* 5[30] *-šu* 9[17] 35[29] *-šu-un* 31[18] *mâta* 61[17] *-šu* 10[21] 21[25] *mâ-ti* 15[11] *-ya* 1[18] *-šu-un* 12[21] *mât* 27[9] *mât-su* 12[20] *-su-nu* 17[19] *ma-tu-uš-šu-un* 17[15] (= *ana mâti-šun*) *mâtâti* 3[22] *mâtâti*$_{pl}$ 3[14] *-šu-nu* 3[15] *ma-ta-a-ta* 40[5] *mâtât*$_{pl}$ 2[24].

מתחץ **mitḫuṣu** cf. מחץ.

מתחר **mitḫariš** cf. מחר.

מתי **matíma** (= *matî* + *ma*) ever, at any time *ma-tí-ma* 21[8].

מתק **mítíḳu** cf. אתק$_4$.

מתן **mutninnû** pious (?), reverent (?) *mut-nin-nu-u* 27[26]. St. אנה$_4$ (?).

נ

נאה (?) to destroy (?) *a-ni-'i* 15[31]; *mu-ni-'i* (II 1) 9[15].

נאד **nâdu** to be high, exalted *at-ta-'i-id* 34[25] *it-ta-'i-id* 19[24]; **nâ'idu, nâdu** exalted *na-'i-du* 9[11] 33[2] *na-a-du* 6[4]; **tanittu** pl. *tanâdâti* exaltation, majesty *ta-nit-ti* 28[20] 33[22] *ta-nit-ta-šu-un* 20[16] *ta-na-da-tí* 6[7].

נא$_1$ל **nâlu** to lie down III–II to cast down *uš-na-il* 2[14] 4[20].

נא$_2$ר **nâru** pl. *nârâti* stream *nâri* 17[3] 40[16] *nârâti*$_{pl}$ 62[2,3]; *ilu* **Nâri-iš** like the stream-god 16[10].

נא$_4$ש **níšu** lion 61[15] *nišî*$_{pl}$ 50[22].

נבא$_1$ **nabû** to speak, say, name, appoint *i-nam-bu-šu* (*nam* for *nab*) 39[15] *na-bu-u* 5[16] (part.) 33[21] (perm.) 62[4]; *at-ta-bi* 19[8] *it-ta-bi* 40[7]; *u-nam-bi* 59[4]; **nibu** number *ni-bi* 11[25] *ni-ba* 12[9] *-šu-un* 40[17]; **nibîtu** name *ni-bit* 19[19] *-su* 19[8] *-sun* 20[16] *ni-bi-it-su* 40[7].

נבא$_4$ **namba'u** spring (of water) *nam-ba-'i* 31[24].

נבט **nabâṭu** to shine, be bright *u-ša-an-bi-iṭ* 36[26]; **nubattu** celebration (?), festival (?) *nu-bat-tu* 31[8] (= *nubaṭ-tu*).

נבל **nabâlu** to destroy *ab-bul* 2[1] 3[26] 4[15,24] 13[21] 18[9] *a-bul* 8[23]; **nablu** destruction *nab-li* 32[32].

נבל **nabalu** dry land *na-ba-li* 21[4] 42[19,22].

נבן **nabnîtu** cf. בנה.

נבר **nibirtu** cf. אבר$_4$.

נגה **nigûtu** joy, rejoicing *ni-gu-tu* 10[11].

נגו **nagû** province, district *na-gu-u* 22[9] 60[1] *na-gi-í* 28[6,8].

נגר **nagiru** leader *amîlu na-gi-ru* 15[34].

נדה **nadû** to lay, cast, throw *ad-di-i* 18[19] *ad-di* 6[23] 18[12] 36[18] 39[4] *-šu* 33[20] *šu-nu-ti* 31[17] *ad-da* 36[2] *id-du* 11[21] *-šu* 26[7] *na-du-u* (perm.) 16[5] 41[23] *na-da-ta* (perm.) 33[26]; *at-ta-di* 33[19] *at-ta-ad-di* 26[32] 30[20]; *in-na-di* 23[8] *in-na-du-u* 40[3] *li-na-di* (var. *li-in-na-di*) 23[1].

נדב **nindabû** sacrificial offering *nin-da-bi-í* 39[9].

נדבך **nadbaku** cf. דבך.

נדן **nadânu** to give *i-nam-di-nu* 33[28] *ad-din* 12[20] *-šu* 48[14] *a-din-šu* 21[11] *id-din* 60[8] *-šu-nu-ti* 27[28] *id-di-na* 32[2] *id-di-nu-šu* 11[22] *id-din-u-ni* 28[2]; *na-dan* 11[18] 12[21,32] 33[28]; *at-ta-din* 58[9]; **nudunnu** dowry, gift *nu-dun-ni-í* 21[14,23]; **mandantu** *mandattu, maddattu, mâdattu,* **mâdâtu** gift, tribute *man-da-at-tu* 10[27] 12[6,21] *-ti* 12[32] *-ta-šu* 27[23] *ma-da-at-tí* 1[3] *-ta* 4[3] *ma-da-tu* 8[3] *-ta* 1[21].

נדן **nidnu** . . . . . *ni-id-ni* 32[6].

נדר **nadâru** to rage, be furious *an-na-dir* (IV I) 15[21].

נוח **nâḫu** to become quiet *i-nu-uḫ* 59[18]; *u-ni-iḫ* 27[2] *u-ni-ḫu* 1[5] *u-ni-iḫ-ḫu* 26[27]; **munîḫu** a superior *mu-ni-ḫa* 2[23] 9[7].

נון **nûnu** a fish *nûnî* 59[10] *nûnî*$_{pl}$ 26[26] *nu-u-ni* 18[21].

נור **nûru** light *nu-u-ru* 52[9] *-ra* 52[7] *nu-ur* 38[17].

נזז **nazâzu** to take position, stand *iz-za-az* 61[24] *i-zi-zu* (sing.) 34[4] *iz-zi-zu* (pl.) 35[16] *iz-zi-zu-ni* 4[7] *i-zi-zu-u* 25[25]; *i-zi-zi* (impv.) 52[23]; *u-ší-ziz* 7[28] *-zi-iz* 6[25] *uš-zi-iz* 36[28] *uš-zi-zu* (sing.) 46[20] *ul-ziz-su-nu-ti* 22[8] 25[30] *u-ša-zi-zu-in-ni* 34[31]; **manzazu, manzaltu** position, seat *man-za-zu* 32[29] 60[9,11] *man-za-az* 25[22] 50[15] *man-za-al-ti-šu-nu* 50[15].

נזם **nazâmu** to weep, wail **tazimtu** wailing *ta-zi-im-ti-ši-na* 39[27].

נחל **naḫlu** brook *na-aḫ-li* 13[30].

נטל **naṭâlu** to look, entreat *at-ta-ṭal* 58[5].

ניר **nâru** to subjugate *i-na-ru* 20[18] 26[5] *a-nir* 33[31] *i-ni-ru* 7[18]; **nîru** a yoke *nîri-ya* 21[5] *ni-ri-ya* 11[9] *nîr* 22[29].

נכד **nakâdu** to cast, lay, to fall down, to fall prostrate (?) *ak-ku-ud* 36[1] 37[28]; **nakuttu** the act of prostrating oneself (?) *na-kut-ti* 36[1] 37[28].

נכל **nakâlu** to be cunning, skilled *u-nak-ki-lu* 36[21]; **nikiltu** craft, cunning *ni-kil-ti* 24[19].

נכם **nakâmu** II I to heap up **nakmu, nakamtu** treasure *nak-mu* 18[22] *na-kam-tí* 10[18] *na-ka-ma-a-ti* 26[33].

נכס **nakâsu** to cut, cut off, cut down *i-nak-ki-su-u* 25[11] *ak-ki-is* 3[5] *ak-kis* 8[22] *ak-ki-sa* 18[22] 19[12] *a-kis* 7[27] *ik-ki-su* (sing.) 25[10]; *u-nak-kis* 16[6] *u-na-ak-kis* 16[14] *u-na-kis* 16[18] *u-ni-ki-is* 4[20] *lu-na-ki-sa* 1[14]; **nukkusu** cut off *nu-uk-ku-su-u-ti* 26[24]; **niksu** act of cutting off *nik-si* 12[11] *ni-kis* 25[9] 26[12].

נכר **nakâru** to be hostile, to rebel *ik-ki-ru* 27^{11}; II I to change (?) *u-nak-ka-ar* 39^{17} *u-nak-ki-ir* 37^{21} 38^{15} *u-na-ki-ir* 6^{19}; *u-šam-kĭr* 27^{30}; **nakru** enemy, hostile 19^{7} *na-ak-ru* 38^{29} 39^{7} *nakri* 9^{16} $15^{19,29}$ *-šu* 22^{31} 23^{2} *nak-ri* 25^{4} 26^{6} *nakrûti* pl 2^{19} 5^{11} 10^{7} *-ya* 32^{29} *-ka* 22^{14} *na-ak-ru-ti-ya* 37^{14}; **nakiru** enemy *na-ki-ri* 9^{6} $15^{26,32}$; **nak-riš** 11^{22}.

נכש **nukušu** part of a door, hinge (?) *nu-ku-ší-í* 38^{9}.

נמב **namba'u** cf. נבא$_4$.

נמד **nimídu** cf. אמד$_4$.

נמכר **namkuru** cf. מכר.

נמצר **namṣaru** cf. מצר.

נמק **nimíḳu** cf. אמק$_4$.

נמר **namâru** to be bright, to shine, to be joyful *im-mi-ru* 40^{28}; *u-nam-mir* 23^{31} *-mi-ir* 37^{3}; **namru** bright *nam-ru* 58^{20} *na-am-ra* 37^{17}; **namri(r)ru** brilliance *nam-ri-ri* 7^{4} 44^{7} *nam-ri-ir-ri-šu-nu* 58^{18}; **namurratu** brilliance *na-mur-ra-tí* 9^{5}.

נמרץ **namraṣu** cf. מרץ.

ננדב **nindabû** cf. נדב.

ננר **nannaru** (= *nanharu* st. נאר$_2$ (?)) illuminator *na-an-na-ri* $35^{15,30}$.

נסא$_4$ **nisû** distant *ni-su-tí* 2^{24} (pl.).

נסח **nasâḫu** to wrench away, carry off *i-na-as-saḫ* 58^{15} *i-na-saḫ-u* 46^{14} *as-suḫ* $18^{11,18}$ 50^{15} *as-su-ḫa-am-ma* 11^{11} *na-si-iḫ* $9^{14,20}$.

נסך **nisakku** prince 9^{1}; **nasikku** prince *amîlu na-sik-ka-ni* 16^{27}.

נסק **nisiḳtu** precious stones (?) *ni-siḳ-ti* 12^{27} 17^{31} 23^{30} 36^{14} 38^{4} 50^{11}.

נפח **nipḫu** ascent, rise (of the heavenly bodies) *ni-ip-ḫi* 37^{12} 38^{23}.

נפחר **napḫaru** cf. פחר.

נפלק **napalḳatu** cf. פלק.

נפר **niprîtu** cf. פרא.

נפרך **naparku** cf. פרך.

נפש **napâšu** to expand, breathe, thrive *na-pa-aš* 20^{26}; **napištu** pl. *napšâti* life *na-piš-tu* 24^{29} 26^{30} *-tí* 31^{27} *-ti* 61^{6} *-ti-šu-nu* 27^{7} *napiš-tim* 33^{1} *-šu* 29^{10} 44^{11} 50^{4} *-šu-nu* 29^{7} 31^{25} *na-piš-ta-šu-nu* 3^{32} *nap-ša-tuš* 14^{13} *nap-šat-su* 26^{7} 33^{24} 48^{9} *-su-un* 26^{10} *-su-nu* 21^{5} *napšâti* pl 57^{18} *-šu* 8^{20} *-šu-nu* 16^{30} *nap-ša-tí* 15^{25} *-šu-nu* 16^{7} $17^{15,20}$ *nap-ša-a-ti* 17^{1}; **nappašu** a window *nap-pa-ša* 59^{22}.

נצא **nîṣu** cf. וצא$_1$.

נצר **naṣâru** to keep, guard, observe *iṣ-ṣu-ra* 27^{25} 33^{4} *-ru* (sing.) 21^{2} 22^{27} *iṣ-ṣur-u* 27^{20} *ni-iṣ-ṣu-ru* 32^{25} *iṣ-ṣu-ru* (pl.) 32^{10} 46^{10} *na-ṣir* 29^{31}; *u-ša-an-ṣir* 31^{25} *-šu* $28^{22,33}$ 33^{21}; **naṣiru** observance *na-ṣir* 20^{3}; **maṣartu** watch, guard *maṣarâti* pl 31^{24} 46^{6}; **niṣirtu** treasure, possession *ni-ṣir-tu* 12^{29} *-ti* 18^{25}.

נקה **naḳû** to pour out, sacrifice *aḳ-ḳi* 10[11] *aḳ-ḳí* 37[1,22] 38[16] *aḳ-ḳa-a* 50[25] *lik-ḳí* 24[17] *li-iḳ-ḳí* 39[17]; *at-ta-ḳí* 60[15]; **niḳu** a sacrifice *kirru niḳa* 24[17] *ni-ḳa-a* 60[15] *niḳâni* 60[20] *kirru niḳâni* 36[34] 37[22] 38[15] 39[17] *kirru niḳâni*$_{pl}$ 7[25] 34[21].

נקב **naḳâbu** II I to pierce *u-na-ḳib* 32[29] *mu-naḳ-ḳib* 36[27]; **naḳbu** canal *naḳbî*$_{pl}$*-šu* 20[24].

נקם **naḳmûtu** cf. קמה.

נקר **naḳâru** to devastate *aḳ-ḳur* 2[1] 3[27] 4[15,25] 13[21] 18[10] *a-ḳur* 8[23].

נרב *an* **nirba** a species of grain 20[27]. For **niribu** cf. ארב$_5$.

נרכב **narkabtu** cf. רכב.

נרם **narâmu** cf. ראם$_3$.

נרפד **nir-pad-du**$_{pl}$ bones, skeleton *-šu* 23[1,3] *-šu-nu-ti* 26[31].

נרר **nararûtu, nirarûtu** aid, help *na-ra-ru-u-ti* 42[24] *ni-ra-ru-ut-tí* 2[12] *ni-ra-ru-ti-šu-nu* 3[23].

נשא$_1$ **našû** to lift up *ta-na-ša-aš-ši* 52[23] *aš-ši* 42[14] *aš-ša-a* 4[22] *iš-ši* 60[22] *iš-šu-u* 58[17] *iš-šu-u-ni* 23[3] *iš-šu-nim-ma* 11[8] 42[20] *liš-šu-u-ni* 23[1]; *i-ši* (impv.) 35[18]; *na-ša-a-ta* (perm.) 32[31]; *na-a-ši* 60[3] *na-ši* 7[9] 62[1] *na-a-aš* 1[3] *na-ša-ta* 38[27]; **nišu** elevation *ni-iš* 23[7] 29[13,17] 33[16] 37[11]; **nišîtu** elevation, favorite *ni-šit* 5[1] 9[1].

נשא **nišû** people cf. אנש$_1$.

נשא **nišû** (perhaps error for *nisû*) distant, remote (?) *ni-šu-tu* 20[11].

נשא **nišû** excrement *ni-ša-a-šu-un* 17[15] (parallel passage *ni-ṣu* 16[33]).

נשב **nišbû** cf. שבא$_4$.

נשק **našâḳu** to kiss *iš-ši-ḳu* 11[8]; *u-na-aš-šiḳ* 21[19,24] 25[13,21] *-ši-ḳa* 21[15] *-ši-ḳu* 22[2] 40[23] 41[18] 42[21] 50[6].

נשר **našru** eagle *našri iṣṣuru* 17[20] *našrî iṣṣuru pl* 26[25].

נת **nîtu** . . . . . *ni-tum* 14[13] *ni-i-ti* 17[26]. St. נאה (?).

ס

סבא$_4$ **sibû** seventh *sibu-u* 64[2,23] *si-bu-u* 59[16] *sibi-í* 13[1] *siba-a* 60[7].

סבס **sabsu** angry, enraged *sab-sa-a-tí* 27[2].

סגל **sugullatu** herd *su-gul-lat* 3[27].

סגר **si-gar** festival (?) 19[26].

סדר **sidru, sidirtu** order, array *si-id-ru* 11[26] *si-dir-ta* 15[15] 17[6].

סום **sâmu** II I to adorn *u-si-im-ši* 6[25]; **sîmtu** adornment, insignia *si-ma-ti* 23[21] *-šu-nu* 41[8] *si-ma-tí-šu* 14[17] *si-mat* 15[22] 48[11]; **simânu** trophy, insignia *si-ma-ni* 16[8,14]; **simânu** third month of the Bab.-Assyr. year *arḫu simâni* 30[16].

סום **sisû** horse *sisî* 20[15] 35[17] *sisî*$_{pl}$ 3[27] 4[2] 11[24] 12[12] 14[28] 21[19] 48[14] 50[13] *-ya* 16[34] *-ši-na* 16[22].

סוק **sâḳu** II I to bring low, oppress *u-si-iḳ* 21[5] *u-si-ḳa* 14[13]; **sûḳu** road, street *sûḳî pl* 26[31].

סחה **saḫû** (?) to rebel *is-si-ḫu* (I 2) 14[6]; **siḫû** rebellion *siḫ-u* 14[12].

סחף **saḫâpu** to cast down *as-ḫu-up-šu* 17[26] *is-ḫup-šu-nu-ti* 17[14] *is-ḫu-up* 16[29] *-šu* 48[22] *-šu-nu-ti* 26[14] *is-ḫu-pu-šu* 10[20] 12[23] 44[8] *-šu-nu-ti* 10[25].

סחר **saḫâru** to turn, return, surround *sa-ḫi-ir-šum-ma* 35[21] *sa-ah-ra* 40[2]; *is-saḫ-ra* (= *istaḫira*) 60[9,11,14]; *u-sa-ḫi-ir* 40[4]; **siḫirtu** enclosure, wall, extent *si-ḫír-ti* 4[24] *-ša* 1[22] 5[24] 6[15] *si-ḫir-ti* 12[1] 33[32] *-šu* 50[10] *-ša* 32[2]; **suḫḫurtu** enclosure, discomfiture *suḫ-ḫur-ta-šu-nu* 15[31]; **siḫru** a band, troop *siḫ-ru* 15[6]; **suḫiru** . . . . . *su-hi-ru* 32[18].

סכה **sikatu** . . . . . *si-kat* 6[26].

סכל **sukkallu** messenger, servant 33[2] 37[18] *sukkalli-ša* 64[8].

סכף **sakâpu** to cast down; **sikiptu** defeat *si-kip-ti* 17[8]; **askuppu** threshold *as-kup-pu* 38[9] *askuppî pl* 64[10,14].

סכר **sakâru** to speak *u-ša-as-kĭr-šu* 29[13].

סכר **sikkuru** a bolt *sik-ku-ru* 52[17] *iṣu sikkuri* 52[11].

סלא **salatu** near (?) (fem. adj.) *sa-la-tu* 20[11] *sa-lat-ya* 57[19] (my near kin).

סלה **salû** to lift up, cast off *is-la-a* 27[21] *is-lu-u* 22[29] 27[13].

סלה **sullû** street (?) *su-ul-li-í-šu-nu* 27[1].

סלח **salâḫu** to sprinkle *is-luḫ-ši* 64[16] *su-luḫ-ši* 64[12].

סלם **salâmu** to turn, be favorable *is-li-mu* 35[13]; **salimu, sulummu** favor, treaty, alliance *sa-li-mí* 46[15] *su-lum-mu-u* 46[16]; **sa-li-mi-iš** graciously 40[34].

סמם **summatu** *iṣṣuru* a dove (?) 60[8] *summata* 60[8] *summati* 16[31].

סנן **sinuntu** *iṣṣuru* a swallow 60[10] *sinunta* 60[10].

סנק **sanâḳu** to bind, press, submit *as-ni-ḳa-šu-nu-ti* 3[17] *is-ni-ḳa* 14[29] *sa-an-ḳu* 33[27]; *is-sa-an-ḳa-am-ma* (IV I) 29[28]; **sunḳu** want, famine *su-un-ḳu* 24[28] 32[13] *su-un-ḳí* 26[12,29] 29[6].

ספא **sipû** to pray *u-sap-pu-u* 25[6] (sing.); **supû, suppû** prayer *su-pu-u-šu* 39[19] *su-pi-í-a* 15[20] 37[19] *su-up-pi-í* 25[6].

ספח **sapâḫu** to overthrow *u-sap-pi-iḫ* 17[9] 35[27].

ספן **sapânu** to cover, overpower, cast *i-sap-pan-nu* 59[15] *as-pu-un* 18[13] 26[24] *is-pu-nu* (sing.) 26[22] *li-is-pu-un* 37[15] *is-pu-nu* (pl.) 23[5] *sa-pi-nu* 18[17] *sa-pi-in* 36[28] *sa-pi-na-at* 15[23] 16[11] 38[28] 39[7].

ספסף **sapsapâtí** extremities, limbs *sa-ap-sa-pa-tí* 16[13].

ספף **sippu** threshold *si-ip-pu* 52[18].

ספר **saparu** net *sa-par* 26[13].

ספר **siparru** copper *siparri* 4[26,29] *siparri pl* 6[26,28].

סרד **surdû** *iṣṣuru* owl 34[15].

סרי **si-ri-ya-am** coat of mail 15[21].

סרם **sarmu** . . . . . *sa-ar-ma-šu-nu* 41^{9}.

סרק **sarâḳu** to pour out; **surḳînu** libation *sur-ḳi-nu* 60^{16} *-ni* 60^{25} 61^{1}.

סרר **surratu** opposition, sedition *sur-ra-a-ti* 46^{12} *-tí* 27^{24}.29^{32} *-tí-šu-un* 46^{24}.

סתה **sittu, sititu** the rest, remainder *si-it-ti* 13^{25} 16^{19} 26^{21} 27^{5} 48^{1} *si-tí-it* 1^{16} 2^{1} *si-it-tu-ti* 29^{5} *-šu-nu* 33^{32} *-tí-šu-nu* 12^{2} *si-it-tu-u-ti* 24^{28} 31^{28}.

סתך **sattukku** daily sacrifice *sat-tuk-ku* $39^{8,23}$ *-ki* 23^{26} *-ki-šu-un* 27^{3} *-ki-ši-na* 23^{21}.

סתר **sutaru** . . . . . *su-ta-ri* 41^{17}.

פ

פא *abnu* **pa** *pl* ideogram for a kind of stone $64^{10,14}$.

פגל **pagâlu** to be great *pu-ug-gu-lu* 35^{21}.

פגר **pagru** body, corpse *pa-gar* 2^{14} *-šu* 22^{31} 23^{2} *pag-ri* (pl.) $16^{12,30}$ *-šu-un* 12^{1} *amilu pagrî pl* 26^{28} *-šu-nu* 15^{33} 17^{28} 33^{31} 48^{4} *pag-rat* (pl. fem.) 59^{21}.

פדה **padû** indulgent, sparing *pa-du-u* 6^{7} *pa-da-a* 5^{17} *pa-du-tí* 6^{10}.

פדן **padânu** way, road *pa-da-nu* 42^{23} *padanî pl* 2^{3}.

פו **pû** mouth, word, speech, command *pî* 36^{13} 62^{3} *-šu* 6^{8} *pi-i* 19^{26} 27^{10} 62^{2} *-šu* 27^{29} $29^{17,32}$ *-šu-un* 31^{26} *-šu-nu* $26^{18,20}$ *pa-a* 6^{10} *-šu* 52^{21} $61^{7,10}$ *-ša* 64^{7}.

פחא **piḫû** to close *pi-ḫi* (impv.) 58^{2} *pi-ḫi-i* 58^{8}; *ap-tí-ḫi* 58^{7}; **piḫâtu** district, governor of a district, satrap *amilu* **piḫâta** 19^{5} *piḫât* 14^{10} *amilu piḫâti pl* 46^{1} 48^{16} 50^{5} *-šu-nu* 33^{27}.

פחר **paḫâru** to assemble, come together *ip-ḫu-ru* 14^{11}; *ip-taḫ-ru* 60^{20}; *u-paḫ-ḫir* 20^{2} *-ḫi-ra* 48^{24} *u-pa-aḫ-ḫi-ra-am-ma* 41^{25} *u-pa-ḫir* 14^{27} 18^{27}; *pu-uḫ-ḫir* (impv.) 14^{22}; *lup-tí-ḫir* 1^{7}; **puḫru** totality *puḫur* 25^{12} 34^{26} *pu-ḫur-šu-nu* 15^{10} 17^{9}; **napḫaru** totality *napḫar* 3^{14} *nap-ḫar* 3^{30} *-ši-na* 7^{16}.

פחר **pu-uḫ-ri-í-ti** (?) . . . . . 59^{13}.

פטר **paṭâru** to open, sever, release *ap-ṭu-ur* 3^{33}; *u-paṭ-ṭi-ra* 20^{24}; *u-ša-ap-ṭi-ir* 41^{9}; *ip-pa-ṭir* 10^{1}; **paṭru** dagger 16^{2} *paṭar* 26^{12} 48^{12} *paṭrî pl* 16^{17}.

פיד **pâdu** side, limit *pad* $6^{5,16}$ 27^{12} 32^{3} *pa-ad* 36^{4} 37^{2} 41^{22}.

פיל *abnu* **pîlu** a kind of stone *pi-li* 6^{24} *pi-i-li* 10^{3}.

פיר **pîru** elephant *pîri* $12^{29\,bis}$ $18^{23,24}$ (*šin pîri* = ivory).

פכה **pakû** fear *pa-ki-í* 40^{25}.

פכד **pakâdu** cf. פקד.

פלו **palû** reign, year of reign *pa-lu-u-a* 37^{13} *pali-ya* 7^{23} 8^{1} 20^{28} *-šu* 24^{14} *pali-í-a* 23^{24} *pa-li-í-a* 35^{11} *-šu* 39^{15} *pa-la-a-šu* 40^{32} *palí pl-ya* 8^{13}.

פלח **palâḫu** to fear, reverence *ap-la-aḫ* 36^{1} *ip-laḫ* 11^{23} 29^{18} 33^{10} *ip-la-ḫu* 16^{21} 26^{10} 31^{20} *pa-la-ḫa* 39^{24} *pa-la-aḫ*(?)*-šu* 41^{3} *pa-li-ḫi-ka* 41^{33} *-šu* 40^{20};

pa-líḫ 6[4] *pa-liḫ* 19[7] *pa-lìḫ-ka* 23[11] *-šu* 24[9] 26[19] *pa-li-iḫ* 35[5] *-šu* 41[11]; *ip-tal-la-ḫu* 22[19] *ip-tal-ḫu* 58[25]; **pulḫu** fear *pul-ḫi* 10[19] 12[23]; **puluḫtu** fear *pu-luḫ-tu* 17[18] *-ti* 29[27] *-ta* 58[6]; **pa-al-ḫi-iš** reverently 35[19].

פלכת IV I to cross, transgress, rebel *ap-pal-kit* 1[9] *ip-pal-kit* 24[31] 25[8] 34[12] *-ki-tu* 33[9]; III I *u-ša-pal-kat* I will break to pieces 52[18].

פלס **palâsu** IV I to look, look upon, favor *ap-pa-lis* 22[3] *-li-is* 59[25] *ap-pa-al-sa* 59[19] *ip-pa-li-is* 40[13] *lip-*[*pa-lis*] 24[8] *lip-pal-sa-an-ni* 37[11]; *na-ap-li-is* (impv.) 38[22] *-li-si* 39[11] *i-tap-lu-si* (IV 2 inf.) 58[6].

פלק **palâḳu** (or *balâḳu*) to destroy **napalḳatu** destruction *na-pal-ḳa-ta-šu* 18[14] *na-pal-ḳa-ti* 17[27] (some implement or mode of attack).

פלש **palâšu** to scatter, break in pieces *ap-lu-uš* 33[18]; *u-pal-li-ša* 15[33].

פנה **panû** face, front, presence *pa-nu-u-a* 20[18] 28[27] 36[2] 37[29] *pa-nu-uš-šu-un* 26[10] 40[24] *pa-ni* 38[32] 46[6] *-a* 6[13] *-ya* 9[27] 42[19,25] *-ki* 63[5] *-šu* 14[18] 23[10] *-ša* 64[6] *pa-na* the past 9[27] 61[25] *pa-an* 1[17] 2[2] 13[23]; **punu** face (?) *pu-na-šu* 58[5].

פסס **pasâsu** to forgive *pa-si-su* 25[28].

מצא **piṣû** white *piṣi-í* 6[24].

פקד **paḳâdu** to visit, inspect, entrust, appoint *ap-ḳíd* 23[29] 48[19] *-su-nu-ti* 46[4] *ap-ki-du* 46[9] (sing.) *ip-ḳíd-du-uš* 48[17] (sing.); *u-pa-ki-du* 42[7] 46[2]; **piḳittu** appointment *pi-ḳít-ti-šu-un* 46[4] *-ta-šu-un* 46[3]; **pitḳudu** thoughtful, provident *pit-ḳu-du* 9[18] 16[1].

פרא to cut off, destroy *pa-ri-'i* 15[25]; *u-par-ri-'i* 16[7,17] 33[1]; **niprîtu** destruction (?), famine (?) *ni-ip-ri-í-tu* 25[32] *-ti* 27[6] *ni-ip-ri-ti* 14[14].

פרא **parû** mule (?), ox (?) *imiru parí pl* 12[12] 14[28] 48[14] *pa-ri-í* 3[28].

פרה *abnu* **parû** a kind of stone *pa-ru-tí* 6[24].

פרב **parab** five sixths 20[26].

פרזל **parzillu** iron *parzilli* 11[21] 22[23] *parzilli pl* 6[28].

פרך **parâku** to separate, bar, hem *pur-ru-ku* 26[31] (II I perm.); **parakku** enclosed space, sanctuary *-ka* 38[19] *parakkî pl* 41[15] *-šu-nu* 26[33].

פרכא **naparkû** cessation *na-par-ka-a* 27[17].

פרם **purimu** wild ass *imiru purimî pl* 30[11].

פרנך **parunakku** enclosure (?) *pa-ru-nak-ki* 20[6].

פרס **parâsu** to divide, cut, decide, hinder *ip-ru-us* 27[22] *pa-ra-as* 27[10]; *u-par-ri-is* 32[4]; **purussu** decision, decree *purussí-šu-nu* 19[21]; **piristu** decision, decree, oracle *pi-ris-ti* 61[19,20].

פרץ **parâṣu** to command *ap-ru-uṣ* 16[26]; **parṣu** command *paraṣ* 7[11] *parṣî pl* 63[2] *-ša* 63[8,11,14,17,20] 64[1,4].

פרר **parâru** to break to pieces *u-par-ri-ir* 17[9] *lu-pi-ri-ir* 4[10] *mu-pa-ri-ru* 5[11].

פרש **paršu** entrails (?), filth, excrement *par-šu* 16[12] 31[29].

פרש **parâšu** IV I to fly *mut-tap-riš-u-tí* (IV 2) 10[11].

פרשד IV I to flee, escape *ip-par-šid* 26^{15} 28^{12} 29^{10} 31^{31} 34^{13} *-ši-du* 1^{17} 2^{2} 32^{11} *na-par-šu-di* 26^{14} (inf.); *it-ta-nap-raš-ši-du* he had fled (IV 3) 34^{14}.

פשה **pašû** cf. בשה.

פשח **pašâḫu** to be quiet, become quiet *u-pa-aš-ši-ḫa* 41^{9}.

פשט **pašâṭu** to scatter, destroy *i-pa-aš-ši-ṭu* 24^{19}.

פשק **pašḳu** strong, steep, difficult [*pa-aš*]*-ḳu* 14^{10} *pa-aš-ḳa-a-tí* 2^{6}; **šupšuḳu** steep *šup-šu-ḳa-a-tí* 2^{26}; **pušḳu** difficulty *pu-uš-ḳu* 40^{25}.

פשש **pašâšu** to cleanse (?), anoint (?) *ap-šu-uš* 37^{21} 38^{15} *lip-šu-uš* 24^{16} 39^{17}.

פתא$_3$ **pitû** to open *ta-pat-ta-a* 52^{16} *ap-ti* 10^{6} *ap-tí* 59^{22} *ap-ta-a* 61^{19} *ip-ta-aš-ši* 63^{8} *ip-*[*tu*] 14^{19} *ip-tu* 17^{22}; *pi-ta-a* (impv.) $52^{14.15}$ *pi-ta-aš-ši* 63^{1}; **putu** opening, entrance, side *pu-ut* 8^{16} *pu-ut-ni* 61^{24} *pu-tí* 15^{29} (pl.); **pitû** open *pi-tu-tí* 2^{28}.

פתק **patâḳu** to build, make **pitḳu** a work *pi-tiḳ* 50^{14}.

פתקד **pitḳudu** cf. פקד.

צ

צא$_1$ן to be good, favorable *u-ṣa-'i-i-nu-in-ni* 44^{9}; **ṣínu** good *ṣi-ni* 16^{11}.

צא$_1$ן **ṣínu** sheep and goats *ṣínî* 30^{27} *ṣi-í-ni* 12^{13} 18^{26} $31^{4.33}$ 32^{3}.

צא$_2$ר **ṣíru** the top, back; lofty, exalted; upon, against *ṣi-i-ru* $7^{2.16}$ *ṣi-i-ri* 37^{18} 38^{22} *ṣi-ru-u-a* 15^{12} *ṣi-ru-uš-šu* 10^{28} 12^{6} $14^{11.15}$ 36^{24} *-šu-un* 12^{22} *ṣîr* 24^{23} 27^{19} 30^{4} 34^{31} *-uš-šu* 21^{20} 24^{31} 25^{8} *-uš-šu-un* 27^{16} 42^{9} *ṣi-ir* 15^{26} 16^{8} *ṣirûti*$_{pl}$ 50^{14} *ṣi-ru-tu* 36^{23} *ṣir-tu* 34^{11} *ṣir-ti* 15^{23} 36^{1} 41^{14} *ṣi-ra-tí* 2^{20} *ṣi-ra-a-ti* 38^{9} 50^{22} *-tí* 9^{10} 42^{15}.

צא$_4$ר **ṣíru** a plain *ṣíri* 3^{20} 24^{27} 25^{8} 30^{24} 44^{5} $57^{20\ bis}$ *ṣíra* 16^{13} 46^{3}.

צבא$_1$ **ṣâbu** man, soldier *ṣâbî*$_{pl}$ 1^{9} 2^{9} *amílu ṣâbî*$_{pl}$ 11^{23} 13^{5} 26^{18} 44^{3} *-šu* 12^{24}.

צבה **ṣabîtu** gazelle *ṣabîti*$_{pl}$ 30^{11}.

צבב *iṣu* **ṣumbu** a kind of wagon *ṣu-um-bi* 14^{28}.

צבח *abnu* **ṣab-ḫi**$_{pl}$ pearls (?), necklace (?) $63^{12.13}$ 64^{21}.

צבת **ṣabâtu** to seize, take, embrace, build, work *aṣ-bat* 4^{2} 7^{26} 15^{25} [17^{29}] 34^{6} 38^{12} 44^{12} 46^{6} 50^{7} *aṣ-ba-at* 36^{32} *iṣ-bat* 25^{22} 33^{5} 35^{28} 60^{3} 61^{22} *-su-nu-ti* 25^{32} *iṣ-ba-ta* 23^{9} 34^{18} 48^{27} *li-iṣ-ba-at* 37^{19} *iṣ-ba-tu* $1^{6.18}$ $22^{17.19}$ 29^{11} 31^{20} *iṣ-ba-tu-ni* 1^{4} *-nim-ma* 15^{7} 28^{32} *iṣ-bat-u-nim-ma* $46^{23.25}$ *ṣa-bat* (impv.) 22^{18} *ṣab-tu* (perm.) 15^{15} *ṣa-bit* 5^{14} *ṣa-ba-tí* 4^{27}; *aṣ-ṣa-bat* (= *aṣ-ta-bat*) 13^{32} *iṣ-ṣa-bat* 13^{27}; *u-ṣab-bit* 21^{4} 31^{16} *-bi-ta* 24^{26}; *u-ša-aṣ-bit* 6^{18} *-su-nu-ti* 34^{24} 42^{23} *-bi-it-su* 40^{14}; **ṣibtu** seizure *ṣi-bit* 33^{18}; **ṣubtu** garment, clothing *ṣu-bat* 52^{10} $64^{2.8.17}$.

צח **ṣu-ḫi** . . . . . *ṣu-ḫi-šu* (?) 60^{22}.

צחר **ṣaḫâru** to be small *u-ṣa-aḫ-ḫir* 12^{20} *li-ṣa-aḫ-ḫi-*[*ir*] 61^{15} *li-ṣa-*[*ḫi-ir*] 61^{16}; **ṣiḫru, ṣaḫru** small *ṣiḫru* 10^{22} 12^{12} *ṣiḫra* 17^{28} 20^{2} 48^{2} *ṣiḫrûti*$_{pl}$ 12^{9} 13^{20} *ṣa-aḫ-ri* 35^{26}.

צלא **ṣiltu** battle *ṣi-il-tí* 15[22].

צלה **ṣalû** to beg, entreat *u-ṣal-li* 22[30] 42[14] *u-ṣal-la-a* 25[25]; **taṣlîtu** prayer *ta-aṣ-li-ti* 38[25].

צלל **ṣalâlu** to fall, sink *iṣ-lal* 6[13].

צלל **ṣalâlu** to cover **ṣalulu** shadow, protection *ṣalu*(?)-*lum* 24[2] *ṣa-lu-lu* 6[7]; **ṣululu** shadow, cover, roof *ṣu-lu-li-šu* 38[8] *ṣu-lul-ši-na* 30[8]; **ṣillu** shadow *an ṣil-li* dungeon 11[22] (*an* = receptacle).

צלם **ṣalmu** image *ṣa-lam* 7[27] 8[25].

צלם **ṣalmu** fem. *ṣalimtu* black *ṣa-lim-tum* 58[11] *ṣal-mat* 40[10].

צמא₁ **ṣummu** thirst *ṣu-um-mí* 30[10,22,32] 31[26] *-šu-nu* 31[29].

צמד **ṣamâdu** to arrange, harness *ṣa-an-du* 40[17] (perm.) *ṣa-mid-su* 20[15]; **ṣimdu, ṣindu, ṣimittu** span *ṣi-in-di-šu* 14[29] *ṣi-mit-ti* 16[9].

צמר **ṣamâru** II I to plan *u-ṣa-am-mí-ru-šu* 17[25].

צף **ṣi-pa** a kind of stone (?) 4[25].

צפף **ṣippatu** a kind of reed *ṣip-pa-a-ti* 20[27].

צפר **iṣṣuru** bird cf. אצר.

צצה **ṣuṣû** a sprout (?) *ṣu-ṣa-a* 62[9].

צצה **ṣiṣṣu** bond *iṣu ṣi-iṣ-ṣi* 22[22].

צרח **ṣarâḫu** to be angry *iṣ-ṣa-ru-uḫ* 42[13].

צרר **ṣirritu** . . . . . *ṣir-ri-tu* 33[19].

צתם **ṣutmu** . . . . . *ṣu-ut*(?)-*mu* 32[6].

ק

קבא₄ **ḳibû** to say, speak, announce, inform, call, command *iḳabî* 61[7,10] *i-ḳab-bi* 52[21] 64[7] *aḳ-bi* 12[4] 13[28] 27[7] 59[7,8] *aḳ-bu-u* 59[6] *taḳ-bu-u* 35[21,23] *iḳ-bi* 25[13] 40[14] *iḳ-ba-a* 48[28] *iḳ-bu-u* 25[10] (sing.) *li-iḳ-ba-a* 37[16] *iḳ-bu-u* 19[22] (pl.) 20[1,17] 26[19] 34[10] *-šu* 19[24] *li-iḳ-bu-u* 37[18] 39[22] 41[33]; **ḳibîtu** command *ki-bit* 6[8] *-su* 39[20] *ki-bi-it* 38[28] *-su-nu* 35[31] [*kibîti-šu*] 41[14] *ki-bi-ti* 41[28] *-šu-nu* 36[1].

קבל **ḳabâlu** to meet **muḳṭablu** (I 2) warrior *muḳ-ṭab-li-šu-nu* 1[9] 2[9,14] 4[19]; **ḳablu** fight *ḳabli* 2[23] 3[16] 4[7] 8[7] 44[2] *ḳab-li* 40[18] 58[23] *ḳab-la* 59[8,16] *ḳa-bal-šu* 48[26]; **ḳablu** midst *ḳabal* 10[20] 11[31]; **ḳabaltu** midst, waist *ḳa-bal-ti* 32[5] *ḳablâti pl-ya* 63[19] *-ša* 63[18] 64[19] *-šu-nu* 16[17].

קוה II I to wait *u-ḳi* 1[8].

קול **ḳûlu** voice *ḳu-lu* 59[19].

קוף **ḳâpu** to decay, fall *i-ḳu-pu* 24[4] 37[28].

קוף **ḳâpu** to entrust *i-ki-pu-nu* 36[7]; *amílu* **ḳîpu** keeper, chief, governor 52[21] 63[1,3,7,10,13,16,19,22] 64[3] *ḳípi* 52[13,14] *ḳípa-šu-nu* 8[2] *amílu ḳípâni pl* 22[21,22] *amílu ki-pa-a-ni* 42[24] 46[1] 50[5] *amílu ki-í-pa-a-ni* 42[7].

קות **ḳâtu** to give *iḳ-u-tu* 36^{18}.

קטר **ḳuṭru** smoke *ḳu-ṭur* 13^{22}.

קיש **ḳâšu** to give, present *a-ḳis-su* 48^{15} *i-ki-ša* 34^{1}.

קלל **ḳullultu** shame, disgrace *ḳul-lul-ti* 12^{3}.

קלקל **ḳalḳaltu** hunger *ḳal-ḳal-ti* $30^{10,22,33}$ 31^{27}.

קמה **ḳamû** to burn *aḳ-mu* 13^{22} 18^{10} *iḳ-mu-u* 28^{13}; **naḳmûtu** conflagration *na-aḳ-mu-ti-šu-nu* 13^{22}.

קמץ **ḳamâṣu** to press together II 2 to crouch *uḳ-tam-mi-iṣ* 59^{23}; III 2 to press together *uš-taḳ-mi-iṣ* 61^{23}.

קנה **ḳanû** reed *ḳanâ* 60^{18}.

קנן **ḳanânu** to place, lay (?) *ḳun-nu-nu* 59^{2} (II 1 perm.) they crouch; **ḳinnu** family, nest *ḳin-nu* 30^{25} *-šu* 25^{17} 31^{3}.

קפד **ḳapâdu** to plan, devise, meditate *iḳ-pu-ud* 14^{7} 46^{11} *iḳ-pu-du* 25^{32} 48^{2} *iḳ-pu-du-u-ni* 26^{20}; III 1 to entrust (?) *u-šaḳ-pi-du* 26^{9}.

קפף **ḳuppu** cage *ḳu-up-pi* 12^{15}.

קצר **ḳaṣâru** to bind, collect, devise *aḳ-ṣur* 23^{27} 33^{33} *iḳ-ṣu-ru* 20^{11} *ka-ṣir* 25^{28}; *ku-uṣ-ṣur* 32^{32}; *ki-iṣ-ṣu-ra* (= *kitṣura* I 2) 62^{9}; *ul-taḳ-ṣi-ru* 3^{16}; **ḳiṣiru** possession *ḳí-ṣir* 33^{33}; **ḳiṣru** might *ki-iṣ-ri* 5^{11} *ki-ṣir* 9^{29} *-šu-nu* 4^{10}.

קקד **ḳaḳḳadu** (= *ḳadḳadu*) head *ḳaḳḳadi* $25^{10,11}$ 40^{10} *-ya* 63^{7} *-ša* 63^{6} 64^{28} *ḳaḳ-ḳa-su* 18^{22} 19^{13} *ḳaḳḳadî*$_{pl}$ 19^{14} *-šu-nu* 1^{13} 4^{20}.

קקר **ḳaḳḳaru** ground, earth *ḳaḳ-ḳa-ru* $25^{14,21}$ $30^{12,29,32}$ 31^{9} *-ri* 9^{29} 52^{1} *ḳaḳ-ḳar* 18^{15} 30^{22}.

קרא$_1$ **ḳarû** to call, invite, pray *aḳ-ri* 10^{9}; *iḳ-tí-ra* 15^{7} *iḳ-tir-u* 27^{9} *iḳ-tí-ru-nim-ma* 11^{25}.

קרב **ḳarâbu** to approach *aḳ-rib* 11^{33} *iḳ-ru-bu* 15^{9}; *aḳ-ṭí-rib* 8^{2}; *šu-uḳ-ri-ba* 39^{13}; **ḳirbu** midst *ki-ir-bi* 41^{30} *-šu* 35^{19} *kir-bi-šu-un* 12^{14} *ki-ir-ba* 41^{18} *-šu* 36^{34} *ki-rib* midst, within (used after prepositions or alone) 2^{10} 4^{19} *-šu* 10^{7} *-šu-un* 13^{6} *-ši-na* 23^{20} *ki-ri-ib-šu* 35^{9}; **kir-bí-tí-šu-nu** (pl. of *kirbu* (?)) 3^{28}; **ḳitrubu** approach, attack *ḳít-ru-ub* 12^{10} 16^{23} *ḳi-it-ru-ub* 6^{9}; **taḳribtu** prayer *taḳ-rib-ti* 27^{3}; **iḳribu** prayer *iḳ-ri-bi*[-*šu*] 24^{17}.

קרד **ḳarâdu** to be strong *iḳ-ri-da* 58^{3}; **ḳardu** fem. *ḳarittu* strong, warrior *ḳar-du* 5^{5} 7^{7} 9^{6} 20^{19} $32^{13,32}$ *ḳar-du-tí* 7^{11} *ḳa-rit-tu* 31^{7} 33^{3}; **ḳarradu, ḳurâdu** strong, warrior *ḳar-ra-du* 32^{33} *ḳu-ra-du* $61^{10,11}$ *ḳu-ra-di* 2^{21} 61^{7} *-ya*$_{pl}$ 2^{5} *-šu-nu* 1^{11} 3^{19} 4^{12} 16^{12} *ḳu-ra-a-di-šu-nu* 2^{16}; **ḳurdu** might *ḳur-di* 25^{26}.

קרן **ḳarnu** horn *ḳarnâti*$_{pl}$*-ša* 32^{30}.

קרר **ḳaruru** decrease *ḳa-ru-ra* 60^{13}.

קש **ḳaštu** bow 15^{24} *ḳašti* 11^{24} 20^{14} 31^{7} 38^{27} *-ya* 19^{3} *ḳašâti* (?)$_{pl}$ 60^{22} (arches of the rainbow (?)).

קתה **ḳatû** completed *ḳa-ta-a* 23[29].

קתה **ḳâtu** hand 33[14] *ḳâtû* (= *ina ḳâti*) 13[7] *ḳâtu-u-a* 26[16] *ḳâtu-šu* 9[15] *-uš-šu* 39[24] *ḳâtuš-šu-un* 46[28] *ḳa-tu-u-a* 38[25] *ḳa-tu-uš-šu* 40[7,20] *ḳâti* 22[16] 23[8] 31[32] *ḳâti-ya* 6[14] *ḳa-ti* 3[30] 10[16] 50[19] *-ya* 61[22] *-šu-un* 16[15] *ḳa-a-ta* 40[12] *ḳât* 18[1,2] *-su* 5[13,26] 9[19] *ḳâta-a-a* 11[31] 16[22] 17[12] 31[5] 50[11] *ḳa-ta-a-šu* 40[10] *ḳâtî* 27[26] 31[17] 34[6] 46[26] *-ya* 33[16,18] 42[14] 63[22] *-ša* 63[21] 64[18].

קתח **ḳuttaḫu** spear *ḳut-ta-ḫu* 15[25] 32[33] *ḳut-ta-ḫi* 17[7].

ר

רא$_4$ה **rî'u** to pasture, shepherd, rule *ir-tí-'i-u* 30[12]; **ri'u** shepherd, ruler 9[8] *amilu* *ri'u* 6[7] *amilu* *ri'i* 5[7]; **ri'ûtu** dominion *ri'u-ut* 19[20] *-su* [40[33]] *ri'û-si-na* 28[2]; **rîtu** pasturage, food *ri-i-ti* 10[24].

רא$_2$ב **ra'âbu** to be angry, rage *ir-'-ub* 64[6].

רא$_3$ב **rîbitu** place, square, street *ri-bit* 9[12] 17[28] 19[16] *ri-ba-a-ti* 26[31].

רא$_4$ד **râdu** storm *ra-a-di* 9[29].

רא$_1$ם **rîmu** wild ox *ri-i-mu* 36[27].

רא$_3$ם **râmu** to pity, love *ir-a-mu* 40[32]; **rîmu** grace *ri-í-mu* 21[10] 25[29] 27[6] 29[12] 33[23] 48[9] *ri-í-ma* 3[31]; **rîmu** fem. *rîmtu* beloved *ri-im-tu* 32[27]; **narâmu** fem. *narâmtu* love, favorite *na-ra-mi-ka* 38[19] *-šu* 37[16] *na-ram* 20[19] 30[13] 32[26] *na-ra-am* 5[2] 35[12] *na-ram-ti* 34[23].

רא$_3$ק **rûḳu** far *ru-u-ḳu* 9[14] 22[10] *rûḳûti*$_{pl}$ 13[27] [62[16]] *ru-ḳu-u-tí* 9[24] *-ti* 30[6]; **rûḳu, ruḳḳu, rûḳítu** distance *ru-ki* 62[3] *ru-u-ki* 62[2] *ru-uk-ki* 10[20] *ru-ki-í-ti* 28[12].

רא$_1$ש **râšu** head *ra-šu-u-a* 15[22]; **ríšu** head, summit, chief *ri-í-šu* 27[26] *ri-í-ši-i-šu* 24[6] *ríš* 5[25] (*ríš í-ni* = fountain head) 8[25] *ri-íš* 35[14] *ríšî* (?)$_{pl}$ 27[15]; **ríštu** pl. *ríšîti* summit *ri-ší-í-tí* 9[5]; **ríštû** first, chief, former *riš-tu-u* 30[16] 62[6] *ri-iš-tum* 37[1] *riš-ti* 7[10].

רא$_4$ש **rišâtu** rejoicings *ri-ša-a-ti* 23[24] 36[15,33] 38[5,13] *-tí* 20[6] *-tim* 41[1].

רבא$_4$ **arba'i** fem. *irbittu* four *arba'-i* 2[22] 9[8] *irbit-ti* 23[14] *ir-bit-ti* 35[2] *ir-bi-it-tim* 40[29] *irbit-ta* 5[7] 7[14]; **ribû** fourth *ribu-u* 63[15] 64[20] *ri-ba-a* 60[5].

רבא$_4$ **riba** decline, sunset *ri-ba* 37[12] 38[23].

רבה **rabû** to be great, become large *ir-bu-u* 20[9] 62[14]; *mu-šar-bu-u* 5[16] 7[12]; **rabû** large 12[12] *rabu-u* 7[1] *ra-bu-u* 35[1,8] *rabî* 8[8] 58[15] *rabi-í* 5[4] *rabâ* 20[2] *raba-a* 17[28] 63[6,7] *ra-ba-a* 64[23] *rabûti* 35[6] *rabûti*$_{pl}$ 2[22] 61[19] *amilu* *rabûti*$_{pl}$ 17[10] *-šu* 16[2] *-šu-un* 19[15] *-šu-nu* 16[19] *rabî-ti* 10[15] 39[10] 52[22] *rabî-tí* 5[23] *rabâti*$_{pl}$ 60[22]; *amilu* **rab-***alu* **ḫal-ṣu** commander of a fortress 13[7]; **rubû** prince 6[13] 9[11] *rubu-u* 6[8] *ru-bi-í* 40[22] (pl.) *rubûti*$_{pl}$ 25[18] *amilu* *rubûti*$_{pl}$ 11[19,34]; **rabi-iš** 7[20]; **tarbîtu** product *ta-ar-bi-it* 36[23].

רבץ **rabâṣu** to lie down *rab-ṣu* (perm.) 59[2].

רבש **murbašu** stroke, blow *mur-ba-šu* 16^{28} 17^{13}.

רגג **raggu** bad, wicked *rag-gu* 39^{7} *ra-ag-gu* 38^{29} *rag-gi* 16^{11}.

רגם **rigmu** word, cry *rig-ma* 59^{4}.

רגר **rig-gír** ideogram for some kind of wood 60^{18}.

רדה **radû** to tread, subdue, beget (?), march, pursue, flow *ar-di-í* 31^{10} 42^{26} *ar-di-šu-nu-ti* 3^{24} *ir-du-u* 20^{10} (he begat (?)) 30^{6} (pl.)^{15,21,33}; *ar-tí-di* 8^{21} *mur-tí-du-u* 7^{14}; II I to join *u-rad-di* 12^{22} 34^{2}; III I to cause to flow *u-šar-di* 58^{16} *u-šar-da-a* 16^{8} *lu-šar-di* 1^{13} 2^{11} $4^{14,21}$; **ridûtu** cohabitation (*bît ridûti* harem) *ridu-u-ti* 20^{6} *ri-du-u-ti* 19^{18}.

רדד **radâdu** to pursue *ar-du-ud* 4^{11} *ra-da-di-šu-nu* 16^{34}.

רוב **râbu** II I to extinguish *mu-rib* 6^{7}.

רוץ **riṣu** helper *ri-ṣi-í-šu* 29^{5}; **riṣûtu** help *ri-ṣu-tu* 25^{4} 27^{28} *ri-ṣu-tí* 5^{19} *ri-ṣu-ti* 15^{20} 33^{8} *-šu* 19^{9} 25^{24} *-šu-nu* 17^{5} *ri-ṣu-u-tu* 29^{3} *-ti* 25^{26} *ri-ṣu-ut* 4^{5} *ri-ṣu-us-su-un* 11^{25}.

רחה(?) **riḫîtu** consumption, destruction *ri-ḫi-it* 26^{30}.

רחץ **raḫâṣu** to overflow *ra-ḫi-ṣi* 1^{12} 5^{22}; **riḫiltu** overflow *ri-ḫi-il-ti* 3^{19}.

רכה **markîtu** refuge *mar-ki-i-tu* 26^{13} *mar-ki-tu* 31^{30} *mar-ki-ti-šu* 34^{14} *-šu-nu* 31^{31}.

רכב **rakâbu** to mount, ride *ar-ta-kab* 15^{23}; **râkibu, rakbu** courier, messenger *ra-ki-bu-ši-in* 16^{23} *rak-bu-šu* 12^{33} $22^{15,25}$ *rak-bi-í-šu-un* $46^{16,23}$; **rukubu,** riding, chariot, equipage *ru-ku-pi-ya* 16^{9} *ru-ku-bi-ka* 35^{17} *ru-kub* 20^{14} 48^{15}; **narkabtu** chariot *narkabti* 20^{15} *-ya* 3^{4} *narkabat* 15^{22} 16^{11} *narkabâti pl* 1^{7} 2^{5} *-ya* 2^{7} *-šu* 8^{19} *-šu-nu* 3^{15}.

רכל **rikiltu** slander *ri-kil-ti* 14^{14}.

רכס **rakâsu** to bind, erect *ar-ku-us-šu* 28^{22}; *u-rak-kis* 12^{16} 21^{4} *-ki-sa* 22^{7} 46^{7} 48^{12} *ruk-ku-sa* 16^{4}; **riksu** bond, support *rik-su-šu* 10^{2} *rik-sa-a-tí* 20^{5} 46^{7}; **markasu** enclosure, retreat *mar-kas* 20^{7}.

[רכש **rukušu** possession *ru-ku-ši-šu-nu* 31^{28}.

רמה **ramû** to dwell, inhabit *ar-ma-a* 41^{1} *ir-mí* 23^{26} *ra-mu-u* 35^{9} *ra-mi-í-ka* 38^{20}; *u-šar-ma-a* 39^{8} 41^{24} *šu-ur-ma-a* 35^{19}.

רמה **ramû** to settle, fall *ir-mu-u* 10^{2}.

רמה **ru-um-mí** . . . . . 61^{14}.

רמך **ramâku** to pour out *ri-it-mu-ku* 16^{12} (I 2 perm. blood and filth clave to the chariot).

רמם **ramâmu** to speak, thunder *ir-tam-ma-am-ma* 58^{12}.

רמן **ramânu** self *ra-ma-nu-uš-šin* 16^{24} *ra-man-i-šu* 22^{27} 42^{6} *ra-ma-ni-šu-nu* 18^{1} 27^{10} *ra-man-šu* 25^{23} 28^{18} *-šu-un* 46^{13}.

רסף **rasâpu** II I to thrust through *u-ra-sa-pu* 17^{2} *u-ras-sip* 25^{1} *u-ra-as-sip* 28^{10} *-si-pa* 32^{33}.

רפש **rapâšu** to be widespread, numerous *u-rap-pi-šu* 20^{11} *mu-rap-piš* 9^{17}; **rapšu** broad *rap-šu* 25^{27} (*libbu rapšu* large-hearted) 30^{8} *rap-ši* 44^{5} *rapšû*$_{pl}$*-ti* 3^{28} *rap-šu-ti* 13^{23} 15^{13} *rapšâti*$_{pl}$ 3^{18} *rap-ša-a-ti* 35^{27} *-tim* 40^{16}; **ritpašu** broad *ri-it-pa-šu* 41^{2}.

רצף **raṣâpu** to join, build *ar-ṣip* 4^{29} 10^{5} *ra-ṣa-pi* 4^{28}.

רקק **riḳḳu** plant, aromatic plant *riḳḳî*$_{pl}$ 36^{15} 38^{4}. St. ורק.

רשה **rašû** to possess, grant, permit *ar-ší-í* 36^{1} 37^{29} *ar-ši-šu* 21^{10} 25^{29} 33^{23} 48^{9} *-šu-u-ma* 29^{12} *-šu-nu-ti* 27^{6} *ar-ša-šu-nu-ti* 3^{31} *ir-šu-u* 12^{26} 35^{13} *ra-aš* 14^{4}; *ir-ta-ši* 40^{4}; *u-šar-ši* 41^{6} *u-šar-ša-a* 22^{26}; **maršîtu** possession *mar-šit* 3^{28}.

רשב **rašâbu** to be mighty *ra-aš-bu* 4^{24}; **rašubtu** might, majesty *ra-šub-bat* 10^{24} 48^{21}.

רשד **rašâdu** III I to establish, found *u-šar-ši-id* 36^{30} *šur-šu-da* 9^{29} (perm.).

רשש **ruššû** genuine *ru-uš-ši-i* 16^{4}.

רת$_4$א **ritû** II I to erect, establish *u-ra-at-ti* 38^{10} *u-ra-at-ta-a* 36^{25} *u-ri-ti* 6^{27}.

רתפש **ritpašu** cf. רפש.

רתת **rittu** hand (?) *rit-tu-u-a* 15^{26} *rit-tí-í-šu* 48^{12} *-šu-un* 22^{7} *rit-ti-šu-un* 16^{4} *-šu-nu* 16^{16}.

ש

ש **ša** relative pronoun who, which, whoever, and genitive particle $1^{2,13}$ 3^{28} 4^{11} 24^{18}; when 7^{20}; that, quod 50^{8}.

ש$_4$אה to see, seek, look after, devise *i-ša-'a-u* 30^{11} *a-ší-'i-a* 41^{3} *ší-'i* 62^{9} (perm.); *aš-tí-'i* 24^{5} *aš-tí-'i-í* 41^{7} *iš-tí-'i-í* 40^{6}; *iš-tí-ni-'i-í-ši-na-a-tim* 40^{11} *iš-tí-ni-'i-u* 46^{20} 48^{6}.

ש$_1$אל **ša'âlu** to ask, request *iš-'a-a-la* 29^{28} *iš-'a-a-lu* 29^{27} *iš-a-lu* 25^{3} *ša-'a-al* $22^{15,25}$ 27^{22}; **muštalu, multalu** provident, prudent *mul-ta-lu* 7^{9}; *iš-ta-na-'a-a-lum* 32^{22}; *u-ša-'i-lu* 11^{27} 15^{15}.

ש$_1$אר **šîru** flesh, kinsman *šîr* 29^{7} 32^{14} *šîri* 24^{10} *šîra* (?) 33^{18} *šîrî*$_{pl}$ 26^{1} *-šu-nu* 26^{24}.

ש$_4$אר **šâru** wind, storm *ša-a-ru* 59^{15} *šârî*$_{pl}$ 60^{15}.

ש$_3$את **šîtu** (?) to flee, to refuse (?) *a-ší-it* 36^{2} *i-ší-tu-u-ni* 26^{13} 27^{6}.

שב **šubu** . . . . . *šu-bí* 2^{14} 4^{19} *šu-u-bí* 4^{13}.

שב$_4$א **šíbû** to be satisfied, have enough *liš-bi* 24^{12}; *u-šab-bu-u* (II I) 32^{20}; **šíbû, nišbû** sufficiency, satisfaction *ší-bi-í* 24^{10} *niš-bi-í* 30^{31}.

שבב **šibbu** girdle *šib-bu* $63^{18,19}$ 64^{19} *šib-bi* $16^{8,17}$ 48^{12}.

שבט **šibṭu** staff, scepter, stroke, slaughter *šib-ṭu* 33^{29} *šib-ṭi* 27^{5}.

שבל **šubultu** ear of grain *šu-bul-tu* 20^{26}.

שבר **šabâru** to break to pieces *a-šab-bir* 52^{17}; *u-šab-bi-ru* 18^{3}; **šibirru** weapon, mace (?) *ši-bir-ri* 38^{25}.

שבר **šibru** Babylonian for *šipru* work *ši-bi-ir-šu* 36[21,28] 38[11] 39[5].

שבת **šubtu** cf. ושב.

שגה **šigû** prayer 27[3].

שגם **šagâmu** to cry out, roar *aš-gu-um* 5[22] 15[27].

שגר **šigâru** cage *iṣu ši-ga-ru* 28[21,34] 33[22].

שגש **šagaltu** destruction *ša-gal-ti* 3[18].

שדה **šadû** mountain *šadu-u* 28[19] 31[11] 58[14] 60[3,4,5,6] *šadi-i* 1[18] 19[8] (pl.) 60[16] *šadi-í* 4[18] *šada-a* 2[5] *šad-da-a* 17[20] *šadî pl* 3[3] *šadî pl-í* 6[8,24] *šad-di-i* 13[27,31].

שדד **šadâdu** to draw, drag *iš-du-du* 34[25]; **šiddu** border, coast *ši-di* 8[1] *ši-di-í* 11[6] *šid-di* 15[28].

שדד **šadâdu** to love, compassionate (?) *šu-du-ud* 61[14].

שדל **šadlu** fem. *šadiltu* broad, extended *šad-lu-ti* 11[7] *ša-di-il-tí* 16[9].

שו **šû** he, it, that one *šu-u* 6[13,14] 12[23] 13[26] 14[24] 16[26] 28[11,24] 29[10,16] 33[10] 42[4] 58[3] 59[16]; **šâšu** he, him, himself, that one *ša-a-šu* 11[10] 12[14] 24[25] 25[1,29] 28[30] 35[9,13,23] 37[7] 39[4]; **šû'atu, šâtu** pl. *šâtunu* this, that *šu-a-tu* 4[21,27] 9[28] 17[3,[27],31] 18[12,15] 44[11] 50[10] *šu-a-ti* 10[13] 24[15] *šu-a-tim* 35[10,20] 36[21] 37[10,27,28,31] 39[10,15] *ša-a-tu-nu* 4[29] 26[18,23] 42[21] 48[27] *ša-tu-nu* 3[31].

שוד **šídu** bull deity *ilu šídi* 26[21].

שוט **šâṭu** to draw, bear *i-ša-aṭ* 11[14] *i-šu-ṭu* 21[22] 27[22] *la-šu-ṭa* (= *lu* + *a-šu-ṭa*) 23[11].

שוף **šípu** foot *ší-pu-u-a* 10[26] 41[19] *ší-pu-uš-šu* 23[16] 40[23] *-uš-šu-un* 31[6] *šípi* 12[10] *ší-pi-šu* 40[9] *šípî* 22[12] *-ya* 11[8] 63[22] *-šu* 7[17] *-ša* 63[21] 64[18] *-šu-nu* 15[12] *šípî pl-ya* 1[17] *-šu* 5[24]; **šíptu** base (?) *ší-pit-su* 10[1]; **šûpu** battering-ram (?) *šu-pi-i* 12[10].

שוק **šûḳu** abundance 20[29].

שור **šûru** ox *šu-u-ri* 16[4].

שזן **šazânu** to lie (?), boast (?) *il-zi-nu* 25[16].

שח **šaḫu** a kind of wild beast *šaḫî pl* 26[25,30].

שחה **šaḫû** to swim *i-ša-aḫ-ḫi* 60[14].

שחט **šaḫâṭu** to strip, flay *aš-ḫu-uṭ* 34[7] [*iš*]-*ḫu-ṭu* 48[5].

שחף **šaḫâpu** to overthrow (= *saḫâpu*) *aš-ḫu-up* 4[17].

שחרר to be narrow, contracted *uš-ha-ri-ir* 59[18].

שחת **šaḫâtu** to bow, cast oneself down *aš-ḫu-ut* 37[28].

שטח **šaṭâḫu** to march (?) *i-ša-aṭ-ṭi-ḫa* 40[17] 41[4].

שטר **šaṭâru** to write *i-šaṭ-ṭa-ru* 24[20] *aš-ṭur* 48[13] *al-ṭu-ur* 4[28] *liš-ṭur* 24[16] *šaṭ-ru* (perm.) 24[18] *šaṭ-ra* 32[15]; **šiṭru** writing *ši-ṭir* 23[31] 39[16,18] *ši-ṭi-ir* 37[20] 38[14].

שי **ší'u** grain, crop *ší-am* 20[25].

שים **šâmu** to fix, appoint *i-šam-mu* 32[5] *li-šim* 24[11] *i-ši-mu* 35[4] *-šu-nu-ti* 32[15]; *mu-šim* 7[3] *mu-ši-mu* 7[11]; **šîmatu, šîmtu, šitimtu** fate, destiny *ši-ma-tu* 62[11] *ši-ma-ti* 24[11] *ši-im-ti-šu* 14[2] *šîmat* 48[22] *ši-ma-at* 35[4] *-su* 35[4] *šîmâti*$_{pl}$ 7[4,12] *ši-tim-ti-šu-nu* 17[22].

שין **šînâti** urine *ši-na-tí-šu-un* 16[32].

שכב **šakbitu** overthrow (?) *šak-bi-ti* 27[6].

שכן **šakânu** to set, lay, make, appoint, establish, accomplish *i-šak-ka-nu* 24[21] 30[25] 17[18] *aš-kun* 1[11] 60[16] *-šu* 22[3] 28[22,33] 29[15] 48[11] *aš-ku-un* 3[19] *aš-ku-na* 16[5] 44[5] *aš-ku-nu* 10[7] 34[20] 50[6] *taš-[kun]* 61[12] *taš-ku-nu* 61[15-18] *iš-kun* 8[17] [52[2]][3] (*šakânu uznu*, to resolve) *iš-ku-na* 25[8] *-nam-ma* 57[21] *iš-ku-nu* 9[13] (sing.) 61[2] *liš-kun* 24[17] 39[18] *iš-ku-nu* (pl.) 2[5] 24[29] 26[29] 29[9] 31[27] *šak-nu* (perm.) 29[9] 48[2]; *ša-kin* 5[14] *ša-kín* 59[19]; *ša-kan* 46[15]; *aš-ta-kan* 11[28] 17[6] 50[18] *al-ta-kan* 6[8] *aš-tak-ka-na* 24[27] 27[14] *iš-ta-kan* 27[29] *iš-tak-kan* 23[20] *[iš]-tak-ka-an* 39[28] *šit-ku-nu* (perm.) 11[26] 15[14] 16[3]; *u-ša-aš-kin* 6[11] *-ki-na* 31[6]; *iš-ša-kín* 23[10] 32[13] *liš-ša-kín* 46[17] 61[17] *-ki-in* 37[7] *iš-šak-nu* 25[32] *iš-ša-ak-nu* 4[6]; **šaknu** governor *ša-ak-nu* 9[1] *amîlu šaknûti*$_{pl}$ 27[13] *amîlu šak-nu-tí-ya* 6[2]; **šiknu** work, appointee *ši-kín* 18[13] 24[30] 27[14]; **maškanu** station *maš-kan-i-šu* 18[19] 48[18] *-šu-un* 46[4]; **šakkanakku** governor 23[18] *šakkanakkî*$_{pl}$ 36[5] *amîlu šakkanakkî*$_{pl}$ 11[19,33] *šak-ka-nak-ka* 40[22].

שכר **šakâru** (also *sakâru*) to speak, swear (?) promise (?) *u-ša-aš-kĭr-šu-nu-ti* 20[5].

שכר **šakâru** . . . . . *u-ša-kir* 15[32] 31[26].

שלא$_3$ **šalû** to cast, shoot (the bow) *ša-li-í* 20[14].

שלה (?) **šulûtu** royalty *šu-lu-ti-ya* 13[5].

שלה **šalû** to float, swim *i-šal-lu-u* 16[10] *u-šal-lu* 59[21].

שלה **šillatu** wickedness (?) blasphemy (?) *šil-la-tu* 26[18,19].

שלג **šalgu** snow *šal-gu* 13[30].

שלח **šalḫû** wall, rampart *šal-ḫu-u* 18[10]; **šal-ḫu-tim** . . . . . 39[26].

שלט **šalâṭu** to rule *šit-lu-ṭa-at* 32[29]; III 2 *ul-tal-li-ṭu* 2[23]; **šal-ṭiš** victoriously 30[30].

שלל **šalâlu** to plunder, carry away *aš-lu-la* 8[24] 11[17,32] 12[17] 13[5,21] 18[25] 31[13,33] 33[30] 50[17]; **šallatu** booty *šal-la-tu* 50[16] *-ti* 12[2] 46[8] *šal-lat* 31[17] *-su* 31[13] *šal-la-sun* 11[17,32] 13[5,21] *-su-nu* 1[15,23] 3[25] 8[24]; **šallûtu** captivity *šal-lu-su-nu* 3[32]; **šal-la-tiš** as booty 12[14].

שלם **šalâmu** to be whole, well, completed, executed *iš-lim-ma* 23[2]; *u-šal-lim* 24[1] *mu-šal-li-ma-at* 38[28] *-mat* 39[6]; **šalmu** favorable, peace *šal-mu* 38[2] *ša-al-mu* 36[11] *šal-mí* 27[4]; **šalimtu** peace *ša-lim-tim* 41[13] *ša-li-im-tim* 41[7,28]; **šulmu** peace, greeting, rest, sunset *šu-lum* 25[8] 29[27,29] *šul-mí* 7[24] *-ya* 22[15,25] 27[22]; **šulmâniš, šalmiš** peacefully *šu-ul-ma-niš* 41[5] *šal-míš* 30[6] 46[8] 50[19] *-mi-iš* 30[10] *-mí-iš* 30[30]; **šalamtu** corpse *ša-lam-ta-aš* 40[4] *šal-mat* 2[16] *-ma-at* 1[11] 3[19] 4[12].

שלם **šalummatu** . . . . . *ša-lum-ma-tí* 6[6].

שלק **šalâḳu** to cut, cut out *aš-lu-uḳ* 26[20]; II I to rip open *u-šal-li-ḳu* 31[28].

שלר **šallaru** a wall *šal-la-ar-šu* 36[19].

שלש **šalšu, šalultu** third *šal-šu* 63[12] *šal-ši* 10[18] 21[1] *šal-ša* 60[5] 64[19] *ša-lu-ul-ti* 35[25].

שלת **šulûtu** cf. שלה.

שם **šumu** name *šu-ma* 62[5,11] *šu-mí* 24[15,18,19] *šumi-ya* 5[16] *šu-mi-ya* 39[16] *-šu* 9[4] 39[18] *šum* 19[9] *-šu* 12[29] *-ki* 52[24] *šu-um* 37[20] 38[14].

שמא₄ **šímû** to hear *i-šim-mí* 24[18] *aš-mí-í* 22[30] *iš-mí* 13[28] 50[2] 61[20] *iš-mí-í* 27[24] 44[2] *iš-mi-í* 29[25] *iš-ma-a* 44[7] *iš-mu-u* 21[8] (sing.) *li-iš-mí-í* 37[19] *iš-mu-u* 15[20] (pl.) 22[10] 25[7] 33[9] 46[22] *li-iš-mu-u* 39[19].

שמא₁ל **šumílu** the left 36[29] *šumíli* 10[5].

שמה **šummânu** bond, fetter *šum-man-nu* 16[5].

שמה **šamû** pl. *šamî, šamâmu, šamûtu* heaven *šamí* 44[10] *šami-í* 7[5] 15[18] 58[11,19,24] 59[1] *ša-ma-mu* 62[4] *ša-ma-mi* 38[23] *ša-mu-tu* 58[1,4] *-tum* 13[29] 16[8].

שמח **šamâḫu** to thrive *šu-um-mu-ḫa* 20[27].

שמם **šumma** if *šum-ma* 52[16].

שמן **šamnu** eighth *šamni-í* 14[6].

שמן **šamnu** oil *šam-ni* 36[19].

שמן **šummannu** cf. שמה.

שמר **šamâru** to be great, powerful, violent *iš-tam-ma-ru* 40[26]; **šamru** violent *šam-ri* 15[29] 17[7]; **šumru, šumurratu** violence *šu-mur* 3[17] 4[8] *šu-mur-ra-as-su* 58[19]; **šam-riš** violently 4[18].

שמר **šimiru** a ring *šimir*$_{pl}$ 22[7] 48[12] 63[21,22] *ší-mir* 64[18] *šimirî*$_{pl}$ 16[8,15].

שמש **šamšu** the sun *ilu šam-šu* 7[14] *šamši* 38[30] *ilu šam-ši* 6[10] 7[24]; *mâtu ilu šam-ši* (?) the extreme east (?) 9[25].

שמש **šutmašu** . . . . . *šut-ma-ši* 2[10] *-ší* 3[21].

שנה **šanû** to be different II I to change, defeat (?) *u-ša-an-ni* 28[19]; **šanumma** another *ša-nu-um-ma* 46[18] *ša-nim-ma* 19[2] 37[30]; **šattu** pl. *šanâti* year *šatti* 35[25] *šat(?)-ti* 24[6] *šanâti*$_{pl}$ 18[7] 37[27,33] 38[32] *-ya* 20[29] 37[13] *šanâ*$_{pl}$*-tí* 1[2]; **šattišam(ma)** yearly *šat-ti-šam* 10[27] *šatti-šam-ma* 17[3] (= that year) *šat-ti-šam-ma* 21[20] 27[17].

שנה **šanû** to be double II I to repeat, inform *u-ša-an-na-a* 22[17] 42[12] *lu-ša-an-ni* 52[24]; **šanîtu** repetition, time 8[18]; **šanû** second *šani-i* 17[24] *šana-a* 60[4] 63[9] 64[18]; **šani'ânu** a second time *ša-ni-ya-a-nu* 25[18] 29[9].

שנג **šangu** priest 27[26] *-u* 7[15] *šangi* 5[1] 7[18]; **šangûtu** priesthood *šangût-su* 7[16].

שנך **mašnaktu** . . . . . *maš-nak-ti* 28[23] 33[21].

שנן **šanânu** to contend with, to rival *ša-na-an* 23[14]; **šâninu** rival *ša-ni-nu* 2[19] *-na* 2[23] 9[8] *ša-nin-šu* 5[7] 40[12]; *al-ta-na-an* 1[10].

שנן **šinnû** tooth *šinni* 12[28 bis] *šin* 12[29] 18[24] (*šin pîri* = ivory).

שנת **šunatu** cf. ושן.

שסה **šasû** to call, cry out, speak *i-šiš-si* 59[3] *al-sa-a* (= *aš-sa-a*) 15[27].

שסף **šispu** milk *ši-is-pu* 32[19].

שף **šaptu** lip, command *šap-tu-uk-ka* 37[7] *šaptí-ya* 25[7] *šap-tí-ya* 21[3] *šap-ta-šu-nu* 59[13].

שפת **šiptu** cf. אשף$_1$.

שפח **šapâḫu** to spread *ša-pu-uḫ* 52[11].

שפך **šapâku** to pour out, heap up *aš-pu-uk* 10[4]; *lu-ší-pi-ik* 1[15]; **sipku** mass *ši-pik* 10[3].

שפל **šapâlu** to be low, deep *u-šap-pi-il* 37[32] *u-ša-pil* 6[19]; **šaplu** fem. *šaplitu* lower, under *šap-li-šu-nu* 60[18] *ša-pal-šu* 23[4] 40[22] *šapliti-ya* 34[25] *šap-li-ti* 36[5] *-tim* 41[16] *šap-lit* 20[3] 23[16] *šap-la-ti* 24[21] (=things on earth); **šupiltu** lower part, pudenda *šupil-ti* 64[2,3,17] *-ta-šu-un* 16[14]; **šupalû** the lower *šupalî* 5[27]; **mušpalu** depth *muš-pa-li* 6[20]; **šapliš** below 62[5].

שפן **šapânu** to cover, overpower, cast *iš-pu-nu* 7[18]. Cf. ספן.

שפר **šapâru** to send, rule *aš-pur* 48[16] *iš-pur* 22[30] *iš-pu-ra* 12[32] 29[27] *iš-pur-am-ma* 22[16] 23[8] 27[29] *iš-pu-ru* 22[15]; *iš-ta-nap-pa-ra* 22[26]; *ul-taš-pi-ru* 9[9]; **šipru, šipirtu** mission, letter, work *ši-ip-ri* 36[13] *ši-pìr* 23[29] 24[5,14,19] 26[33] *šip-ra-a-ti-šu-nu* 46[23]; **šu-par** (?) . . . . . 44[9] 59[11].

שפרשק **šuparšaḳu** officer, general *šu-par-šaḳ-ya* 19[5] *šu-par-šaḳî pl-ya* 46[22] 48[15].

שפשק **šupšuḳu** cf. פשק.

שצל *iṣu* **ša-ṣil-li** a kind of chariot 26[16].

שקה **šaḳû** to drink **mašḳîtu** drink *maš-ki-ti* 10[24].

שקה **šaḳû** to be high *iš-ḳu* 20[25]; **šaḳû** high *ša-ḳu-u* 7[4] *ša-ḳu-u-tí* 30[7].

שקף **šaḳâpu** to erect, set up *aš-ḳup* 8[26].

שקר **šûḳuru** cf. וקר.

שרה **šurru, šurratu** beginning *šur-ru* 1[1] *šur-rat* 7[20]; *arḫu* **tišrîtu** month Tishri *tišrîti* 38[2].

שרח **šarâḫu** to be strong, powerful *u-šar-riḫ-ši* 6[25]; *mul-tar-ḫi* 5[11]; **tašriḫtu** power *taš-ri-iḫ-ti* 36[34].

שרמן **šurmínu** cypress *iṣu šurmíni* 6[20,27].

שרף **šarâpu** to burn (trans.) *ašru-up* 8[24] *aš-ru-up* 2[1] 3[26] 4[15,23].

שרק **šarâḳu** to give, present *iš-ru-ku-uš* 9[10].

שרר. **šarâru** to be bright, shine; **šarurû** brilliance *ša-ru-ru-šu* 37[3]; **šarru** king 1[4] *šarri* 5[3] *-šu-nu* 11[12] *šarra-šu* 18[20] *-šu-nu* 11[20] *šar* 3[6] *šarrâni* 41^{14} *šarrâni*$_{pl}$ 2^{19} *šarrâ*$_{pl}$*-ni* 2^{24} *-šu-nu* 1^{2}; **šarratu** queen *šar-ra-ti* 52^{24} $_{ilu}$*šarrat* 28^{29} $_{ilu}$*šar-rat* 19^{28} 20^{21} 26^{3} 29^{22} 30^{8} 32^{17} 33^{12} 34^{28}; **šarrûtu** royalty *šarrû-tu* 20^{4} *šarru-u-tu* 35^{4} *šarrû-ti* 7^{20} *-a* 5^{16} 6^{22} 8^{25} *-ya* 1^{1} *-šu* 8^{21} *-šu-un* 20^{27} *-šu-nu* 4^{1} *šarru-u-ti* 19^{20} *-ya* 35^{12} *-šu* 40^{23} *šarru-u-ut* 23^{28}.

שש **šiššu** sixth *šiš-šu* 63^{21} 64^{22} *šiš-ši* 24^{23} *šiš-ša* 60^{6}; **šušu** sixty *šu-ši* $3^{21,22}$.

שש **šâšu** cf. שו.

שש **šaššâniš** adv. like marble (?) *ša-aš-ša-ni-iš* 36^{26}.

ששדד $_{iṣu}$**ša-ša-da-di** a kind of chariot 26^{16} 34^{24}.

ששכל **šuškal** . . . . . *šu-uš-kal* 9^{18}.

שת $_{abnu}$**šit**$_{pl}$ ideogram for a kind of stone 30^{19}.

שתה **šatû** to drink *iš-tu-u* 30^{31}; *iš-ta-at-tu-u* 31^{29}; **maštîtu** drink *maš-ti-tu* 31^{26} *maš-ti-ti-šu-nu* 30^{21}.

שתך **maštaku** chamber, dwelling-place *maš-ta-ki-šu-nu* 41^{29}.

שתם **šitimtu** cf. שים.

שתר **šûturu** cf. ותר.

שתת **šuttu** cf. ושן.

ת

ת $_{abnu}$**tu** ideogram for some costly stone $63^{18,19}$ 64^{19}.

תא₂ם **tâmtu, ti'amtu** sea $59^{18,25}$ *tâmti* 2^{24} 3^{24} 5^{23} 22^{9} *tam-ti* 8^{6} *tam-tim* 10^{20} 17^{5} 18^{17} *tam-di* $7^{24,25}$ 8^{25} *tam-ta-am-ma* 59^{10} *tâmâti*$_{pl}$ $6^{9,24}$ *ta-ma-ta* 59^{19} *ti-amat* 21^{8} 62^{7}.

תבא₄ **tibû** to come, approach *it-ba-a* 24^{30} *it-ba-am-ma* 28^{25} *lit-ba-am-ma* $61^{15,16,18}$ *it-bu-ni* 3^{17} 8^{8} *it-bu-nim-ma* 23^{4} *it-bu-u-ni* 28^{10} *tí-bí* 61^{5} *tí-bu-ni* 15^{8} *tí-bu-u-ni* 15^{11}; *u-šat-ba-am-ma* 33^{3} (1st pers.) 35^{10} (3rd pers.) *u-šat-bu-niš-šum-ma* 35^{25} *šu-ut-bu-u* 9^{6}; **tibu** approach *ti-ib* $15^{29,30}$; **tibûtu** approach *ti-bu-ut* 15^{10} 33^{7} 46^{2}.

תבך **tabâku** to pour out, heap up *at-ta-bak* 60^{18} *it-ta-bi-ik* 17^{19}.

תבל **tabâlu** to take away *it-ta-bal* $63^{6,9,12,15,18,21}$ 64^{2} *ta-at-bal* $63^{7,10,13,16,19,22}$ 64^{3}.

תבר **tabrâtí** . . . . . St. ברה (?).

תבש **tabšûtu** . . . . . *ta-ab-šu-tu* 39^{26}. St. באש₃ (?).

תדך **tidûku** cf. דוך.

תור **târu** to turn, return *i-tar-ri* 60^{14} *a-tu-ṛa* 46^{8} 50^{19} *i-tur* 59^{5} *i-tu-ra* 59^{20} *i-tu-ram-ma* $60^{8,10}$ *i-tur-ru* 37^{5} *i-tu-ru-ni* 17^{16} *-nim-ma* 30^{30} *ta-a-a-ri* 35^{13} *ta-a-a-ra* 40^{5}; *u-tir* (II I) 3^{27} $4^{15,25}$ 5^{30} 13^{31} 21^{11} 27^{4} 41^{24} 46^{8} *-šu* 48^{18} *-šu-nu-ti* 18^{8} *u-tí-ir* 37^{22} 38^{16} 41^{25} *u-tir-ra* 3^{29} 12^{17} 16^{25} *u-tir-ram-ma* 13^{6} *u-tir-ru* 14^{26} 27^{10} 42^{11} *lu-tir* 39^{18} *u-tir-ru* (pl.) 18^{2}

mu-tir 9^{23}; *ut-tí-ir-ši* 64^{17-23} *ut-tir-ru* 58^{20}; **târtu** return *ta-a-a-ar-tu* 17^{18} *-ti-ya* 33^{25} *târat* $52^{1.12}$ 63^{5} 64^{5} *ta-a-a-rat* 52^{6}; **titurru** bridge *ti-tur-ra-a-ti* 3^{5}.

תזם **tazimtu** cf. נזם.

תחז **taḫazu** cf. $אחז_1$.

תחלב **taḫlubu** cf. חלב.

תחת **taḫtû** cf. חתה.

תכל **takâlu** to trust *it-ka-lu* 1^{5}; *at-ta-kil* 19^{11} *it-ta-kil* 8^{15} 19^{8} 22^{28} 42^{6} *it-tak-lu* 8^{7} 19^{11}; *u-tak-kil-an-ni* 13^{1} 29^{25}; **tiklu** confidence, help, helper *tik-li-a* 5^{20} *-ya* 23^{7} 27^{12} *ti-ik-li-ya* 15^{19} *-šu* 23^{15} *ti-ik-li-í-šu* 19^{24}; **tukultu** confidence, reliance, aid *tukul-ti* 1^{6} 2^{21} 5^{6} *tu-kul-ti* 40^{24}. *tu-kul-ta-šu* 16^{2} *tu-kul-ta-ni* 14^{23}.

תכף **tikpu** some measure of length *tik-pi* 6^{19}.

תל **tilu** heap, mound, hill 6^{18} *tili* 3^{27} $4^{15.25}$ *til* 4^{16}.

תלח **talâḫu** . . . . . *tul-lu-ḫu* 36^{2} 37^{29}.

תלם **talâmu** III I to give *u-šat-li-ma* 15^{24} *u-šat-li-mu-uš* 50^{22}; **tâlimu** brother *ta-li-mí* 23^{28} *ta-lim-ya* $24^{12.18}$.

תלת **talittu** cf. ורד.

תמה **tamû** to speak, swear *a-ta-ma-a* 35^{20} *i-ta-ma-a* 35^{16} 35^{22} *li-ta-mu-u* 41^{31}; *u-tam-mi-šu-nu-ti* 4^{1}.

תמזז **tam**(?)**-zi-zi-iš** . . . . . 15^{33}.

תמח **tamâḫu** to hold, seize, present *at-muḫ* 15^{26} *it-muḫ* 5^{17} *it-mu-ḫa* 16^{22}; *it-ta-ma-aḫ* 40^{6}; *u-tam-mí-iḫ* 22^{23} *lu-tí-mí-iḫ* 3^{22} *u-tam-mí-ḫu* 46^{25}; *tu-šat-mi-ḫu* 38^{25}.

תמחר **tamḫaru** cf. מחר.

תמטר **tâmṭiru** cf. מטר.

תמן **tímínu** memorial tablet, foundation stone *tí-mí-ín-na* $36^{16.17}$ 37^{32} 38^{5} 39^{3} *tí-mí-ín-šu* 36^{21} $37^{26.31}$ 39^{2} *tim-mi-in-šu* 10^{3}.

תמר **tâmirtu** cf. $אמר_1$; **tamartu** cf. $כאר_2$.

תן **ta-a-an** determinative after numbers and measures 32^{19} 60^{1} (cf. *a-an*).

תנש **tínišítu** cf. $אנש_1$.

תנת **tanittu** cf. נאר.

תפף **tappû** helper *tap-pi-í* 40^{15}.

תקא **tiḳu** attack (?) *ti-iḳ* 10^{1}.

תקם **tuḳumtu** (*tuḳuntu*) battle *tuḳunti* 5^{8} 6^{6} 14^{8} *tuḳ-ma-ti* 15^{11}.

תקן **taḳânu** to be firm, safe *mu-ta-ḳi-in* (II I) 9^{16}.

תקרב **taḳribtu** cf. קרב.

תרה **tarû** . . . . . *ta-ru-u* 40^{12}.

תרה **tírítí** . . . . . *tí-ri-í-tí* 7^{6}.

תרב **tarbîtu** cf. רבה.

תרגל **targullu** . . . . . *tar-gul-li* 58^{15}.

תרח **taraḫḫu** enclosure (?), wall (?) *ta-ra-aḫ-ḫu-uš* 36^{19}.

תרח **tirḫatu** gift, dowry *tir-ḫa-ti* $21^{10,17}$.

תרך **tarâku** to yield, shrink back *i-tar-ra-ku* 16^{32} [17^{21}]; *it-[ta]-rik* 59^{16}.

תרץ **tarâṣu** to direct, lay, place *u-ša-at-ri-iṣ* 36^{24} *u-šat-ri-iṣ* 38^{8} *u-šat-ri-ṣi* 24^{2}; **tarṣu** direction, time *tar-ṣi* 13^{3} 18^{5}.

תשר **tûšaru** cf. ושר; **tišrîtu** cf. שרה.

תתר **titurru** cf. תור.

CORRECTIONS.

Page	xxvii	line	25	read	א$_{3-5}$.
"	xxviii	"	21	"	*balṭûs-su.*
"	xxxii	"	36	"	בְּלוֹ.
"	xxxviii	"	14	"	*išṭur.*
"	xlv	"	2	"	*ippalkit.*
"	67	"	5	"	*ìkallu, ì.*
"	67	"	17	"	*ìkal.*
"	71	"	18	"	*ḫu-li-ya-am.*
"	84	"	21	"	תּוֹר.
"	85	"	36	"	Aššur.
"	86	"	16	"	אִלְפָּא.
"	94	"	6	"	wherefore?
"	101	"	27	"	*mi-ri-iḫ-tu.*
"	122	"	2	"	*lik-ḳí.*
"	123	"	3	"	*si-ḫu.*
"	123	"	10	"	*su-ḫi-ru.*
"	135	"	11	"	**šipku.**

Hippocrene's Beginner's Series...

Do you know what it takes to make a phone call in Russia? O how to get through customs in Japan? This new language instructio series shows how to handle oneself in typical situations by introduc- ing the business person or traveler not only to the vocabulary, grammar, and phrases of a new language, but also the history, customs, and daily practices of a foreign country.

The Beginner's Series consists of basic language instruction, which also includes vocabulary, grammar, and common phrases and review questions, along with cultural insights, interesting historical background, the country's basic facts and hints about everyday living-driving, shopping, eating out, and more.

Arabic For Beginners
186 pages • 5¼ x 8¼ • 0-7818-01141 • $9.95pb • (18)

Beginner's Chinese
150 pages • 5½ x 8 • 0-7818-0566-x • $14.95pb • (690)

Beginner's Bulgarian
207 pages • 5½ x 8½ • 0-7818-0300-4 • $9.95pb • (76)

Beginner's Czech
200 pages • 5½ x 8½ • 0-7818-0231-8 • $9.95pb • (74)

Beginner's Esperanto
400 pages • 5½ x 8½ • 0-7818-0230-x • $14.95pb • (51)

Beginner's Hungarian
200 pages • 5½ x 7 • 0-7818-0209-1 • $7.95pb • (68)

Beginner's Japanese
200 pages • 5½ x 8½ • 0-7818-0234-2 • $11.95pb • (53)

Beginner's Maori
121 pages • 5½ x 8½ • 0-7818-0605-4 • $8.95pb • (703)

Beginner's Persian
150 pages • 5½ x 8 • 0-7818-0567-8 • $14.95pb • (696)

Beginner's Polish
200 pages • 5½ x 8½ • 0-7818-0299-7 • $9.95pb • (82)

Beginner's Romanian
200 pages • 5½ x 8½ • 0-7818-0208-3 • $7.95pb • (79)

Beginner's Russian
200 pages • 5½ x 8½ • 0-7818-0232-6 • $9.95pb • (61)

Beginner's Swahili
200 pages • 5½ x 8½ • 0-7818-0335-7 • $9.95pb • (52)

Beginner's Ukrainian
130 pages • 5½ x 8½ • 0-7818-0443-4 • $11.95pb • (88)

Beginner's Vietnamese
517 pages • 7 x 10 • 30 lessons • 0-7818-0411-6 • $19.95pb • (253)

Beginner's Welsh
210 pages • 5½ x 8½ • 0-7818-0589-9 • $9.95pb • (712)

About out Mastering Series...

These imaginative courses, designed for both individual and classroom use, assume no previous knowledge of the language. The unique combination of practical exercises and step-by-step grammar emphasizes a functional approach to new scripts and their vocabularies. Everyday situations and local customs are explored variously through dialogues, newspaper extracts, drawings and photos. Cassettes are available for each language.

MASTERING ARABIC

320 pp • 5¼ x 8¼ • 0-87052-922-6 • USA • $14.95pb • (501)
2 cassettes: 0-87052-984-6 • (507)

MASTERING FINNISH

278 pp • 5½ x 8½ • 0-7818-0233-4 • W • $14.95pb • (184)
2 Cassettes: 0-7818-0265-2 • W • $12.95 • (231)

MASTERING FRENCH

288 pp • 5½ x 8½ • 0-87052-055-5 • USA • $14.95pb • (511)
2 Cassettes: • 0-87052-060-1 USA • $12.95 • (512)

MASTERING ADVANCED FRENCH

348 pp • 5½ x 8½ • 0-7818-0312-8 • W • $14.95pb • (41)
2 Cassettes: • 0-7818-0313-6 • W • $12.95 • (54)

MASTERING GERMAN

340 pp • 5½ x 8½ • 0-87052-056-3 • USA • $11.95pb • (514)
2 Cassettes: • 0-87052-061-X • USA • $12.95 • (515)

MASTERING ITALIAN

360 pp • 5½ x 8½ • 0-87052-057-1 • USA • $11.95pb • (517)
2 Cassettes: 0-87052-066-0 • USA • $12.95 • (521)

MASTERING ADVANCED ITALIAN

278 pp • 5½ x 8½ • 0-7818-0333-0 • W • $14.95pb • (160)
2 Cassettes: 0-7818-0334-9 • W • $12.95 • (161)

MASTERING JAPANESE

368 pp • 5½ x 8½ • 0-87052-923-4 • USA • $14.95pb • (523)
2 Cassettes: • 0-87052-983-8 USA • $12.95 • (524)

MASTERING NORWEGIAN

183 pp • 5½ x 8½ • 0-7818-0320-9 • W • $14.95pb • (472)

MASTERING POLISH

288 pp • 5½ x 8½ • 0-7818-0015-3 • W • $14.95pb • (381)
2 Cassettes: • 0-7818-0016-1 • W • $12.95 • (389)

MASTERING RUSSIAN

278 pp • 5½ x 8½ • 0-7818-0270-9 • W • $14.95pb • (11)
2 Cassettes: • 0-7818-0271-7 • W • $12.95 • (13)

MASTERING SPANISH

338 pp • 5½ x 8½ • 0-87052-059-8 • USA • $11.95 • (527)
2 Cassettes: • 0-87052-067-9 • USA • $12.95 • (528)

MASTERING ADVANCED SPANISH

326 pp • 5½ x 8½ • 0-7818-0081-1 • W • $14.95pb • (413)
2 Cassettes: • 0-7818-0089-7 • W • $12.95 • (426)

DICTIONARY & PHRASEBOOK SERIES

AUSTRALIAN DICTIONARY AND PHRASEBOOK

Helen Jonsen

Displaying the diversity of English, this book provides terms connected with specific situations such as driving, size conversion charts, travel options, and sightseeing trips are just a few of the many topics provided.

131 pp • 3¾ x 7 • 1,500 entries • 0-7818-0539-2 • W • $11.95pb • (626)

BASQUE-ENGLISH/ENGLISH-BASQUE DICTIONARY AND PHRASEBOOK

240 pages • 3¾ x 7 • 1,500 entries • 0-7818-0622-4 • W • $11.95pb

BOSNIAN-ENGLISH/ENGLISH-BOSNIAN DICTIONARY AND PHRASEBOOK

175 pp • 3¾ x 7 • 1,500 entries • 0-7818-0596-1 • W • $11.95pb • (691)

BRETON-ENGLISH/ENGLISH-BRETON DICTIONARY AND PHRASEBOOK

131 pp • 3¾ x 7 • 1,500 entries • 0-7818-0540-6 • W • $11.95pb • (627)

BRITISH-AMERICAN/AMERICAN-BRITISH DICTIONARY AND PHRASEBOOK

160 pp • 3¾ x 7 • 1,400 entries • 0-7818-0450-7 •W • $11.95pb • (247)

CHECHEN-ENGLISH/ENGLISH-CHECHEN DICTIONARY AND PHRASEBOOK

160 pp • 3¾ x 7 • 1,400 entries • 0-7818-0446-9 • NA • $11.95pb • (183)

GEORGIAN-ENGLISH/ENGLISH-GEORGIAN DICTIONARY AND PHRASEBOOK

150 pp • 3¾ x 7 • 1,300 entries • 0-7818-0542-2 •W • $11.95pb • (630)

GREEK-ENGLISH/ENGLISH-GREEK DICTIONARY AND PHRASEBOOK

175 pages • 3¾ x 7 • 1,500 entries • 0-7818-0635-6 •W • $11.95pb • (715)

IRISH-ENGLISH/ENGLISH-IRISH DICTIONARY AND PHRASEBOOK

160 pp • 3¾ x 7 • 1,400 entries/phrases • 0-87052-110-1 NA • $7.95pb • (385)

LINGALA-ENGLISH/ENGLISH-LINGALA DICTIONARY AND PHRASEBOOK

120 pp • 3¾ x 7 • 0-7818-0456-6 •W • $11.95pb • (296)

MALTESE-ENGLISH/ENGLISH-MALTESE DICTIONARY AND PHRASEBOOK

175 pp 3¾ x 7 • 1,500 entries • 0-7818-0565-1 •W • $11.95pb • (697)

POLISH DICTIONARY AND PHRASEBOOK

252 pp • 5½ x 8½ • 0-7818-0134-6 •W • $11.95pb • (192)
Cassettes—Vol I: 0-7818-0340-3 •W • $12.95 • (492)
Vol II: 0-7818-0384-5 •W • $12.95 • (486)

RUSSIAN DICTIONARY AND PHRASEBOOK, *Revised*

256pp • 5½ x 8½ • 3,000 entries • 0-7818-0190-7 •W • $9.95pb • (597)

UKRAINIAN DICTIONARY AND PHRASEBOOK

205pp • 5½ x 8½ • 3,000 entries • 0-7818-0188-5 •W • $11.95pb • (28)

Practical Dictionaries From Hippocrene:

AFRIKAANS-ENGLISH/ENGLISH-AFRIKAANS PRACTICAL DICTIONARY

430 pages • 4½ x 6½ • 14,000 entries • 0-7818-0052-8 • NA • (134)

ALBANIAN-ENGLISH/ENGLISH-ALBANIAN PRACTICAL DICTIONARY

400 pages • 4³/₈ x 7 • 18,000 entries • 0-7818-0419-1 •W except Albania • $14.95pb • (483)

BULGARIAN-ENGLISH/ENGLISH-BULGARIAN PRACTICAL DICTIONARY

323 pages • 4³/₈ x 7 • 6,500 entries • 0-87052-145-4 • NA • $14.95pb • (331)

DANISH-ENGLISH/ENGLISH-DANISH PRACTICAL DICTIONARY

601 pages • 4³/₈ x 7 • 32,000 entries • 0-7818-0823-8 • NA • $14.95pb • (198)

FRENCH-ENGLISH/ENGLISH-FRENCH PRACTICAL DICTIONARY, *with larger print*

386 pages • 5½ x 8¼ • 35,00 entries • 0-7818-0355-1 •W • $9.95pb • (499)

FULANI-ENGLISH PRACTICAL DICTIONARY

264 pages • 5 x 7¼ • 0-7818-0404-3 •W • $14.95pb • (38)

GERMAN-ENGLISH/ENGLISH-GERMAN PRACTICAL DICTIONARY, *with larger print*

400 pages • 5½ x 8¼ • 35,000 entries • 0-7818-0355-1 • W • $9.95pb • (200)

HINDI-ENGLISH/ENGLISH-HINDI PRACTICAL DICTIONARY

745 pages • 4³/₈ x 7 • 25,000 entries • 0-7818-0084-6 • W • $19.95pb • (442)

ENGLISH-HINDI PRACTICAL DICTIONARY

399 pages • 4³/₈ x 7 • 15,000 entries • 0-87052-978-1 • NA • $11.95pb • (362)

INDIONESIAN-ENGLISH/ENGLISH-INDONESIAN PRACTICAL DICTIONARY

289 pages • 4¼ x 7 • 17,000 entries • 0-87052-810-6 • NA • $11.95pb • (127)

ITALIAN-ENGLISH/ENGLISH-ITALIAN PRACTICAL DICTIONARY, *with larger print*

488 pages • 5½ x 8¼ • 35,000 entries • 0-7818-0354-3 • W • $9.95pb • (201)

KOREAN-ENGLISH/ENGLISH-KOREAN PRACTICAL DICTIONARY

365 pages • 4 x 7¼ • 8,500 entries • 0-87052-092-x • Asia and NA • $14.95pb • (399)

LATVIAN-ENGLISH/ENGLISH-LATVIAN PRACTICAL DICTIONARY

474 pages • 4³/₈ x 7 • 16,000 entries • 0-7818-0059-5 • NA • $16.95pb • (194)

POLISH-ENGLISH/ENGLISH-POLISH PRACTICAL DICTIONARY

703 pages • 5¼ x 8½ • 31,000 entries • 0-7818-0085-4 • W • $11.95pb • (450)

SERBO-CROATIAN-ENGLISH/ENGLISH-SERBO-CROATIAN PRACTICAL DICTIONARY

400 pages • 5 3/8 x 7 • 24,000 entries • 0-7818-0445-0 • W • $16.95pb • (130)

UKRAINIAN-ENGLISH/ENGLISH-UKRAINIAN PRACTICAL DICTIONARY, *Revised edition with menu terms*

406 pages • 4¼ x 7 • 16,000 entries • 0-7818-0306-3 • W • $14.95pb • (343)

YIDDISH-ENGLISH/ENGLISH-YIDDISH PRACTICAL DICTIONARY, *Expanded edition*

215 pages • 4½ x 7 • 4,000 entries • 0-7818-0439-6 • W • $9.95pb • (431)

All prices are subject to change. To order Hippocrene Books, contact your local bookstore, call (718) 454-2366, or write to : Hippocrene Books, 171 Madison Ave. New York, NY 10016. Please enclose check or money order adding $5.00 shipping (UPS) for the first book and $.50 for each additional title.